To some, UN Police are the most useful tool in post conflict situations. Others argue that the diverse, disparate nature of UN Police components in peacekeeping operations makes them unfit for purpose. Hunt's methodological approach to monitoring and evaluating UN Police performance has the real potential to assist in developing a clearer understanding of the effectiveness of international policing and in identifying areas that require strengthening and support, or even a total rethink.

Andrew Hughes, APM, Commissioner (retd.) – Police Adviser to the UN and Director of the Police Division, DPKO, 2007–09

Hunt's innovative study tackles two key questions in contemporary peace operations: what impact do these missions have on host societies and how might they be improved? Using detailed research on the roles of civilian police in UN missions and the case of UNMIL in Liberia in particular, Hunt makes the case that the key to effective policing lies in organizational learning and that this can be facilitated by a reformed approach to monitoring and evaluation. This book offers students and practitioners of peace operations much food for thought on how to design monitoring and evaluation frameworks that capture the complexity of contemporary peace operations and their interactions with the host society.

Paul D. Williams, George Washington University, USA

Charles Hunt's work is not only highly relevant for academics, it is also inspiring for programme managers and M&E practitioners questioning the limits of conventional systems and 'hungry for guidance' on how to improve them.

Stefan Rummel-Shapiro, Senior M&E Advisor, United Nations Peace Building Support Office (UN-PBSO)

UN Peace Operations and International Policing

This book addresses the important question of how the United Nations (UN) should monitor and evaluate the impact of police in its peace operations.

UN peace operations are a vital component of international conflict management. Since the end of the Cold War one of the foremost developments has been the rise of UN policing (UNPOL). Instances of UNPOL action have increased dramatically in number and have evolved from passive observation to participation in frontline law enforcement activities. Attempts to ascertain the impact of UNPOL activities have proven inadequate.

This book seeks to redress this lacuna by investigating the ways in which the effects of peace operations – and UNPOL in particular – are monitored and evaluated. Furthermore, it aims to develop a framework, tested through field research in Liberia, for Monitoring and Evaluation (M&E) that enables more effective impact assessment. By enhancing the relationship between field-level M&E and organisational learning this research aims to make an important contribution to the pursuit of more professional and effective UN peace operations.

This book will be of much interest to students of peace operations, conflict management, policing, security studies and IR in general.

Charles T. Hunt is a lecturer in International Security in the School of Political Science and International Studies, University of Queensland, Australia. He is co-editor of *Making Sense of Peace and Capacity-Building Operations* (2010) and co-author of *Forging New Conventional Wisdom Beyond International Policing* (2013).

Routledge Studies in Peace and Conflict Resolution
Series Editors: Tom Woodhouse and Oliver Ramsbotham
University of Bradford

Peace and Security in the Postmodern World
The OSCE and conflict resolution
Dennis J.D. Sandole

Truth Recovery and Justice after Conflict
Managing violent pasts
Marie Breen Smyth

Peace in International Relations
Oliver P. Richmond

Social Capital and Peace-Building
Creating and resolving conflict with trust and social networks
Edited by Michaelene Cox

Business, Conflict Resolution and Peacebuilding
Contributions from the private sector to address violent conflict
Derek Sweetman

Creativity and Conflict Resolution
Alternative pathways to peace
Tatsushi Arai

Climate Change and Armed Conflict
Hot and Cold Wars
James R. Lee

Transforming Violent Conflict
Radical disagreement, dialogue and survival
Oliver Ramsbotham

Governing Ethnic Conflict
Consociation, identity and the price of peace
Andrew Finlay

Political Discourse and Conflict Resolution
Debating peace in Northern Ireland
Edited by Katy Hayward and Catherine O'Donnell

Economic Assistance and Conflict Transformation
Peacebuilding in Northern Ireland
Sean Byrne

Liberal Peacebuilding and Global Governance
Beyond the metropolis
David Roberts

A Post-Liberal Peace
Oliver P. Richmond

Peace Research
Theory and practice
Peter Wallensteen

Reconciliation after Terrorism
Strategy, possibility or absurdity?
Judith Renner and Alexander Spencer

Post-War Security Transitions
Participatory peacebuilding after asymmetric conflicts
Edited by Veronique Dudouet, Hans Giessman and Katrin Planta

Rethinking Peacebuilding
The quest for just peace in the Middle East and the Western Balkans
Edited by Karin Aggestam and Annika Björkdahl

Violent Conflict and Peacebuilding
The continuing crisis in Darfur
Johan Brosché and Daniel Rothbart

Peacebuilding and NGOs
State–civil society interactions
Ryerson Christie

Peace Negotiations and Time
Deadline diplomacy in territorial disputes
Marco Pinfari

History Education and Post-Conflict Reconciliation
Reconsidering joint textbook projects
Edited by Karina V. Korostelina and Simone Lässig

Conflict Resolution and Human Needs
Linking theory and Practice
Edited by Kevin Avruch and Christopher Mitchell

Human Rights Education and Peacebuilding
A comparative study
Tracey Holland and J. Paul Martin

Post-Conflict Studies
An Interdisciplinary Approach
Edited by Chip Gagnon and Keith Brown

Arab Approaches to Conflict Resolution
Mediation, negotiation and settlement of political disputes
Nahla Hamdan and Frederic S. Pearson

UN Peace Operations and International Policing
Negotiating complexity, assessing impact and learning to learn
Charles T. Hunt

Civil Resistance and Conflict Transformation
Transitions from armed to nonviolent struggle
Edited by Véronique Dudouet

UN Peace Operations and International Policing

Negotiating complexity, assessing impact and learning to learn

Charles T. Hunt

LONDON AND NEW YORK

First published 2015 by Routledge

2 Park Square, Milton Park, Abingdon, Oxon OX14 4RN
711 Third Avenue, New York, NY 10017, USA

Routledge is an imprint of the Taylor & Francis Group, an informa business

First issued in paperback 2016

Copyright © 2015 Charles T. Hunt

The right of Charles T. Hunt to be identified as author of this work has been asserted by him/her in accordance with sections 77 and 78 of the Copyright, Designs and Patents Act 1988.

All rights reserved. No part of this book may be reprinted or reproduced or utilised in any form or by any electronic, mechanical, or other means, now known or hereafter invented, including photocopying and recording, or in any information storage or retrieval system, without permission in writing from the publishers.

Notice:
Product or corporate names may be trademarks or registered trademarks, and are used only for identification and explanation without intent to infringe.

British Library Cataloguing-in-Publication Data
A catalogue record for this book is available from the British Library

Library of Congress Cataloging-in-Publication Data
Hunt, Charles T.
UN peace operations and international policing : negotiating complexity, assessing impact and learning to learn / Charles T. Hunt.
  pages cm. – (Routledge studies in peace and conflict resolution)
  Includes bibliographical references and index.
  1. United Nations–Peacekeeping forces. 2. International police. 3. Peace-building–International cooperation. 4. Conflict management–International cooperation. 5. International relations. 6. Security, International. I. Title.
  JZ4971.H86 2014
  341.5'84–dc23   2014005763

ISBN: 978-0-415-74237-5 (hbk)
ISBN: 978-1-138-65032-9 (pbk)

Typeset in Baskerville
by Wearset Ltd, Boldon, Tyne and Wear

In memory of those loved but lost. In particular, this is for my Grandmas, Marjorie Goodwin and Irene Hunt. Their unwavering encouragement and (often unwarranted) lavish praise indisputably contributed to me thinking I was capable of undertaking a project like this. I will always be grateful for the influence of such wise and generous women.

Contents

List of illustrations   xiii
Acknowledgements   xiv
List of abbreviations   xvi

Introduction   1

PART I
Context-setting   25

1 UN peace operations and policing: policing change, changing police   27

2 Monitoring and evaluation in peace operations: measuring progress, assessing impact and gauging success   63

PART II
Theory and framework building   101

3 Complexity, peace operations and M&E: the need for a paradigm shift?   103

4 A framework for monitoring and evaluating the impact of UNPOL   136

PART III
Empirical case study and implications   167

5 Conflict and consequence in Liberia   169

6	**M&E in practice: strengths, comparative advantages and potentialities**	208
7	**M&E in practice II: weaknesses, latent problems and naïveté**	243
	Conclusion: overcoming the convenience of simplicity	266
	Index	279

Illustrations

Figures

1.1	The core business of multidimensional UN peacekeeping operations	30
2.1	Benchmarking logic	73
2.2	Classical 'logframe' representation	79
3.1	Complex adaptive system	108
4.1	Diagram of overall M&E framework	137
4.2	Field-level M&E process	140

Table

4.1	UNPOL tasks	142

Acknowledgements

The release of this book would not have been possible without the advice and perseverance of a few key individuals. Most of all I am thankful to Alex Bellamy for enabling this project, guiding me through it and sticking with me; for reading half-baked early (and not-so-early) drafts and for all the opportunities he has presented me I will always be extremely grateful. I am also indebted to Paul Boreham for support and guidance throughout the process. His combination of wisdom and wit has been the perfect tonic for my confusion and self-doubt along the way. Thanks also go to Phil Orchard for helping to panel-beat final drafts into shape, as well as Will Skadden for bringing a keen editorial eye to the manuscript and being a great help across the final furlong. Finally, I am grateful to the three anonymous reviewers whose suggestions undoubtedly improved this manuscript.

The field research for this book would not have been possible without the willing participation of the United Nations Mission in Liberia. For that, I am deeply grateful to the former Special Representative of Secretary-General, Ms. Ellen Margrethe Løj, and her Special Assistant, Mr. Andres Smith-Serrano. I would also like to thank each and every participant I was able to interview whose time and candid contributions enabled and enriched this study. I am also thankful to Kwesi Aning and all the staff at the Kofi Annan International Peacekeeping Training Centre in Accra, Ghana, for affording me academic hospitality as well as delightful company before and after my field trip to Liberia – *medawase paaa*! I give further thanks to all those who I met with at the United Nations Secretariat and other organisations including the International Peace Institute in New York as well as William Durch at the Stimson Center and Michael Dziedzic at the United States Institute of Peace in Washington DC. Their contributions have been invaluable.

The research presented in this book was supported in part by a grant from the International Deployment Group (IDG) within the Australian Federal Police entitled "Measuring the Impact of the IDG's Contribution to Peace Operations and International Capacity Building." I would like to express sincere thanks to the IDG for their generous financial support, which contributed to my capacity to complete the research. I also acknowledge the reproduction of some content originally appearing in: Bryn Hughes, Charles T. Hunt and Jodie Curth-Bibb, *Forging New Conventional Wisdom Beyond International Policing* (Boston: Martinus Nijhoff, 2013), pp. 15–34 and 243–78.

To the team who worked on the IDG project, I am fortunate to have benefited from your collegiality and insights. In particular, to Bryn Hughes and Jodie Curth-Bibb for being impressive colleagues and co-authors, for informing my thinking and for encouraging me – I owe a lot to you both.

To all those I have worked alongside at the Asia Pacific Centre for the Responsibility to Protect I am likewise grateful – particular thanks go to Tim Dunne, Noel Morada, Marie Hobman, Jocelyn Vaughn, Sara Davies, Alex Pound, Jess Gifkins, Stephen McLoughlin, Luke Glanville and Bronwyn Crook. In the School of Political Science and International Studies at the University of Queensland I could not have asked for more supportive institutional surroundings. I would like to thank Gillian Whitehouse, Richard Devetak, Seb Kaempf, Martin and Heloise Weber and Andrew Phillips. Particular mention is owed to Warren Laffan and Meg Tighe for their support and genuine concern for my wellbeing in these sunburned lands a long way from 'home'.

Retaining my sanity was down to the camaraderie of the best friends anyone could ask for. I am fortunate to have them and owe a debt of Greek proportions to them all for putting up with me and being so much fun. In Australia, to Sarah Teitt thank you for the dizzying highs and lows, the tos and the fros. Terry James Blair Hallifax 'Rocky' Slight and Will 'Harvs' Skadden, you guys are gold and rarely broke the cardinal rule on rent – bravo! Jodie Curth-Bibb deserves another mention here for there is as much to appreciate about her fellowship as there is her scholarship. To the residents of Borva 1 and 2, past and present – particularly Sofia 'Mops' Walker, Katie 'Kaff' Linnane, Jake 'cobes Kurtzer, Samid Suliman, Rebecca Peart and Natty Gregg – thanks for being my sanctuary, particularly after long days languishing in Up-Skirt Alley. Katy Roberts, you are smart, funny, real pretty and a most welcome intervention. You made finalising this manuscript a very smiley affair. Thank you. Across the seas there are too many to reference but worth special mention are Erin Weir, Jen Pedersen and Vicky 'Smudge' Smith for believing in me more than most, and Mark Malan who was the notable *agent provocateur* in all this, as well as a great mate.

Lastly, but decisively, I am eternally grateful to my family. My brother, James, deserves mention for being a stellar role model and helping/forcing me to realise there was more to this world than the Humber estuary and its environs. The most special thanks is reserved for my parents – Dad, Mum and Geoff – for their faithful support and encouragement, but more than anything for going to great lengths (and some significant depths) to ensure I have had the opportunities that they did not. Thank you.

Brisbane, Australia

Abbreviations

ACS	American Colonization Society
AFL	Armed Forces of Liberia
ATU	Anti-Terrorism Unit
AU	African Union
BCR	Bureau of Corrections and Rehabilitation
BIN	Bureau of Immigration and Naturalisation
BPO	Best Practices Officer
CAS	Complex Adaptive System
CDW	Consolidation, Drawdown and Withdrawal plan
CES	Complex Evolving Systems
CIVPOL	Civilian Police
COP	Communities of Practice
CPA	Comprehensive Peace Agreement
CPAC	Civilian Police Analysis Cell
CPF	Community Policing Forums
CRC	Central Revolutionary Council
CSO	Civil Society Organisation
DDR	Disarmament, Demobilisation and Reintegration
DDRR	Disarmament, Demobilisation, Rehabilitation and Reintegration
DEA	Drug Enforcement Agency
DFS	Department of Field Support
DPA	Department of Political Affairs
DPKO	Department of Peacekeeping Operations
DSRSG	Deputy Special Representative of the Secretary-General
ECOMIL	ECOWAS Mission in Liberia
ECOMOG	ECOWAS Cease-Fire Monitoring Group
ECOWAS	Economic Community of West African States
ERU	Emergency Response Unit
EU	European Union
FPU	Formed Police Unit
GA	General Assembly
GEMAP	Governance and Economic Management Assistance Program

HQ	Headquarters
ICRC	International Committee of the Red Cross
IGNU	Interim Government of National Unity
IMPIP	Integrated Mission Priorities and Implementation Plan
IMPP	Integrated Missions Planning Process
INPFL	Independent National Patriotic Front of Liberia
iPRS	interim Poverty Reduction Strategy
IPTF	International Police Task Force
IR	International Relations
ITS	Integrated Training Service
JMAC	Joint Mission Analysis Cell
JOC	Joint Operations Centre
KM	Knowledge Management
LFF	Liberian Frontier Force
LNP	Liberian National Police
LNTG	Liberian National Transitional Government
LPRC	Liberian Petroleum Refining Corporation
LURD	Liberians United for Reconciliation and Democracy
MDG	Millennium Development Goal
MINUSTAH	United Nations Stabilisation Mission in Haiti
MIP	Mandate Implementation Plan
M&E	Monitoring and Evaluation
MODEL	Movement for Democracy in Liberia
MONUC	United Nations Organisation Mission in the DR Congo
MONUSCO	United Nations Organisation Stabilization Mission in the DR Congo
NBI	National Bureau of Investigation
NGO	Non-Governmental Organisation
NPA	National Ports Authority
NPFL	National Patriotic Front of Liberia
NPM	New Public Management
NTC	National Telecommunications Corporation
NTGL	National Transitional Government of Liberia
OECD	Organisation for Economic Co-operation and Development
OIOS	Office of Internal Oversight Services
ONUMOZ	United Nations Operation in Mozambique
ONUSAL	United Nations Observer Mission in El Salvador
OROLSI	Office for Rule of Law and Security Institutions
OSCE	Organisation for Security Cooperation in Europe
PBPS	Peacekeeping Best Practices Section
PBSO	Peacebuilding Support Office
PET	Policy, Evaluation and Training Division
PIF	Pacific Islands Forum
POLCOM	Police Commissioner
PRC	People's Redemption Council

PRIME	Police Reform Indicators and Measurement Evaluation
PRS	Poverty Reduction Strategy
PSU	Police Support Unit
P-5	Permanent five member states on the UN Security Council
QIP	Quick Impact Project
RAMSI	Regional Assistance Mission to the Solomon Islands
RBB	Results-Based Budgeting
RBM	Results-Based Management
RFTF	Results-Focused Transitional Framework
ROL	Rule of Law
ROLIP	Rule of Law Indicators Project
RRR	Reform, Restructuring and Rebuilding
RUF	Revolutionary United Front
SALW	Small Arms and Light Weapons
SC	Security Council
SCSL	Special Court for Sierra Leone
SMLG	Senior Mission Leadership Group
SOD	Special Operations Division
SOP	Standard Operating Procedures
SRSG	Special Representative of the Secretary-General
SSR	Security Sector Reform
SSS	Special Security Services
SWAPOL	Southwest African Police
TAM	Technical Assessment Missions
TCU	Transnational Crime Unit
TRC	Truth and Reconciliation Commission
ULIMO	United Liberation Movement for Democracy in Liberia
UN	United Nations
UNAMA	United Nations Assistance Mission in Afghanistan
UNAMID	United Nations-African Union Hybrid Mission in Darfur
UNAMIR	United Nations Assistance Mission in Rwanda
UNAVEM	United Nations Angola Verification Mission
UNDAF	United Nations Development Assistance Framework
UNFICYP	United Nations Peacekeeping Force in Cyprus
UNMIBH	United Nations Mission in Bosnia and Herzegovina
UNMIH	United Nations Mission in Haiti
UNMIK	United Nations Mission in Kosovo
UNMIL	United Nations Mission in Liberia
UNMIS	United Nations Mission in the Sudan
UNOCI	United Nations Operation in Côte d'Ivoire
UNOL	United Nations Office in Liberia
UNOMIL	United Nations Observer Mission in Liberia
UNOSOM	United Nations Operation in Somalia
UNOTIL	United Nations Office in Timor-Leste
UNPD	United Nations Police Division

UNPOL	United Nations Police
UNTAC	United Nations Transitional Authority in Cambodia
UNTAES	United Nations Transitional Administration in Eastern Slavonia, Baranja and Western Sirmium
UNTAET	United Nations Transitional Administration in East Timor
UNTAG	United Nations Transition Assistance Group in Namibia
UNTEA	United Nations Temporary Executive Authority (in West New Guinea/West Irian)
USG	Under-Secretary-General
WACI	West African Coast Initiative
WCPC	Women and Children Protection Centres

Introduction

> To date the UN, like many other large bureaucracies, has proven more adept at repeating mistakes, than at learning lessons. Time to change.[1]

United Nations (UN) peace operations are a vital component of the international community's conflict management toolkit. They are one of the main tools used by the Security Council to manage complex crises that pose a threat to international peace and security. Since the end of the Cold War, peace operations have grown and adapted in response to the changing nature of conflict and in relation to the evolving peacebuilding agenda and architecture.[2] Today, over US$7 billion is spent annually on maintaining an array of UN peace operations deploying over 115,000 uniformed and civilian personnel in conflict-affected countries that has become the operational face of the UN in international peace and security.

One of the most significant trends has been the rise of international policing, evolving from a passive observation role to frontline law enforcement activities and an intrusive reform and capacity-building function.[3] UN Police (UNPOL) are now perceived by some to be a lynchpin in most UN peace operations.[4] So much so that according to Bull, perceived shortcomings in UNPOL efforts and corresponding deficits in the security and justice domains have been responsible for the recurrence of violent conflagrations in places like Cambodia, Kosovo and Timor-Leste and resulted in accusations of mission failure or ineffectiveness.[5] Therefore, the short-term restoration of law and order and the more protracted development of domestic police, and the criminal justice system more generally, following armed conflict have come to be seen as a *sine qua non* for missions that aim to lay the foundations for sustainable and durable peace and development.[6] The former Under-Secretary-General for Peacekeeping, Alain Le-Roy, captured the centrality of UNPOL endeavours when he commented that, "Without law and order there can be no peace; without peace there can be no law and order."[7]

These unprecedented quantitative and qualitative changes to the role of police in peace operations – in terms of the growth in numbers deployed and the normative shift towards reform of domestic law enforcement services – as well as the increasing dependency on effective rule of law institutions as a hinge for a mission exit strategy raise important, as yet unanswered, questions about the effectiveness and management of these elements. Attempts to evaluate the effectiveness of peace operations have heretofore focused on a limited and limiting dichotomy between success and failure.[8] Furthermore, the current literature has by and large failed to address the policing component of peace operations.[9] Recent scholarship has begun to point to 'organisational learning' as a central factor related to the success of certain types of peacekeeping missions or the UN peace operations bureaucracy as a whole.[10] This organisational learning is said to occur at two levels: firstly, within missions at the field-level to enable adaptation to changing circumstances; and secondly, between missions for inter-mission learning consolidated at the headquarters level. These are what Howard refers to as First- and Second-level learning, respectively.[11] These studies identify mechanisms for gathering information or knowledge acquisition in the field as the crucial ingredients of organisational learning.

Monitoring and Evaluation (M&E) is the modality through which this data-collection, information analysis and knowledge acquisition, so important to organisational learning, can take place. However, despite its importance for adapting missions to evolving conditions and building a repository of institutional knowledge based on lessons from the field, the UN has thus far struggled to develop M&E that can accurately assess the impact of its peace operations in a way that facilitates learning in both the short and longer-term.[12] Doing so in the realm of UNPOL is a relatively new but crucial part of this endeavour.[13] Furthermore, the extant literature in this area has failed to sufficiently examine and unpack the relationship between M&E, organisational learning and more effective peace operations.

The aim of this book is therefore to address this deficit. The book has two main objectives. The first is to investigate the ways in which the effects of peace operations – and UNPOL in particular – are monitored and evaluated. The second is to develop a framework for M&E that enables more effective impact assessment in order to contribute to organisational learning in the field and at headquarters. It therefore asks how the UN should monitor and evaluate the impact of police in its peace operations. Ultimately, the book argues that enhanced M&E, drawing on and embracing the "spirit of epistemological uncertainty",[14] entrenching flexibility and embedded in holistic mission management framework, can lead to more effective organisational learning and, in turn, to more efficacious peace operations. In doing so, the book offers an antidote to the frailties of current orthodoxy and presents the opportunity for improved practice for UNPOL in peace operations, as well as related fields.

This introduction proceeds in seven sections. The first articulates the research problem by explaining why M&E is particularly important but uniquely difficult in peace operations. The second situates this research in relation to existing literatures. The third section describes and justifies the approach taken, the fourth articulates the research method that underpins the investigation and the fifth section lays out the central argument and its underlying logic. The sixth section specifies the contribution the book makes to the study of peace operations in international relations and the implications of its findings. The final section traces an outline of the book structure.

Research problem

Whilst M&E[15] is central to how all organisations understand the effects of their actions, and how they learn and evolve, for peace operations it is particularly *important*, albeit comparatively *difficult*.[16] M&E in this setting is particularly *important* in three key ways. First, in the context of scarce financial resources, member states implementing austerity measures at home increasingly desire a better understanding of the cost-effectiveness of these peace interventions abroad.[17] M&E constitutes a means of demonstrating accountability and transparency, linking commitments and contributions to achievements.[18] For accountability purposes, M&E also constitutes a solid foundation from which to garner and sustain political will amongst decision-makers, troop/police-contributing countries and donors as well as to respond to critics.[19] Ultimately, it is this political support and material resource that remains the umbilical cord to field operations. Second, a recurrent and vexing challenge for UN peace operations is to gauge whether or not these expeditions are having the intended impact and if so, to what extent. In simple terms, one of the key management challenges in peace operations is to monitor and evaluate how the mission and components therein contribute to achieving mandated objectives and how this is impacting upon society. As a means of impact assessment, M&E provides a way of demonstrating success, substantiating intended outcomes and conferring legitimacy to policy decisions.[20] Furthermore, it provides a way of managing programming and garnering buy-in to the processes underway.

Finally, the ad hoc and evolutionary nature of peace operations demands that lessons from good and bad practice are efficiently identified and committed to institutional memory.[21] M&E has the potential to facilitate such organisational learning. The results of systematic and periodic M&E can provide the material necessary to build institutional knowledge that can in turn inform future mission planning and design, undergird guidance and doctrinal development and serve as a training needs assessment. Furthermore, the ability of a mission to function effectively is enhanced when its agents are provided with significant information on performance and progress and any lessons are identified from ongoing experiences. M&E of day-to-day activities can empower mission managers to identify implementation gaps and make real-time tactical adjustments in what is often a rapidly changeable environment.[22] These assessments can further inform the development of tactical directives or Standard Operating Procedures (SOPs). Therefore, M&E arguably has the potential to contribute to more effective peace operations and their ultimate success in a number of important ways. In addition to these fundamental uses, there are also a number of policing-specific arguments for M&E.

Incisive M&E in the realm of policing can provide insights into what effect UNPOL activities are having, as opposed to simply recording and documenting what they have done and inferring impacts from that. The idiosyncrasies of UNPOL missions – i.e. the way they are constructed, and the work they perform – mean that additional benefits accrue when M&E can be tailored to the policing context. Given the expansion in both magnitude and functionality of UNPOL deployments in recent times, it is perhaps more salient than ever to develop ways to monitor and evaluate their impact. As Mobekk attests, "While crucial lessons have been learned, there is still significant progress to be made in ensuring high-quality efficient international policing and subsequently successful local police reform."[23] Police-building and supporting the provision of safety and justice is more than a formal institutional restructuring process and is better understood as an attempt to transform organisational and socio-cultural behaviours. Such processes of social change require genuine local ownership and participation which has not been the strength of UNPOL missions to date.[24]

Ascertaining a clear picture of how providers are performing in a range of areas as well as how their actions are received in this complex environment lies at the heart of enhancing efficacy and producing sustainable outcomes. Furthermore, despite the groundswell of opinion in favour of policing as an integral part of peace operations, the relative infancy of police reform and the varied results to date leave the validity of the modalities and methods through which it is implemented open to question. Arguably, even the normative assumptions of change that underpin this intervention logic (i.e. change theory) are far from accepted. M&E that reflects upon these uncertainties promises better learning about these evolving practices. Similarly, dilemmas surrounding if, and if so how, to engage non-state sources of security and justice present peace operations with difficult decisions in the restoration of law and order and the building of local capacity in the aftermath of conflict. M&E that incorporates the roles and influences of these stakeholders promises a more holistic picture of what is happening in relation to rule of law experiences amongst the host population. Furthermore, it can support managers in the field and future mission architects to better address these issues.

Finally, there are numerous cross-cutting benefits associated with an M&E regimen. One example relates to identifying and developing strategies to mitigate the negative impacts and unintended consequences of peace operations on host populations.[25] Another dimension relates to presenting illuminating information on the level of coordination vertically (i.e. between the strategic, operational and tactical functional strata within the mission), as well as integration and collaboration horizontally (i.e. across different mission components as well as with external partners).[26] M&E has the potential to produce detailed analysis of interdependent programming in these increasingly integrated endeavours, further improving the chance that operations will be efficacious.

M&E is particularly *difficult* because UN peace operations deploy to some of the world's most insecure locations, characterised by residual armed violence and abject poverty. As a result, areas of responsibility are insufficiently secure and predictable to meet the access needs synonymous with many conventional M&E approaches. These constraints are exacerbated by a scarcity of conventional data sources and the reality that obtainable information is unreliable. Furthermore, peace operations deploy and function in highly dynamic and complex environments. In the aftermath of violent conflict, things happen quickly and a war-to-peace transition does not follow a predictable trajectory.[27] This makes the attribution of accomplishments and claims of causality particularly difficult. Another impediment is that the questions are extremely difficult to engage with analytically – as Downs and Stedman describe in relation to multidimensional peace operations, "It is difficult to think of an environment that is less conducive to the conduct of evaluation research."[28] Similarly, Schumacher points out that, "a conflict zone presents an environment antithetical to the systematic ordering of causality and epistemology towards which evaluation aspires."[29]

To compound this, peace operations are politically sensitive undertakings and there are often normative and political imperatives that prevent 'learning' from what is actually happening in the field and result in an aversion to admit or demonstrate failure. For example, the growing cost of peace operations is a perennial bone of contention for some member states and missions are at times dependent on fragile host state consent. In this context, the UN Secretariat has been understandably reticent to admit failure for fear that politically sensitive funding sources will dry up or missions may be prematurely withdrawn.[30] As a result, a pervasive culture of (and pressure to achieve) 'success' amongst the peace operations bureaucracy militates against accepting failure or recognising negative consequences in periodic assessments.[31] In the realm of policing, these challenges are more pronounced as policing organisations – be they local and host country or international and multinational – are notorious for being cautious, even secretive and resistant to change.[32] The resultant high-pressure operational environments have contributed to a reluctance to participate and value M&E processes, rendering them and their findings of limited utility. Finally, UN peace operations suffer from a shortage of the institutional capacity, as well as material and human resources required to conduct M&E that can be an expensive and time-consuming undertaking.[33]

Notwithstanding these difficulties, the importance of M&E in peace operations – serving a number of different purposes both for those who deploy missions as well as the stakeholders/communities who receive and host them – suggests that developing relevant ways of doing it deserves attention. However, the current state of underdevelopment regarding M&E for UNPOL in UN peace operations belies the potential utility of an insightful M&E system. Consequently, there is a significant practical question about the most appropriate ways to monitor and evaluate the impact of police in UN peace operations. For instance, how should the effectiveness of UNPOL efforts be measured? What impact does UNPOL have on building sustainable peace? To what extent can positive changes in peace and stability be attributed to the work of UNPOL? What is the strength and validity of the theories of change that undergird the UNPOL project? How these questions are answered has significant ramifications for the ability of particular missions, and the peace operations apparatus as a whole, to better contribute to desired goals. Understanding the relationship and increasing the linkages between M&E in the field and organisational learning is central to enhancing the important work of ongoing and future missions in saving lives, abating violence and planting the seeds of sustainable peace in societies emerging from conflict. As yet, this has not been examined satisfactorily. The primary research question guiding this study is therefore, *how should the UN monitor and evaluate the impact of police in its peace operations?*

Research context

Whilst monitoring and evaluating peace operations has long-since been a preoccupation of funders, policy-makers and researchers alike, academic scholarship has thus far neglected the vexing practical questions relating to challenges of monitoring and evaluating the impact of field activity. In doing so, it has missed the opportunity to further research an integral dimension of peace operations and a potential factor in their success. This constitutes a significant gap in the extant literature as the lack of attention to suitable M&E approaches is indicative of the absence of widely used approaches in praxis. As an academic inquiry, this research sits at the confluence of two subfields of the international relations discipline: first, the theory and practice of peace operations; and second, international policing, rule of law and security sector reform (SSR).

The body of literature on peace operations has occurred in three distinct waves.[34] The first spanned the Cold War years and documented what was a new and innovative interpretation of the UN Charter.[35] The second, in the immediate aftermath of the Cold War, initially reflected the optimism of a UN system relieved of the inhibitive dynamics of great power struggles in the Security Council[36] but soon became tendentious to the travesties in UN peacekeeping during the mid-1990s.[37] The most recent wave followed the return to peacekeeping at the turn of the century, with ambitious operations in Kosovo, Sierra Leone, DR Congo and Timor-Leste. Although much of the peacekeeping literature remains descriptive in character, this third wave of scholarship since the mid-2000s is indicative of a maturation of the disciplinary literature. The use of the term 'peace operations' to capture the multifunctional nature of these missions, including a more explicit focus on peacebuilding mandates and modalities, was a hallmark of this work.[38] Furthermore, it brought with it more sophisticated analyses including more robust theoretical inquiries,[39] as well as a readiness to use rigorous social science research methods to address empirical questions associated with the impact of peacekeeping.[40]

As part of this evolution, a number of authors have contributed to debates on how success in peace operations should be conceptualised and evaluated.[41] This was followed by a number of authors looking at dichotomous notions of success and failure in peacekeeping using advanced statistical modelling and methods.[42] Other contributions suggested that multiple factors contributing to the eventual success of peace operations needed to be better understood,[43] always including high politics of the security council (P-5 in particular), host state and domestic spoilers,[44] some also include regional arrangements, and the alignment between these three levels of interests.[45] Furthermore, other authors have written on the topic of success in peacebuilding missions and endeavours specifically broadening the framework for analysis significantly.[46]

Recent scholarship makes a persuasive case that peacekeeping 'works' as it significantly reduces the likelihood of relapse to armed violence – even in the most difficult of cases.[47] Furthermore, these findings seem to sit well with the Human Security Report Project's assessment that the post-Cold War growth of peace operations correlates to an overall reduction in number and toll of intra-state conflicts – more likely to be concluded through settlement than military triumph.[48] However, most of the academic assessments or evaluations about the effectiveness of peacekeeping are grounded in extremely limited and limiting dichotomy of 'success' and 'failure' that perpetuates what Pugh has referred to as the "hegemonic positivism that claims to measure the 'success' or otherwise of operations."[49] In other words, the majority of this literature misses the complexity of the transformative processes at play and has neglected the causal ambiguity inherent in peace operations. Consequently, whilst assessment of the success of peace operations as a policy tool after the fact has made significant strides, examining the impact of activities towards these macro-level results and unpacking the cause-effect relationships between mission outputs and societal outcomes – particularly in relation to specific components of missions – remains an underexplored yet critical area of peace operations research.[50] In short, existing research on the effectiveness of peace operations has failed to sufficiently tackle the issue of organisational performance at the implementation level.[51] This study takes this literature as its point of departure, and therefore seeks to open up the 'black box' of causality in peace operations to add to the understanding of when, how and why missions have desired impacts, as well as when and why this sometimes falls outside of what is feasible.

As mentioned previously, modern research has increasingly pointed to 'organisational learning' as an important factor affecting the outcomes of peace operations.[52] However, there is a paucity of studies on how M&E can assist in improving the UN's peace operations, including how the organisation could more effectively learn lessons during and in the wake of its peace operations. There are two notable exceptions. Firstly, Howard's 2008 book, which highlights the primary importance of 'first-level' or intra-mission learning – i.e. "learning while doing" – as one of three core factors in achieving effective mission outcomes.[53] Secondly, Benner *et al.*'s 2011 book which focuses on identifying the structural and political factors that enable or inhibit organisation-wide processes of learning – i.e. questioning and changing organisational rules in order to change organisational practice through 'knowledge acquisition, advocacy and institutionalization' – within what they refer to as the UN peace operations bureaucracy.[54] Both bring empirical research to bear and shed light on the importance of this understudied element of effectiveness in peace operations. Building on the work of Howard and Benner *et al.* in this area, this book draws together these different strands and levels of learning into a holistic framework for organisational learning. Furthermore, it drills down into the specific area of knowledge acquisition/data gathering firmly grounded in field experiences that is deemed to be a prerequisite for organisational learning – further exploring the relationship between field-level M&E, organisational learning and more effective peace operations.

Historically, policing has been a lesser-studied area of peace operations[55] – falling between the military-centric focus of traditional international security scholarship and the 'alternative' paradigms dominant in the peace research community.[56] However, more recently, there has been an upsurge in scholarship on the role of civilian police in post-conflict situations. This literature focuses on the modalities of international policing within peace operations increasingly implementing mandates at the peacekeeping-peacebuilding nexus.[57] Consequently it is closely tied to the realm of 'Policebuilding', SSR, the Rule of Law and their importance in the study of international affairs, peace and conflict, development and a fledgling international criminology discipline.[58] Research on police in peace operations often points to the lack of effective M&E as an enduring challenge in the realm of international policing producing knowledge gaps and accountability deficits.[59] However, aside from the Benner *et al.*'s book – which traces the UN's experience of organisational learning relating to 'police assistance' in three cases – targeted studies on how to gauge the impact of international policing endeavours and learn from their experiences remain few and far between.[60] Therefore, building on existing research, this study seeks to address some of these gaps by developing a framework for facilitating learning from the insights emanating from the field in the specific context of policing in UN peace operations. Moreover, it goes beyond the majority of the disciplinary literature in this area to develop possible answers to as yet unanswered questions. These literatures and bodies of work act as the launching pad for this inquiry as they provide fertile ground from which to deduce hypotheses and identify the building blocks for a heuristic M&E framework.

Approach

To answer the research question, I adopted a *retroductive* research design.[61] That is an approach that combines deduction (i.e. deriving hypotheses from theoretical literature and other sources) and induction (i.e. abstracting meaning from empirical investigation and observations).[62] This is the most appropriate overarching research strategy for the book because it enabled the field research to stimulate 'back-tracking' such that the study works back from empirical findings to a possible explanation as to that framework's utility. The commonly cited problem with retroductive designs relates to how the initial hypothesis and research inquiry is generated.[63] In other words, how are the mechanisms and structures that are perceived to produce observed phenomena identified or imagined? In this case this genesis was less of a problem as the hypothesis that 'improved M&E might contribute to more effective peace operations through organisational learning' has been advanced by other scholars[64] and is often an (albeit understudied) recommendation of much literature in this area. Similarly, M&E is a known mechanism for associating impact assessment with improvements in practice.

In effect, the deductive process in Part I of the research process laid the groundwork for my theory/framework building in Part II, whilst the inductive process in Part III was followed in order to test my M&E framework and draw out the most pertinent insights and elements to support its suitability for use in this general context. Furthermore, given that the study applies the framework to one case study, a retroductive research strategy was deemed suitable given the inevitable conclusion that this book constitutes only the beginning to a research process. For the framework developed herein to gain greater validity and credence, it is important that further cycles of deduction and induction are conducted in alternative cases to buttress and further revise and refine the findings of this book. The retroductive research strategy followed a seven-step approach.

The first step involved identifying the key trends in international policing and the main strategic/operational challenges facing the UNPOL apparatus. This was deemed necessary to build an awareness of the contemporary issues at stake to be able to incorporate these into a tailored M&E framework and if necessary weight its design in favour of these pressing issues. The second step explored the existing M&E architecture within the UN peace operations system. This step satisfied the need to establish both the 'lay of the land' and the 'state of the art' in this domain. This allowed me to engage critically with the recurring themes and assumptions in current thinking and survey the models utilised in peace operations and related fields. The third step involved evaluating the strengths and weaknesses of these extant approaches. This was crucial for highlighting the key conceptual issues and methodological/practical features that could constitute an improvement in current practice in the specific context of UNPOL in peace operations.

Based on this critical analysis, the fourth step explored the value of using complexity theory as a guiding paradigm for understanding the complexities of peace operations environments, as well as the ramifications of doing so for the task of M&E. Complexity theory was deemed to be useful due to its analytical utility for understanding change and mitigating causal ambiguity in multidimensional systems that are dynamic and continually evolving. The following step utilised this theoretical frame (i.e. concepts and ideas from complexity theory), deductive observations garnered from earlier steps, and insights from initial primary research with practitioners and experts to develop a holistic M&E framework. This alternative framework for M&E was developed due to the need for a tailored approach in the context of inappropriate current orthodoxy.

The penultimate step concerned interrogating the validity, relevance and usefulness of this framework in a case study – United Nations Mission in Liberia (UNMIL)[65] – and was carried out in three parts. The first provided a detailed exploration of the case study context to situate subsequent analyses. The second – based on insights from the field research – identified the strengths, comparative advantages and potentialities of the framework vis-à-vis existing approaches employed in the field. The third highlighted weaknesses, problems and potential naïveté with the framework evidenced in a real-world setting. This approach was selected to allow for thorough and balanced testing of the framework, as well as to facilitate the final step in the approach which was to reflect on how the framework should be refined and revised to take account of these inductive findings.

Case selection

The study utilises one detailed case study for two main reasons. Firstly, the nature and demands of the research question require a large amount of contextual detail. Context-specificity is an important component of the framework developed herein and therefore an exploration of a case study's past; as well as its present it was deemed to be important for understanding the contemporary challenges to building sustainable peace in its post-conflict scenario. In particular, unpacking the historical *modus operandi* and general perceptions of the state security sector were thought to be vital building blocks for efforts to understand progress in the restoration of law and order and the reconstruction of the police and criminal justice system. Second, the book does not call for the development of a 'one-size-fits-all' framework for M&E. Each peace operation is *sui generis* due to the differences in the conflicts and peace processes they deploy to address and support. Whilst there are thematic and programmatic similarities across missions, it would be dangerous to assume that circumstances are replicated across different contexts. Therefore, the commonly cited benefits of multiple case studies do not necessarily apply in this context and a 'small N' study was deemed to be most suitable. The caveat, and a significant one, is that the general validity of my M&E framework cannot be asserted. The conclusions promulgated only hold on the basis of this one case study. However, this can be understood to lay the foundations for further research opportunities.

Given these criteria, UNMIL was selected as the case study for five main reasons. Firstly, the type and content of its mandate made UNMIL a suitable choice. UNMIL epitomises the multidimensional UN peace operations that are most prevalent across the world today. As others have pointed out, as of mid-2013, over 90 per cent of UNPOL were deployed in eight large multidimensional peace operations, six of which are in Africa.[66] Furthermore, UNPOL had a clear and significant part in the mission mandate from the beginning of the mission – not the case in all missions. UNMIL has embodied a kind of hybrid UNPOL mission whereby it was initially and still is furnished with pseudo-executive policing functions but always and increasingly focused on the reform, restructuring, and rebuilding of domestic law enforcement agencies.[67] In this sense, UNMIL's police mandate encapsulates the dualism associated with many contemporary UNPOL deployments.

The second reason for case selection relates to on-the-ground realities. In short, the scenarios that UNMIL has faced throughout its existence capture the major challenges associated with the 'New International Policing', *inter alia*: balancing operational support and capacity-building imperatives; managing a partnership with (transitional) governments; eventual transition of internal security responsibilities to local authorities; and a significant role of non-state actors in security and justice provision. Third, UNMIL has constituted a crucible for new and evolving efforts regarding the role and function of UNPOL in UN peace operations. For example, UNMIL has been a site of emerging thinking and mission-structuring around more holistic and integrated law and justice programming under the rubric of security sector reform. Furthermore, UNMIL was the first UN mission to develop a comprehensive plan for the police component in its concept of operations and to define the role and operational tasks of FPUs in its operational plan.[68]

Fourth, the mission's currency facilitated ease of access to both pertinent information sources as well as past and present mission personnel. This allowed for thorough case study analysis. Finally, UNMIL in Liberia is increasingly spoken about as one of the latest 'success stories' of UN peace operations.⁶⁹ Regardless of the validity of these claims, the perception that it has been a success suggests that it would be a prime case and rich source of organisational learning. These reasons made UNMIL a suitable case study choice.

Method

On a number of different occasions throughout the project I carried out a series of interviews with over 30 officials and experts at UN Headquarters (primarily within DPKO) and had numerous interactions in other settings such as academic roundtables/conferences and meetings with expert practitioners and policy-makers working in this area. I further benefitted from access to internal documents and evolving policies and procedures at the UN, as well as additional informal discussions with officials, diplomats, policy-makers and senior personnel within member state permanent missions in New York. These engagements enabled me to piece together a clear picture of the current state of affairs within the organisation regarding M&E and organisational learning.

The case study research was designed to ensure that it followed an appropriate methodology and sound application of ethical procedures. This led to insightful theoretical analysis to explain research findings – drawing on multiple theories where appropriate.⁷⁰ Conducting the empirical case study included desk and field research components. The first involved a comprehensive review of primary and secondary sources including: mission documentation, UN Security Council/General Assembly reports and lessons learned reviews; relevant think-tank and NGO publications; as well as academic literature and media commentary. This body of information was augmented by extensive field research and author interviews.

The main method I employed during the fieldwork was 'semi-structured interviews'.⁷¹ It was not feasible to attempt to interview the entirety of key stakeholder groups in the mission and beyond, so an initial sample of interviewees and observation sites was selected using purposive sampling techniques.⁷² The resulting list of interviewees constituted a cross-section of stakeholders, including senior UN mission and police component managers; serving police officers and staff in complementary rule of law components; other UN staff; government Ministers and employees including local police, criminal justice institutions; local and international NGOs and CSOs in the mission area as well as local community leaders and members. In the interviews, I was hoping to ascertain interviewees' perceptions and assessments of existing M&E tools at their disposal, along with their ideas about how they could be improved or what a more useful framework might look like. The aim of this approach was to elicit what they, as both implementers and beneficiaries, understood about the challenges of M&E in the peace operations context.

In addition, 'focus group' and 'participant observation' techniques were also used during field research. On occasion, impromptu focus groups were conducted where circumstances dictated or local organisations requested that discussions take place in a group setting. The method of participant observation was utilised as a useful complementary method for discovering information and perspectives that cannot easily be gleaned from time-constrained interviews/focus groups or formal documentation. This collection of research methods afforded the opportunity to gain a human perspective on M&E in the field and at headquarters.

Pursuant to attaining informed consent, agreement was reached on behalf of the mission and with individual participants regarding whether or not contributions were to be treated anonymously. In order to deal with my own 'positionality' – i.e. me being a white, male, western-educated, academic researcher – I employed a reflexive framework, which was designed to prompt continual reflection on the ethics of my research, writing and analysis process – during and subsequent to this field research.[73] Whilst these measures enabled ethical fieldwork, research in a post-conflict environment also presented a number of logistical challenges.

My fieldwork was authorised in part due to an agreement with UNMIL that they would provide me with basic assistance and security assurances. Whilst this arrangement mitigated some of the challenges to conducting field research, particularly relating to travel around the country, it also obliged me to abide by a stringent code of conduct, restrictions on movement and curfews. This contributed to access-constraints regarding some of the important stakeholder groups beyond UNMIL's employ. This predicament had ramifications for the extent to which I was able to realise the broad-based stakeholder engagement inherent in the methodological principles advocated in this study in line with complexity theory. The potential disconnect between the methodologies advocated and those employed herein rendered by this scenario are taken up in further detail in a section addressing the limitations of the study in the concluding chapter.

Central argument

The central claim of this book is that, if it is to realise its full potential, M&E needs to be both re-thought and re-positioned. That is to say: first, it needs to bring new epistemological thinking to bear in the focus and design of an approach and associated selection of methods for its execution; and second, it needs to be embedded in the machinery of peace operations such that it is an intrinsic part of the way peace operations are planned and managed.

In making this claim, this book argues that M&E can and should be understood as critical to effective peace operations insofar as it can facilitate organisational learning in both the immediate and specific context, as well as the more protracted and general sense – i.e. first and second level learning, respectively.[74] That is, M&E can improve real-time decision-making in the field as well as feeding into organisational learning and knowledge management at headquarters' level within – and potentially between – missions. This in turn can enable improved planning and optimising contributions to desired outcomes/impacts – including mitigating the negative unintended consequences of action – and ultimately lead to more efficacious peace operations. However, the book argues that existing templates and models are inadequate and unsuitable in the face of myriad and unique challenges. It therefore argues for – and develops – a framework for approaching M&E of UNPOL in peace operations, drawing and building upon different elements of existing literature and practice. And, it augments this thinking with insights from complexity theory.

Regarding the re-thinking of M&E, the book asserts that as peace operations and international policing are complex undertakings and evolutionary practices, they require a modality for understanding and assessing them as such. Furthermore, it argues that whilst there is an implicit theory of change (be it stabilisation or peacebuilding focused) associated with restoration and building the capacity of an effective rule of law system, the implementation polices and programming are sufficiently 'experimental' (particularly in any given context) as to require a flexible and adaptive tracking modality which is capable of reflecting the complexity at play.

Regarding the re-positioning, it is argued that for M&E to fulfil its potential for the maximum number of stakeholders at multiple levels of analysis, it must be promoted to the fore of holistic management of peace operations. The benefits accruing from more suitable M&E are ultimately contingent on M&E being conceived broadly and figuring more prominently in the overall management of missions and the peace operations bureaucracy itself. Ultimately, the book concludes that enhanced M&E, drawing on and embracing the "spirit of epistemological uncertainty"[75] and embedded in holistic mission management framework, can lead to more effective organisational learning and, in turn, to more efficacious peace operations.

Contribution to the field

By building on the recent work of Howard and Benner *et al.* on the importance of organisational learning to effective peace operations, this book contributes to debates and thinking in this domain. Moreover, the findings have significant implications for research and policy development regarding M&E, which has heretofore resided in a narrow sphere. A major contribution of this book is to conduct the first systematic analysis of M&E for peace operations/UNPOL and to offer a new way of doing it. It draws on the value-add of complexity theory and uses an interdisciplinary approach to generate an innovative critique of current orthodoxy and develops a new framework for M&E that is appropriate for use in uncertain and dynamic post-conflict environments. In doing so, this book adds much-needed analysis and recommendations to this important area of inquiry.

In particular, the book brings M&E in peace operations out of the bureaucratic, external and technical realm into the political, intrinsic and artistic domain. M&E that embraces complexity, rather than simplifies it, has real-world relevance and presents a potentially useful approach for scholars, analysts and practitioners attempting to navigate and make sense of the 'wicked' problems pervasive in this field. The book also contributes to a nascent but growing body of work on the centrality of civilian police in peace operations. In particular, it challenges researchers and practitioners alike to conceptualise how and when non-state actors contribute to and/or are relied upon for progress in peace operations, including how 'progress' is understood and measured. Furthermore, the book presents reflexive M&E that encourages missions to question the validity of assumptions and theories of change upon which they are predicated.

Book structure

The three-stage research approach outlined above is reflected in the structure of the book in three parts. Part I comprises two chapters that contain the engagement with and critical review of existing literature relating to the research question. The first chapter lays out the importance of UNPOL in contemporary peace operations, depicts current practices and identifies the problems and challenges facing today's UNPOL endeavours. It begins by presenting a historical account of the evolution of UN peace operations since their inception. The second section proceeds to focus on the quantitative and qualitative transformation of the role of UN Police in these missions and highlights that as UNPOL have become increasingly mission critical, they have moved deeper into early peacebuilding efforts such as rule of law and security sector reform objectives. The third section highlights the major challenges facing the UN policing apparatus in deploying and executing mandates and the chapter concludes by identifying organisational learning and monitoring and evaluation as a key avenue for addressing these challenges.

The second chapter presents an overview of current M&E practices in UN peace operations and identifies the problems and challenges with existing approaches. The chapter argues that UNPOL require a tailored approach that can overcome the shortcomings with the extant orthodoxy. It proceeds in four sections. First it clarifies what is meant by M&E for the purposes of this book. Second, it reviews and critically assesses current M&E tools within the UN peace operations apparatus.[76] Third, it identifies the extant literature on M&E in (international) policing. Finally, it draws together the major shortcomings and challenges associated with these approaches in relation to the specific M&E needs of police in peace operations.

16 *Introduction*

Part II of the book is an exercise in theory and framework building. The third chapter explores the utility of the study of complexity for explaining and addressing the problems identified in the previous chapters. Specifically, it examines the value of applying some of the insights gained from complexity theory for helping to understand how to better analyse, monitor and evaluate peace operations that can be understood to inhabit complex systems that are highly dynamic and nonlinear. The chapter proceeds in four parts. First, it briefly charts the origins of complexity theory, distils the core concepts of the paradigm, introduces the features of a complex system and notes the increasing application of such concepts to the social sciences as well as enduring contentions. Second, it draws upon the emerging literature viewing peace missions and their operating environments as complex social systems and proceeds to expand on this nascent field using real-world examples to substantiate the suitability of such a representation. The third part demonstrates how the central tenets of complexity theory provide an alternative and pertinent theoretical framework for addressing the weaknesses of extant M&E in peace operations. It considers what employing a complexity lens means for – and brings to – the task of monitoring and evaluating progress and change in complex systems. Finally, the chapter concludes by articulating the core implications of complexity-oriented M&E for contributing to subsequent development of a framework for UNPOL in peace operations.

Chapter 4 develops a framework that substantiates how the ideas in the previous chapter can be made to work in an M&E setting for UNPOL to overcome the challenges identified in Chapters 1 and 2. Based on the insights in Part I and the theoretical insights introduced in the previous chapter, this fourth chapter develops a meta-framework to guide the design and implementation of M&E for UNPOL in peace operations. The chapter proceeds in three main parts. The first section introduces the overarching framework presenting its architecture, the rationale for its design and its key features. The second section explicates the internal field-level 3-step M&E process, describing each step in turn and suggesting the possible tools and methods for its execution as well as relating each step to the others. The third section articulates how the framework facilitates learning processes, including how this is designed to feed back into and inform mission planning. The chapter concludes by summarising the main elements of the framework and its potential benefits as a foundation for the primary field research in subsequent chapters.

Part III of the book tests the framework through reference to a case study – the experience of UNMIL in Liberia. It does so in order to test the relative strength of the framework and highlights remaining challenges faced by such an approach. Chapter 5 provides a backdrop to the case study and has two main parts. The first presents a brief background to Liberia's genesis including the political, economic and social development that occurred between formation and the outbreak of civil war. It proceeds to chronicle the two phases of violent conflict in Liberia stretching from 1989 to 2003, addresses the competing narratives regarding the root causes of the conflict and documents the major consequences of protracted insecurity. The second part introduces the UN peace operation in Liberia, first detailing its mandate then analysing the mission's milestone achievements and examining the UNPOL experience to date. This includes a description of the UNPOL component from inception through to contemporary operational circumstances, including significant changes during the mission lifetime and its primary activities. The final section charts the drawdown of the mission to date and its relevance to UNPOL objectives.

Chapter 6 draws on the analysis of extensive primary research in the field with a wide range of stakeholders to interrogate the validity, utility and applicability of the proposed approach to M&E in this setting. The first section briefly explains the M&E tools and approaches currently employed in UNMIL. The second part identifies and brings empirical insights to bear on the purported strengths, comparative advantages and potentialities of my framework as opposed to current M&E approaches. It emphasises a number of ways in which the framework advances current practice and contributes to organisational learning as observed and revealed in the case of UNMIL in Liberia.

Chapter 7 highlights a number of weaknesses, problems and potential naïveté with the framework in relation to what the case of Liberia reveals, but also what its particular operating environment, mission phase at the time of the field research, and specific mandate may conceal vis-à-vis the settings and possible mandates of UNPOL in other UN peace operations. It points to a number of areas for revision and refinements, as well as recognition of the limitations of the framework.

The final chapter concludes the book with an overview of the research findings and the argument developed throughout the study. It also highlights the original contributions and implications of the study, along with potential avenues for future research. In sum, the book concludes that enhanced M&E, which draws on and embraces the "spirit of epistemological uncertainty",[77] entrenches flexibility and which is embedded in a holistic mission management framework, can lead to more effective organisational learning and, in turn, to more efficacious peace operations.

Notes

1 Sergio Vieira de Mello, "How Not to Run a Country: Lessons for the UN from Kosovo and East Timor", (Dili: unpublished paper, 2000), 21, cited in "Australia's Involvement in Peacekeeping Operations", (Canberra: Senate Standing Committees on Foreign Affairs, Defence and Trade, Parliament of Australia, 2008), 49.
2 Alex J. Bellamy, Paul Williams, and Stuart Griffin, *Understanding Peacekeeping*, 2nd ed. (Cambridge: Polity, 2010), 93–152.
3 Garth den Heyer, *The Role of Civilian Police in Peacekeeping: 1999–2007*

(Washington, DC: Police Foundation, 2012), 13–22; B. K. Greener, "UNPOL: UN Police as Peacekeepers", *Policing and Society* 19, no. 2 (2008); W. J. Durch, "United Nations Police Evolution, Present Capacity and Future Tasks", in *GRIPS State-Building Workshop 2010: Organizing Police Forces in Post-Conflict Peace Support Operations* (2010); John Casey, *Policing the World: The Practice of International and Transnational Policing* (Durham, North Carolina: Carolina Academic Press, 2009).
4 William J. Durch and Madeline L. England, eds., *Enhancing United Nations Capacity to Support Post-Conflict Policing and Rule of Law*, Stimson Center Report No. 63, Revised, Project on Rule of Law in Post-Conflict Settings, Future of Peace Operations Program (Washington DC: The Stimson Center, 2010), 1; Bethan K. Greener, "The Rise of Policing in Peace Operations", *International Peacekeeping* 18, no. 2 (2011).
5 Carolyn Bull, *No Entry without Strategy: Building the Rule of Law under UN Transitional Administration* (Tokyo/New York/Paris: United Nations University Press, 2008), 1. See also: Gordon Peake, "Partnerships and International Policing: The Reach and Limits of Policy Processes", *International Peacekeeping* 18, no. 5 (2011).
6 Till Blume, "Security, Justice and the Rule of Law in Peace Operations", *International Peacekeeping* 15, no. 5 (2008); Jane Stromseth, David Wippman, and Rosa Brooks, eds., *Can Might Make Rights: Building the Rule of Law after Military Interventions* (Cambridge: Cambridge University Press, 2006), 56–60; Rekyo Huang, "Securing the Rule of Law: Assessing International Strategies for Post-Conflict Criminal Justice", (New York: International Peace Academy, 2005); Jessica Howard and Bruce Oswald, "The Rule of Law on Peace Operations" (paper presented at the "Challenges of Peace Operations" Project, Melbourne Law School, University of Melbourne, 11–13 November 2002); Marcus Brand, "Promoting the Rule of Law, Transparency and Fighting against Corruption", in *'Building Capacity for Democracy, Peace and Social Progress' – The 6th International Conference of New or Restored Democracies (ICNRD-6)* (Doha, Qatar: UNDP, 2006); Annika S. Hansen and Sharon Wiharta, "The Transition to a Just Order: Establishing Local Ownership after Conflict", in *Research Report* (Folke Bernadotte Academy, 2007), XVI.
7 UN Press Release, OBV/998, PKO/271, 25 May 2011, www.un.org/News/Press/docs/2011/obv998.doc.htm.
8 See, for example: Paul F. Diehl and Daniel Druckman, *Evaluating Peace Operations* (Boulder, CO: Lynne Rienner, 2010); V. P. Fortna, *Does Peacekeeping Work? Shaping Belligerents' Choices after Civil War* (Princeton, NJ: Princeton University Press 2008); Michael W. Doyle and Nicholas Sambanis, "International Peacebuilding: A Theoretical and Quantitative Analysis", *The American Political Science Review* 94, no. 4 (2000); Nicholas Sambanis, "Short- and Long-Term Effects of United Nations Peace Operations", *The World Bank Economic Review* 22, no. 1 (2008).
9 For an overview, still extremely relevant, see: Stephen John Stedman, "Introduction", in *Ending Civil Wars: The Implementation of Peace Agreements*, ed. Stephen John Stedman, Donald Rothchild, and Elizabeth M. Cousens (Boulder, CO: Lynne Rienner, 2002), 3–20.
10 See, in particular: L. M. Howard, *UN Peacekeeping in Civil Wars* (Cambridge: Cambridge University Press, 2008); Thorsten Benner, Stephan Mergenthaler, and Philipp Rotmann, *The New World of UN Peace Operations: Learning to Build Peace?* (Oxford: Oxford University Press, 2011). See also: Susanna P. Campbell, "When Process Matters: The Potential Implications of Organisational Learning for Peacebuilding Success", *Journal of Peacebuilding and Development* 4, no. 2 (2008).
11 Howard, *UN Peacekeeping in Civil Wars*, 8, 330–9.
12 Cedric de Coning and Paul Romita, "Monitoring and Evaluation of Peace Operations", (New York, Oslo: International Peace Institute & Norwegian

Institute of International Affairs, November 2009); Thorsten Benner, Stephan Mergenthaler, and Philipp Rotmann, "The Evolution of Organizational Learning in the UN Peace Operations Bureaucracy", in *Research DSF No. 31* (German Foundation for Peace Research, 2011).
13 William Durch and Madeline England, eds., *Enhancing United Nations Capacity to Support Post-Conflict Policing and Rule of Law*, 48; Benner, Mergenthaler, and Rotmann, *The New World of UN Peace Operations: Learning to Build Peace?*, 74.
14 Michael Barnett cited in Benner, Mergenthaler, and Rotmann, *The New World of UN Peace Operations: Learning to Build Peace?*, 225.
15 Monitoring and Evaluation broadly conceived to include: impact assessment, measuring success, results-based management, performance management, measures of effectiveness, systematic review, etc.
16 Campbell, "When Process Matters: The Potential Implications of Organisational Learning for Peacebuilding Success", 27.
17 That is, peace operations are relatively expensive in terms of assessed/required member state contributions to the UN.
18 This is particularly true in the context of limited involvement and/or consultation of troop and personnel contributors in opaque Security Council processes.
19 Gordon Peake and Kaysie Studdard-Brown, "Policebuilding: The International Deployment Group in the Solomon Islands", *International Peacekeeping* 12, no. 4 (2005): 529.
20 Agnes Hurwitz and Kaysie Studdard, "Rule of Law Programs in Peace Operations", in *The Security-Development Nexus Program* (New York: International Peace Academy, 2005), 13.
21 Joshua G. Smith, Victoria K. Holt, and William J. Durch, "Enhancing United Nations Capacity for Post-Conflict Policing and Rule of Law", in *The Project on Rule of Law in Post-Conflict Settings* (Washington DC: The Henry L. Stimson Center, 2007b), 43–4.
22 David H. Bayley, "Community Policing: Evaluation Programs", (New York: Civilian Police Division, DPKO, United Nations, 2005), 3.
23 Eirin Mobekk, "Identifying Lessons in United Nations International Policing Missions", in *Policy Paper 9* (Geneva: Geneva Centre for the Democratic Control of Armed Forces (DCAF), 2005), 3.
24 Hansen and Wiharta, "The Transition to a Just Order: Establishing Local Ownership after Conflict".
25 Christian van Stolk, Tom Ling, Anais Reding, and Matt Bassford, *Monitoring and Evaluation in Stabilisation Interventions: Reviewing the State of the Art and Suggesting Ways Forward* (Santa Monica, CA: RAND Corporation, 2011), 3.
26 de Coning and Romita, "Monitoring and Evaluation of Peace Operations", 2.
27 E.D. Mansfield and J. Snyder, "Turbulent Transitions: Why Emerging Democracies Go to War in the Twenty-First Century", in *Leashing the Dogs of War: Conflict Management in a Divided World*, ed. C. Crocker, F. O. Hampson, and P. Aall (Washington, DC: United States Institute for Peace, 2007); M. Mann, *The Rise of Classes and Nation-States, 1760–1914* (New York: Cambridge University Press, 1993); L. Diamond, *Developing Democracy: Toward Consolidation* (Baltimore: Johns Hopkins University Press, 1999).
28 George Downs and Stephen John Stedman, "Evaluation Issues in Peace Implementation", in *Ending Civil Wars: The Implementation of Peace Agreements*, eds. Stephen John Stedman, Donald Rothchild, and Elizabeth M. Cousens (Boulder, CO: Lynne Rienner, 2002), 43.
29 Joseph Schumacher, "What to Measure in Peace Operations", *The Pearson Papers* 10, no. 1 (2007): 45.
30 David Chuter, "Measures of Effectiveness for Peace Operations and Crisis Management", in *Measuring What Matters in Peace Operations and Crisis Management*,

ed. Sarah Jane Meharg (McGill-Queen's University Press, 2009), 187; Helen Lewis, "Evaluation and Assessment of Interventions", (Colorado: Beyond Intractability, 2004), 4.
31 Cheyanne Church and Julie Shouldice, "The Evaluation of Conflict Resolution Interventions: Framing the State of Play", (Letterkenny: INCORE, 2002), 45–7; Chuter, "Measures of Effectiveness for Peace Operations and Crisis Management", 187.
32 Jim Parsons *et al.*, "Developing Indicators to Measure the Rule of Law: A Global Approach" in *VERA International Indicators Group* (Vera Institute of Justice, 2008), 26; S. Rynn and D. Hiscock, "Evaluating for Security and Justice: Challenges and Opportunities for Improved Monitoring and Evaluation of Security System Reform Programmes", (Saferworld, 2009), 11–12.
33 Some M&E practitioners in related fields have estimated that approximately 5–10 per cent of mission/programme costs should be dedicated to the M&E if it is to be effective. (See, for example: DfID, "Measuring and Managing for Results in Fragile and Conflict-Affected States and Situations", in *Interim Guidance Note* [London: Department for International Development/UK Aid, 2010], 18; Rynn and Hiscock, "Evaluating for Security and Justice: Challenges and Opportunities for Improved Monitoring and Evaluation of Security System Reform Programmes", 18; INCAF, "Draft Justice and Security Monitoring and Evaluation Toolkit – Version 2", [OECD International Network on Conflict and Fragility – Task Team on Peacebuilding, Statebuilding, Security, 2010], 24.) These suggestions sit in stark contrast to anecdotal evidence suggesting that DPKO currently commits closer to 0.1 per cent of total mission budgets to these endeavours. (Interview: DPKO official – New York, United Nations, February 2009; Benjamin de Carvalho, IPI Workshop presentation, May 2009).
34 Virginia Page Fortna and Lise Morje Howard, "Pitfalls and Prospects in the Peacekeeping Literature", *Annual Review of Political Science* 11, no. 1 (2008): 284.
35 See, for example: A. L. Burns and N. Heathcote, *Peace-Keeping by U.N. Forces: From Suez to the Congo* (New York: Praeger, 1963); L. P. Bloomfield, *International Military Forces: The Question of Peacekeeping in an Armed and Disarming World* (Boston: Little, Brown, 1964); A. James, *The Politics of Peace-Keeping* (New York: Praeger, 1969); L. L. Fabian, *Soldiers without Enemies: Preparing the United Nations for Peacekeeping* (Washington, DC: Brookings Institute, 1971); H. Wiseman, ed. *Peacekeeping: Appraisals & Proposals* (New York: Pergamon and International Peace Academy, 1983); Indar Jit Rikhye, *The Theory and Practice of Peacekeeping* (London: C. Hurst and Company, 1984); E. B. Haas, *Why We Still Need the United Nations: The Collective Management of International Conflict, 1945–1984* (Berkeley: Institute of International Studies, University of California, Berkeley, 1986).
36 See, for example: Paul F. Diehl, *International Peacekeeping* (Baltimore, MD: John Hopkins University Press, 1993); William J. Durch, *The Evolution of UN Peacekeeping: Case Studies and Comparative Analysis* (New York: St. Martin's Press, 1993); Steven Ratner, *The New UN Peacekeeping: Building Peace in Lands of Conflict after the Cold War* (New York: St. Martin's, 1995); T. G. Weiss, ed. *The United Nations and Civil Wars* (Boulder, CO: Lynne Rienner, 1995); William J. Durch, "Keeping the Peace: Politics and Lessons of the 1990s", in *UN Peacekeeping, American Politics, and the Uncivil Wars of the 1990s*, ed. William J. Durch (Basingstoke, U.K: Macmillan, 1997); J. Hillen, *Blue Helmets: The Strategy of UN Military Operations* (Washington DC: Brassey's, 1998).
37 See, for example: R. Thakur and C. A. Thayer, eds., *A Crisis of Expectations: UN Peacekeeping in the 1990s* (Boulder, CO: Westview 1995); T. Findlay, ed. *Challenges for the New Peacekeepers* (Oxford: Oxford University Press, 1996); W. Clarke and J. Herbst, eds., *Learning from Somalia: The Lessons of Armed Humanitarian*

Intervention (Boulder, CO: Westview, 1997); J. Coulon, *Soldiers of Diplomacy: The United Nations, Peacekeeping, and the New World Order* (Toronto/Buffalo: University of Toronto Press, 1998); E. Moxon-Browne, ed. *A Future for Peacekeeping?* (New York: St. Martin's, 1998); D. C. Jett, *Why Peacekeeping Fails* (New York: St. Martin's, 1999); E. N. Luttwak, "Give War a Chance", *Foreign Affairs* 78, no. 4 (1999); F. H. Fleitz, *Peacekeeping Fiascoes of the 1990s: Causes, Solutions, and U.S. Interests* (Westport, CT: Praeger, 2002).

38 This literature also reflected the evolution of UN peace operations. See, for example: Erwin A. Schmidl, *Peace Operations between War and Peace* (Portland, OR: Frank Cass, 2000); Ramesh Thakur and Albrecht Schnabel, eds., *United Nations Peacekeeping Operations: Ad hoc Missions, Permanent Engagement* (New York: United Nations University Press, 2001); J. Boulden, *Peace Enforcement: The United Nations Experience in Congo, Somalia, and Bosnia* (Westport, CT: Praeger, 2001); E. M. Cousens, C. Kumar, and K. Wermester, eds., *Peacebuilding as Politics: Cultivating Peace in Fragile Societies* (Boulder, CO: Lynne Rienner, 2001); C. Crocker, F. O. Hampson, and P. Aall, eds., *Turbulent Peace* (Washington, DC: US Institute of Peace Press, 2001); K. H. Hawk, *Constructing the Stable State: Goals for Intervention and Peacebuilding* (Westport, CT: Praeger, 2002); Trevor Findlay, ed. *The Use of Force in UN Peace Operations* (Oxford: Oxford University Press, 2002); Esref Aksu, *The United Nations, Intra-State Peacekeeping and Normative Change* (Manchester: University of Manchester Press, 2003); J. Krasno, B. Hayes, and D. Daniel, eds., *Leveraging for Success in United Nations Peace Operations* (Westport, CT: Praeger, 2003); Alex J. Bellamy, Paul Williams, and Stuart Griffin, *Understanding Peacekeeping* (Cambridge: Polity, 2004); Simon Chesterman, *You, the People: The United Nations, Transitional Administration, and State-Building* (Oxford: Oxford University Press, 2004); R. Paris, *At War's End: Building Peace after Civil Conflict* (New York: Cambridge University Press, 2004); John Terence O'Neill and Nicholas Reece, *United Nations Peacekeeping in the Post-Cold War Era* (London: Routledge, 2005); William J. Durch, ed. *Twenty-First-Century Peace Operations* (Washington, D.C.: United States Institute of Peace and the Henry L. Stimson Center, 2006); Norrie MacQueen, *Peacekeeping and the International System* (London: Routledge, 2006); B. Pouligny, *Peace Operations Seen from Below: UN Missions and Local People* (Bloomfield, CT: Kumarian, 2006); Paul F. Diehl, *Peace Operations* (Cambridge: Polity, 2008).

39 See, for example: A. J. Bellamy, "The 'Next Stage' in Peace Operations Theory?", *International Peacekeeping* 11, no. 1 (2004); Eli Stamnes, "Critical Security Studies and the United Nations Preventive Deployment in Macedonia", *International Peacekeeping* 11, no. 1 (2004); M. Pugh, "Peacekeeping and Critical Theory", *International Peacekeeping* 11, no. 1 (2004); S. Whitworth, *Men, Militarism, and UN Peacekeeping: A Gendered Analysis* (Boulder, CO: Lynne Rienner, 2004); Laura Zanotti, "Taming Chaos: A Foucauldian View of UN Peacekeeping, Democracy and Normalization", *International Peacekeeping* 13, no. 2 (2006).

40 Fortna and Howard, "Pitfalls and Prospects in the Peacekeeping Literature", 288–91.

41 Robert C. Johansen, "Peacekeeping: How Should We Measure Success?", *Mershon International Studies Review* 38, no. 2 (1994); Duane Bratt, "Assessing the Success of UN Peacekeeping Operations" *International Peacekeeping* 3, no. 4 (1996); Duane Bratt, "Explaining Peacekeeping Performance: The UN in Internal Conflicts" *International Peacekeeping*, 4, no. 3 (1997); Diehl, *International Peacekeeping*; Downs and Stedman, "Evaluation Issues in Peace Implementation"; Daniel Druckman and Paul C. Stern, "Perspectives on Evaluating Peacekeeping Missions", *International Journal of Peace Studies* 4, no. 1 (1999).

42 Fortna, *Does Peacekeeping Work? Shaping Belligerents' Choices after Civil War*; Doyle

and Sambanis, "International Peacebuilding: A Theoretical and Quantitative Analysis"; Michael Doyle and Nicholas Sambanis, *Making War and Building Peace: United Nations Peace Operations* (Prinecton: Princeton University Press, 2006); Sambanis, "Short- and Long-Term Effects of United Nations Peace Operations"; Diehl and Druckman, *Evaluating Peace Operations*.

43 *Inter alia*: the existence of conflict-fuelling economic resources (e.g. diamonds, precious metals); mobilisation/termination of proxy assistance from external powers; quality of leadership by UN senior management, etc.

44 Adekeye Adebajo, *UN Peacekeeping in Africa: From the Suez Crisis to the Sudan Conflicts* (Boulder, CO: Lynne Reinner, 2011), 7; Howard, *UN Peacekeeping in Civil Wars*.

45 Adebajo, *UN Peacekeeping in Africa: From the Suez Crisis to the Sudan Conflicts*, 7.

46 See, for example: Charles T. Call "Knowing Peace When You See It: Setting Standards for Peacebuilding Success". *Civil Wars* 10, no. 2 (2008): 173–94; Ken Menkhaus, "Measuring Impact: Issues and Dilemmas", in *Occasional Paper Series* (Geneva: InterPeace, 2003); Neclâ Tschirgi, "Post-Conflict Peacebuilding Revisited: Achievements, Limitations, Challenges", in *Security-Development Nexus Program, Policy Paper* (New York: International Peace Academy, 2004); Michael Lund, "What kind of peace is being built? Taking stock of post-conflict peacebuilding and charting future directions", Discussion paper for the 10th anniversary of Agenda for Peace (International Development Research Centre [IDRC], Canada, January 2003).

47 Fortna, *Does Peacekeeping Work? Shaping Belligerents' Choices after Civil War*. See also: Doyle and Sambanis, *Making War and Building Peace: United Nations Peace Operations*; Sambanis, "Short- and Long-Term Effects of United Nations Peace Operations"; V. P. Fortna, "Does Peacekeeping Keep Peace? International Intervention and the Duration of Peace after Civil War", *International Studies Quarterly* 48, no. 2 (2004); V. P. Fortna, "Inside and Out: Peacekeeping and the Duration of Peace after Civil and Interstate Wars", *Intetrnational Studies Review* 5, no. 4 (2003); Michael J. Gilligan and Ernest J. Sergenti, "Do UN Interventions Cause Peace? Using Matching to Improve Causal Inference", *Quarterly Journal of Political Science* 3, (2008).

48 HSRP, "Human Security Brief 2007", (Vancouver, BC: School of International Studies, Simon Fraser University, 2007), 33–7.

49 Pugh, M. 'Cover Comments' in Higate and Henry, *Insecure Spaces: Peacekeeping, Power and Performance in Haiti, Kosovo and Liberia*.

50 One notable exception that attempts to delve into the causal mechanisms of peace operations is: Fortna, *Does Peacekeeping Work? Shaping Belligerents' Choices after Civil War*. Whilst this book examines some causal mechanisms of peacekeeping (including military, political and economic strategies, *inter alia*: changing the incentive structure for belligerents; reducing uncertainty/mistrust that drive security dilemma spirals; preventing events that trigger a reversion to violence; and, supporting political transformation to avoid disgruntlement-driven resumption of hostilities), it does not explore the cause-and-effect associated with the programmes and activities of particular components such as UNPOL.

51 Michael Lipson, "Performance under Ambiguity: International Organization Performance in UN Peacekeeping", *The Review of International Organizations* 5, no. 3 (2010): 261–7.

52 Howard, *UN Peacekeeping in Civil Wars*; Benner, Mergenthaler, and Rotmann, *The New World of UN Peace Operations: Learning to Build Peace?*

53 Howard, *UN Peacekeeping in Civil Wars*, 330–9.

54 Benner, Mergenthaler, and Rotmann, *The New World of UN Peace Operations: Learning to Build Peace?*

55 Annika S. Hansen, "From Congo to Kosovo: Civilian Police in Peace Operations", *Adelphi Papers* 41, no. 343 (2002): 33.

56 Espen B Eide and Tor Tanke Holm, "Introduction", in *Peacebuilding and Police Reform*, ed. Espen B Eide and Tor Tanke Holm (London: Frank Cass, 2000), 2.
57 See, for example: B. K. Greener, *The New International Policing*, Global Issues (Basingstoke, England: Palgrave Macmillan, 2009); Hansen, "From Congo to Kosovo: Civilian Police in Peace Operations"; Peter Andreas and Ethan Nadelmann, *Policing the Globe: Criminalization and Crime Control in International Relations* (Oxford: Oxford University Press, 2006); D. H. Bayley and Robert Perito, *The Police in War: Fighting Insurgency, Terrorism, and Violent Crime* (Boulder, CO: Lynne Rienner Publishers, 2010); Casey, *Policing the World: The Practice of International and Transnational Policing*; Robert B. Oakley, Michael J. Dziedzic, and Eliot M. Goldberg, eds., *Policing the New World Disorder: Peace Operations and Public Security* (Washington, DC: National Defense University, 1998); Erwin A. Schmidl, *Police in Peace Operations* (Vienna: Landesverteidigungsakademie, Militarwissenschaftliches Buro, 1998).
58 See, for example: D. Bayley, *Changing the Guard: Developing Democratic Police Abroad* (New York: Oxford University Press, 2006); Espen B. Eide and Tor Tanke Holm, *Peacebuilding and Police Reform* (London: Frank Cass, 2000); Alice Hills, *Policing Post-Conflict Cities* (London: Zed Books, 2009); Charles T. Call, ed. *Constructing Justice and Security after War* (Washington DC: United States Institute of Peace Press, 2007); Andrew Goldsmith and James Sheptycki, eds., *Crafting Transnational Policing: Police Capacity-Building and Global Policing Reform*, Onati International Series in Law and Society (Oxford: Hart Publishing, 2007); Hans Born and Albrecht Schnabel, eds., *Security Sector Reform in Challenging Environments*, Dcaf Yearbook (Geneva/Vienna: DCAF/LIT Verlag, 2009); Clem McCartney, Martina Fischer, and Oliver Wils, eds., *Security Sector Reform – Potentials and Challenges for Conflict Transformation*, vol. 2, Berghof Handbook Dialogue Series (Berlin: Berghof Research Center for Constructive Conflict Management, 2004); Alan Bryden and Heiner Hänggi, eds., *Reform and Reconstruction of the Security Sector* (Münster: LIT Verlag, 2004).
59 See, for example: Hansen, "From Congo to Kosovo: Civilian Police in Peace Operations", 31; Ylber Bajraktari, Arthur Boutellis, Fatema Gunja, Daniel Harris, James Kapsis, Eva Kaye, and Jane Rhee, "The Prime System: Measuring the Success of Post-Conflict Police Reform", (Princeton, NJ: Princeton University: Woodrow Wilson School of Public and International Affairs, 2006); William G. O'Neill, "Police Reform in Post-Conflict Societies: What We Know and What We Still Need to Know", in *The Security-Development Nexus Program* (New York: International Peace Academy, 2005), 11; Peake and Studdard-Brown, "Policebuilding: The International Deployment Group in the Solomon Islands": 528–9; Dennis. Smith, "Managing Civpol: The Potential Performance Management in International Public Services", in *Rethinking International Organizations: Pathology and Promise*, eds. D. Dijkzeul and Y. Beigbeder (New York: Berghahn, 2003); Mobekk, "Identifying Lessons in United Nations International Policing Missions", 22; Hurwitz and Studdard, "Rule of Law Programs in Peace Operations", 13; Benner, Mergenthaler, and Rotmann, *The New World of UN Peace Operations: Learning to Build Peace?*, 70–1; Durch and England, eds., *Enhancing United Nations Capacity to Support Post-Conflict Policing and Rule of Law*, 33, 47–8.
60 One noteworthy example is: Bajraktari *et al.*, "The Prime System: Measuring the Success of Post-Conflict Police Reform".
61 See: A. Sayer, *Method in Social Science: A Realist Approach*, 2nd ed. (London: Routledge, 1992), 107; Norman Blaikie, *Designing Social Research*, 2nd ed. (Cambridge: Polity, 2009), 87–9.
62 "Retroduction means that the researcher develops a preliminary model through the use of analogies and deduction from theories from related fields that fit the observation that is to be explained. A first set of preliminary

hypotheses is drawn from the model and 'fitted' to the empirical reality, i.e. tested to which extent it fits the actual field of research. This testing is not to be confused with the testing of causal hypotheses but must rather be seen as a much earlier step to develop or adapt such hypotheses. With the help of such empirical work new variables might be found, others refined or even rejected. After several repetitions of theoretical deduction and empirical induction in a spiral process of theory development, the candidate hypotheses will be generated with these new and refined variables". (Thorsten Benner, Andrea Binder, and Philipp Rotmann, *Learning to Build Peace? United Nations Peacebuilding and Organizational Learning: Developing a Research Framework*, Gppi Research Paper Series No. 7 [Berlin: German Foundation for Peace Research, 2007], 21–2.)

63 Blaikie, *Designing Social Research*, 87.
64 Howard, *UN Peacekeeping in Civil Wars*; Benner, Mergenthaler, and Rotmann, *The New World of UN Peace Operations: Learning to Build Peace*; Campbell, "When Process Matters: The Potential Implications of Organisational Learning for Peacebuilding Success".
65 For discussion of the reasons for case selection, see below.
66 DPKO, UN Police Magazine 11th Edition (New York: United Nations, July 2013), 32–3.
67 Interview with Author: UNMIL Senior Official, UN Police – Monrovia, Liberia, September 2010.
68 Benner, Mergenthaler, and Rotmann, "The Evolution of Organizational Learning in the UN Peace Operations Bureaucracy", 22.
69 See, for example: UN News Service, "Outgoing UN peacekeeping chief hails achievements of blue helmets", 4 August 2011, www.un.org/apps/news/story.asp?NewsID=39234&Cr=Le+Roy&Cr1=.
70 Elisabeth Porter, "Conclusion: Reflections on Contemporary Research in Africa", in *Researching Conflict in Africa: Insights and Experiences*, ed. Elisabeth Porter, *et al.* (Tokyo: United Nations University Press, 2005), 158.
71 In addition, some focus groups and participant observation were also used – see below.
72 M. Q. Patton, *Qualitative Evaluation and Research Methods*, 2nd ed. (Newbury Park, CA: Sage Publications, 1990); Bruce L. Berg, *Qualitative Research Methods for the Social Sciences*, (Boston: Allyn and Bacon, 2001), 32; Jane Morse, "Designing Funded Qualitative Research", in *Handbook of Qualitative Research*, ed. Norman Denzin and Yvonna Lincoln (Thousand Oaks, CA: Sage Press, 1994), 222.
73 Marsha Henry, Paul Higate, and Gurchathen Sanghera, "Positionality and Power: The Politics of Peacekeeping Research", *International Peacekeeping* 16, no. 4 (2009): 469–78; Paul Higate and Marsha Henry, *Insecure Spaces: Peacekeeping, Power and Performance in Haiti, Kosovo and Liberia* (London: Zed Books, 2009), 1–7.
74 Howard, *UN Peacekeeping in Civil Wars*, 19–20; Benner, Mergenthaler, and Rotmann, *The New World of UN Peace Operations: Learning to Build Peace?*
75 Michael Barnett cited in Benner, Mergenthaler, and Rotmann, *The New World of UN Peace Operations: Learning to Build Peace?* 225.
76 This account is based on publicly available UN reports and documents, as well as a series of interviews (conducted by the Author) with UN Secretariat officials and experts on the workings of the various departments and management structures conducted during 2009 and 2010.
77 Michael Barnett cited in Benner, Mergenthaler, and Rotmann, *The New World of UN Peace Operations: Learning to Build Peace?* 225.

Part I
Context-setting

1 UN peace operations and policing

Policing change, changing police

Introduction

In this chapter I examine the evolution of UN peace operations, focusing particularly on the place of policing. The chapter identifies substantive change in UN policing, as well as the increasing importance attached to police and rule of law initiatives as part of UN peace operations. As such, it lays the foundations for the inquiry in the chapters that follow. The chapter proceeds in three parts. Firstly, it traces the trajectory of quantitative, qualitative and normative change in the peace operations architecture at the UN from their inception to the present day. This section highlights the move towards multidimensional missions and points to the reality that they are engaged in early peacebuilding efforts. The second part charts the evolving role of police within peace operations and their place in emerging thinking that places resurrecting the rule of law as a cornerstone of war-to-peace transitions under the auspices of UN multidimensional peace operations. The section demonstrates that as UNPOL have become increasingly central, they have also become ever more involved in intrusive reform activities at the peacekeeping-peacebuilding nexus that implicate a broader security and rule of law system. The third part highlights key challenges relating to generating and deploying missions as well as implementing mandates once in theatre. In particular, this section argues that the UNPOL apparatus faces significant hurdles due to structural constraints to recruitment of sufficient quantity and quality of UNPOL and unproven assumptions underpinning the modalities and even the ethic of the UNPOL project. It is argued that these enduring and emerging issues have significant implications for the impact of UNPOL. The chapter concludes by identifying organisational learning and monitoring and evaluation as key avenues for addressing these challenges.

UN peace operations: from peacekeeping to peacebuilding

Since its baptism in the Middle East in 1948, UN peacekeeping[1] has evolved significantly.[2] Traditionally, peacekeeping was predominantly military in character, designed to observe ceasefires and provide a buffer between opposing forces of inter-state wars.[3] Early operations were characterised by their adherence to what has been termed the 'holy trinity' of peacekeeping: consent; impartiality; and, the minimum use of force.[4] One of the major characteristics of these missions was an unwillingness to promote any particular form of governance given the prevailing ideological struggles associated with the Cold War.[5]

Whilst this traditional conception of peacekeeping retains some currency, and a number of long-standing missions continue,[6] UN peace operations have adapted in response to changes in the international peace and security environment. Following the end of the Cold War, the peacekeeping architecture went through what Bellamy *et al.* refer to as a quantitative, qualitative and normative "triple transformation".[7] This transformation was manifested in a significant increase in the number of peace operations deployed, and although not entirely sequential, a parallel substantive development in the more ambitious character of mission mandates in response to an increase in intra-state conflict.

The focus of new missions deployed to Namibia (UNTAG), Angola (UNAVEM I and II) and Cambodia (UNTAC) was on assisting in the implementation of peace agreements and creating a sustainable peace following intra-state conflict. These operations came to embody an unprecedented level of UN involvement in the internal matters of sovereign states – unimaginable during the Cold War years of superpower rivalry and Security Council paralysis. These developments were captured in Secretary-General Boutros-Ghali's seminal 1992 'An Agenda for Peace',[8] which laid out a framework for the UN's peace and security operations, based around preventive diplomacy, peacemaking, peacekeeping and post-conflict peacebuilding. Most progressive in this was the definition of post-conflict peace-building as, "action to identify and support structures which will tend to strengthen and solidify peace in order to avoid a relapse into conflict".[9] This laid the platform for UN peace operations to become increasingly transformative in their objectives, *inter alia*, assisting in the conduct of democratic elections.

'An Agenda for Peace' incorporated the mandates of several UN departments and agencies beyond the Department of Peacekeeping Operations (DPKO) under the rubric of peacebuilding. It paved the way for the deployment of their resources in pursuit of an ambitious but strategically undifferentiated set of goals, as the final phase of international assistance with conflict resolution. Furthermore, it shifted attention from the strategic issues of where, when and how to intervene, to the operational challenges of linking together the activities of a multiplicity of agencies and actors with different mandates, budgets and cultures. The ensuing focus on the mechanics and techniques of cooperation and coordination in pursuit of an elusive unity of effort tended to displace efforts at determining strategic priorities, and the questions of who should set them and how.

Whilst the multidimensional missions of the 1990s met with varying degrees of success,[10] it was the catastrophes that unfolded under the watch of UN peace operations in Somalia, Rwanda and Bosnia that precipitated a system-wide retreat from UN peacekeeping in the second half of the 1990s.[11] However, the world continued to witness an increase in intra-state conflict leaving intractable problems even after the fighting had stopped. Devastated economies, the collapse of civil institutions, humanitarian emergencies and mass displacement were perpetuating cycles of conflict and human insecurity. By 1999, the international community had re-engaged with peace operations, as the UN Security Council authorised new missions in Sierra Leone, the Democratic Republic of the Congo, Timor-Leste and in Kosovo. The atavism was unambiguous, not only in quantitative terms, but also in quality due to the nature of these large multifunctional operations. Particularly significant was the scope of the missions in Kosovo and Timor-Leste, as the UN established civil administration and assumed full executive responsibilities.

The apparent failures of peacekeeping in the 1990s and the ambitious missions in Kosovo and Timor-Leste, led to the creation of a High-Level Panel on UN Peace Operations in 2000. Its findings, better known as the 'Brahimi Report', constituted a comprehensive review of UN peace operations and reflected an accumulation of lessons identified both in the field and at headquarters.[12] In addition to attempts to delineate the scope of peace operations, the Brahimi Report constituted a 'root and branch' reassessment of the UN's involvement in peacekeeping and contained twenty-two sets of recommendations. It recognised, among others:

- the importance of peacebuilding as integral to the success of peacekeeping operations;
- the desirability of defining and identifying elements of peacebuilding before they are incorporated into the mandates of complex peace operations; and
- the fact that peacebuilding support offices can also be established as a follow-on to other peace operations.

The report also emphasised the need for the UN and DPKO to professionalise its conduct, stating that, "not enough has been done to improve the system's ability to tap that (field) experience or to feed it back into the development of operational doctrine, plans, procedures or mandates".[13]

Since 1999, despite a suite of potential mission alternatives, the majority of UN peace operations deployed have existed as multidimensional and increasingly integrated endeavours.[14] These modern missions employ tools across the conflict prevention, management and resolution spectrum, encompassing peacemaking, humanitarian operations, peacebuilding and at times peace enforcement. These operations tend to be located at the peacekeeping-peacebuilding nexus. That is, whilst they might not be mandated, or responsible, for overseeing the full transition of conflict-affected societies from war to peace, they are invariably engaged in the business of early peacebuilding in an attempt to prevent a relapse into conflict. The landmark 2008 'Principles and Guidelines' document states that, "in the short-term, a United Nations peacekeeping operation may have little choice but to initiate longer-term institution and capacity-building efforts, due to the inability of other actors to take the lead".[15] This development was further reflected in the 2009 and 2012 reports of the Secretary-General on post-conflict peacebuilding[16] and a 2011 DPKO/DFS Strategy on the contribution of peacekeepers to early peacebuilding.[17]

This new generation of multifaceted or complex peace operations have tended to deploy in the aftermath of internecine conflict, employing military, police and civilian components to assist in the implementation of comprehensive peace agreements.[18] Missions are mandated to play some role in a wide range of tasks and activities, *inter alia*:

- Disarmament, Demobilisation and Reintegration (DDR)
- Organising democratic elections
- Combating 'spoilers'
- Strengthening institutions of state, addressing governance issues – political impunity and accountability
- Security Sector Reform (SSR), resurrecting Rule of Law and coercing/co-opting organised criminality
- Reforming dysfunctional economies
- Return and resettling refugees and IDPs
- Protection of civilians

The cross-cutting and interdependent nature of many of these objectives has led to attempts to enhance the level of integration of operations. The 'integrated missions concept'[19] attempts to harness the capacities of the UN system as a whole and develop coherent and mutually reinforcing strategies

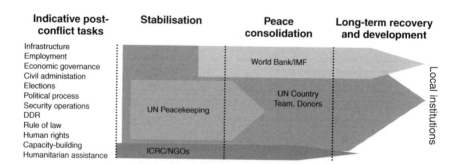

Figure 1.1 The core business of multidimensional UN peacekeeping operations.[20]

for the UN family and partner institutions in a given situation.[21] The overlapping responsibilities and spheres of influence in multidimensional missions are depicted in the diagram above.

Ultimately, there has been a trend towards contemporary peace operations being in the business of assisting societies in a war-to-peace transition – combining the restoration of a secure environment associated with traditional peacekeeping with the transformative agenda of 'post-conflict'[22] peacebuilding encompassing a wide range of objectives.[23]

Based on the mixed experiences of these multidimensional missions and their forerunners since 1989,[24] around 2004 a number of scholars coalesced around the conclusion that a major flaw in the strategies of these missions was a lack of focus on the development of effective and legitimate governmental institutions.[25] This, in turn, breathed life into arguments that the UN's peace operations would have a greater chance of success if they focused more attention on 'statebuilding' – i.e. creating more resilient state institutions to manage the vulnerability of the war-to-peace transition including rapid democratization and marketization.[26] On the other hand, this notion met with resistance from a number of scholars, some who perceived the ambitious statebuilding agenda as beyond the remit and capacity of peace operations, and others who deemed it to represent the uncomfortable and unproven imposition of a liberal, even neo-colonial, peacebuilding dogma or imperialism.[27] As Johnstone has astutely distilled the debate,

> This ambitious agenda raises questions about whether peace operations are exercises in social engineering, based on liberal democratic models, as well as concerns about the transformative capacity of outside intervention: even if the creation of liberal democratic states is a worthy goal, what can outsiders do to achieve that goal?[28]

In this context, some missions that were previously heralded as successes were experiencing regression, as happened when violence flared up in Kosovo in 2004 and law and order disintegrated in Timor-Leste in 2006, requiring the UN to return and deploy its UNMIT mission.[29] These and other events led to frustrations amongst practitioners and academics alike about the effectiveness of peacebuilding strategies of peace operations.[30] In particular, the ability of missions to reform/rebuild police and criminal justice systems capable of maintaining the peace upon their withdrawal was brought into question.[31] Reflecting these debates, there was a marked amplification of Rule of Law discourse across a wide range of UN actors leading to two significant reports of the Secretary-General on the subject.[32] However, the importance of rule of law dimensions and in particular the role of police in peace operations has a much longer history. The following section maps out the operational and bureaucratic evolution of UN policing.

Civilian police in UN peace operations

Traditionally, civilian police components were treated by mission architects and member states as a 'bolt-on' capacity – an addendum to military-dominated mission structures.[33] However, this tendency has diminished as police components have become increasingly recognised as mission-critical.[34] Many now argue that 'getting policing right' is at the core of successful peace operations.[35] UN Police (UNPOL)[36] have been present in UN peacekeeping since they were first deployed in the ONUC mission in Congo Leopoldville in 1960. In the intervening years, civilian police have been part of more than 30 UN missions on 4 continents.[37] More telling, the number of UNPOL deployed has burgeoned since the end of the Cold War. In 1988 there were only 35 civilian police, whereas by mid-2013 DPKO was authorised to deploy over 16,700.[38]

However, reflecting general trends in peacekeeping, the UN is not the only actor operating in this realm. In parallel, the European Union (EU), Organisation for Security Cooperation in Europe (OSCE), and increasingly the African Union (AU), have deployed police in their own operations both within and beyond their respective regions.[39] Furthermore, a number of states have developed their own capacities to deploy police overseas such as the Australian Federal Police's International Deployment Group[40] and the Royal Canadian Mounted Police's International Peace Operations Branch,[41] to name two in the vanguard. In July 2003, the first police-led international peace operation – the Regional Assistance Mission to the Solomon Islands (RAMSI) – was deployed under the auspices of the Pacific Islands Forum (PIF)[42] and interventions in Iraq and Afghanistan have also highlighted the important role of police in assisting societies affected by conflict.[43] These broader developments are captured by what some refer to as the 'new international policing' architecture.[44]

Despite the growing number of non-UN providers, the quantity of UNPOL deployed increased by 80 per cent since 2007.[45] As of July 2013 around 12,500 police from over 80 countries were deployed in 18 UN missions,[46] making the UN the biggest provider of policing support in post-conflict environments.[47] These police now represent approximately 15 per cent of all uniformed personnel in UN peace operations, compared to only 2 per cent as recently as 1995. These trends have contributed to conceptualisations of peace operations becoming 'more blue, less green'[48] – reflecting the quantitative increase of police in missions but also the perception that UNPOL play a relatively important role in mission exit strategies compared to the military.[49] In short, the UN relies more and more on police in its mission to maintain international peace and security.

In reaching its current manifestation, UN policing has gone through a number of metamorphoses.[50] The following section charts these developments, presenting a typology of UNPOL missions and an account of the emerging rule of law architecture as it unfolded 'in the field', while highlighting important corollary developments 'in the office' at the UN Secretariat and DPKO.

'In the field and in the office'

The role and posture of UNPOL has changed dramatically since their inaugural deployment. In the absence of clear mandates or guidance for their implementation, 'mission-creep' in one case has often been refined and reapplied in subsequent ones.[51] However, despite this ad hoc-ism, one can trace an approximately sequential development in their character. In essence, the role of police in peace operations has broadened and deepened, evolving from passive observation of domestic police agencies to a more intrusive reform function and even assuming full law enforcement responsibilities.[52]

As mentioned above, the first deployment of civilian police was in the Congo in 1960–4 where UNPOL were mandated to support Congolese police in maintaining law and order. This was closely followed by their inclusion in the UN Temporary Executive Authority (UNTEA) from 1962–3 which installed a foreign chief of police to lead the Papuan Police Force and deployed Filipino officers as the mission oversaw the transition of West New Guinea/West Irian from Dutch colonial rule to Indonesian control. These were followed by the larger UNFICYP mission in Cyprus, first deployed in 1964 but which continues today.[53] It was here that UN police were first given the moniker of 'CIVPOL' and tasked to monitor the zone between Greek and Turkish Cypriot communities, as well as to liaise and facilitate cooperation between the respective police agencies.[54]

There were few new missions deployed during a hiatus until the end of the Cold War. Those that were had no significant policing contingent and those present were not usually recognised as an independent component and generally limited to supporting military observers or conducting unobtrusive monitoring roles.[55] However, despite a significant time-lag, elements of these early policing mandates did lay the foundations for what is commonly implemented by UNPOL in contemporary peace operations.[56] Following the end of the Cold War, civilian police in peace operations began to take more coherent form, were assigned a specific role, and deployed strategically in pursuit of overall mission goals. Nevertheless, mandates continued to evolve.

Monitoring and advising

Police peacekeepers operated under the military component until 1989 when, with the inception of the UN Transitional Assistance Group in Namibia (UNTAG), the police component became an independent entity. UNPOL in UNTAG were required to monitor the human rights situation, but also played a role in facilitating democratic elections by both monitoring the conduct of the disruptive Southwest African Police (SWAPOL) and by participating on election observation teams.[57] This was new ground for UNPOL and subsequently perceived to have a big impact on the overall success of the mission – demonstrating the potentially important role police could play in peace operations.[58] UNTAG also represented a rebirth of policing deployments, as subsequent missions of increasing size and frequency were mandated to monitor, observe and report upon local police services in relation to their obligations under peace agreements. The UN operation in Mozambique (ONUMOZ) followed in a similar vein as did the UNAVEM II and III missions in Angola.

Capacity-building and institutional development

Mandates for UNPOL continued to expand in the early 1990s requiring engagement in an inflated set of tasks.[59] The most significant augmentation was the move towards building the capacity of indigenous police services. This change occurred in two dimensions. The first was through the provision of training, initially part of ad hoc arrangements in the UNTAC mission in Cambodia[60] but more formally incorporated into the UN missions in Somalia (UNOSOM) and Rwanda (UNAMIR) in the mid-1990s.[61] These missions required UNPOL to support, train and mentor with the aim of professionalising domestic police services. Collectively, these functions came to be known as 'SMART' policing – an acronym for: *S*upport for human rights, *M*onitoring, *A*dvising, *R*eporting, and *T*raining – instituted as the basic framework for international policing in 1995.[62]

The second and more intrusive development was into the realm of reforming, restructuring and rebuilding domestic police institutions (RRR). This programming had its antecedent in ONUSAL in El Salvador[63] and was first included in the mandate for UNMIH in Haiti,[64] but was most prevalent in the International Police Task Force (IPTF) that made up the bulk of the UN Mission in Bosnia and Herzegovina (UNMIBH) – beginning its operations in 1995 but engaging in such efforts after changes to the initial mandate.[65] Under these mandates, UNPOL officers were involved in overhauling or building from scratch national police services, 'de-militarizing' existing corps, removing known human rights abusers, and often down-sizing.[66] This has included selecting, recruiting, vetting, advising and mentoring officers for fundamentally reconstituted police services in addition to developing and teaching on curricula at policing academies and providing field training. RRR still involved providing technical and logistical support to develop effectiveness of local police, whilst deeper reforms have also included UNPOL providing assistance with: legislation; systems; procedures; codes; values; organisation; management; logistics; and, communications. The timing and nature of this shift was in keeping with the general trends in UN peace operations increasingly engaging in peacebuilding tasks aimed at buttressing the institutions believed to lay firm foundations for a lasting peace.

Executive policing

The most ambitious functional expansion came in 1999 as new missions in Kosovo and Timor-Leste were mandated with complete executive authority for law enforcement activities. That is, as the UN established civil administrations over both territories and embarked on nation-building, UNPOL assumed full responsibility for the interim maintenance of law and order, including the right to bear arms and execute powers of arrest and detention.[67] In addition, officers and units were required to perform a disparate array of tasks including *inter alia*: conducting investigations; directing traffic; providing border security; collecting, analysing and utilising criminal intelligence as well as forensic evidence; and managing the organisation and administration of the police force.[68] In both cases, processes of reconstituting, or creating anew, indigenous police services – capacity-building and institutional development – were conducted in parallel.

Although this type of mandate had forerunners in the UN Transitional Authority in Eastern Slavonia, Baranja and Western Sirmium (UNTAES) and the IPTF in Bosnia, UNMIK and UNTAET represented a culmination of increasing authority for UNPOL and potentially constituted a paradigmatic shift.[69] However, despite the critical role envisaged for UNPOL in plugging the public security gap in the short-term and building self-sustaining police services in the longer-term, the number of police in these missions continued to be dwarfed by the military component. The UN's transitional administrations in Kosovo and Timor-Leste induced much debate around international transitional authority and the DPKO capacity to reproduce such executive policing functions in future operations. However, these mandates have not been replicated since and it seems that such executive authority remains an anomaly, not the rule.[70]

In response to these emerging demands on UNPOL, the Brahimi report advocated a 'doctrinal shift', such that the utilisation of police in peace operations should "...focus primarily on the reform and restructuring of local police forces in addition to traditional advisory, training and monitoring tasks" – whilst maintaining and developing its capacity to respond effectively to civil disorder and for self-defence.[71] It also argued for the role of UN police to be "better understood and developed".[72]

Multidimensional policing

The emergence of multidimensional and integrated missions has had a significant effect on the operational objectives of UNPOL. Contemporary policing missions are increasingly "tools both of immediate crisis management and of development assistance and democratisation."[73] Each mission environment is unique and displays idiosyncratic political, economic and social circumstances that inevitably dictate the scope of the mandate and the rules of engagement. However, under these mandates, UNPOL has increasingly focused on transformative activities whilst continuing to assist in limited law enforcement activities. These functions are elaborated on below.

Rather than signify a return to the rule of law, the cessation of hostilities can usher in a period of lawlessness.[74] Societies emerging from war often experience minimal public security, a breakdown in law and order and increased levels of criminality – ranging from opportunistic petty transgressions to pervasive organised crime.[75] That is, the collapse of the rule of law can be both a cause and consequence of conflict.[76]

Durch *et al.* suggest there are two main reasons for this.[77] First, and somewhat counter-intuitively, this can occur as a result of peace agreement. Incomplete disarmament programmes render communities awash with small arms and light weapons (SALW), whilst insufficiently designed and resourced demobilisation and reintegration initiatives have left ex-combatants without the necessary skills and/or employment opportunities, such that the resort to criminality becomes incentive compatible.[78] This transition from 'fighters' to 'felons' is facilitated by the relative ease with which paramilitary activities can be transformed into criminal enterprises, particularly if deterrence is low and impunity high.[79] These maladies are often exacerbated by the psychological impact of war in desensitising former militia-men and women to violence and danger.[80] In addition, if residual social divisions, ethnic tensions and justice issues are not sufficiently addressed, this can lead to conflict over privilege to political power, rights to land and access to scarce resources. In this context, without tangible preventive strategies, upsurges in criminality and challenges to the rule of law are a predictable consequence of a peace agreement.[81]

Second, the destructive and divisive nature of conflict can mean that the capacity of a conflict-affected society to tackle criminal activity and enforce law and order is severely reduced in the immediate post-violence phase. Public security and criminal justice institutions such as the police service are often politicised, corrupted and co-opted during conflict as part of the pursuit of political power.[82] It is common that sections of the security apparatus are implicated in abuses or indeed that the country in question has no historical legacy of providing equitable public security to its population per se.[83] In addition, the neglect and degradation of these institutions that can occur during periods of instability render the state unable to respond to breaches of law and further exacerbate a volatile post-conflict environment. Similarly, the non-state realm, often a major provider of security and justice services in states where UN peace operations tend to be deployed,[84] can also be affected by conflict. Traditional sources of authority and legitimacy can have their reputation degraded and informal mechanisms for provision of security are also susceptible to becoming politicised/ethnicised during internecine conflict.[85]

This lack of capacity within post-conflict societies leads to what has been referred to as the 'enforcement' and 'institutional' gaps[86] – deficits that threaten to undercut peacebuilding initiatives[87] and allow the space for pernicious elements to operate and for organised criminality to flourish and gain a foothold which becomes increasingly hard to dislodge.[88] Where alternative non-state sources of security are also absent or eroded beyond utility, as Linden *et al.* explain, "Securing order for governance is central to the international police mandate."[89] This was the scenario that UNPOL faced in cases such as El Salvador, Mozambique, Kosovo, Liberia and Haiti.

For these reasons, UNPOL often play a pivotal role in plugging the institutional civil law enforcement gap. As described above, on occasion, this has been manifest in executive authority missions where UNPOL officers and units are directly responsible for all law enforcement functions. More commonly, the multidimensional non-executive mandates dictate that UNPOL support national law enforcement agencies in the execution of their functions. Oftentimes, modern UNPOL missions have been mandated under chapter VII of the UN charter to provide 'direct operational assistance' to host governments in all policing functions necessary for the restoration and maintenance of the rule of law, public safety and order.[90] For example, the UNPOL component in Haiti (MINUSTAH) first deployed in 2004 has been integral in tackling the gangs of Port-au-Prince and combating organised crime, reflecting its 'muscular' posture.[91] Similarly, UNMIL's large police component in Liberia has provided robust operational support to the Liberian National Police (LNP) in riot control and other policing functions. The important distinction between this multidimensional policing and executive policing is that, in this posture, UNPOL officers are not considered law enforcement officials under the legislation of the host government or the Security Council mandate.

This immediate – although often continuing – restoration function meets a short-term stabilisation requirement and has been labelled as 'police peacekeeping' by some.[92] However, it is argued that the durability of a secure environment depends upon effective national policing capacity and self-sustaining rule of law. As Hansen notes, "security is the key to a 'new social contract' between the population and its government or society in which the population is willing to surrender the responsibility for its physical safety into government hands."[93] The second area of focus for UNPOL in multidimensional missions therefore relates to activities aimed at achieving this outcome and is increasingly known as 'policebuilding'.[94]

In multidimensional missions, UNPOL have frequently been called upon to implement police reform with the intention of delivering comprehensive capacity-building measures to develop professional, democratic, self-sustaining local police services.[95] Whilst these aims were incorporated in operations as described above, the nature of RRR has changed over the years as it has become more intrusive.[96] A common understanding of 'the police' is that they are "responsible for the preservation of internal order and security of the state through enforcement of the rule of law and using, if necessary, state-sanctioned powers of coercion and force".[97] The democratic policing ideal holds that domestic police services "…play a crucial role in maintaining public security and order and in legitimizing the state's monopoly on the use of force through a commitment to the rule of law. The nexus between good governance, rule of law, and public security makes effective policing an important component of well-functioning, modern societies."[98] The UN has therefore increasingly engaged in building host countries' policing capacity to maintain law and order.

As mentioned above, this approach traditionally involved a technical approach addressing issues such as "low levels of vocational skills, equipment shortages, and defective infrastructure".[99] However, arguably since 2005, there has been a shift away from a technocratic approach focused on training individual officers and providing technical and material assistance, towards a more political approach that involves reform of organisational culture and conduct to make it an effective and accountable institution of state in line with democratic policing norms.[100]

This move towards addressing the political and organisational nature of police institutions holistically came in response to the recognition that no amount of technical capacity-building provided through the SMART approach to individual officers through training and mentoring or to the organisation in the form of 'laptops and landcruisers' would transform parts of the security apparatus into democratic (i.e. accountable and responsive) policing services if they remained corrupt and/or captured by powerful stakeholders (as well as degraded and dysfunctional). RRR is therefore underpinned by attempts to address the political and economic dimensions of a conflict-affected police service. In the absence of such an approach, UNPOL may run the risk of empowering through technical assistance whoever had managed to commandeer and politicise the police during conflict.[101] As DPKO's RRR policy states, "an important element of sustainable success is to achieve a cultural change of police and law enforcement officials' attitudes and behaviour: this cannot be changed merely through recruitment and training."[102]

As a result, UNPOL now regularly engage in policebuilding, enacting and supporting the reform, restructuring and rebuilding of police and other law enforcement agencies, as well as targeting change in the ministries and departments of government that oversee the law and justice sector. These efforts to strengthen domestic policing are indicative of how UNPOL activities are increasingly located at the nexus between peacekeeping and peacebuilding. As Greener has noted, "Police are increasingly being used as peacebuilders rather than being restricted to narrower peacekeeping roles."[103]

In every case, UNPOL are just one of myriad international, regional and non-governmental organisations (often led by other agencies such as UNDP as well as bilateral donors and international financial institutions such as the World Bank and the IMF) who manage, support and fund a wider engagement in transforming the security and justice architecture of a country more holistically that will likely continue after the peace operation has departed.[104] The protracted timelines associated with policebuilding diminish the role of UNPOL in the longer term.[105] Indeed, there are enduring debates about the extent to which peace operations should engage in policebuilding and in what ways.[106] However, in the short-term, they play an integral role in setting the wheels in motion for early peacebuilding. 'Policebuilding' has therefore become the process aimed at launching capacity-development of local police such that they are capable of creating and sustaining law, order and public trust; ensuring that local law enforcement officers and institutions are respecting international human rights standards and protecting fundamental freedoms in the medium to long term.

In addition, multidimensional policing has seen UNPOL increasingly involved in many additional cross-cutting mission objectives, including: supervision of cease-fires; facilitating safe returnee programmes; combating organised crime in support of economic reconstruction; as well as emerging roles in the provision of civilian protection.[107] Furthermore, UNPOL are also expected to play a central role in protecting UN personnel and facilities.[108] Whilst most of these are not new tasks for UNPOL, this modern modality represents an accumulation of most tasks conducted throughout UNPOL's history (with the notable exception of executive powers of arrest and detention). Aside from the ongoing observer missions in the Middle East and south Asia, practically all UN operations are now furnished with a significant police component. The relatively short space of time which saw new UNPOL efforts of this type deployed to Liberia, Haiti, Côte d'Ivoire, Sudan (UNMIS and UNAMID) as well as revamping of the mission in the DR Congo was indicative of this trend.

Regardless of how policing components are configured, efforts are not conducted in a vacuum. As UNPOL functions have expanded, there has also been a development in the way policing objectives are conceived of within a broader security and rule of law system. One of the major lessons identified as far back as UNTAC in Cambodia, but particularly following the missions in Kosovo and Timor-Leste, was that getting policing right was only part of the law and order puzzle in post-conflict situations.[109] There has been an increasing recognition that effective police are contingent upon effective justice and corrections institutions and processes.[110] If the judicial system lacks the capacity to process those that the police enter into the criminal justice system then the problem becomes one of high rates of pre-trial detention. Sequentially, if/when judicial decisions lead to penal or corrective punishment, if the prisons or corrective institutions do not have the capacity to incarcerate or support then again the system breaks down. Ultimately, the success of police reform will be retarded if transformation of the criminal justice apparatus – i.e. other elements of the rule of law 'triad' – does not proceed at a similar rate.[111] In other words, reform efforts are mutually dependent. The interdependence of these elements demands that UN peace operations address the rule of law elements as a system, not as isolated component parts.

The recognition of these systemic challenges led to most new missions created since 2003 including provisions for capacity-building of the criminal justice sector, to include penal and judicial reform. The absence of dedicated staff and resources led to increasing UNPOL involvement in a broader range of activities – from securing prisons and ensuring the rights of prisoners to assisting in overseeing due legal process. In the absence of criminal justice specialists, the mainstreaming of rule of law programming was another contributing factor to the unprecedented demand for UNPOL.[112]

Following major recommendations in the Brahimi Report and other subsequent thematic developments, the UNPOL apparatus has become embedded in an overarching Rule of Law architecture at HQ. A 2007 organisational reform saw the Police Division brought under the authority of an integrated *Office for Rule of Law and Security Institutions* (OROLSI), along with the Criminal Law and Judicial Advisory Section, Disarmament, Demobilisation and Reintegration Section, the Security Sector Reform Section, and the Mine Action Service. Despite a lag in organisational response, these developments are increasingly reflected in mission structures to include customs and corrections officials, with UNPOL working much closer with legal and judicial elements of missions to provide advice and support. Furthermore, it is now UN practice for UNPOL to be considered part of a holistic approach to restoring and reforming the rule of law and security system. At field-level, this was first formalised in 2007 when the African Union-United Nations Hybrid Mission in Darfur (UNAMID) was authorised with over 6,000 UNPOL deployed under an integrated Rule of Law concept of operations.[113]

In summary, in multidimensional missions, "The United Nations police officer is no longer a passive onlooker but an active partner in consolidating peace and building democratic institutions that underpin the long-term stability and prosperity in peaceful societies."[114] The move towards transformational objectives, whilst retaining a muscular posture for assisting fledgling police services in maintaining law and order, in the context of a holistic rule of law approach, has significant ramifications for future UNPOL requirements and how these missions should be managed. A clear understanding of these mission types is vital to understanding the intentions, core tasks and objectives of UNPOL missions, including those that implicate other mission sections, when assessing the impact of these efforts.

Whilst there have been significant reforms and developments 'in the office' of UN policing, in general, change 'in the field' has far outpaced that in the supporting bureaucracy which has suffered chronic lack of capacity to plan, manage and oversee its field missions.[115] Of course, the UN Police Division (UNPD) is beholden to the good will and contributions of the Member States for mandating and staffing UNPOL missions – and this will remain the case. However, the evolution of UNPOL practice and management structures presents a number of key challenges. The ability of both Headquarters and field operations to address these will be a key factor in whether police in peace operations can meet the expectations that their increasing centrality has created. The following section addresses key issues facing UNPOL.

Opportunities and challenges for UNPOL

Numerous studies have been undertaken to identify lessons from UNPOL missions and areas for improvement.[116] Many others have emphasised issues in the broader realm of international policing and SSR.[117] Collectively, these point to an array of conceptual and practical challenges that international policing missions face in meeting their objectives. This section briefly touches on issues relating to generating and deploying UNPOL then explores the most pressing challenges surrounding the implementation of UNPOL mandates.

Generating and deploying UNPOL

Throughout its existence, the Police Division has faced perennial challenges in recruiting, training, deploying and ensuring the accountability of a sufficient quantity and quality of personnel from senior management to junior officers.[118] UNPOL continue to suffer from an overall shortage of officers as unprecedented demand exceeds extant supply.[119] The problem has reached the extent that there is regularly competition between UN missions for this scarce human resource.[120] The insufficient overall quantity of personnel is exacerbated by the systemic inability to resolve asymmetric regional and linguistic representation as well as severe gender imbalances amongst those who are recruited.[121] Many have also noted that police, as contributed to UN missions undertaking policebuilding tasks, are not necessarily the best agents of change.[122] The prevalence of capacity-building mandates means that international policing is increasingly 'not like the day job'. Despite the escalating technicality of UNPOL activities and the specific skill sets required of police peacekeepers, the spiralling demand for police since 1999 has primarily been met through the deployment of Formed Police Units (FPUs).[123] By mid-2013, approximately half of all authorised UNPOL were in the form of FPUs.[124]

Renowned UN official, Sergio Vieira de Mello, then SRSG of UNTAET, said in 2000, "UN police are slow to arrive and seldom effective. They are made up of police officers from up to sixty different countries, all with their own attitudes towards policing, uneven training standards and varying levels of individual competence."[125] Over a decade later, the same issues endure and the quantity and quality of UNPOL human resources remains a major challenge.[126]

Implementing UNPOL mandates

The major challenges identified in relation to UNPOL's ability to achieve its mandate revolve around the politics of policebuilding and the role of non-state providers.

The politics of policebuilding

As described above, efforts over the years to close the 'institutional gap' by building up the capacity of indigenous police services have changed and the nature of RRR has become ever more intrusive. RRR has targeted the overhaul of policing organisations to ensure observance of principles of democratic policing – that is policing that protects and promotes human rights.[127] More specifically, the concept is based on the premise that police should be a service (representative of that society's composition), not a force; focused on ensuring the security of individuals in a transparent fashion, and accountable to law.[128] Furthermore, RRR has typically been heavily state-centric, focusing on building the capacity of state institutions, including targeting change in the ministries and departments of government that oversee the law and justice sector.

As a result, 'policebuilding' as it is currently conceived of in UNPOL missions is inherently political when compared to less intrusive monitoring and even the more technical capacity-building approach of days gone by.[129] On a local level, police reform is political because it creates winners and losers. It involves making decisions which affect existing power balances and political agendas as well as bureaucratic structures.[130] Internationally, the aims of policebuilding interventions are values-based and, in addition to developing technical institutional capacity, also target cultural transformation of police organisations and their practices in line with a particular normative framework.[131] As Eide and Holm explain, "Reforming police forces is not merely a technical issue – it is a commitment to a specific political development at the expense of other possible developments."[132] Greener goes as far as to say that policebuilding constitutes both a challenge to and reinforcement of state sovereignty, declaring that it is, "a strategy aimed at reconstructing one of the very core parts of statehood in order to rebuild functioning states, albeit in very different forms from those that were in place prior to these efforts."[133] Regardless of the level of analysis, these politics frame the intervention logic or theory of change underlying the UNPOL project and have profound consequences for the meaning attached to efforts to monitor and evaluate progress in line with it.

It is widely stated that in 'post-conflict' settings, where there is a peace agreement and often a political transition there is both a need and an opportunity to (re-)establish the rule of law and begin a process of transformation in the public security and justice sector. As an encompassing moniker, the 'Rule of Law' has become a major rhetorical pillar upon which visions of sustainable peace are predicated.[134] Its prominence has risen to the point that it has been depicted as the "preeminent legitimating political ideal in the world today",[135] surpassing democracy and liberal economics as the dominant paradigm in the post-Cold War era.[136] To borrow from Claude Ake, rule of law driven peacebuilding is increasingly akin to a "global theology".[137] Bull claims that the rule of law theory of change constitutes, "the self-declared cornerstone of [the UN's] statebuilding agenda".[138] Emphasised in seminal peace operations reviews 'An Agenda for Peace'[139] and the 'Brahimi Report', the rule of law and police reform came increasingly into focus following relapse into violence in Cambodia (1997), Kosovo (2004) and Timor-Leste (2006) – all missions with significant police reform efforts.[140]

The inference in this change theory is that building an accountable criminal justice system capable of maintaining the rule of law and public trust is a vital element of peacebuilding.[141] The argument goes that institutional change in the police and wider security system can contribute to strengthening law and order, engender social change and support conflict prevention.[142] Indeed, there is widespread consensus that a semblance of stability and public security is a prerequisite to peacebuilding and development.[143]

However, as described above, policebuilding espouses liberal, democratic and human rights values and is consequently intrinsically political. There are those who argue that such theories of change are grounded in the liberal peace thesis.[144] That is to say, they are based on the assumptions that liberal-democracies are more stable because of their liberal-democratic institutions, including the police.[145] There are those such as Barnett et al., who note that, on the contrary, there is "relatively little knowledge regarding what causes peace or what the paths to peace are".[146] Others concur that the assumptions of the liberal peace have not been sufficiently validated as to go unquestioned.[147] For instance, Paris adds that "we know relatively little about how to transform war-torn countries into stable societies".[148] Bull contends that re-creating liberal democratic models of ROL in societies emerging from conflict as a prerequisite for durable peace is at best an 'educated guess' and that "the presumed causal linkages have seldom been explained".[149] Other research similarly questions the veracity of 'democratic policing' or 'rule of law' change theories as a firm foundation for peacebuilding.[150] The allegation that follows is that: "...the move to reforming, restructuring and rebuilding police forces means that this approach is not merely a temporary security provision but may also be a form of political and social engineering".[151] Conversely, proponents of change theories closely tied to rule of law and transforming state security institutions in line with liberal norms argue that scholarship critical of liberal peacebuilding has failed to propose a 'post-liberal' alternative – in effect putting forward vague notions of an 'emancipatory peacebuilding' or variations on the liberal approach.[152] Consequently, commentators such as Paris believe that, whilst there is much that can be improved within the paradigm, there is currently no viable alternative political framework for peace operations to follow and work to.[153]

Given the shift towards inherently political transformational objectives in the last 10 years, the validity of the change theories undergirding UNPOL missions and the robustness of the rule of law as a cornerstone of a war-to-peace transition remains unconvincing to some. The mixed record of rule of law and police reform in peace operations to date suggest there is much more learning to be done about how UNPOL can best contribute towards durable peace. It, therefore, seems vital that UNPOL operations remain reflexive in relation to these assumptions and the ways and means by which they attempt to construct rule of law – particularly in light of what the dominant paradigm privileges as well as precludes. An emerging criticism of the liberal-democratic policebuilding approach is its hitherto dogmatic state-centrism and its blindness to a multi-actor security and justice landscape that exists in many of the places where peace operations deploy. In essence, these critics argue that the orthodox imagination is narrowed implicitly by a top-down, formal-institutional and state-centric premise.[154] Dominant approaches to police and rule of law reform has thus far been characterised by only a cursory understanding and/or engagement with traditional forms of order and existing informal mechanisms.[155] This has had important implications for the effectiveness of UNPOL missions. The following section examines the issues related to non-state security and justice actors as they relate to UN peace operations.

Non-state providers – grappling with hybrid conceptions of policing and the ROL

There is a growing body of empirical research emphasising the importance of non-statutory sources of security and justice to social order – particularly in the aftermath of violent conflict.[156] Indeed, development agencies and organisations heavily involved in SSR have begun to explicitly recognise their importance to restoring security in post-conflict environments.[157] These 'alternative' providers of rule of law type services are variously referred to as non-state, informal, customary or traditional mechanisms and systems of policing, security and/or justice. They comprise a myriad of public, community-based and private actors and commonly include traditional chieftaincies/councils of elders, village, tribal, religious figures, customary dispute resolution processes/rituals.[158] Their authority to make adjudication and apply sanctions is based on high levels of local legitimacy and is often restorative as well as retributive in nature.[159]

The relationship between non-state actors and the formal state is complex and mutable.[160] As Albrecht and Kyed describe, "There may be full recognition and close collaboration, limited partnership, unofficial acceptance, competition and even open hostility."[161] However, it is often the case that there is more symbiosis between non-state policing providers and the state than is disclosed in formal procedural accounts. Informal systems usually co-exist alongside the state, sometimes with a de facto division of labour, but can also substitute for it where the formal security and justice apparatus is inaccessible or dysfunctional.[162] In other words, it may be that non-statutory actors are doing the work the police cannot or will not do, but with tacit approval and even some material assistance – although this remains fluid and often obscured in the official record.[163] Ultimately, they are indisputably part of the same system.[164] As Baker posits, "the case for state and non-state policing being very distinct is imagined for political reasons but does not correspond with reality."[165] Furthermore, there are both practical and normative reasons to reveal and understand these non-state providers of security and justice in the context of peace operations.[166]

In a practical sense, where state security providers are discredited and capacity is low, but risk and threats to security are high, it may be both pragmatic and morally incumbent – not to mention more efficient and effective – for peace operations to engage informal sources to provide security and justice in the immediate aftermath of violent conflict.[167] This is further supported by empirical research that suggests most people in these predicaments look to informal providers first and foremost for policing-type services.[168] This preference is often explained due to the fact informal mechanisms are regularly more accessible to more segments of society and the timeliness and low transaction costs associated with their service provision.[169] Furthermore, they are often advocated because they commonly reflect processes and values more compatible with customary traditions, such as the emphasis on harmony rather than blame, and getting past offences in order to restore peace said by some to be redeeming qualities not often associated with retributive systems synonymous with Western frameworks.[170] As Baker and Scheye have noted:

> There are many reasons for the vitality and strength of non-state delivery, including their: physical, linguistic and cultural accessibility;

legitimacy; efficacy; timeliness of decisions; low transactional costs; support for restitution and restorative justice rather than punishment or incarceration; and degree of participation afforded to disputants.[171]

In a normative sense, the argument goes that informal sources often enjoy more trust, credibility, salience and with it legitimacy than statutory authorities such as the police and court system which have often been implicated in the conflict.[172]

The case has been made that UNPOL efforts in peace operations have met with limited success, in part because they failed to recognise the importance of non-state providers and what they represent about the rule of law in some settings.[173] Others go further to suggest that it might be more practical, effective and sustainable to improve non-state providers (possibly in partnership with the state) than attempt to create a state-centric system "that is neither sustainable nor the option of choice for most of the population."[174] However, there are many who caution against the potential ills of engaging with and empowering non-state actors vis-à-vis the state. Non-state providers are not immune to the eroding or corrupting afflictions of conflict and can be deeply flawed. Furthermore, whilst these mechanisms can enjoy high levels of legitimacy locally, there can also be disparities in accessibility (e.g. women and youth vs. men), inconsistencies in outcomes and disconnects between international human rights 'standards' and the methods used/punishments meted out by way of resolution.[175] Perhaps one of the biggest question marks relates to the level of accountability such informal mechanisms and actors are held to and by whom.[176]

Others have pointed to the lack of value-add for nationwide policebuilding approaches due to the difficulty in up-scaling informal systems and their asymmetric relevance and utility for rural rather than urban locales. For example, Durch suggests that, "given the limited scalability of informal systems – they are, by definition, of very localized legitimacy and reach, useful in rural or village settings but probably less so in larger towns and cities". He goes on to posit that, "Informal self-governance may require both personal relationships and stable rural communities that urban settings and their displaced and mixed populations cannot replicate."[177]

Even proponents of engaging more with non-state providers admit that there is a need to balance desire to harness local models of policing with the reality that what went before was inadequate and/or problematic.[178] It is also important to note the need for support and resources in order to rebuild their capacity and legitimacy is also likely to exist. Bayley goes further, suggesting that "delegation of security beyond the state" might actually make the work of peace operations more difficult and resource-intensive due to the selection and oversight responsibilities and also claims that to do so could have profound political ramifications for emergent social and political order – in the extreme could be seen as colonial in its impact.[179]

It is perhaps unsurprising that non-state entities are often left out of the equation in the theory and practice of peace operations given that these efforts are crafted and funded by either state-based organisations or the researchers largely beholden to these same organisations. As Durch points out, "It is ... very difficult for the professional UN, as an agent of and collaborator with states and other intergovernmental organizations, to reinforce or replicate a 'hybrid state' solution to problems of state weakness."[180] That said, on the one hand overlooking traditional forms of social order can affect and even degrade the vital relationship between a mission and locals. On the other hand, condoning them could constitute supporting systems that contravene international human and civil rights standards to which UN missions are beholden.[181]

Balancing short-term security provision with long-term reform of rule of law systems and the role of non-state providers therein remains an area of contentious debate. What is clear is that UN peace operations have been slow to grapple with these challenges.[182] Questions about if, and if so how, to engage with and incorporate non-state security and justice providers into post-conflict rule of law reform will continue to be a vexing issue for UN peace operations. Nevertheless, it is apparent that any effort to assess the impact of UNPOL endeavours and learn from these experiences needs to be cognisant of the role of non-state actors in this domain.[183]

Conclusion

As UN peace operations have evolved to face the changing nature of conflict, the number of police deployed has burgeoned as their mandates have become increasingly ambitious and complex. From plugging the 'post-conflict' public security gap to instigating and managing police reform programmes, UNPOL are now perceived to be a mission-critical and indelible component of contemporary peace operations attempting to lay the foundations for sustainable peace.[184]

This rapid evolution of UNPOL form and function has precipitated a number of significant conceptual, institutional and operational challenges. First, structural-bureaucratic constraints relating to the way member states contribute police to peace operations render shortages of quantity and quality of the personnel deployed to the field. In the absence of organisational reform in the areas of recruitment and pre-deployment training requirements, DPKO will continue to struggle to deploy effective UNPOL in a timely fashion.

Second, once deployed, the immediate need to stabilise societies in the aftermath of violent conflict presents field operations with significant challenges to find effective ways to provide (or at least assist in providing) a semblance of public security. Reaching sufficient levels of coverage without a contradictory over-reliance on paramilitary-style FPUs is an enduring challenge and inherently linked to the personnel issue above.

Moreover, the mixed record to date of police reform in multidimensional missions raises question marks over the validity of the politics and logic underpinning the transformative agenda of policebuilding. The lack of consensus surrounding this, render it incumbent on UNPOL to continually question and reflect on the effectiveness of these strategies. Unresolved problems concerning when and how to engage with non-state providers of security and justice compound these challenges as UNPOL face up to ongoing demand for their services.

Addressing these challenges will require a range of measures, not to mention political commitment from Security Council members and police contributing countries. However, in light of the scarce political capital and material resource, recent scholarship has begun to point to the importance of 'organisational learning' within the UN's peace operations architecture as one way of improving the effectiveness of missions.[185] That is, institutionalising knowledge emanating from good and bad experiences in the field and adjusting mission structures, guidance, strategies and tactics in accordance with that learning. Howard conjectures that this occurs in the field (first-level – within a mission) and at headquarters (second-level – between missions) but is often unexplored.[186] However, in practice, UN peace operations have heretofore struggled to ascertain and accurately reflect their relationship to and impact on the specific context to which it is deployed.[187] Furthermore, it has been both slow and selective in effectively learning lessons, elaborating 'best practices' and building institutional memory from what are rapidly evolving field experiences. In the case of UNPOL these shortcomings are equally pertinent and arguably amplified due to the operational challenges, short tours of duty, low retention and shortage of quality pre-deployment training.

Both Howard and Benner *et al.* point to the inadequate learning infrastructure in the peace operations bureaucracy as one of the major inhibiting factors to organisational learning that could improve the efficacy of UN peace operations. In particular, they point to the lack of suitable ways to capture experiences and accumulate knowledge from the field as a major shortcoming in this regard.[188] In other words, organisational learning relating to police in peace operations requires a modality for determining whether or not UNPOL missions are having their intended effects and if not, ascertaining why not.[189] A holistic Monitoring and Evaluation (M&E) framework for UNPOL that targets the impact of UNPOL for organisational learning purposes is a way in which these deficits can be overcome. The challenges faced and the dynamic nature of UNPOL in peace operations make it vital that there is a way of assessing what is working, what is not, and how it could be improved. The following chapter, therefore, takes up the issue of M&E and unpacks the current 'state of the art' as well as the opportunities and challenges associated with current M&E orthodoxy in the realm of UN peace operations, and UNPOL in particular.

Notes

1 Despite attempts to define the term 'peacekeeping' vis-à-vis 'peace support operations', 'peace enforcement' or 'peacebuilding', in UN parlance and practice 'peacekeeping' is a living term. Whilst the UN uses the term 'peacekeeping operations' to cover a range of missions deployed to the field – for instance the C-34 Special Committee on Peacekeeping Operations and the "United Nations Peacekeeping Operations: Principles and Guidelines" – there is much debate over the utility of the terminology given that many of these missions are engaged in a myriad of activities that do not conform to traditional concepts of peacekeeping. In effect, its meaning is continually reconstituted by the evolution of practice. As there is no provision in the UN Charter for peacekeeping per se, it is de facto, whatever the substance of missions authorised by the Security Council and managed by the Secretariat dictate. In this book I use the term 'peace operations' to mean the range of missions that the United Nations deploy in the aftermath of conflict under the auspices of its Department of Peacekeeping Operations (DPKO) and Department of Political Affairs (DPA). These encompass the range of operations engaged in conflict prevention, peacemaking, traditional peacekeeping, peace enforcement and (early) peacebuilding, (early) recovery and transition. The main referent will be the subset of operations referred to as multidimensional missions.
2 Paul F. Diehl, *International Peacekeeping* (Baltimore, MD: Johns Hopkins University Press, 1993); Alex Bellamy, Paul Williams, and Stuart Griffin, *Understanding Peacekeeping*, (Cambridge: Polity, 2004), 71–2: William J. Durch, ed. *Twenty-First-Century Peace Operations*, (Washington DC: United States Institute of Peace and the Henry L. Stimson Center, 2006).
3 "United Nations Peacekeeping Operations: Principles and Guidelines", ed. Peacekeeping Best Practices Section (New York: United Nations, 2008), 21–2.
4 Albeit with some notable exceptions, for example: the UN Operation in the Congo (ONUC) – 1960–4. See: Bellamy, Williams, and Griffin, *Understanding Peacekeeping*, 96.
5 R. Paris, *At War's End: Building Peace after Civil Conflict*, (New York: Cambridge University Press, 2004), 15.
6 For example, the UN Truce Supervision Operation (UNTSO), UN Disengagement Observer Force in the Golan Heights (UNDOF) and the UN Military Observer Group in India and Pakistan (UNMOGIP).
7 Bellamy, Williams, and Griffin, *Understanding Peacekeeping*, 75–81.
8 Boutros Boutros-Ghali, "An Agenda for Peace", in *Report of the Secretary-General* (New York: United Nations, 1992).
9 Ibid., paragraph 21.
10 Michael Doyle and Nicholas Sambanis, *Making War and Building Peace: United Nations Peace Operations*. (Princeton, NJ: Princeton University Press, 1993).
11 Bellamy, Williams, and Griffin, *Understanding Peacekeeping*, 81.
12 UN High-Level Panel on United Nations Peace Operations, "Report of the Panel on United Nations Peace Operations", (New York: United Nations, 2000).
13 Ibid, para 229, 39.
14 "United Nations Peacekeeping Operations: Principles and Guidelines", 24–5. Noteworthy exceptions are the UN Mission in Ethiopia/Eritrea (UNMEE) and UN Mission for the Referendum in Western Sahara (MINURSO).
15 "United Nations Peacekeeping Operations: Principles and Guidelines", 28.
16 "Report of the Secretary-General on Peacebuilding in the Immediate

Aftermath of Conflict", (New York: United Nations, 2012); "Report of the Secretary-General on Peacebuilding in the Immediate Aftermath of Conflict", S/2012/746 (New York: United Nations, 2012).
17 DPKO, "The Contribution of United Nations Peacekeeping to Early Peacebuilding: A DPKO/DFS Strategy for Peacekeepers", (New York: United Nations, 2011).
18 "United Nations Peacekeeping Operations: Principles and Guidelines", 22.
19 See: "United Nations Integrated Missions Planning Process (Impp) Guidelines Endorsed by the Secretary-General on 13 June 2006", *International Peacekeeping* 15, no. 4 (2008).
20 "United Nations Peacekeeping Operations: Principles and Guidelines", 23.
21 Kathleen M. Jennings and Anja T. Kaspersen, "Introduction: Integration Revisited", *International Peacekeeping* 15, no. 4 (2008).
22 The term 'post-conflict' is oft-used but rarely reflects a literal translation. In effect, processes labelled as 'post-conflict' often take place in the context of transition, where violent conflict may have ceased but the conflict may continue in alternative forms where conflict may more accurately be said to have transformed rather than ended.
23 Paris, *At War's End: Building Peace after Civil Conflict*, 19.
24 Doyle and Sambanis, *Making War and Building Peace: United Nations Peace Operations*.
25 For example: Stephen D. Krasner, "Sharing Sovereignty: New Institutions for Collapsed and Failing States", *International Security* 29, no. 2 (2004); James D. Fearon and David D. Laitin, "Neotrusteeship and the Problem of Weak States", *International Security* 28, no. 4 (2004); Simon Chesterman, *You, the People: The United Nations, Transitional Administration, and State-Building*, (Oxford: Oxford University Press, 2004); Paris, *At War's End: Building Peace after Civil Conflict*.
26 By 'Statebuilding' I mean the concept defined by: Roland Paris and Timothy Sisk, eds., *The Dilemmas of Statebuilding: Confronting the Contradictions of Postwar Peace Operations* (London and New York: Routledge, 2009), 14–15. That is: Statebuilding is not synonymous with Peacebuilding – i.e. former is a sub-element of the latter.
27 See, for example: Alejandro Bendana, "From Peacebuilding to Statebuilding: One Step Forward and Two Steps Back", *Development* 48, no. 3 (2005); Mark Duffield, "Development, Territories, and People: Consolidating the External Sovereign Frontier", *Alternatives* 32, no. 2 (2007); Mark Duffield, *Development, Security and Unending War* (London: Polity, 2007); Oliver Richmond, "The Problem of Peace: Understanding the 'Liberal Peace'", *Conflict, Security & Development* 6, no. 3 (2006); O.P. Richmond, "UN Peace Operations and the Dilemmas of the Peacebuilding Consensus", *International Peacekeeping* 11, no. 1 (2004): 90, 95; Jeremy Weinstein, "Autonomous Recovery and International Intervention in Comparative Perspective", in *Working Paper No. 57* (Washington DC: Center for Global Development, 2005); Pierre Engelbert and Dennis M. Tull, "Postconflict Reconstruction in Africa: Flawed Ideas About Failed States", *International Security* 32, no. 4 (2008); J. Herbst, "Let Them Fail: State Failure in Theory and Practice – Implications for Policy", in *When State Fail: Causes and Consequences*, ed. Robert I. Rotberg (Princeton: Princeton University Press, 2003); David Chandler, *Empire in Denial: The Politics of State-Building* (London: Pluto, 2006), Chapter 6.
28 Ian Johnstone, "Managing Consent in Contemporary Peacekeeping Operations", *International Peacekeeping* 18, no. 2 (2011): 173.
29 Ludovic Hood, "Missed Opportunities: The United Nations, Police Service and Defence Force Development in Timor-Leste, 1999–2004", *Civil Wars* 8,

no. 2 (2006); UN, "Report of the United Nations Independent Special Commission of Inquiry for Timor-Leste", (Geneva: United Nations, 2006).
30 Engelbert and Tull, "Postconflict Reconstruction in Africa: Flawed Ideas About Failed States".
31 See, for example: Keith Krause and Oliver Jutersonke, "Peace, Security and Development in Post-Conflict Environments", *Security Dialogue* 36, no. 4 (2005): 451–2; Carolyn Bull, *No Entry without Strategy: Building the Rule of Law under UN Transitional Administration* (Toyko, New York, Paris: United Nations University Press, 2008), 3.
32 Kofi Annan, "The Rule of Law and Transitional Justice in Conflict and Post-Conflict Societies", in *Report of the Secretary-General* (New York: United Nations, 2004); Kofi Annan, "Uniting Our Strengths: Enhancing United Nations Support for the Rule of Law", in *Report of the Secretary General* (New York: United Nations, 2006). The Secretary-General defined 'rule of law' in the former as: "a principle of governance in which all persons, institutions and entities, public and private, including the state itself, are accountable to laws that are publicly promulgated, equally enforced and independently adjudicated, and which are consistent with international human rights norms and standards. It requires, as well, measures to ensure adherence to the principles of supremacy of law, equality before the law, accountability to the law, fairness in the application of the law, separation of powers, participation in decision-making, legal certainty, avoidance of arbitrariness and procedural and legal transparency", 4.
33 Chuck Call and Michael Barnett, "Looking for a Few Good Cops: Peacekeeping, Peacebuilding and Civpol", *International Peacekeeping* 6, no. 4 (1999): 46–7.
34 Annika S. Hansen, "From Congo to Kosovo: Civilian Police in Peace Operations", *Adelphi Papers* 41, no. 343 (2002): 108; Espen B. Eide and Tor Tanke Holm, "Introduction", In *Peacebuilding and Police Reform*, ed. Espen B. Eide and Tor Tanke Holm (London: Frank Cass, 2000), 4.
35 See, for example: Garth den Heyer, "Post-Conflict Civilian Police Reform: 1999 to 2007", Working Paper No 44. (Geneva: International Police Executive Symposium [IPES] and the Geneva Center for the Democratic Control of the Armed Forces [DCAF] and Coginta, 2012), 4–5; Gordon Peake and Kaysie Studdard-Brown, "Policebuilding: The International Deployment Group in the Solomon Islands", *International Peacekeeping* 12, no. 4 (2005): 530.
36 The police serving in field missions have officially been referred to as 'UNPOL' since 2005.
37 UN Police Division Website, www.un.org/Depts/dpko/police/division.shtml.
38 DPKO, *UN Police Magazine 11th Edition* (New York: United Nations, July 2013), 33.
39 For a detailed account of regional and individual state deployments of police in parallel to, or partnership with, the UN, see: B. K. Greener, *The New International Policing*, Global Issues (Basingstoke, England: Palgrave Macmillan, 2009), 8–31.
40 Australian Federal Police, International Deployment Group, www.afp.gov.au/policing/international-deployment-group.aspx. For more detail see: Alex J. Bellamy, "The International Deployment Group", in *Policing in Context: An Introduction to Police Work in Australia*, ed. Roderic G. Broadhurst and Sara E. Davies (South Melbourne, Vic.: Oxford University Press Australia & New Zealand, 2009), 195; Abby McLeod and Sinclair Dinnen, "Police Building in the Southwest Pacific – New Directions in Australian Regional Policing" in *Crafting Transnational Policing: Police Capacity-Building and Global Policing Reform*, ed. Andrew Goldsmith and James Sheptycki (Oxford: Hart Publishing,

2007); Elsina Wainwright and John MacFarlane, "Police Join the Front Line: Building Australia's International Policing Capability", (Canberra: Australian Strategic Policy Institute, 2004).
41 For further detail, see: www.rcmp-grc.gc.ca/po-mp/index-eng.htm.
42 Peake and Studdard-Brown, "Policebuilding: The International Deployment Group in the Solomon Islands".
43 Graham Day and Christopher Freeman, "Policekeeping Is the Key: Rebuilding the Internal Security Architecture of Postwar Iraq", *International Affairs* 79, no. 2 (2003).
44 Greener, *The New International Policing*, 3. See also: Bayley and Perito, *The Police in War: Fighting Insurgency, Terrorism, and Violent Crime* (Boulder, CO: Lynne Rienner Publishers, 2010); Peter Grabosky, *Community Policing and Peacekeeping* (CRC Press, 2009); John Casey, *Policing the World: The Practice of International and Transnational Policing* (Durham, NC: Carolina Academic Press, 2009); Goldsmith and Sheptycki, eds., *Crafting Transnational Policing: Police Capacity-Building and Global Policing Reform.*
45 *Annual Review of Global Peace Operations 2012*, Briefing Paper (New York: Centre for International Cooperation, NYU, 2012), 2.
46 DPKO, *UN Police Magazine 11th Edition* (New York: United Nations, July 2013), 58.
47 NYU Centre for International Cooperation, *Annual Review of Global Peace Operations 2010* (Boulder, CO: Lynne Reinner, 2010); Joshua Smith, Victoria Holt, and William Durch, "Enhancing United Nations Capacity for Post-Conflict Policing and Rule of Law", In *The Project on Rule of Law in Post-Conflict Settings* (Washington, DC: The Henry L Stimson Center, 2007), 15.
48 Interview with the author: Research Associate, Henry L. Stimson Center – Washington, DC, February 2009; Greener, *The New International Policing*, 5.
49 William Durch, "United Nations Police Evolution, Present Capacity and Future Tasks", In *GRIPS State Building Workshop 2010: Organizing Police Forces in Post-Conflict Peace Support Operations* (2010): 18.
50 Garth den Heyer, *The Role of Civilian Police in Peacekeeping: 1999–2007* (Washington, DC: Police Foundation, 2012), 15–19; Nina M. Serafino, "Policing in Peacekeeping and Related Stability Operations: Problems and Proposed Solutions", in *CRS Report for Congress* (Congressional Research Service: The Library of Congress, 2004); Hansen, "From Congo to Kosovo – Civilian Police in Peace Operations", 15–31; Eirin Mobekk, "Identifying Lessons in United Nations International Policing Missions "In *Policy Paper 9* (Geneva, Geneva Centre for the Democratic Control of Armed Forces [DCAF], 2005), 1–3.
51 Hansen, "From Congo to Kosovo: Civilian Police in Peace Operations", 16–31.
52 Greener, *The New International Policing*, 24.
53 For in depth accounts of these missions, see: Nassrine Azimi, "The Role and Functions of Civilian Police in United Nations Peacekeeping Operations: Debriefing and Lessons", in *Report and Recommendations of the International Conference, Singapore* (London: Kluwer Law International and United Nations Institute for Training and Research, 1996), 11–23; Duncan Chappell and John Evans, "The Role, Preparation and Performance of Civilian Police in United Nations Peacekeeping Operations", *Criminal Law Forum* 10, no. 2 (1999): 179–90; Erwin A. Schmidl, "Police Functions in Peace Operations: An Historical Overview", in *Policing the New World Disorder: Peace Operations and Public Security* eds. Robert B. Oakley, Michael J. Dziedzic, and Eliot M. Goldberg (Washington DC: National Defense University, 1998).
54 Greener, *The New International Policing*, 10–11.
55 Hansen, "From Congo to Kosovo: Civilian Police in Peace Operations", 9;

Roxane D.V. Sismandis, "Police Functions in Peace Operations", in *Workshop Report* (Washington DC: United States Institute of Peace, 1997), 2.

56 For example, the police units in ONUC were involved in some training for a new Congolese police force which would return to UN police mandates in the 1990s. Moreover, the police involved in UNTEA were required to perform some law enforcement tasks during the transition – a clear antecedent to the executive law enforcement mandates seen in Timor-Leste and Kosovo.

57 Stephen Fannin, "UN Peace Settlement Plan for Namibia (UNTAG)" (paper presented at the The Role and Functions of Civilian Police in United Nations Peacekeeping Operations: Debriefing and Lessons, Singapore, 1995), 114.

58 Roger Hearn, *UN Peacekeeping in Action: The Namibian Experience* (New York: Nova Science Publishers, 1999), 73; Virginia Page Fortna, "United Nations Transition Assistance Group", in *The Evolution of UN Peacekeeping*, ed. William Durch (New York: St. Martin's Press, 1993).

59 For example, police in ONUMOZ were also required to monitor processes related to the conduct of free and fair democratic elections. See: Ali Mahmoud, "UN Operations in Mozambique (ONUMOZ)", (paper presented at the The Role and Functions of Civilian Police in United Nations Peacekeeping Operations: Debriefing and Lessons, Singapore, 1995), 43–4. Also, later in the life cycle of UNAVEM, CIVPOL became involved for the first time in verifying the disarmament and demobilisation of former soldiers and their integration into the police services. See: Muhammad Anwarul Iqbal, "An Overview of the Civpol Operations in Angola (UNAVEM)" (paper presented at the The Role and Functions of Civilian Police in United Nations Peacekeeping Operations: Debriefing and Lessons, Singapore, 1995), 95–6.

60 Whilst accounts of its success are mixed, for UN policing UNTAC represented "a significant leap forward in terms of mandated authority and operations". Durch, "United Nations Police Evolution, Present Capacity and Future Tasks", 4.

61 Mettle Selwyn, "Operation in Somalia (UNOSOM)" (paper presented at the The Role and Functions of Civilian Police in United Nations Peacekeeping Operations: Debriefing and Lessons, Singapore, 1995), 54; Cheik Oumar Diarra, "United Nations Assistance Mission for Rwanda" (paper presented at the The Role and Functions of Civilian Police in United Nations Peacekeeping Operations: Debriefing and Lessons, Singapore, 1995), 101–2.

62 Serafino, "Policing in Peacekeeping and Related Stability Operations: Problems and Proposed Solutions", 6; Hansen, "From Congo to Kosovo: Civilian Police in Peace Operations", 22.

63 Gino Costa, "The United Nations and Reform of the Police in El Salvador", *International Peacekeeping* 2, no. 3 (1995).

64 Chetan Kumar, "Peacebuilding in Haiti", in *Peace-Building as Politics. Cultivating Peace in Fragile Societies*, eds. Elizabeth M. Cousens and Chetan Kumar (Boulder, CO: Lynne Rienner Publishers, 2001), 24–35.

65 Michael Doyle, "Too Little, Too Late? Justice and Security Reform in Bosnia-Herzegovina", in *Constructing Justice and Security after War*, ed. Charles T. Call (Washington, DC: US Institute of Peace Press, 2007), 242–3.

66 Rama Mani, "Contextualizing Police Reform: Security, the Rule of Law and Post-Conflict Peacebuilding" *International Peacekeeping* 6, no. 4 (1999): 12.

67 Renata Dwan, "Introduction", in *Executive Policing: Enforcing the Law in Peace Operations*, ed. Renata Dwan (Stockholm: Stockholm International Peace Research Institute [SIPRI], 2002), 3–4.

68 Hansen, "From Congo to Kosovo: Civilian Police in Peace Operations", 28.

69 Dwan, "Executive Policing: Enforcing the Law in Peace Operations", 2–3; Hansen, "From Congo to Kosovo: Civilian Police in Peace Operations", 25.

54 Context-setting

70 Anja T Kaspersen, Espen Barth Eide, and Annika S. Hansen, "International Policing and the Rule of Law in Transitions from War to Peace", in *Challenges to Collective Security – Working Paper* (Oslo: UN Programme, NUPI, 2004), 10–11; Dwan, "Conclusions", 123.
71 UN High-Level Panel on United Nations Peace Operations, "Report of the Panel on United Nations Peace Operations", paras 39 and 119.
72 Ibid., para 40.
73 Hansen, "From Congo to Kosovo: Civilian Police in Peace Operations", 108.
74 Sergio Vieira de Mello, "How Not to Run a Country: Lessons for the UN from Kosovo and East Timor", in *Interfet Detainee Management Unit in East Timor*, ed. Michael Kelly (Chavannes-de-Bogis/Genève: SLAC, 2000), 4.
75 Kirsti Samuels, "Rule of Law Reform in Post-Conflict Countries: Operational Initiatives and Lessons Learnt", in *Social Development Papers: Conflict Prevention and Reconstruction, Paper No. 37* (The World Bank, 2006), 7.
76 Annika Hansen and Sharon Wiharta, "The Transition to a Just Order: Establishing Local Ownership after Conflict", In *Research Report* (Folk Bernadotte Academy, 2007), 1.
77 William Durch and Madeline England, eds., *Enhancing United Nations Capacity to Support Post-Conflict Policing and Rule of Law*. Stimson Center Report no. 63, REV. 1 ed. Vol. Revised/Updated, Project on Rule of Law in Post-Conflict Settings, Future of Peace Operations Program (Washington DC: The Stimson Center, 2010), 10.
78 Hansen, "From Congo to Kosovo: Civilian Police in Peace Operations", 31.
79 For more detailed discussion of these dynamics, see Cockayne & Lupel's framework depicting *predatory*, *parasitic* and *symbiotic* organised criminal elements and the transition between groups: James Cockayne and Adam Lupel, "Introduction: Rethinking the Relationship between Peace Operations and Organized Crime", *International Peacekeeping* 16, no. 1 (2009): 11. See also: Jaremey McMullin, "Reintegration of Combatants: Were the Right Lessons Learned in Mozambique?", *International Peacekeeping* 11, no. 4 (2004): 626.
80 Chrissie Steenkamp, "The Legacy of War: Conceptualizing a Culture of Violence to Explain Violence after Peace Accords", *The Round Table* 94, no. 379 (2005): 264.
81 Charles T. Call and William Stanley, "Protecting the People: Public Security Choices after Civil Wars", *Global Governance* 7, no. 2 (2001): 151.
82 Halvor Hartz, Laura Mercean, and Clint Williamson, "Safeguarding a Viable Peace: Institutionalizing the Rule of Law", in *The Quest for a Viable Peace: International Intervention and Strategies for Conflict Transformation*, eds. Jack Covey, Michael J. Dziedzic, and Leonard R. Hawley (Washington DC: United States Institute of Peace Press, 2005), 157–60.
83 Mobekk, "Identifying Lessons in United Nations International Policing Missions", 6.
84 For example, some estimates suggest up to 80 per cent of people receive their security and justice provision from non-statutory sources. See: B. Baker and E. Scheye, "Multi-Layered Justice and Security Delivery in Post-Conflict and Fragile States", *Conflict, Security and Development* 7, no. 4 (2007). For further discussion on non-state policing providers, see section below.
85 David H. Bayley, "The Morphing of Peacekeeping: Competing Approaches to Public Safety", *International Peacekeeping* 18, no. 1 (2011): 57; Bryn Hughes and Charles Hunt, "The Rule of Law in Peace and Capacity Building Operations: Moving Beyond a Conventional State-Centred Imagination", *Journal of International Peacekeeping* 13, no. 3 (2009): 284.
86 M. J. Dziedzic, "Introduction", in *Policing the New World Disorder*, eds. Robert B.

Oakley, Michael J. Dziedzic, and Eliot M. Goldberg (Washington, DC: National Defense University, 1998), 11–15.
87 Michael Brzoska and Andreas Heinemann-Gruder, "Security Sector Reform and Post-Conflict Reconstruction under International Auspices", in *Reform and Reconstruction of the Security Sector*, eds. Alan Bryden and Heiner Hänggi (Baden-Baden: Nomos Verlagsgesellschaft, 2004); Seth G. Jones, Jeremy Wilson, Andrew Rathmell, and K. Jack Riley, *Establishing Law and Order after Conflict*, vol. 1 (Santa Monica, CA: RAND Corporation, 2005), 8–12.
88 Colette Rausch, ed. *Combating Serious Crimes in Postconflict Societies: A Handbook for Policymakers and Practitioners* (Washington D.C.: US Institute for Peace Press, 2006); Cockayne and Lupel, "Introduction: Rethinking the Relationship between Peace Operations and Organized Crime".
89 Rick Linden, David Last, and Christopher Murphy, "Obstacles on the Road to Peace and Justice: The Role of Civilian Police in Peacekeeping", in *Crafting Transnational Policing: Police Capacity-Building and Global Policing Reform*, eds. Andrew Goldsmith and James Sheptycki (Oxford: Hart Publishing, 2007), 150.
90 Durch and England, eds., *Enhancing United Nations Capacity to Support Post-Conflict Policing and Rule of Law*, 22.
91 Michael J. Dziedzic and Robert Perito, "Haiti: Confronting the Gangs of Port-Au-Prince", in *Special Report* (Washington, DC: United States Institute of Peace, 2008).
92 Annika S. Hansen, "Policing the Peace: The Rise of United Nations Formed Police Units", in *Policy Briefing* (Berlin: ZIF, 2011); UNPD, "Developing Doctrine for International Police Peacekeeping", in *IAPTC Annual Convention* (Sydney, Australia, 2009).
93 Hansen, "From Congo to Kosovo – Civilian Police in Peace Operations", 35.
94 Peake and Studdard-Brown, "Policebuilding: The International Deployment Group in the Solomon Islands"; Sinclair Dinnen, Abby McLeod, and Gordon Peake, "Police-Building in Weak States: Australian Approaches in Papua New Guinea and Solomon Islands", *Civil Wars* 8, no. 2 (2006); Tonita Murray, "Police-Building in Afghanistan: A Case Study of Civil Security Reform", *International Peacekeeping* 14, no. 1 (2007).
95 For example, UNAMSIL in Sierra Leone (1999–2005), MONUC/MONUSCO in DR Congo (1999–present), UNMIL in Liberia (2003–present), and UNMIS in Sudan (2005–11).
96 Greener, *The New International Policing*, 24; den Heyer, "Post-conflict Civilian Police Reform", 12–14. For further discussion, see section below on 'The Politics of Policebuilding'.
97 Tony Murney and John McFarlane, "Police Development: Confounding the Challenges for the International Community", in *Community Policing and Peacekeeping*, ed. Peter Grabosky (Boca Raton, FL: CRC Press, 2009), 203.
98 Smith, Holt, and Durch, "Enhancing United Nations Capacity for Post-Conflict Policing and Rule of Law", 10.
99 Murney and McFarlane, "Police Development: Confounding the Challenges for the International Community", 212.
100 Thorsten Benner, Stephan Mergenthaler, and Philipp Rotmann, *The New World of UN Peace Operations: Learning to Build Peace?* (Oxford: Oxford University Press, 2011), 68.
101 Ibid., 95–6.
102 "Support for the Reform, Restructuring and Rebuilding of Police and Law Enforcement Agencies", in *DPKO Policy* (2006), para 5.13.17.
103 B. K. Greener, "UNPOL: UN Police as Peacekeepers", *Policing and Society* 19, no. 2 (2008): 11. For further discussion of policebuilding and its dilemmas, see section below 'The Politics of Policebuilding'.

104 See, for example: OECD, "OECD-DAC Handbook on Security System Reform", (2007); "Security Sector Reform and the Rule of Law", in *Stabilisation Issues Note* (London: UK Stabilisation Unit, 2010); Hans Born, "Security Sector Reform in Challenging Environments: Insights from Comparative Analysis", in *Security Sector Reform in Challenging Environments*, eds. Hans Born and Albrecht Schnabel (Geneva/Vienna: DCAF/LIT Verlag, 2009).
105 For good accounts of challenges of more protracted police development, see: Vandra Harris, "Building on Sand? Australian Police Involvement in International Police Capacity Building", *Policing and Society: An International Journal of Research and Policy* 20, no. 1 (2010); Murney and McFarlane, "Police Development: Confounding the Challenges for the International Community".
106 Durch and England, eds., *Enhancing United Nations Capacity to Support Post-Conflict Policing and Rule of Law*, 5.
107 See: Durch and England, eds., *Enhancing United Nations Capacity to Support Post-Conflict Policing and Rule of Law*, 89–91, Table A1.2. for a full list of UNPOL activities from 1999–2010. See also: Linden, Last, and Murphy, "Obstacles on the Road to Peace and Justice: The Role of Civilian Police in Peacekeeping", 151; Cockayne and Lupel, "Introduction: Rethinking the Relationship between Peace Operations and Organized Crime"; Charles T. Hunt and Alex J. Bellamy, "Mainstreaming the Responsibility to Protect in Peace Operations", *Civil Wars* 13, no. 1 (2011): 8, 10, 13.
108 "Report of the Comprehensive Analysis of the Police Division, Office of Rule of Law & Security Institutions, DPKO", (New York: United Nations, December 2008), 9.
109 Lynn M. Thomas, "Peace Operations and the Need to Prioritize the Rule of Law through Legal System Reform: Lessons from Somalia and Bosnia", *Small Wars & Insurgencies* 15, no. 2 (2004): 70–6.
110 Call and Stanley, "Protecting the People: Public Security Choices after Civil Wars", 168.
111 D. H. Bayley, *Democratizing the Police Abroad: What to Do and How to Do It* (US Dept. of Justice, Office of Justice Programs, National Institute of Justice, 2001), 42; Rachel Neild, "Democratic Police Reforms in War-Torn Societies", *Conflict, Security & Development* 1, no. 1 (2001): 31–4.
112 Durch and England, eds., *Enhancing United Nations Capacity to Support Post-Conflict Policing and Rule of Law*, 3.
113 DPKO, *UN Police Magazine 6th Edition* (New York: United Nations, January 2011), 24–5.
114 "Report of the Comprehensive Analysis of the Police Division, Office of Rule of Law & Security Institutions, DPKO", 5.
115 Durch, "United Nations Police Evolution, Present Capacity and Future Tasks", 15; Greener, "UNPOL: UN Police as Peacekeepers", 10.
116 See, for example: Otwin Marenin, "Restoring Policing Systems in Conflict Torn Nations: Process, Problems, Prospects", in *Occasional Paper No. 7* (Geneva: Geneva Centre for the Democratic Control of Armed Forces [DCAF], 2005); Hansen, "From Congo to Kosovo: Civilian Police in Peace Operations".; Azimi, "The Role and Functions of Civilian Police in United Nations Peacekeeping Operations: Debriefing and Lessons", 114–34; Goldsmith and Sheptycki, eds., *Crafting Transnational Policing: Police Capacity-Building and Global Policing Reform*; Mobekk, "Identifying Lessons in United Nations International Policing Missions"; Ylber Bajraktari, Arthur Boutellis, Fatema Gunja, Daniel Harris, James Kapsis, Eva Kaye, and Jane Rhee, "The Prime System: Measuring the Success of Post-Conflict Police Reform" (Princeton, NJ: Princeton University: Woodrow Wilson School of Public and

International Affairs, 2006); Durch and England, eds., *Enhancing United Nations Capacity to Support Post-Conflict Policing and Rule of Law.*
117 See, for example: Bayley, *Democratizing the Police Abroad: What to Do and How to Do It*; Bayley and Perito, *The Police in War: Fighting Insurgency, Terrorism, and Violent Crime*; Casey, *Policing the World: The Practice of International and Transnational Policing*; Goldsmith and Sheptycki, eds., *Crafting Transnational Policing: Police Capacity-Building and Global Policing Reform*; Greener, *The New International Policing*; Alice Hills, *Policing Post-Conflict Cities* (London: Zed Books, 2009); Frank Upham, "Mythmaking in the Rule of Law Orthodoxy", in *Carnegie Paper* (Washinbton D.C.: Carnegie Endowment for International Peace, 2002).
118 Wibke Hansen, Tobias Gienanth, and Roderick Parkes, "International and Local Policing in Peace Operations: Lessons Learned and the Way Forward to Integrated Approaches", in *International Berlin Workshop Report* (Berlin: ZIF, 2007), 14–16; Bruce Oswald and Adrian Bates, "Privileges and Immunities of United Nations Police", in *Making Sense of Peace and Capacity-Building Operations: Rethinking Policing and Beyond*, eds. Bryn W. Hughes, Charles T. Hunt, and Boris Kondoch (Leiden: Martinus Nijhoff, 2010).
119 Durch and England, eds., *Enhancing United Nations Capacity to Support Post-Conflict Policing and Rule of Law*, 42–7.
120 Interview with the author: UN DPKO Official – New York, February 2009
121 Notwithstanding attempts to address these problems such as the Global Effort to recruit more female police.
122 Peake and Studdard-Brown, "Policebuilding: The International Deployment Group in the Solomon Islands": 528.
123 FPUs are national contingents, typically 120–140 in number, drawn from member state paramilitary/gendarmerie forces. Their major benefits are that FPUs deploy rapidly and as a 'ready-made' law enforcement unit, self-sufficient logistically, demonstrating a clear chain of command and history of joint training and functional coherence. They are usually armed and trained for more volatile situations than patrolling officers, such as riot control, and have the flexibility to calibrate their use of force, as circumstances dictate. See: Hansen, "Policing the Peace: The Rise of United Nations Formed Police Units", 1–2. For more on the reasons behind ready provision of FPUs for deployment, see: Durch, "United Nations Police Evolution, Present Capacity and Future Tasks", 13–14.
124 DPKO, *UN Police Magazine 11th Edition*, 48. The UN's penchant for FPUs has provoked both positive and negative consequences in the field. First and foremost, their use has helped to constrict the 'public security gap' in a way that has mitigated the pitfalls of employing military to deal with public disorder. (Peter Viggo Jakobsen, "Military Forces and Public Security Challenges", in *The United Nations and Regional Security: Europe and Beyond*, eds. Michael Pugh and Waheguru Pal Singh Sidhu (London/Boulder: Lynne Rienner Publishers, 2003)). However, these units continue to attract controversy. Despite their comparative advantage over military law enforcement alternatives, these stability policing teams still resemble paramilitaries in image and at times in conduct. There have been numerous accusations of FPUs being overly 'heavy-handed' and over-stepping their rules of engagement. (Benjamin Agordzo, "Filling the 'Security Gap' in Post-Conflict Situations: Could Formed Police Units Make a Difference?", *International Peacekeeping* 16, no. 2 (2009): 288.) This has deleterious consequences for the differentiation mentioned above and importantly for public trust and confidence. (Alice Hills, "The Inherent Limits of Military Police Forces in Policing Peace Operations", *International Peacekeeping* 8, no. 3 (2003): 92.)

125 Vieira de Mello, "How Not to Run a Country: Lessons for the UN from Kosovo and East Timor".
126 For further details, see: William J. Durch and Michelle Ker. "Police in UN Peacekeeping: Improving Selection, Recruitment, and Deployment". *Providing for Peacekeeping*, 6 (New York: International Peace Institute, November 2013).
127 den Heyer, "Post-Conflict Civilian Police Reform", 20.
128 For detailed discussion and definition of democratic policing, see: Bayley, *Changing the Guard: Developing Democratic Police Abroad* (New York: Oxford University Press, 2006); Peter Grabosky, "Democratic Policing", in *Community Policing and Peacekeeping*, ed. Peter Grabosky (Boca Raton, FL: CRC Press, 2009); Bayley, *Democratizing the Police Abroad: What to Do and How to Do It*, 13–15; Marenin, "Restoring Policing Systems in Conflict Torn Nations: Process, Problems, Prospects", 37–8, 60.
129 Bayley, *Democratizing the Police Abroad: What to Do and How to Do It*, 35–6. The rare executive law enforcement missions in Timor and Kosovo brought their own political questions regarding accusations of neo-trusteeship, etc.
130 Hansen and Wiharta, "The Transition to a Just Order: Establishing Local Ownership after Conflict"; Robert M. Perito, "Police in Peace and Stability Operations: Evolving Us Policy and Practice", *International Peacekeeping* 15, no. 1 (2008).
131 Kaspersen, Eide, and Hansen, "International Policing and the Rule of Law in Transitions from War to Peace", 5.
132 Eide and Holm, "Introduction", 4–5. See also: Cousens, Kumar, and Wermester, eds., *Peacebuilding as Politics: Cultivating Peace in Fragile Societies*.
133 Greener, *The New International Policing*, 117, 124.
134 Rekyo Huang, "Securing the Rule of Law: Assessing International Strategies for Post-Conflict Criminal Justice". (New York: International Peace Academy, 2005); Jessica Howard and Bruce Oswald, "The Rule of Law on Peace Operations" (Paper presented at the 'Challenges of Peace Operations' Project, Melbourne Law School, University of Melbourne, 11–13 November, 2002); Jane Stromseth, David Wippman, and Rosa Brooks, eds., *Can Might Make Rights: Building the Rule of Law after Military Interventions* (Cambridge: Cambridge University Press, 2006), 56–60; Marcus Brand, "Promoting the Rule of Law, Transparency and Fighting against Corruption". In *Building Capacity for Democracy, Peace and Social Progress – The 6th International Conference of New or Restored Democracies (ICNRD-6)(Doha: UNDP)*; Hansen and Wiharta, "The Transition to a Just Order: Establishing Local Ownership after Conflict", XVI.
135 Brian Z. Tamanaha, *On the Rule of Law: History, Politics, Theory* (Cambridge: Cambridge University Press, 2004), 4.
136 Brand, "Promoting the Rule of Law, Transparency and Fighting against Corruption", 5.
137 Claude Ake, *Democracy and Development in Africa* (Washington DC: Brookings Institution, 1996), 287.
138 Bull, *No Entry without Strategy: Building the Rule of Law under UN Transitional Administration*, 10.
139 "There is an obvious connection between democratic practices – such as the rule of law ... – and the achievement of true peace and security in any new and stable political order". Boutros-Ghali, "An Agenda for Peace", paragraph 59.
140 Bull, *No Entry without Strategy: Building the Rule of Law under UN Transitional Administration*, 1.
141 Neclâ Tschirgi, "Post-Conflict Peacebuilding Revisited: Achievements, Limitations, Challenges", in *Security-Development Nexus Program, Policy Paper* (New York: International Peace Academy, 2004); Charles T. Call, "Ending Wars,

Building States", In *Building States to Build Peace*, eds. Charles T. Call and Vanesa Wyeth (Boulder: Lynne Rienner Publishers, 2008), 13–16; Chris Ferguson, "Police Reform, Peacekeeping and SSR: The Need for Closer Synthesis", *Journal of Security Sector Manangement* 2, no. 3 (2004); Alan Bryden, Timothy Donais, and Heiner Hänggi, "Shaping a Security Governance Agenda in Post-Conflict Peacebuilding", in *Policy Paper No. 11* (Geneva: Geneva Centre for the Democratic Control of Armed Forces (DCAF), 2005).

142 Durch and England, eds., *Enhancing United Nations Capacity to Support Post-Conflict Policing and Rule of Law*, 10–12; Stromseth, Wippman, and Brooks, eds., *Can Might Make Rights: Building the Rule of Law after Military Interventions*; Hansen and Wiharta, "The Transition to a Just Order: Establishing Local Ownership after Conflict", 1; Mobekk, "Identifying Lessons in United Nations International Policing Missions", 6; Hansen, "From Congo to Kosovo: Civilian Police in Peace Operations", 25.

143 Hills, *Policing Post-Conflict Cities*, 70; Agnes Hurwitz and Kaysie Studdard, "Rule of Law Programs in Peace Operations", In *The Security-Development Nexus Program* (New York: International Peace Academy, 2005), 1–6.

144 Greener, *The New International Policing*, 117; Eide and Holm, *Peacebuilding and Police Reform*, 1–8; Bull, *No Entry without Strategy: Building the Rule of Law under UN Transitional Administration*, 16–43.

145 See: Larry Diamond, "Promoting Democracy in the 1990s: Actors and Instruments, Issues and Imperatives", in *Report to the Carnegie Commission on Preventing Deadly Conflict* (New York: Carnegie Corporation, 1995), 9.

146 Michael Barnett, Hunjoon Kim, Madalene O'Donnell, and Laura Sitea, "Peacebuilding: What Is in a Name?", *Global Governance* 13(2007): 45.

147 See, for example: Stephen Golub, "A House without a Foundation", in *Promoting the Rule of Law Abroad: In Search of Knowledge*, ed. Thomas Carothers (Washington DC: Carnegie Endowment for International Peace, 2006), 110. Moreover, in relation to policing, others point out that the liberal-democratic model is more an ideal than something actually achieved by many/any. See: Murney and McFarlane, "Police Development: Confounding the Challenges for the International Community", 205.

148 Roland Paris, "Understanding the 'Coordination Problem' in Post-War Statebuilding", in *The Dilemmas of Statebuilding: Confronting the Contradictions of Postwar Peace Operations*, eds. Roland Paris and Timothy Sisk (London and New York: Routledge, 2009).

149 Bull, *No Entry without Strategy: Building the Rule of Law under UN Transitional Administration*, 48.

150 See, for example: Marcus Cox, "Security and Justice: Measuring the Development Returns", (London: Agulhas Applied Knowledge, 2008), vii–viii; Maria Derks, "Security Sector Reform as Development Policy: A Closer Look at the Link between Security and Development", in *ISA Annual Convention* (San Francisco, 2008), 24; Robert Egnell and Peter Haldén, "Laudable, Ahistorical and Overambitious: Security Sector Reform Meets State Formation Theory", *Conflict, Security & Development* 9, no. 1 (2009): 47–8.

151 Greener, *The New International Policing*, 110.

152 See, for example: David Chandler, "Back to the Future? The Limits of Neo-Wilsonian Ideals of Exporting Democracy", *Review of International Studies* 32, no. 3 (2006); Michael Barnett, "Building a Republican Peace", *International Security* 30, no. 4 (2006); Oliver P. Richmond, "Emancipatory Forms of Human Security and Liberal Peacebuilding", *International Journal* 62, no. 3 (2007); Duffield, *Development, Security and Unending War*.

153 Roland Paris, "Saving Liberal Peacebuilding", *Review of International Studies* 36, no. 02 (2010): 357–62.

154 Golub, "A House without a Foundation", 105.
155 Kirsti Samuels, "Rule of Law Reform in Post-Conflict Countries: Operational Initiatives and Lessons Learnt", in *Social Development Papers: Conflict Prevention and Reconstruction, Paper No. 37* (The World Bank, 2006), 16–23.
156 *Inter alia*: "Special Edition: Policing Post-Conflict Societies", *Policing and Society: An International Journal of Research and Policy* 19, no. 4 (2009); Dinnen, McLeod, and Peake, "Police-Building in Weak States: Australian Approaches in Papua New Guinea and Solomon Islands"; Bruce Baker, *Security in Post-Conflict Africa: The Role of Nonstate Policing*, Advances in Police Theory and Practice (Boca Raton, FL: CRS Press, 2009); Andrew Goldsmith and Sinclair Dinnen, "Transnational Police Building: Critical Lessons from Timor Leste and Solomon Islands" *Third World Quarterly* 28, no. 6 (2007); Abby McLeod, "Police Capacity Development in the Pacific: The Challenge of Local Context", *Policing and Society* 19, no. 2 (2009); Thomas Carothers, "Promoting the Rule of Law Abroad: The Problem of Knowledge", in *Carnegie Paper* (Washington DC: Carnegie Endowment for International Peace, 2003); Deborah H. Isser, ed. *Customary Justice and the Rule of Law in War-Torn Societies*, Peacebuilding and the Rule of Law (Washington DC: United States Institute of Peace,2010); Eric Scheye, "Statebuilding in the Fragile and Conflict-Affected States: Flawed Approaches and Misconceptions", *unpublished manuscript* (2009).
157 See, for example: OECD, "OECD-DAC Handbook on Security System Reform", 17; DfID, "Non-State Justice and Security Systems", (London: DfID, 2004), 3–4.
158 Bruce Baker, *Multi-Choice Policing in Africa* (Uppsala: Nordiska Afrikainstituter, 2008); Ian Clegg, Robert Hutton, and Jim Whetton, eds., *Policy Guidance to Support Policing in Developing Countries*, (Swansea: University of Wales, 2000), 54–61; Alice Hills, "Police Reform in Post-Colonial States", in *Working Paper 36* (Geneva: Geneva Centre for the Democratic Control of Armed Forces (DCAF), 2002), 7–8.
159 Bruce Baker, "Grasping the Nettle of Nonstate Policing", In *Making Sense of Peace and Capacity Building Operations: Rethinking Policing and Beyond*, eds. Bryn Hughes, Charles T. Hunt, and Boris Kondoch (Leiden: Martinus Nijhoff, 2010), 80–3.
160 Baker, *Security in Post-Conflict Africa: The Role of Nonstate Policing*.
161 Peter Albrecht and Helene Maria Kyed, "Justice and Security: When the State Isn't the Main Provider", in *DIIS Policy Brief* (Copenhagen: Danish Institute for International Studies (DIIS), 2010), 2.
162 Madeline L. England, "Security Sector Reform in Stabilization Environments: A Note on Current Practice", in *Future of Peace Operations* (Washington, DC: Henry L. Stimson Center, 2009), 11–14.
163 Christian Lund, "Twilight Institutions: Public Authority and Local Politics in Africa", *Development and Change* 37, no. 4 (2006): 688.
164 Anna Kantor and Mariam Persson, "Understanding Vigilantism: Informal Security Providers and Security Sector Reform in Liberia", (Folke Bernadotte Academy, 2010), 27–9.
165 Baker, *Security in Post-Conflict Africa: The Role of Nonstate Policing*, 46.
166 Bruce Baker, "A Policing Partnership for Post-War Africa? Lessons from Liberia and Southern Sudan", *Policing and Society: An International Journal of Research and Policy* 19, no. 4 (2009); Bruce Baker, "Police Reform in Sierra Leone: The Role of the UK", in *GRIPS State'Building Workshop 2010: Organizing Police Forces in Post-Conflict Peace Support Operations* (2010).
167 Bayley, "The Morphing of Peacekeeping: Competing Approaches to Public Safety", 53–4.

168 Some have put this number at as much as 80 per cent (OECD, "OECD-DAC Handbook on Security System Reform", 17.). Stephan Golub, "Beyond Rule of Law Orthodoxy: The Legal Empowerment Alternative", (Carnegie Endowment for International Peace, 2003), 16; Kritz cited in Bull, *No Entry without Strategy: Building the Rule of Law under UN Transitional Administration*, 55; Hurwitz and Studdard, "Rule of Law Programs in Peace Operations", 5.
169 Dinnen, McLeod, and Peake, "Police-Building in Weak States: Australian Approaches in Papua New Guinea and Solomon Islands", 101.
170 Brian Z. Tamanaha, *A General Jurisprudence of Law and Society* (New York: Oxford University Press, 2001), 145–6.
171 Baker and Scheye, "Multi-Layered Justice and Security Delivery in Post-Conflict and Fragile States", 512.
172 Howard and Oswald, "The Rule of Law on Peace Operations", 276–7; Eric Scheye, "Pragmatic Realism in Justice and Security Development: Supporting Improvement in the Performance of Non-State/Local Justice and Security Networks", (The Hague: Netherlands: Institute of International Relations, 2009).
173 In relation to UN missions in Cambodia, Timor-Leste and Kosovo, see: Bull, *No Entry without Strategy: Building the Rule of Law under UN Transitional Administration*, 9–10.
174 Bruce Baker and Eric Scheye, "Access to Justice in a Post-Conflict State: Donor-Supported Multidimensional Peacekeeping in Southern Sudan", *International Peacekeeping* 16, no. 2 (2009): 181; Baker, "A Policing Partnership for Post-War Africa? Lessons from Liberia and Southern Sudan", 387.
175 Bayley, "The Morphing of Peacekeeping: Competing Approaches to Public Safety", 56–9.
176 England, "Security Sector Reform in Stabilization Environments: A Note on Current Practice", 11–14.
177 Durch, "United Nations Police Evolution, Present Capacity and Future Tasks", 19–20.
178 Charles T. Call, "Challenges in Police Refrom: Promoting Effectiveness and Accountability", in *From Promise to Practice: Strengthening UN Capacities for the Prevention of Vuiolent Conflict* (New York: International Peace Academy, 2003), 4.
179 Bayley, "The Morphing of Peacekeeping: Competing Approaches to Public Safety", 53, 59–62.
180 Durch, "United Nations Police Evolution, Present Capacity and Future Tasks", 19–20.
181 Mobekk, "Identifying Lessons in United Nations International Policing Mission", 10.
182 Bull, *No Entry without Strategy: Building the Rule of Law under UN Transitional Administration*, 8.
183 Roger MacGinty, "Indigenous Peace-Making Versus the Liberal Peace", *Cooperation and Conflict* 43, no. 2 (2008); Tanja Chopra, "When Peacebuilding Contradicts Statebuilding: Notes from the Arid Lands of Kenya", *International Peacekeeping* 16, no. 4 (2009).
184 den Heyer, *The Role of Civilian Police in Peacekeeping: 1999–2007*, 3; Peake and Studdard-Brown, "Policebuilding: The International Deployment Group in the Solomon Islands": 530.
185 See, in particular, L. M. Howard, *UN Peacekeeping in Civil Wars* (Cambridge: Cambridge University Press, 2008); Benner, Mergenthaler, and Rotmann, *The New World of UN Peace Operations: Learning to Build Peace?* See also: Susanna P. Campbell, "When Process Matters: The Potential Implications of Organisational Learning for Peacebuilding Success", *Journal of Peacebuilding and Development* 4, no. 2 (2008).

186 Howard, *UN Peacekeeping in Civil Wars*, 330–9.
187 See, for example: Sarah Jane Meharg, ed. *Measuring What Matters in Peace Operations and Crisis Management* (McGill-Queen's University Press, 2009); Cedric de Coning and Paul Romita, "Monitoring and Evaluation of Peace Operations". (New York, Oslo: International Peace Institute & Norwegian Institute of International Affairs: November 2009); Joseph Schumacher, "What to Measure in Peace Operations". *The Pearson Papers* 10, no. 1 (2007).
188 See, respectively: Howard, *UN Peacekeeping in Civil Wars*, 333–4; Benner, Mergenthaler, and Rotmann, *The New World of UN Peace Operations: Learning to Build Peace?*, 219.
189 den Heyer, "Post-Conflict Civilian Police Reform", 21.

2 Monitoring and evaluation in peace operations
Measuring progress, assessing impact and gauging success

Introduction

The previous chapter charted the evolution of UNPOL form and function in UN peace operations and identified some of the major challenges they face in deploying missions and implementing mandates. This chapter explores one avenue for addressing those challenges: Monitoring and Evaluation (M&E). It has been argued that M&E is crucial for realising effective peace operations.[1] However, despite its purported importance, current efforts have not been able to meet the needs of the peace operations apparatus.[2] M&E is critically important to the smooth functioning of UN peace operations but it is particularly difficult to conduct given the unique operational circumstances, methodological challenges and a context of political pressure.

This chapter examines current convention in this domain. It proceeds in four sections. First it clarifies what is meant by M&E. Second, it reviews and critically assesses current M&E tools within the UN peace operations apparatus.[3] Third, it identifies and analyses the extant literature on M&E in (international) policing. Finally, it draws together the major shortcomings and challenges associated with these approaches in relation to the specific M&E needs of police in peace operations. I argue that the M&E approaches employed by the UN to date may be necessary but are not sufficient for the short- or longer-term needs of UNPOL. The specific context and objectives for police in modern peace missions render unique challenges that defy the application of M&E tools forged in different circumstances but that extant efforts largely fail to reflect this. Therefore, I posit that UNPOL require a tailored approach that can overcome the shortcomings with the extant orthodoxy. Implicit assumptions, a counterproductive incentive structure and problematic dependencies constrict the perspective of current M&E orthodoxy, rendering assessments blinkered to certain phenomena. I argue that overcoming these challenges requires addressing seven sets of criticisms relating to outcome/impact focus, flexibility, data diversity, context-sensitivity, holism, participation and learning-orientation.

64 *Context-setting*

Monitoring and evaluation

What is M&E?

The theory and practice of M&E crosses disciplines and includes both public and private sectors.[4] The term M&E is understood and defined in a variety of different ways depending on the context.[5] For example, in current and competing paradigms many separate the 'monitoring' and 'evaluation' as discrete facets often conducted in different ways by different agents – indeed, some treat the two as entirely separate disciplines. In general, *monitoring* is viewed as an internal, ongoing exercise, whereas *evaluation* is understood as an externally conducted discrete process at the end of a project cycle, operational phase or even mission lifetime.[6] Furthermore, assessments are often perceived to be either formative or summative. Formative evaluation is designed to cultivate and develop the intervention itself, whereas the goal of a summative evaluation is to assess intervention end-states.[7] Indeed, these can be understood to fit loosely into the conventional distinction between monitoring and evaluation.

However, M&E in the context of post-conflict 'interventions' is embryonic to say the least.[8] The environments into which peace operations deploy display certain idiosyncrasies, which defy simplistic adaptations of existing theories and frameworks.[9] As a result, the demand for M&E in these settings has generated disparate modalities for different actors and praxis is typified by methodological anarchy, or at least "methodological orthodoxy has yet to crystallize".[10] Even where practices are emerging the referent under analysis differs. For example, some efforts focus on the UN as an international organisation whilst others focus on specific peace operations or components or even programmes therein. Similarly, the subject of assessments differ as some attempt to label endeavours as successes or failures, others talk about impact or outcomes and some target performance.[11] Furthermore, such notions of success are contingent on whose perspectives dominate.[12]

In practice – particularly in peace operations – the distinctions between monitoring and evaluation are less clear and the two concepts are usually utilised in tandem.[13] This book uses the term M&E to imply a holistic management approach, combining 'M' and 'E' in a closer, interdependent and symbiotic system for both *formative* and *summative* purposes.[14] An M&E 'system' implies a process that synchronises these two activities and embeds the capacity to plan for, disseminate and respond to the findings. Its focus is on field-level impact assessment as a building block for organisational learning.[15] As Campbell writes, "Organisational learning and impact assessment are interdependent. Organisational learning requires incremental impact assessment, or information about the alignment between intention and outcome."[16] As peace operations have evolved, so too have the UN's M&E methods. The following section looks at the culture of M&E in the UN peace operations bureaucracy.

M&E in the UN peace operations apparatus

Many of the tools developed by the UN to monitor and evaluate peace operations implicate both headquarters and field missions and there is consequently no clear distinction between the two due to significant and often intentional overlap. However, there has been a clear development of an organisational learning system within the peace operations bureaucracy.

Having had no clear institutional home for M&E in the first three and a half decades of UN peacekeeping, a small 'lessons learned unit' was created within DPKO in 1995. As a result, the dominant mode of UN self-evaluation has been through 'lessons learned' reports. This approach is primarily concerned with assessing past missions to glean what went well and what went wrong, with the aim of altering future practice as a result.[17] These have tended to reflect upon thematic areas or the experiences of particular missions.[18] While early lessons learned reports were criticised for avoiding critical reporting that might 'tread on toes', this tendency was dramatically reversed with the high-profile and very critical self-assessments following the catastrophes in Srebrenica and Rwanda; however the question remains regarding less contentious and smaller scale reporting.[19] Other critics claim that the majority of these reports have been overly reactive and focused on identifying mistakes from failures rather than good practices from positive experiences. Furthermore, it has been argued that these were invariably produced by people without a social science and/or M&E background leading to uneven quality, deemed insufficiently timely, and were not widely read by staff at headquarters or in the field and hence not amenable to feeding into dynamic implementation planning.[20]

The broad terms of reference of these oversight reports dictates that there is rarely comprehensive reflection on policing components. Some also allude to an unwritten rule that the lessons learned unit traditionally kept out of 'uniformed territory', leaving evaluation of the police (and military) to their respective divisions.[21] What does focus on UNPOL has been of limited utility for practitioners in the field.[22]

The presumed organisational learning associated with these processes has not necessarily followed.[23] That is, they did not lead to improved organisational efficiency and effectiveness as intended.[24] Notwithstanding the ubiquitous recognition that future success in peacekeeping is dependent on effective knowledge management, lessons identified were not necessarily translated into lessons learned.[25] Despite the rapidly changing character of peace operations in the 1990s, the UN had not developed and embedded a suitable learning system.[26]

In 2000, the Brahimi Report noted that, "the work of DPKO's existing Lessons Learned Unit does not seem to have had a great deal of impact on peace operations practice,... the compilation of lessons learned seems to occur mostly after a mission has ended", and that "...not enough has been done to improve the system's ability to tap that [field] experience or to feed it back into the development of operational doctrine, plans, procedures or mandates."[27] Since then there has been a drive towards professionalising the business of peacekeeping at the UN.[28] That is, an attempt to make it a more effective, efficient and ultimately a more reliable tool for contemporary conflict management. A major component of this was improving the learning infrastructure of the peace operations apparatus.[29] This professionalization drive was at the heart of Under-Secretary-General Guehenno's change management process that resulted in the 'Peace Operations 2010' reform agenda launched in 2006.[30] The core goal of transforming the peace operations bureaucracy into a learning organisation resulted in a number of developments in the way the UN/DPKO approached the matter of M&E.

The 'Lessons Learned Unit' subsequently merged with the 'Policy and Analysis Unit' to become the 'Peacekeeping Best Practices Unit' in 2001 (eventually the 'Peacekeeping Best Practices Section' [PBPS] in 2005) with a sharper focus on learning from good as well as bad experiences through more timely reports and training seminars.[31] In addition to the name change and mission refinement, PBPS received increased funding and became home to efforts to institutionalise improved 'Knowledge Management' (KM).[32] The KM Team in partnership with the Guidance Team were designed to, "ensure that lessons identified in the field are reflected in the official guidance materials of the peace operations bureaucracy".[33] For PBPS this signified a shift away from external reports written at the completion of a mission, reflecting the Secretary-General's belief that

> [l]essons learning is a continuous activity best carried out by practitioners in the field ... Given the fluidity of the operational environment and the vast array of new lessons emerging every day in missions, lessons should be captured and used on a continuous basis, not just once a mission has closed.[34]

This enhanced focus on the field as the place where lessons should be identified and the additional workload on field personnel, led to the creation of field-based Best Practices Officers (BPO). They provide a focal point for institutional knowledge in the context of short service periods of most mission personnel.[35] The KM and Guidance teams, in collaboration with the BPOs, developed a number of M&E tools to enhance the institutional learning cycle and work towards field experiences being reflected in official guidance materials developed at headquarters.[36] The resultant 'Best Practices Toolbox', launched in 2005, included four M&E tools aimed at capturing and sharing experiences from the field and gathering the information perceived to be the first stage of organisational learning[37]: after-action reviews; surveys of practice; end-of-assignment reports; and, handover notes.[38]

Nevertheless, the toolkit's utility has been hampered as the field based BPOs have struggled to sufficiently integrate into the work and learning taking place in missions. Furthermore, the capacity for learning varies across missions and the influence of top-down headquarters processes advocating the implementation of these M&E tools is contingent on the will of mission leadership in the field and these tools have been employed with varying consistency and quality.[39] In addition, the perennial coordination challenges between field missions and headquarters exacerbate these disconnects. Consequently, these M&E efforts have not yet provided the bridge for increased flow of information between the field and headquarters that they were intended to be. This in turn limits the extent to which field experiences can inform PBPS analysis and development of knowledge trends for prioritising policy and guidance development at headquarters.

To disseminate the knowledge emanating from the toolkit, PBPS developed two major enabling technologies. First, in addition to the public web-based resource hub for information-sharing,[40] in 2006 the 'Peace Operations Intranet' was launched to facilitate access to a repository of guidance for peacekeepers across all missions. Second, PBPS developed Communities of Practice (CoP) to provide a real-time portal for information sharing. CoPs are facilitated email networks intended to support knowledge transfer between field missions. These initiatives have brought benefits in enabling information management and sharing. However, results have varied with the capacity of managers to implement them and the technological requirements continue to test the IT capabilities of some field operations.[41]

Whilst these developments constitute a significant step forward in embracing organisational learning, the PBPS and the KM architecture continues to suffer from shortages in influence over the peace operations policy-making and mandate implementation apparatus – in large part due to ineffective human resource capacity.[42] Another criticism is that, despite targeting field experiences and using CoPs to accelerate feedback processes, there remains a problematic lag between identification of good and bad practice in missions and evidence of course-correction in their light. That is to say, this KM system is perceived to be sluggish due to the time it takes for 'lessons' to appear in codified guidance and doctrine. An interim assessment of this new learning infrastructure in 2007 suggested that, despite signs of progress, "further efforts are needed to … integrate learning processes into the daily work of staff members".[43]

These developments in learning systems were reflected in a number of other UN Secretariat reforms. For example, in 2008/9 a restructuring of DPKO saw the creation of an integrated *Policy, Evaluation and Training Division* (DPET) comprising the existing *PBPS* and *Integrated Training Service* (ITS), as well as the newly created *Evaluation and Partnerships Section*. The remit of the division includes, "…systematic capturing of best practices and lessons learned ... provide an integrated, unified capacity to evaluate mission performance and mandate implementation".[44]

The Evaluation Unit was tasked with assisting headquarters and field missions in conducting evaluations and developing self-evaluation capacities. The Unit's policy directive states that its location and work was intended to allow it to feed evaluation findings back into policy development and best practices.[45] However, it is not the purpose of these evaluations to ascertain the impact of mission activities as such.[46] Furthermore, the unit is tasked with conducting evaluations of both headquarters and field-missions.[47] Thus far, these have ranged from cross-cutting thematic assessments to annual evaluations of particular missions. At present annual workplans are promulgated following requests by various divisions. However, demand overwhelms capacity to supply – the unit has very limited capacity to conduct and support evaluations[48] – so the workplan is a product of strategic level prioritising and compromise and limited to areas not investigated by the OIOS.[49] Given that this unit is now firmly under the authority of the Under-Secretaries-General for DPKO/DFS, questions remain about its ability to act independently and the implications for transparency when evaluations address problems and/or failures.

The evolution of a culture of M&E and learning within the peace operations bureaucracy is indicative of the increasing recognition of its importance to the effective management of missions. For example, in 2007, a Secretary-General report recognised that "the absence of a formal mechanism, structure and capacity to periodically evaluate ... peace operations grossly limits the ability of the Department of Peacekeeping Operations to take informed decisions and provide guidance to mission leadership."[50]

This has been followed up with further rhetorical statements. For example, the most recent vision for UN peacekeeping – 'A New Partnership Agenda' – includes a dedicated section on the importance of reviewing and reporting on progress.[51] Similarly, the strategic framework document for the newly inaugurated OROLSI included explicit goals to become a "results-oriented, learning and evolving organization" that will "establish strong monitoring and evaluation regimes ... [that] shall feed directly into [a] repository of best practices for recurring areas of work", as well as informing adjustment of "doctrine, guidelines, procedures ... training materials and curriculums".[52]

However, the extant M&E architecture in the peace operations bureaucracy remains underdeveloped.[53] Furthermore, specific tools employed by the UN peace operations system reflect the multiple levels of analysis, range of intended audiences and the ad hoc nature of the field more generally. Beyond the remit of DPET, a number of other modalities govern the way M&E is conventionally conducted in UN peace operations. The following section examines seven key M&E approaches that dominate this space.

Current M&E approaches in UN field operations

Results-based budgeting

The UN's main method of evaluating peace operations performance is through Results-Based Budgeting (RBB). The formal introduction of RBB procedures in 2001 represented a significant move towards an M&E culture within the UN.[54] This was in keeping with the 'New Public Management' (NPM) reform movement that saw public sector organisations – including the UN – adopting private sector performance management techniques and incentive structures.[55] RBB is the primary means of budgetary reporting across the UN system and is mandatory for peace operations via annual financial performance reports. It is therefore the only M&E tool used across all missions and different components within those missions and hence the most systematic.[56]

In peace operations, RBB is ostensibly a budgetary planning and monitoring tool, primarily for accountability purposes but also intended to inform decisions on mandate extensions and the concomitant financial commitments to peace operations.[57] The RBB system constitutes a logical framework pervasive in results-based management approaches. It has been purported to achieve increased budget transparency and accountability by focusing on results and using demonstrable performance indicators to link mission performance with the budget.[58] RBB frameworks identify 'expected accomplishments' based on Security Council mandates and indicators of progress towards these. Targets and actual achievements are reported for each 'expected accomplishment' – occasionally including baselines for these measures from previous reporting periods.

Whilst the relevance of RBB across the UN system has been said to vary,[59] a 2007 OIOS review concluded that, "results-based management has been an administrative chore of little value to accountability and decision-making".[60] Moreover, it has been criticised internally and externally as an ineffective M&E tool for peace operations. For example, OIOS reviews of the use of RBB in missions have noted that:

> There are certain challenges unique to peacekeeping that influence the ultimate effectiveness of RBB as a management and planning tool. Peacekeeping missions frequently operate in an especially fluid and uncertain context of political and security change. This high degree of uncertainty therefore undermines the ideal RBB scenario in which missions could establish a logical framework with clear objectives linked to a set of stable and predictable outputs and performance indicators against which mission performance would be assessed.[61]

A 2008 Secretary-General report noted that the application of RBB had been "inadequate" in part because it had been perceived "as a compliance matter rather than as a management tool for understanding what has worked well and why".⁶² Furthermore, a Joint Inspection Unit review of RBB noted that, "[a]s a general rule, senior management at DPKO just sees RBB as a paper exercise, budget-driven, and not linked to substantive management ... RBB has not yet broken through the managerial culture at DPKO."⁶³ In addition, the former Under-Secretary-General for DPKO, Jean-Marie Guehenno, was quoted as saying, "I think missions have gone through the motions of results-based budgeting but I doubt if it has much impact on improving performance."⁶⁴

The indicators and measures used tend to be quantitative in nature and focus almost exclusively on outputs at the activity level rather than effects at the outcome and impact levels. For example, in regard to UNPOL activities, the process includes reporting of *outputs* such as the number of domestic police deployed and the percentage of female officers maintained,⁶⁵ but there is little (if any) progression to identifying the *outcomes* indicative of effectiveness of stated activities and associated outputs, nor is there any clear rationale for the attribution of causality.⁶⁶ In the absence of explicit baseline assessments, such measures fail to demonstrate relative progress. More importantly, they fall short of indicating the impacts (intended or otherwise) of UNPOL on overarching objectives, such as the level of violent crime or public perception of the police. However, the UN's own report on program performance notes that, "what matters is whether an output induces something to happen (progress in the achievement of an expected accomplishment)", further highlighting the imperative to prioritise "the results obtained by the Organization."⁶⁷ The logical framework at the core of RBB relies upon the identification of fixed objectives and on a clear conception of the cause-effect relationships between activities executed and the attainment of expected accomplishments. This is rarely possible with the goals and change theories of peace operations that are often opaque and, as Brusset suggests, the relationship between activities and the observed outcomes is the 'black box' when it comes to M&E in peace operations.⁶⁸ As Lipson concurs,

> lack of understanding of the causal relations between activities, outputs, and outcomes deprives RBB of validity as a performance measure. In the absence of clear understandings of such cause-effect relations, the association of specific outputs with expected accomplishments in RBB documents represents, at best, educated guesses.⁶⁹

RBB is also ill-suited to the dynamic and changing nature of mission goals as missions move through different phases. RBB frameworks lose their utility in tracking progress against 'expected accomplishments' if these are unfixed and subject to revision. Furthermore, some of the expected accomplishments included in RBB frameworks are beyond the realistic scope of missions such as normalising relations between countries at war as a good example.⁷⁰ Crucially, there is also a lack of integration of

RBB into ongoing mission planning processes. Linkages between RBB findings and subsequent mission support have been limited – in part as a result of internal politics in the General Assembly.[71]

RBB will likely continue to be employed despite its shortcomings. Ultimately, it is an accountability tool to demonstrate the transparent use of resources to member states and "conformity with NPM-influenced standards for management practices ... but is unsuited to the operational requirements of peacekeeping".[72] In sum, RBB is more valuable to the bureaucracy than it is to enhancing the performance and effectiveness of peace operations in the field.

Periodic mission reporting

Another part of the M&E architecture is the periodic (usually bi-annual) Secretary-General's mission reports to the Security Council. This regular reporting mechanism contains a narrative on developments in areas relevant to the mission's mandate but does not assess the performance of peace operations per se. In order to demonstrate progress, the output measures synonymous with RBB are regularly incorporated into these reports. For example, in Timor-Leste, the UN has typically reported the number of local police officers trained and the number of hours of training provision.[73] This reliance on limited RBB outputs is exacerbated by the fact that there is no standardised format or template for what such reports should include. This renders their content somewhat arbitrary and contributes to the ad hoc nature of M&E. Furthermore, the recommendations included in these reports are invariably geared towards budgetary requests and consequently lack focus on strategic direction.

Results-based management in the field

Extemporaneously, individual UN peace operations have employed a range of techniques to highlight ongoing achievements. These have tended to focus on individual programmes or specific objectives of a mission. For example, in collaboration with resident UN country teams, some peace operations have developed results-focused transition strategies and frameworks.[74] Similarly, in recent years missions have increasingly developed an Integrated Mission Priorities and Implementation Plan (IMPIP), including benchmarks for all parts of an integrated UN endeavour, purported to be a tool for joint-programming and monitoring the efforts of UN integrated missions.[75]

However, despite identifying key tasks and specifying expected outcomes, these outcomes are generally conceived of and measured by quantitative outputs and fail to reveal the impacts of such developments. These frameworks have represented a more holistic and integrated approach to post-conflict peacebuilding and are therefore multi-agency in character. Hence, they lack the focus to make disaggregated assessments about the work of particular mission components. In the realm of policing, appraisals to assess the performance of field-based UNPOL officers at all levels were initiated by the UNPD in 2006, however, as of 2008 their completion was found to be variable by an internal OIOS report on the management of UN police operations.[76] UNPOL approaches to gauging the impact of capacity-building and reform processes have included little more than anecdotal reports of spot checks on police departments to ensure compliance with various reporting techniques and administrative bookkeeping.[77] In general, this type of performance management in the field has been ad hoc and a product of innovative leadership rather than clear process.[78]

Office of Internal Oversight Services (OIOS)

In recent years, the 'Inspection and Evaluation' Division within the OIOS has conducted programme evaluations in UNMIS, UNMIL and MINUSTAH, as well as thematic evaluations on DDR, the management of UN police operations, and cooperation/coordination between DPKO/DFS, and regional organisations.[79] Whilst OIOS evaluations may offer benefits through their perceived independence and objective methods, much of this value is offset by inconsistent attention. Their reports are rarely repeated as the focus for OIOS evaluations is variable and subject to changing demands within the organisation. Furthermore, despite OIOS's expertise in evaluation methodologies, their lack of experience in field missions renders them ill-suited to conducting operational level evaluations.[80] Consequently, they are commonly perceived as an internal accountability modality rather than an M&E process aimed at impact assessment and learning.

Ad hoc evaluations

On occasion, evaluation teams are sent from headquarters to assess a particular mission. For example, the Police Division has sent evaluation teams to missions in the context of substantive changes to the mandate, conflict dynamics or occurrence of milestone events such as elections.[81] These evaluations generally produce findings, a third of which are intended for headquarters, the other two thirds aimed at the field.[82] According to the former Under-Secretary-General DPKO, reports from multi-disciplinary evaluation teams conducting field-based assessments provided more useful information about mandate implementation and effectiveness than the ubiquitous RBB.[83] However, as with criticisms of the lessons learned report modality, these ad hoc evaluations are perceived to be reactive and usually sent as a response to a crisis or identified weakness. Consequently, they are not systematic nor do they offer any value in uncovering the weaknesses in the first place.

UN benchmarking for peace consolidation

The utility of a benchmarking approach to M&E in peace operations has been increasingly recognised[84] and gradually employed as a technocratic means of gauging progress towards peace consolidation, draw-down and eventual withdrawal of UN peace operations.[85] In part, this was to formalise a shift in thinking about mission exit strategies from timeline-focused plans towards milestone-driven processes.[86] Consequently, the Security Council now regularly requests benchmarks to monitor progress toward mandate implementation, peace consolidation and eventual transition.[87]

In light of these developments and the hitherto ad hoc process by which these benchmarks have been arrived at, an inter-agency committee including DPKO as well as DPA, UNDP and the UN Peacebuilding Support Office (PBSO) developed a practitioner's guide to benchmarking in 2010.[88] The guide is targeted at UN system strategic planners and M&E specialists as support in their roles of designing and monitoring the implementation of UN system transition plans in conflict-affected countries, by informing and strengthening existing planning tools. Its aim is to better enable UN field presences to measure progress towards or regress away from peace consolidation and is purported as a first step towards formalising specific formats and procedures for establishing benchmarking, data handling and reporting in UN field missions. This fits with longer-term goals of (i) developing a common UN system methodology for measuring peace consolidation in a host country, and (ii) refining tools for reconfiguring assistance in the latter stages of integrated peace operations involving the relevant UN organs and agencies.[89] In essence, it employs a benchmarking approach to M&E targeting strategic level outcomes.

Benchmarking is primarily concerned with assessing the progress of peace consolidation in host countries rather than identifying the impact of mission activity or drawing lessons from these insights for learning purposes. That is, it does not allow for the impact of peacekeepers themselves to be gauged independently of organisational success, nor does it

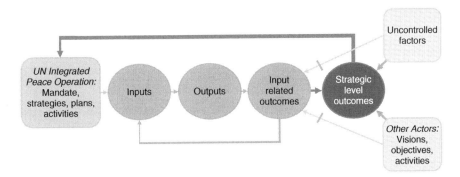

Figure 2.1 Benchmarking logic.[90]

sufficiently conceptualise this success or impact in terms of progress and performance.

The framework puts its faith in a linear representation of the war-to-peace transition and depicts a highly mechanistic relationship between actions and outcomes. Therefore, as with RBB, the benchmarking approach neglects to unpack the 'black box' so as to identify the causal mechanisms responsible for the eventual effects. Unlike the RBB, the benchmarking system does acknowledge the likely existence of external influences and unintended consequences under the 'uncontrolled factors'.

A problem with this approach is that it relies upon extrapolating realistic benchmarks from past successes and failures in peacekeeping. As previously suggested, it is often difficult to pin down clear and realistic visions of success and the inadequate nature of extant lessons learned processes severely limits the ability to do this.[91] Efforts have been undertaken across different UN departments and agencies to develop benchmarks.[92] However, the promulgation of generic benchmarks and potential indicators brings its own questions. For example, who chooses the benchmarks? If this is done 'externally' there is a danger that measures lack sufficient context-specificity and also risk jeopardising local ownership. On the other hand, if they are produced 'internally' – i.e. within the mission or in a participatory fashion with local stakeholders – there is a risk that these may be manipulated to represent progress or eschewed in favour of particular local agendas. Furthermore, questions arise about who measures against the benchmarks and how, raising issues of independence and validity.[93] There is also a heavy focus on protracted peacebuilding processes and political transitions that implicate the broader engagement of the UN system, including the peacebuilding fund and development programming. Although this is an important facet of a mission's lifecycle, this is not particularly elucidating in stabilisation processes or ascertaining the impact of early peacebuilding efforts.

Benchmarking is a relatively recent but increasingly pervasive approach to M&E in UN peace operations. It is premature to draw conclusions on its overall utility and relevance. However, its focus on overall peace consolidation and the transition and drawdown of UN presence in a given situation suggest that it is not well-suited to assessing the impact of missions or contributing to organisational learning. Furthermore, the macro-level focus dictates that not much attention is paid to the specifics of UNPOL and rule of law issues. Importantly, there is presently no clear method for measuring progress against these benchmarks. In the absence of purpose-designed measures of effectiveness, they have hitherto utilised quantitative measures synonymous with the RBB process.[94] The handbook suggests that a range of monitoring tools could feed into the benchmarking process, *inter alia*: UNIFEM's Gender and Conflict Indicators, The World Bank's Post-Conflict/Governance Indicators, and UNDP's Governance Indicators and the *Rule of Law Indicators Project*. Given the latter's focus on rule of law and policing issues, it is worth examining this further.

Rule of law indicators project

As part of efforts within the PD and OROLSI to professionalise the management of peace operations, the UN has recently developed the Rule of Law Indicators Project (ROLIP).[95] Peace operations have commonly deployed without a comprehensive assessment of domestic Rule of Law capacity or population's experience thereof. Instead, mission managers have relied upon anecdotal evidence, and cursory attention in pre-deployment Technical Assessment Missions (TAM) to ascertain the host country's capacity and capability as well as public perception of the police and other rule of law institutions. This has had deleterious consequences for forming baseline assessments as well as associated strategising.[96] The ROLIP is therefore designed to use empirical indicators to evaluate the strengths and weaknesses of the rule of law system, including the police, legal-judicial, and corrections sectors in the theatre of operations in order to assist national authorities in their rule of law reform efforts, including the development of national strategies.[97] Furthermore, the ROLIP is aimed at aiding donors and other stakeholders in effective planning for rule of law support programming.[98] The *Rule of Law Indicators Implementation Guide and Project Tools* was launched in 2011 and consists of around 100 indicators, an implementation guide and *pro forma* questionnaires.[99]

This constitutes an important step towards systematising analyses of mission environments and promises to aid the mission planning process. However, despite pilot field-testing in Liberia and Haiti, and plans to implement the system in three countries in 2011–12,[100] it remains unclear whether or not its eventual results can act as meaningful baseline assessments and, moreover, if it can be an effective means of tracking progress over time. Although the project explicitly focuses on outputs and outcomes (i.e. institutional performance and the effect or consequences of institutional performance, respectively) through indicators that measure performance and track change over time,[101] the instrument is focused on the realm of domestic rule of law performance. This can only implicate the efficacy of the UN presence indirectly or by proxy. That is, it does not target the ways in which UNPOL might have influenced improvements in domestic policing capacity, but rather infers that this is the case. Nor does it articulate how improvements in these indicators contribute to overall mission objectives.

In summary, M&E in UN peace operations has traditionally consisted of predominantly anecdotal accounts and/or after-the-event reviews. The primary motivation for employing M&E, typically at the behest of member states, has been demonstrating accountability and the transparent micro-management of resources. A secondary impetus concerns feeding field-level information into mandate renewal and resourcing decisions. Consequently, the dominant modalities such as RBB and benchmarking reflect this agenda. Where learning-oriented methods have been employed, such as emerging KM systems, they remain contingent on the acumen of individual managers and suffer as a result of an under-developed M&E culture and learning infrastructure both at headquarters and in the field.[102] Indicative of this, a 2009 OIOS internal evaluation of the learning infrastructure was entitled 'Learning lessons for improving organizational efficiency and effectiveness is weak' and identified that the KM tools are subject to varying consistency and quality if completed at all.[103] Importantly, this collection of M&E options remains insufficiently engaged with each other. Nevertheless, the main M&E methods have only been in place for around a decade and their existence and evolution represents a significant shift towards an M&E culture at the UN.

In relation to UNPOL, DPKO has not developed effective ways to monitor and evaluate its impact in restoring public order and longer-term police reform objectives.[104] Comprehensive performance measurements are non-existent and UNPOL decision-makers depend upon rudimentary input and output indicators to measure progress and establish claims of impact. Police Commissioners and other senior mission managers are without the necessary tools to conduct real-time impact assessments of their activities.[105] Measures targeting outcomes are rare and continue to rely heavily on crime statistics, which can be misleading in this context.[106] Furthermore, the UN's peace operations bureaucracy lacks a systematic way of capturing policing experience from missions.[107] Instead, knowledge has been lost, as a handful of senior practitioners such as police commissioners have left the organisation. In short, UNPOL has simply not received much attention when it comes to developing tailored M&E. This was recognised in the Secretary-General's 2009 report on rule of law and policing stating that, "Evaluating the impact of rule of law assistance and measuring its effectiveness remains a major challenge [and] ... an obstacle to effective programming."[108] The following section examines the salience of the small literature on measuring domestic and international policing.

Literature on M&E in (international) policing

Whilst there is a wealth of literature on measuring the performance of policing in a domestic context, predominantly emanating from Western/OECD countries,[109] this is often of limited use in international policing. First, even in societies where the rule of law has strong roots, the eclectic nature of policing functions means that the most appropriate way to measure police performance remains an area of debate.[110] Second, in general, domestic police performance measurement systems are not appropriate for international policing endeavours, as they focus solely on the effectiveness of a police service, not on the effectiveness of police reform per se, nor on other tasks such as UNPOL operational assistance. Therefore, whilst such approaches might be a necessary part of assessing police services that the UN are responsible for reforming, they are not sufficient for the M&E of UNPOL.

Notwithstanding these barriers, Smith has argued that M&E developed in Western policing settings could be used to enhance the performance of police in UN peace operations when viewed as an international public service.[111] He points to the *COMPSTAT* programme, which has been heralded for its impact upon the performance of the New York and Los Angeles Police Departments.[112] This is a sophisticated computerised model using extensive crime statistics to assess the performance of managers against prioritised policing objectives in specific precincts. The model conceptualises cause-and-effect relationships by mapping policing activities through to outcomes.[113] However, post-conflict environments are typically lacking the rich data sets and abundant resources required to employ and maintain such technologies. Furthermore, the extent to which such systems measure complex social phenomena akin to the intended impact of UNPOL is debatable given their managerial focus and dependence upon crime statistics.

With regard to police in peace operations, there are still significant research gaps and the lack of attention to suitable M&E approaches is indicative of the absence of widely used tools.[114] The rare attempts to evaluate UNPOL tend to centre on the longer-term goals of reforming and restructuring of police services.[115] The most sophisticated of such attempts is arguably the 'Police Reform Indicators and Measurement Evaluation' (PRIME) System developed at Princeton University[116], which assesses police reform in post-conflict environments. The system conceptualises the prerequisites for an effective reformed police service and has developed indicators to "measure the extent to which a police service has made overall progress on key outcomes."[117] PRIME claims to provide a 'real world' solution whereby "available and practical data sources"[118] are utilised and comprises sixteen core predominantly qualitative indicators which are divided into four main pillars of 'outcomes' covering: (1) performance effectiveness; (2) management and oversight; (3) community relations; and (4) sustainability.

PRIME's use of a policing lens provides the opportunity to capture the organisational and operational idiosyncrasies associated with UNPOL missions. For example, the results point to some of the enabling competencies within the police component, which may facilitate more effective missions.[119] However, a significant criticism of PRIME is its inability to internalise exogenous factors and unintended consequences.[120] For example, the approach struggles to account for the inhibitive effect of external influences such as organised criminality. Overlooking countervailing issues and the likelihood of externalities runs the risk of exaggerating positive developments but importantly, renders PRIME incapable of identifying and explaining reasons for lack of progress. Ultimately, the decision to locate the domestic police service as the unit of analysis inhibits the ability of PRIME to draw conclusions about the impact of UNPOL in supporting the reform process under scrutiny.[121]

Whilst M&E is a relatively underexplored phenomenon in peace operations in general, international policing has simply not received much attention when it comes to developing tailored M&E dedicated to understanding and assessing their impact.[122] Furthermore, there has been little effort to systematise M&E that targets the impact of UNPOL within a broader learning framework. As some commentators have pointed out,

> The lack of standardized mechanisms for assessing police reform efforts has limited the UN's ability to be flexible in adjusting policy in the field and hindered efforts to develop best practices that can be used to inform the planning and implementation of future missions.[123]

The following section provides a critique of the M&E approaches introduced as they relate to UNPOL.

Critiques of dominant M&E approaches

The M&E deficit in UN peace operations, particularly in the area of UNPOL, has been exacerbated by the inappropriateness of many of the approaches employed.[124] Despite some innovation, the vast majority of efforts have been rooted in conventional M&E approaches drawn from alien contexts and apolitical settings that do not sufficiently recognise the unique distinguishing features of conflict-affected environments.[125] M&E tools utilised by the UN to monitor progress and evaluate impact regarding the implementation of a mandate – in particular the dominant RBB and benchmarking – are informed by so-called 'objective' and mechanistic representations synonymous with the logical framework modality.[126]

The logical framework is the conceptual building block for the ubiquitous Results-based Management (RBM) which has prevailed as a dominant paradigm for performance management in both private and public sectors is pervasive (synonymous with NPM philosophies), particularly amongst Western government agencies and their subsidiaries/proxies. The logical framework also underpins tracking and measuring progress in military, humanitarian and development organisations regularly involved in peace operations.[127] What was originally conceived of as a planning tool typically relies upon measuring and interpreting inputs, outputs, outcomes, results and impacts. This approach assumes clear and demonstrable cause-and-effect relationships between these elements in a linear results-chain.

Monitoring and evaluation in peace operations 79

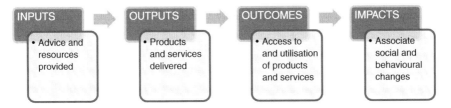

Figure 2.2 Classical 'logframe' representation.[128]

The strengths of these approaches are clear. They are purpose-built to demonstrate success and emphasise accountability by mapping the allocation and utilisation of resources through to tangible outputs. Furthermore, their propensity to distil and standardise data is conducive to consistent reporting and enables some degree of comparative analysis across space and time. Indeed, such systems have oftentimes represented the only way of satisfying multiple and disparate reporting requirements in this context. However, notwithstanding these benefits, the shortcomings of these approaches in general have come under increasing scrutiny in recent years.[129] When applied to the specific business of UNPOL in peace operations, there are a number of challenges associated with these methods that are largely unaccounted for in extant approaches and/or recur in the critical literature.[130] Whilst RBM-inspired M&E might be sufficient for demonstrating productivity in relation to simple traditional UNPOL activities such as patrols, they are less well-suited to ascertaining the impact of the police-building activities increasingly central to UNPOL mandates.

The following critique emanates from the pervasive logical framework modality; however, it applies in differing degree to most of the approaches reviewed here and all those predicated on linear modelling. A combination of assumptions, a perverse incentive structure and potentially distorting dependencies constrain current M&E approaches to a narrow perspective, which leave assessments with blind spots. The seven criticisms most salient to peace operations and UNPOL are presented below.

1 Not outcome/impact focused

The majority of extant M&E approaches for UNPOL are overwhelmingly output-oriented.[131] That is to say that, regardless of what they claim to demonstrate, more often than not, they point to superficial achievements and imply that the successful achievement of results at the output level (commonly as quantitative metrics) constitutes success for a mission. This is perpetuated by the dominance of RBB and benchmarking in monitoring mission progress which typically trace inputs through to outputs but fail to prioritise and identify the outcomes and impact of missions upon underlying conditions in the country. For UNPOL, this is evident in the lack of measures designed to assess behavioural change in regard to reforming law enforcement agencies.[132] The objectives of UNPOL, particularly in relation to police reform, are process-oriented intangibles rather than isolatable products. Increasingly vital aspects of UNPOL work in policebuilding involve targeting changes in public perceptions and psychosocial behaviour. Attempts to capture these through output measures have been unsuccessful on the whole. As Menkaus describes, "[e]fforts to operationalize those concepts by identifying indicators which are amenable to observable, replicable, verifiable measurement are famously problematic."[133] These incomplete accounts are not capable of elucidating the effect of UNPOL efforts or enabling organisational learning.

Moreover, even where these approaches purport to be focused on outcomes or impact, a common area of ambiguity relates to how these tools are supposed to attribute causality. RBB, for example, often infers that results at the output level are indicative of outcomes and impacts in the broader environment. In other words, output measures are used as proxy measures for achievement of grand mission goals. Albeit often with caveats, these models depict direct relationships between micro-level inputs and macro-level outcomes but fail to provide a defensible account of the cause-and-effect between the intervention and the impacts that they imply. For example, to demonstrate progress towards meeting the expected accomplishment of 'enhanced public law and order', the planned and actual indicators of achievement are all generally in the form of quantitative outputs relating to technical capacity-building such as recruits trained or productivity in terms of the number of meetings held, contacts made and documents promulgated. There is no continuation to explain if, and if so how, these outputs had contributed to 'enhanced public law and order'. The ways and means by which that accomplishment was achieved are left unexplained. This leaves questions of causality largely unanswered or open to interpretation. The pervasive assumption of this dominant paradigm is that the phenomena under assessment are characterised by order, certainty and 'knowability'. In relation to UNPOL, this assumes that the behavioural and cultural change associated with the restoration of law and order and the reform of public security actors occur according to a linear trajectory (i.e. they are predictable) and can be broken down into and understood in discrete parts. This leads to an artificially siloed view in which intervention activities are quarantined for precise evaluation. It also assumes that social systems are marked by direct relationships with simple cause-and-effect between elements. In reality, this is not the case where conflict-affected societies pose 'wicked' problems (rather than 'tame' ones)[134] where any attempt to address them is likely to lead to unintended consequences.[135]

In situations of complexity such as peace operations, a multiplicity of exogenous factors (i.e. forces beyond the control of UNPOL and usually the whole mission) impinges upon outcomes and impacts.[136] For example, population perceptions of improved public security are likely to be a product of myriad contributing factors of which UNPOL and its actions will only be one. Furthermore, the combination of UNPOL activities and exogenous factors often contribute to both positive and negative externalities (i.e. unintended consequences).[137] For example, the provision of human rights training to police does not ensure a new approach or that the trainees' superiors will utilise them any differently. Similarly, perceptions of police as human rights abusers may not change if sporadic but high-profile instances of police brutality continue. Importantly, attempts to scale-up successful programmes may not deliver the same results when replicated and can be undermined due to the existence of these unintended consequences. The restricted focus of extant M&E overlooks the important effect of exogenous factors and significance of unintended consequences on outcomes and impacts in the mission area.[138] Failure to incorporate these phenomena has deleterious consequences for learning about what works, what doesn't, and why.

2 Inflexible and ill-suited to adaptation

Extant M&E is by and large inappropriate due to its lack of flexibility.[139] Oftentimes, M&E orthodoxy is fast-tracked or set to fixed, arbitrary and improbable timeframes due to political agendas, institutional reporting requirements and budget cycles dictated from above rather than tailored to the nature of the program being assessed.[140] However, these are rarely suitable for the dynamics of change associated with the types of activities UNPOL engage in – at least not for all of them. For instance, routine public order patrols and riot control work have a direct and immediate effect. Hence, assessing their impact can be conducted in a relatively short timeframe following their implementation. However, reform, restructuring and capacity-building endeavours seek to achieve long-term changes in attitudes and organisational cultures. Achieving such fundamental social change and addressing the root causes of conflict are invariably time-consuming endeavours and are not amenable to definitive measurement within arbitrary timeframes or arguably even the lifetime of a peace operation.

Where impact is likely to require more protracted implementation and patience, these artificial reporting timelines can produce misleading accounts of progress to placate political masters. Moreover, this can lead to a focus on short-term goals and 'quick wins' to demonstrate tangible successes. This concentration can have a perverse effect on the activities prioritised by mission managers in order to re-orient programme work in line with temporal rather than substantive goals. Resources and personnel can be diverted and deployed in pursuit of easily measurable outputs at the expense of more pressing or useful initiatives – albeit ones that have less chance of producing 'results' in quick order. In this instance, M&E of current convention can become a prescriptive instrument rather than a responsive reporting modality perversely creating and incentivising the scenario whereby 'what gets measured, gets done'. The ramifications of this are significant given that such a *modus operandi* can also lead to myopia (i.e. not seeing long-term and big picture) and tunnel vision – problems particularly salient to effective institutional development such as policebuilding.

Ultimately, the dominant modes of M&E employ fixed milestone achievements and targets as benchmarks of progress. This approach is extremely ill-suited to agile adaptation in light of changing goals and conditions symptomatic of peace operations.

3 Dependent on narrow range of data sources

M&E approaches of current convention are heavily dependent on quantitative indicators and data sources. These invariably focus on 'hard', tangible outputs such as the number of police trained, amount of guns collected or an inventory of the 'laptops and landcruisers' delivered. Whilst these are perceived to be less subjective, peace operations environments are tumultuous, dynamic and typically lack the rich data sets required. As a recent review of the UN's peacebuilding architecture recognised:

> Peacebuilding, of its nature, is a complicated process: rebuilding fragile or shattered relationships inevitably takes time. It does not lend itself to compartmentalization or 'boots on the ground' measurement. Organizations such as the United Nations and the international financial institutions can find it inherently difficult to deal with this complexity and interrelatedness. There is inevitably a gravitational pull, for organizations and donors, towards the concrete and more readily measurable.[141]

This often manifests in an over-reliance on crime statistics that are notoriously scarce, untrustworthy or ambiguous and open to interpretation in conflict-affected environments. For example, increases in the number of crimes reported to police could be interpreted as an indication of an increasing crime rate but it could equally be indicative of increased public trust in police, leading to increased reporting of crimes. Trends in crime rates are therefore potentially misleading when taken as an indicator of police effectiveness.[142] Furthermore, this dependency on quantitative metrics fails to situate UNPOL impact in the context of broader political, social and economic conditions and consequently lacks nuance when identifying perceived change in public security.[143] That is to say, these approaches only really 'see what they are looking for'. When trying to ascertain impact, and importantly the reasons for a lack of impact, this becomes particularly inhibitive. As Albert Einstein was quoted as saying, "Not everything that can be counted counts, and not everything that counts can be counted."[144]

4 Context-insensitive

One of the major failings of extant M&E relates to the generic nature of the tool/indicators employed. Despite promoting best practice to the contrary,[145] current approaches such as RBB, benchmarking and the ROLIP employ standardised measures to gauge capacity and track change. As a result, these tools demonstrate a lack of awareness regarding the contextual conditions and exigencies that underpin and interact with the mission and how they should inform assessment.[146]

In particular, baseline data is rarely prioritised and often unreliable or simply absent.[147] For example, the RBB and benchmarking systems occasionally include targets and measures from previous reporting periods, but seldom include comprehensive baseline assessments. It is often argued that this is due to the ad hoc nature of M&E in these settings and this deficit is also attributed to resource implications, scarcity of relevant data and the short timeframe between the Security Council mandating and beginning to deploy a new mission.[148] Regarding UNPOL, the ROLIP has the potential to be an antidote to this problem but until that is proven, M&E of UNPOL lacks a clear picture of what exists. The paucity of baselines has led to M&E findings grounded in a lack of awareness about conflict dynamics and the relevant stakeholders[149] with ramifications for the utility of findings for learning purposes. If the situation at the beginning of an M&E cycle is not analysed and documented, it will be difficult to ascertain if – and the extent to which – there have been changes in the areas UNPOL is working on.[150] The identification of accomplishments and any attempt to attribute them requires a baseline against which progress can be gauged.[151] These deficits lead to the dependency on creating *ex-poste* baseline information of questionable fidelity and/or increased analytical risk associated with 'what if' counterfactuals, which are prone to distorting causal attributions due to their inherent hindsight biases.[152]

The lack of context-awareness renders extant M&E unable to elucidate the unique dynamics at play or establish a solid platform from which to build arguments of change.[153] Irrespective of whether qualitative, quantitative or mixed methods are used, collecting and interpreting baseline data against which progress can be gauged is a central tenet and vital point of departure for incisive M&E.[154]

5 Reductive/Non-systemic

M&E orthodoxy does not reflect the systemic nature of the phenomena under analysis.[155] That is, the assessment of individual mission components

84 *Context-setting*

such as UNPOL is customarily separated from the broader context within which they occur. Extant efforts are invariably 'stove-piped' and focus on programmes and projects, as opposed to the systems within which those programmes and projects take place. For example, RBB and benchmarking efforts to assess the progress of police reform primarily use measures of capacity-building within the domestic police service and qualitative standards such as a national police institution being deemed as 'operational' (i.e. have reached operating capacity and self-sustaining management and funding systems are in place). However, as already suggested, the performance of reforming police services is intrinsically linked to the recovery of the other elements of the criminal justice apparatus. UNPOL's success in restoring law and order will likely be contingent on the support of judicial and penal elements of the criminal justice system, and *vice versa*. The fact that efforts to assess progress in police RRR do not take account of these interdependencies means that they risk providing misleading accounts of the impact of UNPOL activities.

Existing approaches imply that problems can be treated as if they exist in isolation and can be 'fixed' as such. That is to say their 'reductive' nature underplays the extent to which issues are interdependent and outcomes the result of multiple enabling and disabling factors. Furthermore, this reductionism extends to the broader challenge of identifying the impact of UNPOL as a contributing part to an overarching effort. In reality, UNPOL reform efforts are part of a wider engagement in the mission area. For example, as part of multidimensional peace operations M&E of UNPOL will inevitably sit in a broader M&E architecture given shared objectives across the wider rule of law domain and the mission as a whole.[156] Furthermore, UNPOL and its parent UN mission are a component part of the overarching international engagement in a particular country.[157] It is wrong to assume that an M&E system for UNPOL can exist in a vacuum.

The upshot is that M&E orthodoxy does not accurately depict the systemic nature of peace operations and their impact and M&E of UNPOL therefore lacks a holistic and systematic approach.[158] This, in turn, leads to limited and isolated definition and diagnosis of problems with troublesome ramifications for mandate implementation planning that addresses issues holistically. Whilst conventional M&E tools focus on the specific activities of the UN mission and attempts to relate them to macro-level outcomes, they lack the necessary coherence and coordination across various relevant agencies and stakeholders to accurately reflect combined impact and relative contributions to those eventualities.[159]

6 Limited participation

Extant M&E systems often fail to include a wide range of stakeholders, instead privileging external experts and/or a select group of powerbrokers

– oftentimes the political elite. The dominant, top-down conventional approaches tend to rely on interaction with formal and institutionalised actors, making little effort to solicit the input, participation or cooperation from other stakeholders beyond the immediate purview of the mission.[160] This is true of its design, goal-setting, information gathering, interpretation and utilisation. For example, in the dominant modes such as RBB and benchmarking, UNPOL objectives are designed by bureaucrats and political masters external to the mission environment. With the rare exception of public perceptions of the UNPOL presence or reformed law enforcement agencies or ad hoc victimisation surveys, information gathering is highly dependent on formal sources and lacks the voices of many stakeholders beyond the remit of the mission and its immediate partners. Finally, the primary reporting mechanisms are tailored towards and serve audiences within the organisation and at headquarters so as to inform the decision-making within that constituency.

In regularly sidelining a broader cross-section of actors, current convention misses the opportunity to harness and internalise local knowledge. In these circumstances, conventional M&E is perceived as an instrument of the interveners, not something to be understood and embraced by locals.[161] This exclusivity can contribute to a stymieing of local ownership that is arguably crucial to sustainable outcomes in the long-run. However, broad participation in M&E is deemed to be important for three main reasons. First, normatively, people should have oversight and participation in the decisions and developments that affect them when it comes to their safety and security. Second, contextually relevant problem diagnosis, realistic and locally relevant conceptions of success, pathways to get there, realistic timelines for their attainment and the most meaningful criteria and indicator design for gauging progress partially depend upon such expertise.[162] Third, the effectiveness of programs like policebuilding are likely to be dependent on a certain level of national/local ownership.[163] If stakeholders do not have a sense of ownership over the processes underway as well as the M&E tracking them, they are unlikely to value its findings and/or act upon them.[164] This can have deleterious consequences for the legitimacy of the M&E and sustainable outcomes in the long-run.[165]

7 Accountability over learning

The dominant modes for M&E are not oriented towards learning. They are primarily driven by external accountability demands (e.g. RBB) or focused on guiding drawdown and withdrawal of missions (benchmarking). These approaches risk creating perverse incentives and can have very real ramifications for the effectiveness of field missions. For example, the pressure to report can usurp the need to report meaningfully. As one account puts it, "the combined pressure-cooker and fishbowl elements of a high-profile situation influence M&E practices as strongly as

86 *Context-setting*

on-the-ground factors do".[166] That is, the information recounted from the field may provide little insight into the realities on the ground and hence can lead to distorted perceptions and poor decision-making.

The dominant modality of extant approaches as an accountability requirement rather than a learning opportunity further contributes to the change theory at play being treated as being outside the scope of M&E. This means questions are seldom asked about the appropriateness of the modes and methods of UNPOL endeavours. For example, standard measures of effectiveness relating to policebuilding invariably demonstrate the amount of police officers trained or the number of police stations built. The lack of complementary impact assessment means that M&E fails to examine whether or not these types of activities are having the desired effects. In this way, M&E lacks reflexivity and fails to question, 'uncover, assess and test'[167] the implicit/explicit theories of change upon which they are predicated.[168] Inadvertently, conventional M&E becomes about demonstrating the validity of intervention logic rather than interrogating it.[169] It does not facilitate reflection on the soundness of the change theory and produces little reflection on the mode and methods of the peacebuilding approach. Consequently, M&E of current convention is left focusing on whether UNPOL are 'doing things right' rather than if they are 'doing the right things'. This retards innovation and adaptation of mission plans, rendering M&E static and clunky instead of nimble and agile to facilitate learning in the face of complex challenges and dynamic circumstances.

Ultimately, this combination of unrealistic reporting and lack of introspection limit the extent to which current M&E methods facilitate organisational learning. Furthermore, the preeminent modes of M&E have limited linkages to the learning infrastructure in missions and at headquarters. The KM toolkit presents an exception to this rule, but – as mentioned earlier – the effectiveness of these methods has also been called into question. The upshot is that current M&E is not harmonised with the rest of the M&E architecture. This causes a breakdown in feedback loops and inhibits the ability for information from the field to filter up into organisational learning processes. Consequently, there are problematic barriers to in-mission learning from experiences for real-time course correction as well as a jam in the knowledge transition from the field to headquarters.[170] Learning is undermined to the detriment of efforts to improve the efficacy of peace operations.

In summary, M&E approaches tailored for assessing the impacts of UNPOL are few and far between. The major cross-cutting M&E tools used by the UN have a number of shortcomings that render them inappropriate for the unique context of UNPOL in peace operations. They are: not outcome/impact focused and gloss over important issues of ambiguity in causality; inflexible in the face of fluctuating conditions and fast-changing objectives; dependent on narrow and often scarce data sources; not sufficiently context-sensitive to capture important idiosyncrasies; underplay the systemic nature of goals and collectively constituted accomplishments; fail to include important stakeholders in the design and implementation of M&E as well as utilisation of its findings; and, are accountability driven to the detriment of learning objectives and potentialities.

This is not to suggest that conventional approaches are of no use to the overall endeavour of M&E in peace operations. Systems like RBB and its derivatives offer ongoing utility for accounting for the transparent employment of resources. Furthermore, they remain useful for tracking the implementation of more traditional and simple elements of UNPOL mandates such as conducting patrols as part of operational assistance. However, they are inadequate for monitoring and evaluating the impact of the intrusive RRR commonly required by UNPOL in modern missions. Therefore, it is the shortcomings and gaps associated with M&E orthodoxy that need to be better understood and ways of mitigating them incorporated in an approach that harnesses the benefits whilst being more cognisant of the assumptions, perverse incentives, dependencies and blind spots often left unrecognised in M&E of current convention.

Conclusion

Given the ad hoc nature of peace operations, the need to improve the efficacy of rapidly evolving activities in the field and commit lessons learned to institutional memory is clear, present and will continue. At the UN, a growing learning infrastructure coupled with increasing recognition of M&E's utility has been reflected in the incremental institutionalisation of an M&E culture within the peace operations apparatus as part of ongoing professionalization of the business of peacekeeping at the UN.

If M&E is the means by which field experiences can be gathered, analysed and transformed into knowledge for the purposes of organisational learning then the way in which M&E captures, understands and interprets these experiences is crucial. Moreover, the way in which M&E ascertains the impact of missions on observable change and outcomes is pivotal. However, dominant approaches in the UN's M&E architecture – primarily RBB and benchmarking – neglect or gloss over the ways in which UNPOL activities influence overall outcomes and impacts. The mechanisms through which this is presumed to take place are rarely, if ever, interrogated in M&E, leaving the 'black box' unopened and conceptions of causality incomplete. Consequently attributions of accomplishments by UNPOL are inferred and unsubstantiated. Moreover, when desired outcomes do not eventuate, this M&E orthodoxy is incapable of determining why not and hence cannot point to ways in which strategies, operational plans and tactics can be altered and problems overcome. In sum, current attempts to conduct M&E in a way that ascertains the impact of UNPOL missions remain inadequate, whilst obligatory and pervasive M&E tools are largely separate from existing knowledge management systems at

Headquarters. By extension, the linkage between that collation of field level experience and a process of organisational learning within and between missions is inefficient.

Of course, ambiguity surrounding the nature of the problem, organisational goals and causality itself make this extremely difficult to achieve.[171] As Austin *et al.* attest, "there are still no quick and easy answers to the question of how best to assess, monitor and evaluate peace practices."[172] There will remain a need to document and account for the efficient use of resources and conventional approaches are useful in this realm. However, they lack the elucidating value of more hermeneutic approaches that allow for the intangible impacts of peace operations to be identified and interpreted. The peace operations environment is not amenable to simplistic adaptations of frameworks forged in different circumstances or for different purposes. The post-conflict environment is typically data-scarce, unstable and highly politicised. None of these attributes are particularly conducive to effective M&E.

M&E practice has yet to embrace the full implications of assessing the complexity of peace and conflict work and existing approaches are often not viable or of extremely limited utility. Debates and practice of M&E in these settings have heretofore focused and relied upon frameworks, methods, tools and techniques better-suited to simple, mechanistic and linear intervention activities. Although the logical framework modality constituted something of a zeitgeist across a wide range of relevant actors, the critique emerging in the last decade points to some significant shortcomings in this approach, which limit its utility if not discredit its results. When applied to peace operations, these linear mechanics can lead to: faulty thinking; misguided data collection; misleading reporting of results; and, a false sense of reality amongst senior decision-makers who are often far from where change is (or is not) taking place.[173]

UNPOL endeavours at the peacekeeping-peacebuilding nexus are more akin to complex social change than mechanistic and discrete tasks. Therefore, the M&E of these efforts requires a unique and tailored response – associated with police-specific timeframes, institutional reporting and measuring procedures. However, such a design must take into account that UNPOL are part of an interdependent system and the ability to coordinate with, and speak the same language as, partners for peace in the realm of M&E is equally crucial. Ultimately, to be relevant and responsive, M&E needs to provide reliable and actionable information to a wide range of stakeholders, as opposed to wrapping up familiar political arguments in new or different empirical evidence.[174] As Johansen forewarned, "[m]ethodological ease should not take priority over an accurate understanding of complicated realities."[175]

There is a clear need and much value in developing ways to improve the M&E of UNPOL. As Meharg states, "The central challenge remains that peace operations and crisis management environments are significantly complex so as to require different ways to think about measuring the effectiveness of activities."[176] Given the apparent need for systemic assessments, better accounts of causality in relation to unpredictable and intangible non-linear change and greater participation, the following chapter explores the utility of complexity theory for doing so.

Notes

1. Cedric de Coning and Paul Romita, "Monitoring and Evaluation of Peace Operations". (New York, Oslo: International Peace Institute & Norwegian Institute of International Affairs, November 2009); Schumacher, "What to Measure in Peace Operations", *The Pearson Papers* 10, no. 1 (2007): 45–59; Jake Sherman, "Measures of Effectiveness in Peacebuilding and State-Building", in *Measuring What Matters in Peace Operations and Crisis Management*, ed. Sarah Jane Meharg (McGill-Queen's University Press, 2009); Christian van Stolk, Tom Ling, Anais Reding, and Matt Bassford, *Monitoring and Evaluation in Stabilisation Interventions: Reviewing the State of the Art and Suggesting Ways Forward* (Santa Monica, CA: RAND Corporation, 2011).
2. Sarah Jane Meharg, "Mechanisms and Tools", in *Measuring What Matters in Peace Operations and Crisis Management*, ed. Sarah Jane Meharg (Kingston, ON: McGill-Queen's University Press, 2009), 122–8; Stolk *et al.*, *Monitoring and Evaluation in Stabilisation Interventions: Reviewing the State of the Art and Suggesting Ways Forward*, 5.
3. This account is based on publicly available UN reports and documents, as well as a series of author interviews with UN Secretariat officials and experts on the workings of the various departments and management structures conducted during 2009 and 2010.
4. Peter H. Rossi, Mark W. Lipsey, and Howard E. Freeman, *Evaluation: A Systematic Approach*, 7th ed. (USA: Sage Publications, 2003).
5. Sarah Jane Meharg, "The Language of Measuring", In *Measuring What Matters in Peace Operations and Crisis Management*, 57–88.
6. See for example: Evaluation Office UNDP, "Handbook on Planning, Monitoring and Evaluating for Development Results", (UNDP, 2009); International Alert and Saferworld FEWER, "Conflict-Sensitive Monitoring and Evaluation", in *Conflict-sensitive approaches to development, humanitarian assistance and peace building: tools for peace and conflict impact assessment* (FEWER, International Alert and Saferworld, 2003); OECD-DAC, "Guidance on Evaluating Conflict Prevention and Peacebuilding Activities", in *Working Document for Application Period* (OECD-DAC, 2008).
7. Daniel Druckman, *Doing Research: Methods of Inquiry for Conflict Analysis* (London: Sage Publications, 2005), 295–6; Barry K. Beyer, *How to Conduct a Formative Evaluation* (Virginia: Association for Supervision and Curriculum Development, 1995); Michael Scriven, *Evaluation Thesauras*, 4th ed. (London: Sage Publications, 1991).
8. Helen Lewis, "Evaluation and Assessment of Interventions". (Colorado: Beyond Interactability, 2004).
9. Cheyanne Church and Julie Shouldice, "The Evaluation of Conflict Resolution Interventions: Framing the State of Play", (Letterkenny: INCORE, 2002), 5; Stolk *et al.*, *Monitoring and Evaluation in Stabilisation Interventions: Reviewing the State of the Art and Suggesting Ways Forward*, 5–9.
10. Schumacher, "What to Measure in Peace Operations", 46.
11. Meharg, "The Language of Measuring", 57–8.

12 Daniel Druckman and Paul C. Stern, "The Forum: Evaluating Peacekeeping Missions", *Mershon International Studies Review* 41, no. 1 (1997); Robert C. Johansen, "Peacekeeping: How Should We Measure Success?" In *Mershon International Studies Review* 38, no. 2 (1994): 307–10; Charles T. Call, "Knowing Peace When You See It: Setting Standards for Peacebuilding Success", *Civil Wars* 10, no. 2 (2008): 173–94; Duane Bratt, "Explaining Peacekeeping Performance: The UN in Internal Conflicts" In *International Peacekeeping* 4, no. 3 (1997): 45–70.
13 Interviews with Author: DPKO officials – New York: United Nations, February 2009.
14 For the purposes of this book, the 'M' constitutes "the continuous process of gathering, collating and managing information", whilst the 'E' is the business of "synthesising and analysing that data". See: Druckman, *Doing Research: Methods of Inquiry for Conflict Analysis*, 295–309.
15 Steve Barth, "Observations and Reflections About Peacekeeping Best Practice", in *Reflected Knowledge Working Paper* (New York: UN, 2009).
16 Susanna P. Campbell, "When Process Matters: The Potential Implications of Organisational Learning for Peacebuilding Success", in *Journal of Peacebuilding and Development* 4, no. 2 (2008): 27.
17 Paul F. Diehl and Daniel Druckman, *Evaluating Peace Operations* (Boulder, CO: Lynne Rienner, 2010), 5.
18 See, for example: Scott N. Carlson, "Legal and Judicial Rule of Law Work in Multi-Dimensional Peacekeeping Operations: Lessons-Learned Study", (New York: UN Peacekeeping Best Practices Unit, 2006). For example: David Harland, "UN Peacekeeping Operations in Post-Conflict Timor-Leste: Accomplishments and Lessons Learned", ed. UN PBPS (New York: United Nations, 2005). For more examples, see: www.pbpu.unlb.org/PBPS.
19 Durch in Druckman and Stern, "The Forum: Evaluating Peacekeeping Missions", 158.
20 Thorston Benner, Stephan Mergenthaler, and Phillip Rotmann, "The Evolution of Organizational Learning in the UN Peace Operations Bureaucracy", In *Research DSF no. 31* (German Foundation for Peace Research, 2011), 20; Ettore Bolisani and Fabrizio Damiani, "Knowledge Management in Complex Environments: The UN Peacekeeping", *Measuring Business Excellence* 14, no. 4 (2010): 79–80; Lise Morjé Howard, *UN Peacekeeping in Civil Wars* (Cambridge: Cambridge University Press, 2008) 337.
21 Benner, Mergenthaler, and Rotmann, *The New World of UN Peace Operations: Learning to Build Peace?* (Oxford: University of Oxford Press, 2011), 70–1.
22 Agnes Hurwitz and Reyko Studdard, "Rule of Law Programs in Peace Operations", *The Security Development Nexus Program* (New York: International Peace Academy), 13; Dennis Smith, "Managing CIVPOL: The Potential Performance Management in International Public Services", In *Rethinking International Organizations: Pathology and Promise*, eds. Dennis Dijkzeul and Yves Beigbeder (New York: Berghahn, 2003) 279.
23 William J. Durch *et al.*, "The Brahimi Report and the Future of U.N. Peace Operations", (Washington, DC: The Henry L. Stimson Center, 2003), 39–41.
24 OIOS, "Learning Lessons for Improving Organizational Efficiency and Effectiveness Is Weak", in *Thematic evaluation of lessons learned: protocols and practices* (New York: United Nations, 2009), 20; "Peacekeeping Best Practices – Report of the Secretary-General", in *Administrative and budgetary aspects of the financing of the United Nations peacekeeping operations*, ed. General Assembly (New York: United Nations, 2007), 2.
25 Howard, *UN Peacekeeping in Civil Wars*, 14–20; Caty Clement and Adam C. Smith, "Managing Complexity: Political and Managerial Challenges in

United Nations Peace Operations", (New York: International Peace Institute, 2009), 8–9.
26 Thorsten Benner and Philipp Rotmann, "Learning to Learn? UN Peacebuilding and the Challenges of Building a Learning Organization", *Journal of Intervention and Statebuilding* 2, no. 1 (2008): 45–9.
27 UN High-Level Panel on United Nations Peace Operations, "Report of the Panel on United Nations Peace Operations", para 229, 39.
28 Inter alia, the following reports and position 'non-papers' frame these developments chronologically: UN Security Council, "Report of the Independent Inquiry into the Actions of the United Nations During the 1994 Genocide in Rwanda", (New York: United Nations, 1999); UN High-Level Panel on United Nations Peace Operations, "Report of the Panel on United Nations Peace Operations" and subsequent implementation reports of the Secretary-General in 2000 and 2001; Secretary-General, "Comprehensive Report on Strengthening the Capacity of the United Nations to Manage and Sustain Peace Operations", in *Report of the Secretary-General* (New York: United Nations, 2007); "United Nations Peacekeeping Operations: Principles and Guidelines".; DPKO/DFS, "A New Partnership Agenda: Charting a New Horizon for UN Peacekeeping" (New York: UN Department of Peacekeeping Operations and Department of Field Support, 2009).
29 Benner and Rotmann, "Learning to Learn? UN Peacebuilding and the Challenges of Building a Learning Organization", 53.
30 See: DPKO, "'Peace Operations 2010' Reform Strategy (Excerpts from the Report of the Secretary-General)", (New York: United Nations, 2007). Originally published in: "Overview of the Financing of the United Nations Peacekeeping Operations: Budget Performance for the Period from 1 July 2004 to 30 June 2005 and Budget for the Period from 1 July 2006 to 30 June 2007", in *Report of the Secretary-General Administrative and budgetary aspects of the financing of the United Nations peacekeeping operations* (New York: United Nations, 2006), 6–10, paras 6–21.
31 Following this reform the section produced an unprecedented number of reports of increased scope and varying focus, including public perception surveys of four sub-Saharan African missions.
32 UN reports define KM as: 'the systematic creation, organization, storage and sharing of knowledge in order to better achieve organizational goals.' "Report of the Office of Internal Oversight Services on the Thematic Evaluation of Knowledge Management Networks in the Pursuit of the Goals of the Millennium Declaration", (New York: United Nations Economic and Social Council, 2006), 4, para 2.
33 "Peacekeeping Best Practices – Report of the Secretary-General", 6.
34 Ibid., 6.
35 Bolisani and Damiani, "Knowledge Management in Complex Environments: The UN Peacekeeping", 81.
36 Benner, Mergenthaler, and Rotmann, "The Evolution of Organizational Learning in the UN Peace Operations Bureaucracy", 25–6.
37 Bolisani and Damiani, "Knowledge Management in Complex Environments: The UN Peacekeeping", 80–2.
38 "Report of the Office of Internal Oversight Services on the Thematic Evaluation of Knowledge Management Networks in the Pursuit of the Goals of the Millennium Declaration", 20.
39 Benner and Rotmann, "Learning to Learn? UN Peacebuilding and the Challenges of Building a Learning Organization", 55.
40 'Peacekeeping Resources Hub: Policy, Lessons Learned and Training for the Peacekeeping Community', www.pbpu.unlb.org/PBPS.

41 "In 2009, DPKO/DFS CoP project team deployed 27 CoPs engaging 2600 staff members across five continents in eight months". Bolisani and Damiani, "Knowledge Management in Complex Environments: The UN Peacekeeping", 82.
42 Howard, *UN Peacekeeping in Civil Wars*, 337; Benner, Mergenthaler, and Rotmann, "The Evolution of Organizational Learning in the UN Peace Operations Bureaucracy", 29.
43 "Peacekeeping Best Practices – Report of the Secretary-General", 10.
44 "Comprehensive Report on Strengthening the Capacity of the United Nations to Manage and Sustain Peace Operations", 21–2, paragraph 72–7.
45 "Policy Directive: DPKO/DFS Mission Evaluation", (New York: United Nations, 2008), 2.
46 Interview: DPET Evaluation Unit Officer – New York, February 2009.
47 See: "Policy Directive: DPKO/DFS Mission Evaluation"; "Policy Directive: DPKO/DFS Headquarters Self–Evaluation", (New York: United Nations, 2008).
48 Interview: DPET Evaluation Unit Officer – New York, 24th February 2009
49 Michael Lipson, "Performance under Ambiguity: International Organization Performance in UN Peacekeeping", in *The Review of International Organizations*, 5, no. 3. (2010): 268.
50 "Comprehensive Report on Strengthening the Capacity of the United Nations to Manage and Sustain Peace Operations", 21–2, para. 74.A/61/858.
51 DPKO/DFS, "A New Partnership Agenda: Charting a New Horizon for UN Peacekeeping", 15–16.
52 OROLSI, "The Way Forward: A Strategic Approach for the Office of the Rule of Law and Security Institutions, United Nations Department of Peacekeeping Operations", (New York: United Nations, 2008), 7.
53 Benner, Mergenthaler, and Rotmann, "The Evolution of Organizational Learning in the UN Peace Operations Bureaucracy", 29, 31.
54 See: "Results-Based Budgeting", in *Report of the Secretary-General* (New York: United Nations, 1999), and A/54/456 Addendums 1–5; Andrzej T. Abraszewski *et al.*, "Results-Based Budgeting: The Experience of the United Nations System Organizations", (Geneva: United Nations Joint Inspection Unit, 1999).
55 See, for example: H. Shiroyama, "UN Management Reform as a Basis for Managerial Accountability", in *Envisioning Reform: Enhancing UN Accountability in the 21st Century*, eds. Sumihiro Kuyama and Michael Ross Fowler (New York: United Nations University Press, 2009).
56 Sarah Dalrymple, "Survey of the United Nations Organisation's Arrangements for Monitoring and Evaluating Support to Security Sector Reform", in *RESEARCH REPORT* (London: Saferworld, 2009), 5.
57 See: Secretary-General Report (1999) "Results-based Budgeting" (New York, United Nations), A/54/456; General Assembly Resolution (2001), "Results-based budgeting" (New York, United Nations), A/RES/55/231.
58 Abraszewski *et al.*, "Results-Based Budgeting: The Experience of the United Nations System Organizations", 3–4.
59 See: E. C. Luck, "Making the UN Accountable: Political and Managerial Challenges", in *Envisioning Reform: Enhancing UN Accountability in the 21st Century*, eds. S. Kuyama and M. R. Fowler (New York: United Nations University Press, 2009), 30.
60 UN, "Review of Results-Based Management at the United Nations", (New York: United Nations, 2008), 21, para. 45.
61 UN, "Review of Results-Based Budgeting in United Nations Mission in Sudan (UNMIS)", (New York: Office of Internal Oversight Services, Inspection and

Evaluation Division, 2007), 21, para. 45. See also: UN, "Review of Results-Based Budgeting in United Nations Mission in Liberia (UNMIL)", (New York: Office of Internal Oversight Services, Inspection and Evaluation Division, 2007).
62 UN, "Accountability Framework, Enterprise Risk Management and Internal Control Framework, and Results-Based Management Framework", in *Report of the Secretary-General* (New York: United Nations, 2008), 20–1, para. 64.
63 Even Fontaine Ortiz and Tadanori Inomata, "Evaluation of Results-Based Budgeting in Peacekeeping Operations" (Geneva: UN Joint Inspection Unit, 2006), 2, para. 7.
64 Guehenno cited in Lipson, "Performance under Ambiguity: International Organization Performance in UN Peacekeeping", 274.
65 For example, see: UN, "Performance Report on the Budget of UNMIL for the Period 1 July 2006 to 30 June 2007", in *Financing of the United Nations Mission in Liberia* (New York: United Nations, 2008), 14–15.
66 Abraszewski *et al.*, "Results-Based Budgeting: The Experience of the United Nations System Organizations", 12–13.
67 UN, "Programme Performance of the United Nations for the Biennium 2006–2007", in *Report of the Secretary-General* (New York: United Nations, 2008).
68 Emery Brusset, "Significance of Impact Assessment: A New Methodology", in *Measuring What Matters in Peace Operations and Crisis Management*, ed. Sarah Jane Meharg (McGill-Queen's University Press, 2009), 190–4.
69 Lipson, "Performance under Ambiguity: International Organization Performance in UN Peacekeeping", 275.
70 Ibid., 272.
71 Tim Balint, Sarah Schernbeck, and Simone Schneider, "Performance Accountability in the UN Secretariat — the Conflictual Way toward More Flexibility", *Public Administration and Development* 29, no. 5 (2009): 357–8.
72 Lipson, "Performance under Ambiguity: International Organization Performance in UN Peacekeeping", 274.
73 Ylber Bajraktari, Arthur Boutellis, Fatema Gunja, Daniel Harris, James Kapsis, Eva Kaye, and Jane Rhee, "The Prime System: Measuring the Success of Post-Conflict Police Reform", (Princeton, NJ: Princeton University, Woodrow Wilson School of Public and International Affairs, 2006), 89.
74 See, for example: "UNAMSIL/UNCT Transition Strategy: Laying a foundation for durable peace and sustainable development" (UNAMSIL, 2005); "Proxy Indicators: Status of Restoration of State Authority and Recovery in Liberia" (UNMIL Civil Affairs Section, April 2005).
75 Interview: UN DPKO official – New York, February 2009.
76 OIOS, "Management of UN Police Operations", in *Audit Report* (New York: UN Office of Internal Oversight Services, 2008), 20.
77 Joshua G. Smith, Victoria K. Holt, and William J. Durch, "Enhancing United Nations Capacity for Post-Conflict Policing and Rule of Law", in *The Project on Rule of Law in Post-Conflict Settings* (Washington DC: The Henry L Stimson Center, 2007), 44.
78 Bajraktari *et al.*, "The Prime System: Measuring the Success of Post-Conflict Police Reform", 106.
79 For a list of publications, see: www.un.org/depts/oios/pages/other_oios_reports.html.
80 Interview: Office of Military Affairs Official, Policy and Evaluation Section (previously Inspector General) – New York, February 2009.
81 Benner, Mergenthaler, and Rotmann, "The Evolution of Organizational Learning in the UN Peace Operations Bureaucracy", 23.
82 Interview: Office of Military Affairs Official, Policy and Evaluation Section (previously Inspector General) – New York, February 2009.

94 Context-setting

83 Former Under-Secretary-General Jean-Marie Guehenno cited in Lipson, "Performance under Ambiguity: International Organization Performance in UN Peacekeeping", 274.
84 See Secretary-General's comments on value of benchmarking in nascent Peacebuilding Commission: 'Explanatory Note of the Secretary General on the Peacebuilding Commission', *United Nations*, 17 April 2005.
85 "Exit Strategies and Peace Consolidation in State-Building Operations", in *Report on Wilton Park Conference 965* (CIS, University of Oxford, 2009).
86 William J. Durch, "Supporting Peace: The End", *Prism* 2, no. 1 (2010): 52.
87 DPKO/DFS, "A New Partnership Agenda: Charting a New Horizon for UN Peacekeeping", 15; Richard Ponzio, "What Benchmarking Is Needed, and How Can Performance Be Best Evaluated?", in *Exit Strategies and Peace Consolidation in State-Building Operations* (Wilton Park, UK, 2009).
88 UN, "Monitoring Peace Consolidation: United Nations Practitioners Guide to Benchmarking", (New York: United Nations In cooperation with the Fafo Institute for Applied International Studies and the Norwegian Peacebuilding Centre [NOREF], 2010).
89 See: Svein Erik Stave, "The UN Practitioners Handbook for Peace Consolidation Benchmarking", in *Monitoring and Evaluation of Peace Operations Workshop* (New York: IPI and NUPI, 2009), 3.
90 Stave, "The UN Practitioners Handbook for Peace Consolidation Benchmarking", 3.
91 IPI, "Peace Operations", in *Task Forces on Strengthening Multilateral Security Capacity, IPI Blue Paper No. 9* (New York: International Peace Institute, 2009), 19.
92 For example, in the realm of UNPOL, the Stimson Center has been commissioned to identify these in a project entitled, 'Measures of effectiveness and benchmarking', details available at: www.stimson.org/research-pages/restoring-the-rule-of-law/.
93 Dominik Zaum, "Peace Operations and Exit", *The RUSI Journal* 153, no. 2 (2008): 39; George Downs and Stephen J. Stedman, "Evaluation Issues in Peace Implementation", in *Ending Civil Wars: The Implementation of Peace Agreements*, eds. Stephen Stedman, Donald Rothchild, and Elizabeth Cousens (Boulder, CO: Lynne Rienner, 2002), 45–7.
94 "Exit Strategies and Peace Consolidation in State-Building Operations", 7.
95 A joint initiative of the DPKO and Office of the High Commissioner for Human Rights (OHCHR) in partnership with the Vera Institute of Justice/Altus Global Alliance and in cooperation with the Department of Political Affairs (DPA), Office of Legal Affairs (OLA), United Nations Children's Fund (UNICEF), the UN Development Programme (UNDP), the UN Fund for Women (UNIFEM), the UN High Commissioner for Refugees (UNHCR), the UN Office on Drugs and Crime (UNODC) and The World Bank.
96 Durch and England, eds., *Enhancing United Nations Capacity to Support Post-Conflict Policing and Rule of Law*, 47–8.
97 Interview: Policy and Legal Affairs Officer, UN Police Division, DPKO – New York, February 2009; Smith, Holt, and Durch, "Enhancing United Nations Capacity for Post-Conflict Policing and Rule of Law", 5.
98 Interview: Policy and Legal Affairs Officer, UN Police Division, DPKO – New York, February 2009; UN, "The Rule of Law Indicators Project: Faqs", (New York: UN Police Division, 2008).
99 "The United Nations Rule of Law Indicators: Implementation Guide and Project Tools", (New York: United Nations Department of Peacekeeping Operations/Office of the High Commissioner for Human Rights, 2011).
100 Personal communication: Policy and Legal Affairs Officer, UN Police Division, DPKO – February 2011.

101 "The United Nations Rule of Law Indicators: Implementation Guide and Project Tools", 3–4.
102 Benner, Mergenthaler, and Rotmann, "The Evolution of Organizational Learning in the UN Peace Operations Bureaucracy", 33.
103 OIOS, "Learning Lessons for Improving Organizational Efficiency and Effectiveness Is Weak", 12.
104 Smith, Holt, and Durch, "Enhancing United Nations Capacity for Post-Conflict Policing and Rule of Law", 43.
105 Interview: Chief Standing Police Capacity, UN Police Division, DPKO – New York, February 2009.
106 Bajraktari et al., "The Prime System: Measuring the Success of Post-Conflict Police Reform", 106.
107 Benner, Mergenthaler, and Rotmann, *The New World of UN Peace Operations: Learning to Build Peace?* 70–3.
108 "Annual Report of Strengthening and Coordinating United Nations Rule of Law Activities", in *Report of the Secretary-General.* (New York: United Nations, 2009), 16.
109 See, for example: Peter Neyroud, "Past, Present and Future Performance: Lessons and Prospects for the Measurement of Police Performance", *Policing* 2, no. 3 (2008); Nigel Fielding and Martin Innes, "Reassurance Policing, Community Policing and Measuring Police Performance", *Policing and Society: An International Journal of Research and Policy* 16, no. 2 (2006); David I. Ashby, "Policing Neighbourhoods: Exploring the Geographies of Crime, Policing and Performance Assessment", *Policing and Society* 15, no. 4 (2005); "The Policing Performance Assessment Framework", (London: Home Office, UK Government, 2004); Isabelle Lelandais and Julie Bodson, "Measuring Police Performance", (Montreal: International Centre for the Prevention of Crime, 2007); R. Langworthy, *Measuring What Matters: Proceedings from the Police Research Institute Meetings* (Washington DC: National Institute of Justice, 1999).
110 Rick Sarre, "Community Policing – Success or Failure? Exploring Different Models of Evaluation" (AIC Conference Proceedings, no. 5, Canberra 1992); Julie Van Den Eynde, Arthur Veno, and Alison Hart, "They Look Good but They Don't Work: A Case Study of Global Performance Indicators in Crime Prevention", *Evaluation and Program Planning* 26, no. 3 (2003).
111 Smith, "Managing Civpol: The Potential Performance Management in International Public Services", 282.
112 Ibid., 276–9; William J. Bratton and Sean W. Malinowski, "Police Performance Management in Practice: Taking COMPSTAT to the Next Level", *Policing* 2, no. 3 (2008).
113 Moore and Braga, "Measuring and Improving Police Performance: The Lessons of Compstat and Its Progreny".
114 Garth den Heyer, *The Role of Civilian Police in Peacekeeping: 1999–2007* (Washington, DC: Police Foundation, 2012), 174; Ann Fitz-Gerald and Sylvie Jackson, "Developing a Performance Measurement System for Security Sector Interventions", *Journal of Security Sector Management* 6, no. 1 (2008): 1.
115 William G. O'Neill, "Police Reform in Post-Conflict Societies: What We Know and What We Still Need to Know". In *The Security-Development Nexus Program.* (New York: International Peace Academy, 2005); Charles T. Call, "Challenges in Police Reform: Promoting Effectiveness and Accountability". In *From Promise to Practice: Strengthening UN Capacities for the Prevention of Violent Conflict* (New York: International Peace Academy, 2003).
116 Bajraktari et al., "The Prime System: Measuring the Success of Post-Conflict Police Reform".
117 Ibid., 15.

96 Context-setting

118 Ibid., 13.
119 Ibid., 105–6.
120 Unintended consequences of peacekeeping, also known as 'displacement effects' when they have negative connotations, see: Chiyuki Aoi, Cedric de Coning, and Ramesh Thakur, eds., *Unintended Consequences of Peacekeeping Operations* (Tokyo: United Nations University Press, 2007).
121 Another rare example of UNPOL M&E can be found amongst the DPKO-commissioned guidance on Community Policing. See: David H. Bayley, "Community Policing: Evaluation Programs" (New York: Civilian Police Division, DPKO, United Nations, 2005). The compendium includes a manual on how to evaluate programmes promoting community policing in peacekeeping contexts. Although this constitutes a guide rather than a ready-to-use tool, it does propose a method, potential performance indicators and sources of validation.
122 David Lewis, "Reassessing the Role of Osce Police Assistance Programing in Central Asia", in *Occasional Paper Series No. 4* (Open Society Foundations, 2011), 49; den Heyer, *The Role of Civilian Police in Peacekeeping*, 179.
123 Durch and England, eds., *Enhancing United Nations Capacity to Support Post-Conflict Policing and Rule of Law*, 48.
124 den Heyer, *The Role of Civilian Police in Peacekeeping*, 179; Sarah Jane Meharg, "Introduction", in Sarah Jane Meharg, ed. *Measuring What Matters in Peace Operations and Crisis Management* (Kingston, ON: McGill–Queen's University Press, 2009), 4–14.
125 Esra Çuhadar Gürkaynak, Bruce Dayton, and Thania Paffenholz, "Evaluation in Conflict Resolution and Peacebuilding", in *Handbook of Conflict Analysis and Resolution*, ed. Dennis Sandole, *et al.* (London: Taylor and Francis, 2008), 295–8; Stolk *et al.*, *Monitoring and Evaluation in Stabilisation Interventions: Reviewing the State of the Art and Suggesting Ways Forward*, 5.
126 Whilst none of the M&E approaches is a pure application of the logframe, as will be demonstrated here, each has its conceptual roots in this modality, particularly in regard to the inference of causality between results levels.
127 Sarah Jane Meharg, "Measuring the Effectiveness of Reconstruction and Stabilization Activites", *The Pearson Papers* 10, no. 1 (2007), 34–41; DfID, "Guidance of Using the Revised Logical Framework", in *How to Note* (London: Department for International Development [DfID], 2009).
128 INCAF, "Draft Justice and Security Monitoring and Evaluation Toolkit – Version 2", OECD International Network on Conflict and Fragility – Task Team on Peacebuilding, Statebuilding, Security (2010): 13.
129 See, for example: O. Bakewell and A. Garbutt, *The Use and Abuse of the Logical Framework Approach* (Stockholm: Swedish Internaitonal Development Agency [SIDA], 2005); Richard Blue, Cynthia Clapp-Wincek, and Holly Benner, *Beyond Success Stories: Monitoring and Evaluation for Foreign Assistance Results* (USAID, 2009); B. Perrin, "Effective Use and Misuse of Performance Measurement", *American Journal of Evaluation* 19, no. 3 (1998).
130 See, for example: Lewis, "Evaluation and Assessment of Interventions"; Cohen, "Measuring Progress in Stabilization and Reconstruction"; Meharg, "Measuring the Effectiveness of Reconstruction and Stabilization Activites", 43; Cheyanne Church and Julie Shouldice, "The Evaluation of Conflict Resolution Interventions: Part II: Emerging Practice and Theory" (Derry/Londonderry, 2003).
131 Dalrymple, "Survey of the United Nations Organisation's Arrangements for Monitoring and Evaluating Support to Security Sector Reform", 31.
132 Whilst this in part explains why strict accountability usually stops at the outputs level (i.e. peacekeepers cannot be expected to be held responsible for

results at the outcome and impact level) it does not help in ascertaining the effects of the operations or learning from them. See also: GAO, "U.N. Peacekeeping – Transition Strategies for Post-Conflict Countries Lack Results-Oriented Measures of Progress", in *Report to the Chairman, Committee on International Relations, House of Representatives – USA* (Washington DC: United States General Accounting Office, 2003), 18–30; Madeline L. England, "Management of the Security Sector: A Note on Current Practice", in *Future of Peace Operations* (Washington, DC: Henry L. Stimson Center, 2009), 7.
133 Ken Menkhaus, "Measuring Impact: Issues and Dilemmas", in *Occasional Paper Series* (Geneva: InterPeace, 2003), 6.
134 Kenneth J. Menkhaus, "State Fragility as a Wicked Problem", *Prism* 1, no. 2 (2010): 85–97.
135 Church and Shouldice, "The Evaluation of Conflict Resolution Interventions: Framing the State of Play", 49.
136 de Coning and Romita, "Monitoring and Evaluation of Peace Operations", 26.
137 For discussion of unintended consequences of peacekeeping, see: Aoi, de Coning, and Thakur, eds., *Unintended Consequences of Peacekeeping Operations*.
138 Garth den Heyer, "Post-Conflict Civilian Police Reform: 1999 to 2007" *Working Paper* No 44. (Geneva: International Police Executive Symposium [IPES] and the Geneva Centre for the Democratic Control of the Armed Forces [DCAF] and Coginta, 2012), 21.
139 Stolk *et al.*, *Monitoring and Evaluation in Stabilisation Interventions: Reviewing the State of the Art and Suggesting Ways Forward*, 5–6.
140 Gürkaynak, Dayton, and Paffenholz, "Evaluation in Conflict Resolution and Peacebuilding", 294–9.
141 UN, "Review of the United Nations Peacebuilding Architecture", (New York: United Nations, 2010), 9.
142 Ian Clegg, Robert Hutton, and Jim Whetton, eds., *Policy Guidance to Support Policing in Developing Countries*, (Swansea: University of Wales, 2000) 56.
143 Timothy G. Shilston, "One, Two, Three, What Are We Still Counting For? Police Performance Regimes, Public Perceptions of Service Delivery and the Failure of Quantitative Measurement", *Policing* 2, no. 3 (2008); England, "Management of the Security Sector: A Note on Current Practice", 8.
144 Bajraktari *et al.*, "The Prime System: Measuring the Success of Post-Conflict Police Reform", 10.
145 See, for example: OECD-DAC, "Guidance on Evaluating Conflict Prevention and Peacebuilding Activities", 19–23.
146 Church and Shouldice, "The Evaluation of Conflict Resolution Interventions: Framing the State of Play", 5.
147 Dalrymple, "Survey of the United Nations Organisation's Arrangements for Monitoring and Evaluating Support to Security Sector Reform", 5.
148 Ibid., 5; Simon Rynn and Duncan Hiscock, "Evaluating for Security and Justice: Challenges and Opportunities for Improved Monitoring and Evaluation of Security System Reform Programmes", (Saferworld, 2009), 19–20.
149 Interview: UN DPKO official – New York, United Nations, February 2009.
150 Thania Paffenholz and Luc Reychler, *Aid for Peace: A Guide to Planning and Evaluation for Conflict Zones* (Baden-Baden: Nomos, 2007), 42.
151 David C. Becker and Robert Grossman-Vermaas, "Metrics for the Haiti Stabilization Initiative", *Prism* 2, no. 2 (2011): 151.
152 Bruce Russet, "Counterfactuals About War and Its Absence", in *Counterfactual Thought Experiments in World Politics: Logical, Methodological, and Psychological Perspectives*, eds. Philip E. Tetlock and Aaron Belkin (Princeton, New Jersey: Princeton University Press, 1996), 184–6; Druckman, *Doing Research: Methods of Inquiry for Conflict Analysis*, 300.

98 Context-setting

153 Michael Dziedzic, Barbara Sotirin, and John Agoglia, "Metrics Framework for Assessing Conflict Transformation and Stabilization", in *Measuring Progress in Conflict Environments (MPICE)* (New York: United States Institute for Peace, 2008), 5.
154 Druckman and Stern, "The Forum: Evaluating Peacekeeping Missions", 163.
155 den Heyer, "Post-Conflict Civilian Police Reform", 21.
156 UN, "Monitoring Peace Consolidation: United Nations Practitioners' Guide to Benchmarking", 7.
157 Kristiina Rintakoski, "An Organizational Perspective on Measuring the Effectiveness of Crisis Management", in *Measuring What Matters in Peace Operations and Crisis Management*, ed. Sarah Jane Meharg (McGill-Queen's University Press, 2009), 207; Schumacher, "What to Measure in Peace Operations", 46; de Coning and Romita, "Monitoring and Evaluation of Peace Operations", 7.
158 Bajraktari *et al.*, "The Prime System: Measuring the Success of Post-Conflict Police Reform", 106.
159 Rynn and Hiscock, "Evaluating for Security and Justice: Challenges and Opportunities for Improved Monitoring and Evaluation of Security System Reform Programmes", 14–15.
160 UNDP, "Handbook on Planning, Monitoring and Evaluating for Development Results", 25; Dalrymple, "Survey of the United Nations Organisation's Arrangements for Monitoring and Evaluating Support to Security Sector Reform", 32.
161 Rynn and Hiscock, "Evaluating for Security and Justice: Challenges and Opportunities for Improved Monitoring and Evaluation of Security System Reform Programmes", 18.
162 Michael Quinn Patton, *Utilization-Focused Evaluation*, 4th ed. (Thousand Oaks, CA: Sage, 2008); Menkhaus, "Measuring Impact: Issues and Dilemmas", 13; Becker and Grossman-Vermaas, "Metrics for the Haiti Stabilization Initiative", 151.
163 L. Nathan, *No Ownership, No Commitment: A Guide to Local Ownership in Security Sector Reform* (UK Government, Global Conflict Prevention Pool, University of Birmingham, 2007); Annika S. Hansen, "Local Ownership in Peace Operations", in *Local Ownership and Security Sector Reform* ed. Timothy Donais (Geneva/Vienna: DCAF/LIT Verlag, 2008); Eric Scheye and Gordon Peake, "Unknotting Local Ownership", in *After Intervention: Public Security Management in Post-Conflict Societies – from Intervention to Sustainable Local Ownership*, ed. Anja H. Ebnöther and Philipp H. Fluri (Vienna/Geneva: Austrian National Defence Academy/DCAF, 2005).
164 Robert C. Davis, *The Use of Citizen Surveys as a Tool for Police Reform* (New York: Vera Institute of Justice, 2000), 11.
165 Sherman, "Measures of Effectiveness in Peacebuilding and State-Building", 211.
166 USAID, "Monitoring and Evaluation in Postconflict Settings", 2.
167 C. Church and Mark M. Rogers, "Designing for Results: Integrating Monitoring and Evaluation in Conflict Transformation Programs", (Washington DC: Search for Common Ground, 2006).
168 As argued in the previous chapter, such change theories are arguably framed by the liberal peace. This is not problematic per se, but due to their infancy they need to be tested and adapted if necessary.
169 Campbell, "When Process Matters: The Potential Implications of Organisational Learning for Peacebuilding Success", 24.
170 den Heyer, "Post-Conflict Civilian Police Reform", 21.
171 Lipson, "Performance under Ambiguity: International Organization Performance in UN Peacekeeping", 254–5.

172 Alex Austin, Martina Fischer, and Oliver Wils, eds., *Peace and Conflict Impact Assessment – Critical Views on Theory and Practice*, vol. 1, Berghof Handbook Dialogue Series (Berlin: Berghof Research Center for Constructive Conflict Management 2003).
173 Bakewell and Garbutt, *The Use and Abuse of the Logical Framework Approach*, 12.
174 Cohen, "Measuring Progress in Stabilization and Reconstruction", 13.
175 Johansen, "Peacekeeping: How Should We Measure Success?", 310.
176 Meharg, "Mechanisms and Tools", 125.

Part II
Theory and framework building

3 Complexity, peace operations and M&E
The need for a paradigm shift?

> There is always an easy solution to every human problem – neat, plausible, and wrong.[1]

Introduction

The previous chapter identified the shortcomings of extant theory and practice of M&E in relation to UNPOL in UN peace operations. In particular, it highlighted seven key areas where current orthodoxy does not adequately cater for the impact assessment and learning needs of the full gamut of UNPOL activities and objectives. This chapter explores the possibility of harnessing insights from the study of 'complexity' to help understand how to analyse, monitor and evaluate multidimensional UN peace operations that are invariably part of conflict and peacebuilding systems in highly dynamic and nonlinear environments.

There is an increasing recognition in both research and practice that, unlike their traditional antecedents, the majority of modern peace operations are now complex undertakings. In the 1990s, humanitarian agencies began using the phrase 'complex emergencies', while the language of 'complex peace operations' is now ubiquitous throughout the peacekeeping community in describing the multi-agency and multifunctional character of twenty-first-century peace operations.[2] However, regarding attempts to monitor and evaluate the impact of missions, this recognition has been largely a rhetorical one. Whilst there has been widespread acknowledgement that complexity is rife in the business of peacekeeping, this has not been adequately reflected in pervasive M&E practice.[3] Current convention displays a limited appreciation of what complexity means for how the impact of mission activities should be captured and interpreted. This has significant implications for design, planning and ongoing management of missions, to which M&E informed by complexity theory could be a valuable contributor.

In this chapter I argue that complexity theory brings novel insights to the study of peace operations. In particular, I argue that the central claims and concepts of complexity theory correspond well with the challenges

104 *Theory and framework building*

facing M&E for UNPOL that I identified in the previous chapter and that consequently complexity theory can usefully inform the development of more appropriate approaches. The chapter proceeds in four parts. First, it briefly charts the origins of complexity theory, distils the core concepts of the paradigm, introduces the features of a complex system and notes the increasing application of such concepts to the social sciences as well as enduring contentions. Second, it draws upon the emerging literature viewing peace missions and their operating environments as complex social systems and proceeds to expand on this nascent field using real-world examples to substantiate the suitability of such a representation. The third part demonstrates how the central tenets of complexity theory provide an alternative theoretical framework for addressing the weaknesses of extant M&E in peace operations. It proceeds to looks at what employing a complexity lens means for – and brings to – the task of monitoring and evaluating progress and change in complex systems. Finally, the chapter concludes by articulating the core implications of complexity-oriented M&E for contributing to subsequent development of a framework for UNPOL in peace operations.

Complexity theory

Complexity science emanated from theoretical physics and cybernetics,[4] however, today complexity science is best understood as a loose constellation of ideas, principles and influences developed and embedded throughout the physical and natural sciences, particularly in biology, computer simulation, mathematics, physics and chemistry and sub-fields including chaos theory, fractal geometry and cybernetics. Other related disciplines such as systems thinking have also expounded upon and harnessed similar concepts and illustrative models.[5]

In basic terms, the science of complexity and its central tenets provide a framework for explaining systemic change processes evident in physical and organic phenomena. The common thread through these theories, henceforth 'complexity theory', is their contention that fixed linear paradigms – often referred to as Newtonian in character – are both limited and limiting when applied to complex systems.

By its nature, something which is complex is not easily reduced to a discrete categorization. Hence, complexity does not adhere to a precise definition. A commonly used device to explain complexity is to contrast a 'complicated' system with one that is truly 'complex'.[6] A complicated system can have a huge number of constituent parts and their configuration can appear complex. However, the behaviour of a complicated system is ultimately determined.[7] For example, the electronics systems in aircraft are extremely complicated. They are replete with components and utilise various different technologies. Whilst grasping all of this information may be beyond the capacity of any one individual, it is possible to understand its functioning. That is to say, the system is stable and 'knowable'. This means enough of the causal relationships between the system's elements are linear, that this modality applies at all times and locations, and that as a result, system-level outcomes are determined, finite and can be predicted.[8]

On the contrary, interactions between arrays of elements in complex systems are dynamic and non-linear. That is to say those relations transform over time and cannot be understood to trace a simple trajectory of causality. This means that outcomes are undetermined, unpredictable and can be unexpected. Phenomena as diverse as an ant colony, the human nervous system, language, ecosystems, financial markets and political community are examples of complex systems.[9] A system's complexity is the product of its constituent parts interacting and emerges at the systemic level. As Jervis puts it, subtly but significantly altering a popular idiom, "the whole is *different from*, not *greater than*, the sum of the parts"[10] (original emphasis). It is for this reason that the behaviour of a complex system is not reducible to the behaviours of its constituent parts.

Despite these intricacies, it is not necessary for complexity to be perceived as convoluted or esoteric. In short, complex is the opposite of independent, while complicated is the opposite of simple. It does, however, introduce a lexicon and set of ideas somewhat unfamiliar in the social sciences. Complexity theory is furnished with an array of concepts that underpin this distinction between systems that are merely complicated and those that are complex. Therefore, in a generic sense, complex systems possess particular defining features and display certain systemic properties.[11] The first three relate to 'interconnections and interdependence', 'feedback' and 'emergence'.

All systems are comprised of multiple elements. However, it is the existence of *interconnections* between these parts, processes and dimensions that is emblematic of complex systems. Interactions between elements, be they agents, processes or indeed other (sub-)systems, lead to intricate *interdependent* relationships symptomatic of complex systems.[12] This means action by any part of the system can affect another and/or the whole. These are also dynamic, such that interactions can be volatile and changing. The degree of interdependence, often referred to as 'connectivity',[13] dictates how change occurs in the system, the resilience or robustness of the system and with it the magnitude of the 'ripple effects' from disturbance and perturbations (both internal to and external on the environment).

Complex systems are 'controlled' by *feedback mechanisms and processes*. These drive systemic change and can be both negative and positive, which respectively dampen and amplify change.[14] Both types represent the way in which alterations in system components or system-level behaviour is related back to both its original source and other elements of the system. Negative feedback tends to counteract the activating change, reversing the direction of change/restoring initial conditions and acting as a 'control' or 'stabiliser'[15] – in effect reducing overall deviation in the system. Simple examples include the thermostat on a central heating system or the plughole in relation to a bath filling up.[16] Positive feedback tends to propagate the vector or variety of change, 'destabilising' the system, which can lead to significant quantitative and qualitative changes in the system.[17] An oft-used example is when logs are added to a bonfire which eventually exhausts its fuel and burns out.[18] Whilst similar feedback is present in simple systems, the difference in complex systems is that feedback is the conveyance to the system of its own non-linear, unpredictable and dynamical change.[19] Furthermore, in complex systems these are not one-off feedback events, but ongoing feedback 'processes'.[20]

Probably the most archetypal feature of a complex system is *emergence*.[21] Emergent properties refer to the structures, qualities or behavioural patterns of the system as a whole that are difficult to predict based on the characteristics of constituent parts. Emergence is therefore contingent on and produced by the myriad of possible interrelationships between elements within the system.[22] For example, a piano chord is often used as an analogy, as when three or more single notes are played together, the product – a chord – displays a "harmonious combination of sounds [that] has a new attribute which no one of its individual components had".[23] Emergent properties stem from the local 'rules' of interacting elements that are not necessarily known or understood at the macro-level and make systemic behaviour difficult to predict.

The three features explained here combine to have important ramifications for how complex systems change over time. First, they dictate that change occurs in a *non-linear* fashion. That is, the causal interrelations in complex systems are not necessarily proportional and therefore defy a predictive and additive logic.[24] Feedback processes between interacting components and dimensions produce relations that create dynamical and unpredictable change.[25] Clear causal relationships cannot be identified or assumed due to the many and different influencing factors. Nonlinear systems are not anomalies or unusual. In reality, nonlinearity is likely to be the norm when studying systems.[26] Linear or 'tame' problems can be disaggregated and treated independently.[27] Once 'solved', the series of discrete explanations can be accumulated and integrated into a holistic solution – i.e. the whole is *equal* to the sum of its parts. However, linearity is often an approximation of a more complex reality, arrived at through regression techniques. In a complex system, an input to the system may have an uneven impact due to the irregular distribution of system elements and the nature of coupling between them.[28] This makes complex systems intrinsically hard to control or predict with any certainty.

Second, the properties of a complex system ensure that change can happen disproportionately. In complexity terms, this is referred to as *sensitive dependence* and emphasises a system's susceptibility to context and variations in any aspect of the situation.[29] A complex system's behaviour is extremely sensitive to the initial conditions as, due to the nonlinear relationships, minor adjustments in one component of a system may lead to major changes in outcomes under observation.[30] Positive feedback processes are particularly important in this. This phenomenon is often depicted by Lorenz's 'butterfly effect' whereby an event, seemingly trivial in size or importance (e.g. a butterfly flapping its wings in Brasil), can lead to large and significant event (e.g. a hurricane in Japan), through an unpredictable chain of interrelated events.[31]

Third, change in complex systems is said to happen when a system moves within and between peculiar loci (i.e. phase spaces) that frame systemic behaviour known in complexity terms as *attractors*. An attractor encapsulates the long-term qualitative behaviour of a system and expresses the patterns of ordering and phases of the system. This includes the possibility that complex systems may have many equilibria.[32] Eoyang describes how attractors host "emergent behaviour that has a finite bound and infinite variability within the bound."[33] In typological terms, these can be 'periodic' or 'fixed point' attractors,[34] however, it is the 'strange attractor' that is the hallmark of complex systems and relates to systemic behaviour at the 'edge of chaos'.[35]

Minor changes occur regularly within a phase space but occasionally some perturbation can shunt the system into a new attractor with associated global patterning. The nature of complex systems is such that it is not possible to know what type or magnitude of perturbation will constitute a sufficient shove. This creates the potential for a complex system trajectory of large upheavals separated by long periods of global stability, but energetic local activity known as 'punctuated equilibrium'.[36]

When complex systems have the inherent capacity to change, precisely because of the adaptive agency of their constitutive elements – i.e. their ability to respond consciously and strategically to peers and their environment – they fall into a sub-category known as *Complex Adaptive Systems*.[37] More recently, scholars such as Mitleton-Kelly have suggested that these phenomena are better described as *Complex Evolving Systems* (CES) as this better captures the nature of systemic change where elements are simultaneously evolving *with*, not just adapting *to*, a changing environment.[38]

This particular type of complex system is characterised by two further behaviours. First, they are self-organising. *Self-organisation* refers to the reorganising and self-regulation of a system in response to a disturbance or external constraint. Whilst similar to emergence, this characteristic is a peculiar consequence of the interactions, interdependence and multiple feedback processes at play between agents who consciously structure their conduct in accordance with their own visions, goals and calculations of the predicament. In other words, self-organisation is the emergent product of interacting adaptive agents.[39] Chaos and order combine to produce conditions of self-organised complexity sometimes referred to as a 'chaordic' state.[40]

108 *Theory and framework building*

Second, CES are in a continuous process of *co-evolution*. That is to say, system elements interact intricately with each other and their environment (including its emergent properties), influencing the evolution of each. Intrinsic feedback processes cause the nature of relations between agents and between agents and the system to change – themselves subsequently adapting in response to a changed environment. Therefore, in CES, elements have adaptive agency and are engaged in a continuous process of relational evolution.[41] This is critical to describing how complex adaptive systems change over the longer-term. Mitleton-Kelly summarises it astutely when she writes:

> Complex systems are ... made up of interacting agents, whose interactions create emergent properties, qualities, and patterns of behaviour. It is the actions of individual agents and the immense variety of those actions that constantly influence and create emergent macro patterns or structures. In turn the macro structure of a complex ecosystem influences individual entities, and the evolutionary process moves constantly between micro behaviours and emergent structures, each influencing and recreating each other.[42]

The diagram below is a graphical representation of the emergent, self-organising and co-evolutionary character of a complex adaptive (evolving) system.

In summary, a complex system is comprised of interactive and interdependent elements, with constitutive feedback processes which lead to emergent properties. These features mean that complex systems change and produce systemic outcomes through nonlinear trajectories, are sensitive to changes in initial conditions and these occur within and between distinct but variable phase spaces. Complex evolving systems consist of adaptive agents that have a latent capacity to self-organise in response to

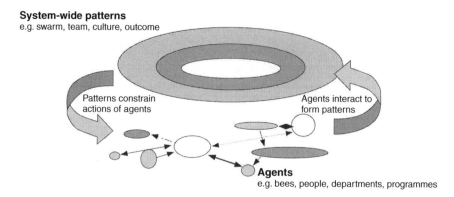

Figure 3.1 Complex adaptive system.[43]

perturbations, as well as co-evolve with each other and with the broader systemic environment.[44]

Complexity theory in the social sciences

In the last 20 years, complexity theory has been advocated for and applied across the gamut of the social sciences – particularly when interaction within and between social entities is conspicuous but predictability of systemic behaviour is low.[45] In this domain, the referent is a *complex social system* whereby the important interactions are the relations between *agents* as opposed to simple components of a system. In the field of International Relations (IR), the unpredictability of episodes in global politics has led scholars to laud the utility of complexity theory and its main tenets as an alternative – or at least addition – to dominant reductive IR theories[46] for better understanding key events in world affairs.[47] In development studies, complexity has drawn increasing attention in the last decade in investigating the value of complexity concepts for better understanding how social change occurs and how this might impact upon development policy-making and implementation.[48] Even in economics – a discipline synonymous with epistemological rigidity – there are signs that complexity theory is gaining traction in challenging neoclassical orthodoxy and advocating for evolving econometric and economic theory based on complexity concepts to explain economic phenomena such as growth and market failure.[49] Segments of organisational, business and management studies have embraced complexity theory in their work addressing practical organisational problems – such as organisational change management – in both the private and public sectors.[50] Complexity concepts have also had a significant effect on disciplines such as sociology,[51] social theory[52] and (social) psychology.[53]

Despite disciplinary difference, the central tenets of complexity theory have proven to be pertinent in the social sciences – particularly in understanding how and why change occurs within social systems. This interdisciplinary approach has enabled scholars to explore its utility for enhancing understanding of political, social and economic phenomena. However, these sentiments are not unanimous and there are many disagreements about the extent to which complexity concepts are transferable to human systems and organisations in the social sciences. Due to its genesis in the 'hard' sciences, there are those who advise caution when transposing complexity concepts into substantively different disciplinary domains. The following addresses the recurrent criticisms of applying complexity theory to social systems under methodological, practical and political concerns.

Hendrick identifies three main methological issues at stake for the critics.[54] First, that there are those who believe it is dangerous to 'cherry pick' and apply only convenient concepts in isolation when complexity theory should be applied as a holistic explanatory framework. These critics argue that, like the elements of a complex system itself, we need to recognise that the complex characteristics of a system are closely related and it is them working in concert that creates new order. Second, there are those who are concerned about the proliferation and diversity of definitions for complexity concepts. The associated fear is that the meaning of terms may become imprecise or distorted, rendering their application arbitrary or even misleading. Finally, theoretical purists are averse to the use of complexity as a vague metaphor or analogy and conjecture that it is not yet fleshed out sufficiently to be useful theory in social science. Whilst these are all valid warnings, such methodological contentions are not alien to the social sciences. Disparate definitions and the corollary assumptions that underpin them are recurrent in research in international relations and peace and conflict studies. It is therefore important to proceed prudently and make explicit the delineation of definitions and the scope of what is – and equally what cannot be – expected from their application.[55]

In practical terms, a persistent criticism of complexity theory is the lack of clarity on how it manifests in practice. This is in part due to the lack of empirical case studies to evidence its utility and leads to the accusation that it does not state explicitly what is to be done. In these scenarios, as Ramalingam concedes, complexity often leads to perplexity amongst practitioners and policy-makers;[56] or worse, to accusations that complexity is "just the latest management jargon" of consultants and complexologists selling their latest nostrum or "peddling managerial snake-oil".[57] Given its infancy in the social sciences, applications of complexity theory are vulnerable to this charge like any new paradigm. Moreover, the thrust of complexity theory is about process rather than product. In this sense, the perceived source of weakness should actually be viewed as the source of its strength – the complexity approach is not about providing *solutions for problems*, but *approaches to problems*. There remains, however, a concomitant need to exercise restraint and to avoid overestimating the applicability of complexity concepts as a panacea to challenges in analysing human systems.

From a political perspective, critics have stated that central tenets of complexity theory such as emergence and self-organisation sound a lot like *laissez-faire* market ideologies.[58] The implication is that complexity is a cloak for a neo-liberal marketization agenda. However, complexity theory notes that not all emergence and self-organisation is objectively 'good'. For example, complexity theory aids a clearer understanding of how negative events such as financial crises or genocides are also emergent outcomes of complex systems. Its application therefore advocates and attempts to create systems that reside at the 'edge of chaos' – i.e. those which are most resilient and robust due to an optimal combination of flexibility and control rather than a dogmatic ideational set of beliefs.[59]

Notwithstanding these contentions, applications of complexity theory across the social sciences reflect common foundational ideas about how we can understand and use empirical sources to evidence change in social systems where interaction and interdependence is high but predictability of systemic outcomes is low. Importantly these ideas do not depend upon a rigid and linear Newtonian cause-and-effect logic. Whilst these developments are significant, to date there has been little research produced on the applicability of complexity theory to conflict prevention, management and resolution[60] and even less so with regard to peace operations.[61] However, the multidimensional nature of contemporary peace missions and their operating environments, make this field a prime candidate for just that. The following section argues that understanding peace operations environments as complex systems can assist in understanding how change occurs as a result of and/or in relation to the activities of a mission.

Peace operations environments and the case for complexity

Peace operations environments can be depicted as CESs because they exhibit the core characteristics of a CES.[62] That is, when understood as a system they are replete with multiple actors that are interconnected in a plethora of ways leading to intricate interdependency. Furthermore, peace operations and the peace processes they assist in implementing are controlled by numerous positive and negative feedback processes. Finally, they continually produce emergent order as a result of their unique composition and partnerships, as well as changeable goals and objectives.

Peace operations environments contain a myriad of international, national and local level stakeholders. Similar to Ramalingam *et al.*'s description of international aid interventions, peace operations happen in "the context of a dense and globalised web of connections and relationships between individuals, communities, institutions, nations and groups of nations".[63] The peace operations bureaucracy itself functions through a distorted hierarchy that includes member states in the SC and GA, managers in the Secretariat and DPKO, senior and middle managers in field operations and the peacekeepers on the ground. The interactions between these actors produce vertical relations between stakeholders at all levels of magnitude. Furthermore, multidimensional missions are comprised of different sectors; *inter alia* the military, police and numerous civilian substantive sections, oversight and management entities, as well as partnership and cooperation with host government and civil society. Consequently, peace operations locales are typified by multiple interlinked elements.

In addition, a broad spectrum of tasks and activities are performed by different configurations of those same stakeholders. The military, police and civilian elements of peace operations conduct programming in security, rule of law, humanitarian, economic, governance, political, developmental and human rights spheres. The relations within each of these pillars are extensive, but the increasingly integrated nature of programmes

112 *Theory and framework building*

– such as Security Sector Reform (SSR), Disarmament, Demobilisation and Reintegration (DDR) or arranging and securing elections – has led to a proliferation of linkages and interdependencies across these functional areas. In this sense, multidimensional UN peace operations are invariably part of an overarching peacebuilding architecture tasked with cooperatively managing change in conflict-affected environments.[64] This adds another layer or dimension of interconnections. Similarly, the institutional capacity-building synonymous with modern missions implicates strong interdependencies between the mission and the host government and community. This means that peace operations environments contain a plethora of horizontal relationships between and across clusters of implementing agents, as well as those with the host state and society.

This is a straightforward and uncontroversial account of how peace operations environments are replete with interconnections and interactions across agents and dimensions of social, economic and political order. This array of vertical and horizontal relations means that these settings display high connectivity and intricate interdependence between elements and dimensions, of which peace operations are one. This is the archetypal quality of a complex social system. Although it is hardly new to highlight the multidimensionality of conflict-affected societies, complexity theory implies that acknowledging this reality and revealing the degree of connectivity between actors and programmes is a necessary precondition for understanding the intensity of feedback processes that 'control' emergent environmental outcomes.

In human systems, *feedback* relates to influence over action and behaviour, albeit dependent on the degree of connectivity between agents.[65] Given the notoriously ad hoc nature of peace operations, they are perennially reacting to both positive and negative events and changing 'on the fly'. This happens in a number of different ways. However, each of the avenues relies upon *feedback* processes to propagate or inhibit the alterations in a peace operation's conduct in relation to its systemic context.

Positive feedback can have a large effect (i.e. amplification) at the HQ level where strategic decisions that influence the character of mission mandates are made. For example, the practice since 1999 to mandate missions to protect civilians substantively changed the nature of peace operations from the top down (i.e. positive feedback). However, the unprecedented nature of much activity in peace operations means that positive feedback can also emanate from the field when a particular mission pioneers new initiatives that prove successful. For example, the innovation of public information components in the missions in Sierra Leone and Liberia were instrumental to changing the way in which these elements have operated since.[66] Negative feedback processes are also prevalent at the strategic level. For example, the predilections of some members of the SC to remain steadfast to a particular conception of peacekeeping based on consent, impartiality and minimum use of force acts as a control for what peace operations can and cannot be designed to do, with ramifications for expectations once deployed. In the field, negative feedback processes are omnipresent due to the prevalence of stringent policies, doctrinal frameworks and standard operating procedures that govern how mandates are implemented and the conduct of peacekeepers themselves.

Feedback processes in peace operations environments are both negative (i.e. they dampen the magnitude of deviation from current systemic behaviour) and positive (i.e. they amplify, and often substantively change, behaviour of the system). Moreover, the feedback processes are multidirectional. That is, they can be instigated from the bottom up, as well as from the top down. Consequently, these feedback processes common to all mission contexts are important to the way in which the actions and behaviours of peace operations transpire. Feedback in the systemic context is essential to the way a peace operation progresses over time and how it, in turn, impacts upon its environment. Complexity theory brings a focus on these feedback processes as well as an explanatory framework for understanding the direction and magnitude of their effects. In other words, enabling and disabling *emergent* behaviours through positive and/or negative feedback processes.

The system level structures and behavioural patterns of peace operations environments are difficult to predict based on simple knowledge of the individual traits and preferences of the agents and inputs involved.[67] For example, peace operations are mandated to accomplish certain core objectives such as DDR. It is straightforward to identify the overarching goals of a DDR programme – i.e. disarm ex-combatants, demobilise them from their chain of command and provide opportunities for them to reintegrate into civilian society. It is also likely that generic guidelines based on previous experiences will inform the design and planning for such a process. However, it is the local rules of interaction between the constituent parts of the system – e.g. the UN and the international donor community, the mission and the host government, the DDR programme and the ex-combatants – that dictate how such processes unfold. These constitutive relationships have a significant impact on how a mission interoperates with its systemic environment that is not easily predictable by observing the behaviours of its constituent parts.

In the realm of policing, mission UNPOL components are made up of multiple national contingents and units. These contributions often possess extremely different backgrounds regarding training and policing philosophy. However, notwithstanding operational challenges, they work together in ways and towards goals that do not necessarily reflect what they would normally (or indeed, preferably) do. Similarly, when these UNPOL operatives are tasked with police reform, the intended impact – i.e. improved local police services – is the emergent property of international-national collaboration and may not be a predictable product of those contributing to the process. Systemic outcomes relating to UNPOL is a product of multiple contributions but different to what might be predicted based on their separate characteristics. Emergence is accentuated further in peace operations due to the high turnover and short tenure of personnel in field missions. The frequent influx of new personnel with little familiarity with the job or the context further contributes to the unpredictability of perpetually new emergent order.

Negative (maladaptive) emergence also occurs in peace operations. For example, a recurrent criticism of peace operations is their ineffective coordination, particularly between military and non-military components. The various civilian, police and military elements of a mission have distinct organisational cultures and operate under their own procedures (at times even sub-sections – e.g. national military contingents operating with national caveats). This is a way unpredictable order emerges in the mission environment – in this instance, undesirable systemic behaviour stemming from the local rules of individual units, leading to incoherence at the systemic/macro-level.[68]

Given the multiagency character of peace operations and the increasingly integrated nature of programming, the form and function of missions is contingent on idiosyncratic organisational cultures, identities and procedures and the myriad of ways in which they interact. Furthermore, peace operations are one element of the broader environment and systemic outcomes that are contingent on the ways in which missions interoperate with other peacebuilding actors, host governments, civil society and local communities. The resultant emergent systemic identity and behaviour is consequently difficult to predict accurately based solely on knowledge of each in isolation. Whilst the challenges of integration and coordination at the systemic level are well-known,[69] complexity theory is a useful framework for uncovering and explaining these phenomena.[70] Although emergence can and should be expected in peace operations environments, its substance is difficult to predict due to the nonlinearity of relationships within the system and therefore hard to achieve by design. Therefore, complexity theory adds weight to the argument that the unique context-specific solutions that transpire in these settings can be understood as leading to new and oftentimes unexpected order and coherence – i.e. the *emergent property* of the system. Importantly, complexity theory also reminds us that this emergence is not always an objectively 'good' thing.

In summary, when a human society is affected by conflict – violent or otherwise – its complex adaptive nature is even more prevalent.[71] Societies embroiled in – or emerging from – conflict, are dynamical and complex environments.[72] Consequently, peace operations environments are multidimensional and have a range of stakeholders with different perspectives whose interrelationships are often non-linear. The feedback between these actors produces 'emergent' and often unpredictable outcomes. The impact of conflict on any specified level or unit of analysis will inevitably have consequences for higher and lower magnitude purlieus within the same system, in turn influencing change in that domain. This means that the social outcomes of peace processes cannot be predicted from looking at single issues in isolation, but has to attend to the influence of constantly changing context – i.e. its dynamics. It is also important to note that the elements of such a system are conscious and creative agents with interests and memory such that history matters to how these system-level outcomes transpire.

Whilst relatively nascent, there is a fledgling community of academic and policy-oriented researchers that advocate using principles and perspectives synonymous with complexity theory to understand UN peace operations as complex social systems.[73] Whilst some of the concepts in complexity theory are clearly relevant to understanding change in the context of peace operations, this is not to suggest that all of the theory is applicable all of the time. For example, it would be to draw an extremely long bow to suggest that the notion of 'attractors' can be transposed to map conflict phases or spaces or that 'self-organisation' best describes how missions are shaped to address new and changing political and operational challenges. The above represents a modest contribution to demonstrating how UN peace operations environments can be understood to display the core characteristics of complex systems. This is not intended to be a conclusive account or proof of peace operations locales as complex evolving systems. However, it can be understood as part of an attempt to build such a case and to explore the possibilities that doing so creates. Whilst I believe there is a compelling case, this can only be a point of departure and specific human systems such as peace operations need to be studied in their own right to overcome the limitations associated with such an importation of theory. Nevertheless, if this is to be believed, then hypothetically, the way in which change occurs in complex systems – i.e. emergent outcomes through non-linear trajectories that are sensitive to initial conditions, bounded by unique loci, and in the extreme, display self-organising and co-evolutionary qualities – may be useful in understanding the impact of peace operations (i.e. the type, extent and rationale for change).

Complex aspects of peace operations environments have significant implications for how missions are implemented, how we can understand them and how these understandings can inform efforts to monitor and evaluate progress. Notwithstanding compelling arguments to the contrary, the majority of peace operations activities are monitored and evaluated as if they are addressing singular or isolated problems or puzzles. This belies the complexity, or 'wickedness', and the systemic nature of conflict, fractured social orders and the way in which attempts to resolve them and rebuild in their wake unfold.[74] The unique perspectives that complexity theory brings to the study of change in such settings might have the potential to shed light on how M&E can better reflect the impact of peace

116 *Theory and framework building*

operations. In this vein, the following section demonstrates how the central claims and concepts of complexity theory correspond well with the challenges facing M&E in UNPOL identified in the previous chapter.

Complexity theory for overcoming the shortcomings with extant M&E

As I argued in Chapter 2, existing approaches to M&E in the context of peace operations suffer from a number of weaknesses. Seven major critiques were presented and in the following section I explore how complexity theory might help overcome them.

Causal ambiguity

The dominant views and theories of change undergirding M&E in peace operations tend to simplify the relationship between mission activities and system-level outcomes to a linear mechanistic results chain:

INPUTS → OUTPUTS → OUTCOMES → IMPACT

These accounts of change are based on three central assumptions: (1) *ceteris paribus* holds; (2) inputs are broadly proportionate to outputs and outcomes; and, (3) system-level outcomes equate to the summative product of sub-system level contributions. On the contrary, complexity theory brings a new perspective to bear on these issues based on its intrinsic treatment of non-linearity, as well as the feature of sensitive dependence.

Regarding *ceteris paribus* – i.e. 'all else remaining constant' – understanding of change rests upon the notion of an 'independent' variable and assumptions of linearity.[75] Complexity theory holds that in circumstances of multivariate change, this is an artificial construct and antithetical to the peace operations setting where systemic effects are the product of multiple interactions, adaptive agency and emergence. For example, with the plethora of actors, inter-linkages and (sometimes competing) agendas discussed above, system-level outcomes such as the creation of sustainable peace are not necessarily a direct result of the activities conducted by a mission. The presence of external influences means that exogenous factors play a constitutive role in eventual outcomes. An example relates to the security conditions in neighbouring territories whereby given their proximity, spill-over effects and associated interdependence, the effectiveness of the MINURCAT mission in Chad/CAR was widely believed to be inextricably linked to security outcomes in Darfur.[76] The same can be said of meddlesome neighbouring governments.[77] Consequently, complexity theory contends that *ceteris paribus* does not hold and that, on the contrary, systemic outcomes in peace operations are driven by a large number of variables – none of which can be understood to be independent – and provides a justification and explanatory framework for how change emerges through non-linear functions.

In relation to *input-outcome proportionality*, common practice is to explain tangible changes observed in a system as being proportional to adjustments in the inputs and therefore allow for some degree of attribution to those responsible for the inputs. Complexity theory contends that in complex systems, inputs and outputs cannot generally be correlated in a linear fashion with outcomes. It promotes two interrelated explanations for this. First, inputs to a complex system tend to diffuse unevenly. This happens because elements often have an irregular distribution and manifest in unequally structured sub-systems. Moreover, the social, economic and political bonds responsible for these distributions in the peace operations context are not likely to be of uniform strength in all parts of the system.[78] For example, in the case of police training, there may be a difference between absorption capacity of police in urban centres as opposed to rural locales due to disparities in, *inter alia*, competency, capacity and career incentives.

Second, this internal irregularity leads to externalities or unintended consequences. Despite good intentions, peace operations do not have exclusively positive and objectively beneficial impacts. On the contrary, their presence in a host country is notorious for having multiple negative 'side-effects' as well.[79] These are often unintended, at least at the macro level. For example, whilst the creation of camps and provision of humanitarian assistance for the internally displaced is often a critical task of peace operations, this can have negative consequences. Camps and what is provided therein can distort the incentive structure for those who are not displaced to emulate displacement if life-sustaining support is more readily available by doing so. Complexity theory articulates how the likelihood of potential repercussions mean that system-level net outcomes are not only the direct result of inputs, but are also a product of unintended consequences, some of which may be positive but others may be negative.[80]

Whilst this causal ambiguity and unpredictability in peace operations leads to 'surprising' outcomes that are disproportionate to inputs, their occurrence should not be surprising. Rather they are a symptom of the fact that peace operations are embedded in complex systems.[81] Complexity theory, therefore, provides theoretical underpinning for the case that no intervention in a complex human system can guarantee an intended, or indeed a singular, effect.[82] In this way, it adds value to understandings of how inputs (i.e. peace operation activities) are related to overall outcomes (e.g. improvement in public security) in non-linear rather than linear ways.

Regarding *summative impacts*, a common simplification of current convention is the view that the outputs and outcomes of a peace operations action are additive. That is, the assumption that:

(Action X → Output A → Outcome 1) + (Action Y → Output B → Outcome 2) = (Action X + Action Y → Output A + B → Outcome 1 + 2)

For example, if Action X was technical assistance (e.g. provision of vehicles, uniforms, etc) and Action Y was capacity-building through training (e.g. human rights course), the arithmetic approach above would suggest that outcomes relating to improved technical capacity to perform duties and enhanced human rights awareness, respectively, might lead to better crime control and realisation of due legal process in addressing post-conflict criminality. In other words, technical interventions are commonly assumed to lead to the behavioural change (e.g. UNPOL efforts to reform domestic police and criminal justice sectors). However, this is often not the case as Actions X and Y and their associated outcomes/impacts will likely have some of the unintended consequences mentioned above and constitute exogenous factors for other interdependent parts of the system. Extending the example above, it has often been the case that improving the effectiveness of the police to arrest and humanely detain criminals has overwhelmed the capacity of the judiciary to try and sentence the suspects. This invariably leads to high rates of lengthy pre-trial detention in terrible conditions ahead of any verdict.

Complexity theory points to the systemic nature of peace operations outcomes and their contingent production (i.e. emergence) as the reason why they defy a simple additive logic when it comes to gauging the cumulative effect of micro-level activities on macro-level outcomes. Ultimately, complexity theory sheds new light on how accumulative conceptions of impact in peace operations may miss the detail of how actions and their outputs interact to create meta-outcomes that are not necessarily additive products of meso-outcomes. In complexity terms, this relates not only to emergence, nonlinearity and externalities, but also to the notion of perturbation of the system and sensitive dependence. Departing from this mechanistic arithmetic, complexity theory offers an alternative and more nuanced view of systemic outcomes based on the concept of sensitive dependence.[83]

In sum, peace operations and their settings are antithetical to linear representations.[84] It is not feasible to make assessments based on *ceteris paribus* conditionality; the relationship between inputs and outcomes is disproportionate due to exogenous factors and externalities, and those same outcomes cannot simply be added together and deemed representative of the whole. Complexity theory brings more clarity to discussions of non-linearity and causality in peace operations. The issue of nonlinear change – i.e. the way in which change intended/desired by a peace operation occurs – is one of the areas that complexity theory holds most promise for attempts to monitor and evaluate the impact of peace operations.

Context-(in)sensitivity

Another critique of extant M&E is that it is not sufficiently context-sensitive and that this has ramifications for understanding and interpreting change. Dominant approaches often involve generic indicators and rarely include accurate baseline assessments. Alternatively, complexity theory emphasises the centrality of a nuanced rendering of the context for two main reasons. First, it is important to have a clear picture of the relevant system elements (i.e. stakeholders) as well as the way they relate due the integral role of local rules of interaction in the emergence of system-level outcomes. That is, if outcomes are to be understood accurately, they need to heed their emergent nature which is contingent on an appreciation of the potential influence of multiple and disparate actors.

Second, a detailed baseline account of initial conditions is crucial to informing the effect of sensitive dependence when interpreting outcomes. Embedded in complex systems, the impact of peace operations activities (equivalent to a perturbation) will be subject to sensitive dependence and hence susceptible to variations in initial conditions such that the observed outcomes can vary dramatically. For example, although activity X was observed to have produced outcome Y, that cause-effect relationship is not necessarily replicable or scalable. That is to say, similar activities will not automatically have the same impact in a different context or time-period. Likewise, expanding or multiplying the amount of the activity will not lead to directly proportional increases in the observed outcome. This is already widely recognised in peacekeeping literature and practice, manifest in the rejection of one-size-fits-all philosophies.[85] However, complexity theory adds an extra level of detail in understanding this and provides a way of explaining how overall outcomes cannot be easily reduced and attributed to initiating actions and inputs.[86]

Un-systemic

The preeminent M&E tools in peace operations tend to focus on units of analysis that underplay the systemic nature of producing outcomes. That is, they are either overly narrow or broad. In the first instance, much of current orthodoxy was seen to artificially silo the activities of sections such as UNPOL and treat their goals and accomplishments as independent of the other mission actors and stakeholders. Oppositely, complexity theory compels analysts to understand outcomes in their systemic context. Here again, the concept of emergence is important to understanding how achievements of systemic change are collectively constituted. Outcomes are the product of multiple contributions, dynamic interrelationships and enabling conditions and thus cannot be easily reduced to the actions of any individual or group of system elements in particular. For example, given the multiagency nature of programming, outcomes such as effective police reform are the result of collaboration between the peace operation and its diverse UNPOL contingent, the host government and a range of other stakeholders and hence not easily attributed to individual actors such as UNPOL. In other words, complexity theory implies that system level outcomes are irreducible to the discrete actions of individual peacekeepers, the programmes of neatly separate units or even of the mission overall. This perspective has the potential to underpin M&E that situates the outcomes in the rule of law domain in the broader context of actors working collaboratively towards these goals and has important ramifications for M&E that contains a more sophisticated treatment of attribution.

On the other hand, strategic level M&E often treats a peace operation and the effort of the 'international community' as a single unit of analysis or monolithic entity. This underplays the agency of sub-sections of missions and indeed the way these sub-entities interact to create emergent order and outcomes. As pointed out by Durch and England, "[i]n peace operations the actions of even small groups ... can have major implications for local stability and the achievement of the mission's mandate."[87] Complexity theory facilitates an analysis that emphasises the system and its inner workings and properties as a means of understanding, explaining and substantiating the emergent outcomes and behaviours observed at the systemic level.

Exclusive methods

Current M&E orthodoxy ensures that the approaches are designed and implemented, as well as interpreted and utilised without the participation of a broad range of relevant stakeholders. Furthermore, dominant modalities are heavily dependent on narrow, homogenous and often scarce data sources. Complexity theory points out that desired outcomes in peace operations are likely to be emergent and therefore a product of the peculiar interactions and interdependencies between the elements that comprise the system. It therefore suggests that to understand change under conditions of complexity, assessments cannot rely on the knowledge of only a limited set of actors or the privileging of a particular type of knowledge. In other words, a partial picture of change in these settings will produce only a partial account of how change has transpired and why. Whilst some scholars have recognised the importance of local and cultural dimensions of conflict environments,[88] complexity theory adds to these perspectives by providing a holistic vision of the relationship between a peace operation and its environment and, therefore, a means of interrogating change in such settings. Consequently, complexity theory presents the rationale to aim for a broad-based and inclusive approach to M&E if the nature and trajectory of emergent outcomes are to be deduced and captured.

Anti-learning

The final, but crucial, critique relates to the notion that dominant M&E in peace operations are primarily focused on accountability rather than learning. This has two significant consequences. First, this proclivity renders extant approaches rigid and inflexible. The unresponsive and inappropriate timeframes synonymous with this accountability modality constrain the frequency and timing of opportunities to update implementation plans and correct course. This periodic modality also inhibits the continuous gathering and accumulating knowledge from field experiences in real-time. Complexity theory contends that in order for a system (i.e. peace operation) to be resilient and to adapt to dynamic situations with rapidly changing conditions and objectives as well as harness new knowledge (i.e. learn), it is dependent on feedback processes. That is, a reliance upon ongoing and frequent ways in which the system's non-linear, inconsistent and emergent change is conveyed back to the elements of the system to inform adjustments (i.e. first-level learning).

Second, as a result of the breakdown or absence of feedback loops, the ability of M&E in the mission to contribute to an organisational learning process (i.e. second-level) is severely restricted. Complexity theory highlights the role of co-evolution in organisational learning. Peace operations and their environments are comprised of adaptive agents that possess the capacity to act consciously.[89] That is, an adaptive agent can perceive one's own state, as well as the state of other actors and their environment.[90] According to complexity theory, this adaptive agency plays a significant role in shaping the system, particularly in the way that feedback occurs, and leads to phenomena akin to self-organisation and co-evolution in peace operations. It further posits that co-evolution occurs when entities are highly connected[91] and, as a result, the evolution of each becomes contingent on the other. In peace operations, this happens between agents of the operation as well as between the mission and its operating environment. For learning-oriented M&E, this clearly points to the need for close connections (via feedback processes) between the learning infrastructure in the peace operations bureaucracy and field missions.

A complexity lens allows us to see that peace operations environments are comprised of adaptive agents who learn and adapt their behaviours, albeit in non-linear and unpredictable ways. This directly impacts upon the system's resilience/adaptability to external changes.[92] Therefore, complexity theory provides the justification that learning already occurs in peace operations continuously in collaborative and relational ways. It furthermore provides the foundation to argue that M&E intended to feed into organisational learning should look to capture these experiences whilst offering some guidance on how holistic M&E can harness the centrality of feedback to the process of co-evolution which is synonymous with iterative learning.[93]

Summary

The central claims and concepts of complexity theory correspond to the challenges to gauging impact of missions and contributing to organisational learning in the peace operations bureaucracy identified in the previous chapter. Therefore, complexity theory may hold potential to guide the design of M&E that can overcome the prevailing challenges relating to causal ambiguity, context-sensitivity, systemic understanding of change and outcomes, knowledge sources and participation, and learning objectives.[94]

There are now a growing number of researchers analysing the value of applying complexity thinking to M&E.[95] Furthermore, albeit very recently, there have been some efforts to develop practical approaches for doing so.[96] Similarly, communities of practice have promoted dialogue around the value of integrating complexity concepts into M&E – particularly in aid and humanitarian programming. All contend that complexity theory offers a useful framework for developing M&E that is better able to reflect unsteady and unpredictable progress towards goals in complex social systems.[97] Eoyang and Berkas clearly state the need for alternative approaches, claiming that as complex adaptive systems,

> ..human systems are dynamic, entangled, scale independent, transformative and emergent. These characteristics challenge the basic assumptions of traditional evaluation methods. They necessitate new evaluation approaches that are as rich and varied as the human systems they are designed to assess.[98]

Others have conjectured that, "complexity [monitoring and] evaluation ... may provide useful insights to help overcome the serious flaws in current practice".[99] However, meeting this challenge – i.e. recognising and facing up to complex realities – has been described as "the greatest torment" of monitoring and evaluating experts.[100]

The purported benefits are pertinent to the challenge of M&E in peace operations that have become increasingly engaged in early peacebuilding efforts, regularly engaging in institutional change in support of social transformation. As identified in Chapter 1, one of the most significant components of these efforts is the increasingly transformational aims and objectives of UNPOL regarding police and rule of law reform. That is, peace operations and their UNPOL components are in the business of addressing 'wicked problems'. However, as yet, there has been little attempt to draw on complexity concepts in the design of M&E for peace operations and their police components. The following section identifies a number of ramifications of applying a complexity-lens to the task of designing M&E for peace operations, including how it can address and potentially remedy the deficiencies of extant approaches.

Ramifications of complexity theory augmented M&E for peace operations

M&E in complex systems requires a different approach to measuring and describing, causal analysis and reporting and using findings.[101] M&E

underpinned by the central tenets of complexity theory therefore has a number of implications for extant practice in peace operations.[102]

First, it implies a shift in its *purpose and scope*. Whilst conventional M&E is often conceived of as a top-down "compliance function",[103] complexity-oriented-M&E is about 'what is (not) working and why' and hence the approach needs to facilitate learning and adaptation.[104] That is, its purpose is not *causal attribution* and *credit-taking* but contribution-centric *impact assessment* and *learning*. The general aims of traditional M&E to account to political masters[105] are superseded by the production of context-sensitive impact assessments based on rapid and iterative feedback that can enable site and situation specific learning for real-time adaptive management of missions in dynamic and unpredictable conditions.[106] Regarding scope, it constitutes a move away from the empirical 'testing' of prescriptive intervention logics, towards a framework that facilitates knowledge acquisition and enables innovation and reflexivity. It is therefore introspective vis-à-vis change theories – continuously reflecting on the extent to which the actions and strategy of the mission suit the system under assessment for longer-term organisational adaptation (i.e. second-level learning). Both of these promise to enhance a mission's agility to learn from experiences, as well as its ability to adapt strategies and tactics accordingly to support emergent outcomes 'as it goes' over the periodic packaging of successes and failures for strategic accountability purposes.[107] Ultimately, the purpose is to shift away from the 'fear of failure' engendered by existing modalities, towards a 'hunger for learning'.[108]

Second, complexity-oriented-M&E constitutes subtle but important adjustments to the referent such that there is a *re-focusing* of M&E. In order to correct the narrow focus of conventional M&E, complexity-oriented approaches focus on the system and its systemic properties and behaviour.[109] This demands assessments that uncover the ways in which a peace operation is intertwined with its systemic environment creating interdependencies, how this occurs in numerous ways, across multiple units of analysis and all different levels and dimensions of the overarching system, as well as what this means for understanding progress and change.[110] Furthermore, in order to reflect the prevalence of emergence, complexity-oriented approaches focus on identifying non-linear and dynamical change,[111] rather than dynamic or static, capturing and harnessing the reality that expectations and outcomes are emergent, rather than predetermined.[112] This means it is fundamentally concerned with identifying critical feedback processes and seeking out the unexpected and surprising, including a focus on the effect of exogenous factors and the nature of unintended consequences rather than retrospectively rationalising the ones that were intended by design.[113] Ultimately, this demands more focus on the 'M' of 'M&E'.[114]

Third, given these shifts in the purpose, scope and focus, complexity-oriented-M&E demands new thinking about the task at hand and therefore requires alterations and augmentation to the *methods and approach* employed. The intrinsic uncertainty and unpredictability implies analysis more akin to historical research that changes the question from 'did x cause y?' to 'what is happening and why'? This requires different and multiple approaches and tools that reveal more effective and triangulated results and identify vicious and virtuous circles to produce dynamic and emergent results about what is happening.[115] Similarly, to reflect the diversity of system elements under analysis, M&E needs to be cognisant and inclusive of divergent and changing perspectives on what is happening, as well as what is valued and should be measured, what constitutes credible evidence and how it should be weighed in the interpretation of findings.[116] This demands inclusive and participatory approaches to the selection information sources and interpretation, including the construction of narratives about events and processes capable of making sense of nonlinearity, sensitive dependence and emergence. Furthermore, the methods and approach employed must be flexible and adaptive, grounded in the belief that M&E must be as nimble and supple as possible to reflect the dynamic nature of the system under analysis.[117] This means privileging the continuous reappraisal of monitoring sources and evaluative criteria so as to retain currency as the system evolves and conditions and objectives change.[118] The more detailed implications for methodology, methods, tools and techniques will be taken up in the following chapter.

Fourth, M&E itself needs to be understood and embraced as part of the complex system it is assessing. Conventional M&E has traditionally been perceived as a rational – even apolitical/neutral – technocratic, data-producing endeavour.[119] Monitors and evaluators are generally characterised as – and often profess to be – external and independent. They usually claim to employ an objective methodology, accordingly designed without much, if any, participation beyond the M&E experts and their commissioners. However, in reality M&E processes co-exist alongside the change they are designed to track. As Imam *et al.* note: "[M&E] can be seen both as a system itself, and as a sub-system that provides feedback to a broader system."[120] Complexity-oriented-M&E therefore recognises its own role in the system – relinquishing any claims to objectivity or impartiality – and attends to its latent capacity to contribute to change as well as track it.[121] Furthermore, the findings of current orthodoxy are invariably targeted at and tailored towards political masters and funders as a primary means of justifying expenditures, demonstrating success and occasionally explaining hold-ups or failures. The implications for methodologies and approach discussed above lead to an inclusive and participatory process, as opposed to a tool with its intellectual engine-room consisting of a centralised pool of M&E 'experts'. Complexity-oriented-M&E further reflects its part in the system by ensuring that the findings are fed back into this stakeholder forum to support local ownership of the process, as well as the M&E itself.

For peace operations, complexity theory presents a framework through which M&E can embrace what have to date been seen as 'messy realities' – a flexible and adaptive alternative to reductive linear modelling with the potential to strengthen understandings of change and progress, as well as elucidating a menu of promising options for action emanating from M&E findings. To realise these benefits requires subtle but significant adjustments to the purpose, scope and focus of assessments, a reconfiguration of the methods employed and an awareness of the intrinsic nature of M&E to affecting as well as tracking change. The qualities and potential insights promised by complexity-oriented M&E offer a possible corrective/antidote to the shortcomings of current orthodoxy. In relation to UNPOL, this is particularly salient in the realm of police reform. It seems that the stage is set for the arrival of complexity thinking in M&E where peace operations are tasked with assisting and managing change in complex social systems.

However, this does not render obsolete existing approaches that are well-established and often entrenched in institutional practice.[122] Some elements of peace operations work are more amenable to linear/mechanistic modelling and assessment than others. For example, the Disarmament and Demobilisation components of a DDR programme are often accurately measured using tangible, quantitative indicators and their impact assessed according to linear logic. It is straightforward to suggest that the number of small arms and light weapons collected at a cantonment site is a good measure of effective disarmament. However the difficulty of assessing the impact of the 'reintegration' component of DDR reiterates why linear models often fall short when it comes to M&E of holistic programmes. Many variables are important to an ex-combatant successfully reinserting themselves into society, ranging from acceptance by family/community, through to access and commitment to educational/vocational training as a means of finding alternative gainful employment. Outcomes relating to this cannot be captured using quantitative metrics of how many people enrolled in the reintegration programme or attended an arbitrary amount of classes. This requires M&E that targets behavioural change and social impact.

Ultimately, the range of different activities undertaken in peace operations demands the employment of a range of methods and approaches as appropriate. What is crucial is that they are utilised in a theoretically coherent fashion and their respective weaknesses are revealed and, where possible, mitigated.[123] In this sense, complexity-oriented M&E is a means to an end, not a means in and of itself.

Conclusion

In this chapter I have highlighted how complexity concepts can be utilised to better understand peace operations and their conflict-affected host societies. The case has been made across the social sciences that the characteristics of natural complex systems are both germane to and appropriate for a human social system. It was argued herein that peace operations' environments can be seen to display the defining features of complex systems and that consequently many of the challenges facing contemporary peace operations are akin to multidimensional and interdependent 'messes' rather than simple, isolated and easily solvable 'puzzles'.[124] Furthermore, the societies that peace operations assist and interact with are open and dynamical systems, reproducing and evolving along contingent trajectories – that is, trajectories influenced but never fully determined by a large number of factors, some of which are intended by the peace operations, others not. Therefore, this is not about saying 'the problem is complex' in a superficial manner or attaching a label to peace operations to describe how complicated their planning, implementation and management might be. Peace operations always have been and always will be difficult endeavours. Rather, it is about representing the peace operations realm as a complex system that has idiosyncratic behaviours, some of which are antithetical to understanding and observing through the exclusive application of simple logics and linear philosophies.

As de Coning suggests, "Peacekeeping operations and the conflict systems within which they operate are truly complex. It follows that planning something that is complex would require an approach that is quite different."[125] Consequently, it is important to understand what complexity theory adds and introduces to our understandings of peace operations. First, complexity theory brings together into a holistic theoretical framework what are otherwise disparate theoretical vignettes. Therefore, complexity theory is not promoted here as a substitute for existing theories of peace operations and how they function, rather as an augmentation and supplement to extant analytical frameworks to plug the important gaps that they leave. However, for all that it simply reinforces in existing theories about peace operations, complexity theory also has novelty value. It offers new insights and perspectives on processes in peace operations environments that are simply deemed to be illogical or idiosyncratic when viewed through the prism of traditional social scientific theory.[126] In particular, complexity theory adds value by providing an explanatory framework that: makes sense of non-linear dynamics and causal ambiguity; prioritises sensitivity to context and initial conditions; privileges a systemic perspective; encourages an inclusive and participatory approach; and promotes a learning-orientation for 'improving' rather than 'proving'. In these ways it offers genuine promise for overcoming the shortcomings associated with current thinking and practice regarding M&E. Furthermore, the complexity approach is not about providing 'solutions *for* problems', but 'approaches *to* problems'.

Based upon this proposition, it was demonstrated that the main claims and concepts of complexity theory map neatly to the challenges facing M&E in peace operations identified in Chapter 2. It was therefore argued that these concepts could have important implications for the design of M&E that is tailored to these endeavours. In particular, it was argued that complexity-oriented-M&E has the potential to illuminate the dynamics of change in the context of peace operations. The chapter proceeded to identify the main ramifications of complexity-oriented-M&E as an adjunct to – and means to overcome the aforementioned deficiencies associated with – extant approaches. It highlighted important alterations to the purpose, scope, focus, methods and perception of M&E such that it can be more outcome and impact focused, flexible, multi-source, context-sensitive, systemic, inclusive and learning oriented.

If there is acknowledgement that peace operations environments behave akin to complex systems then the aim should be to work with those features and properties, rather than ignore, or worse reject, them in the way we engage them analytically. It is therefore important to recognise what this means for their planning, implementation and management. The latent unpredictability dictates that such complexity cannot be overcome or solved. Rather, it must be revealed and attempts made to manage it. As Clement and Smith explain, "In a complex environment predictability is low, unintended consequences are many, and effectively organizing and managing resources becomes both more daunting and more essential."[127] One of the foremost tools at the disposal of peace operations for guiding the employment of scarce resources is M&E. It seems logical that attempts to assess progress in these settings should countenance and reflect that complexity. Whilst this realisation seems straightforward, unlocking the potential benefits of applying complexity concepts in M&E will not only require a change in what is done, but a substantive change and focus on how it is done.

The following chapter develops an M&E framework from which a case-specific methodology can be derived for assessing the impact of UNPOL in multidimensional peace operations that embeds the strengths of extant approaches in an approach underpinned by some of the concepts and ideas introduced here.

Notes

1 Henry L. Mencken, "The Divine Afflatus", *Evening Mail* (New York: November 16, 1917).
2 United Nations Peacekeeping Operations: Principles and Guidelines", ed. Peacekeeping Best Practive Section (New York; UN, 2008) 8, 18, 66; Robert Egnell, *Complex Peace Operations and Civil-Military Relations: Winning the Peace*, Cass Military Studies (Routledge, 2009); Kristine St-Pierre, *Then and Now: Understanding the Spectrum of Complex Peace Operations* (Ottawa: Pearson Peacekeeping Centre, 2008).
3 Cedric de Coning, "Planning for Success", in *Managing Complexity: Political and Managerial Challenges in United Nations Peace Operations*, eds. Caty Clement and Adam C. Smith (New York: International Peace Institute, 2009), 24–5; Cedric de Coning and Paul Romita, "Monitoring and Evaluation of Peace

Operations", (New York, Oslo; International Peace Institute & Norwegian Institute of International Affairs, November 2009) 4–6.
4 See, for example: Norbert Wiener, *Cybernetics* (Cambridge, MA: MIT Press, 1948); Ludwig von Bertalanffy, *General System Theory: Foundations, Development, Applications* (New York: George Braziller, 1968); Gregoire Nicolis and Ilya Prigogine, *Exploring Complexity* (New York: Freeman and Co, 1989).
5 Melanie Mitchell, *Complexity: A Guided Tour* (Oxford: Oxford University Press, 2011); Neil Johnson, *Simply Complexity: A Clear Guide to Complexity Theory* (Oneworld, 2009).
6 For further explanation of differences between simple, complicated, complex (and chaotic) systems, see: R. Ackoff, *Redesigning the Future: A Systems Approach to Societal Problems* (New York: John Wiley and Sons, 1974); D. Snowden, "Cynefin: A Sense of Time and Space, the Social Ecology of Knowledge Management", in *Knowledge Horizons: The Present and the Promise of Knowledge Management*, eds. Charles Despres and Daniele Chauvel (Oxford: Butterworth-Heinemann, 2000).
7 Frances Westley, Brenda Zimmerman, and Michael Q. Patton, *Getting to Maybe: How the World Is Changed?* (Canada: Random House, 2006), 9.
8 Peter Allen, "What Is Complexity Science? Knowledge of the Limits of Knowledge", *Emergence: Complexity & Organization* 3, no. 1 (2001): 27–9, 36–9.
9 P. Coveney and R. Highfield, *Frontiers of Complexity: The Search for Order in a Chaotic World* (London: Faber & Faber, 1996), 5–10.
10 Robert Jervis, *System Effects: Complexity in Political and Social Science* (Princeton, New Jersey: Princeton University Press, 1997), 12–13.
11 The following features and properties are a synthesised list drawing on numerous attempts across different disciplines to summarise the core characteristics of complex systems. See, *inter alia*: D. Hendrick, "Complexity Theory and Conflict Transformation: An Exploration of Potential and Implications", in *Working Paper* (Bradford: Department of Peace Studies, University of Bradford, 2009), 6–7; B. Ramalingam, "Exploring the Science of Complexity Ideas and Implications for Development and Humanitarian Efforts", in *Working Paper 285* (London: Overseas Development Institute, 2008); Eve Mitleton-Kelly, "Ten Principles of Complexity and Enabling Infrastructures", in *Complex Systems and Evolutionary Perspectives on Organisations: The Application of Complexity Theory to Organisations*, ed. Eve Mitleton-Kelly (Oxford: Elsevier, 2003).
12 P. H. Longstaff, "Security, Resilience, and Communication in Unpredictable Environments Such as Terrorism, Natural Disasters and Complex Technology", (Harvard University Program on Information Resources Policy, 2005), 88.
13 Connectivity is defined by tight and loose 'coupling' – i.e. degree of 'epistatic interaction'.
14 Russ Marion, *The Edge of Organization: Chaos and Complexity Theories of Formal Social Systems* (Thousand Oaks: Sage, 1999), 74–9.
15 Jervis, *System Effects: Complexity in Political and Social Science*, 125.
16 Glenda H. Eoyang, "A Brief Introduction to Complexity in Organizations", (Circle Pines, MN: Chaos Limited, Inc., 1996), 5; S. Kauffman, *At Home in the Universe: The Search for Laws of Complexity* (Oxford: Oxford University Press, 1996), 21.
17 F. Heylighen, *The Science of Self-Organization and Adaptivity* (Brussels, Belgium: Center Leo Apostel, Free University of Brussels, 2001); Jervis, *System Effects: Complexity in Political and Social Science*, 125.
18 Eoyang, "A Brief Introduction to Complexity in Organizations", 5.
19 D. Byrne, *Complexity Theory and the Social Sciences: An Introduction* (London: Routledge, 1998), 172.

20 Ramalingam, "Exploring the Science of Complexity Ideas and Implications for Development and Humanitarian Efforts", 17.
21 James McGlade and Elizabeth Garnsey, "The Nature of Complexity", in *Complexity and Co-Evolution: Continuity and Change in Socio-Economic Systems*, eds. E. Garnsey and J. McGlade (Cheltenham, UK: Edward Elgar, 2006), 5; Marion, *The Edge of Organization: Chaos and Complexity Theories of Formal Social Systems*, 29–32.
22 Steven Johnson, *Emergence: The Connected Lives of Ants, Brains, Cities and Software* (New York: Penguin Books, 2001), 11–17.
23 Reuben Ablowitz, "The Theory of Emergence", *Philosophy of Science* January (1939): 2–3.
24 Westley, Zimmerman, and Patton, *Getting to Maybe: How the World Is Changed?*
25 R. Stacey, *Complexity and Creativity in Organisations* (San Francisco: Berrett-Koehler Publishers, 1996), 23–8.
26 To emphasise the point, Ulam compared the prevailing view of nonlinear systems to the idea of 'non-elephant animals at the zoo'. Ulam cited D. Campbell *et al.*, "Experimental Mathematics: The Role of Computation in Nonlinear Science", *Communications of the Association for Computing Machinery* 28, no. 4 (1985).
27 S. Rihani, *Complex Systems Theory and Development Practice* (London: Zed Books, 2002), 3.
28 Longstaff, "Security, Resilience, and Communication in Unpredictable Environments Such as Terrorism, Natural Disasters and Complex Technology", 88.
29 Stacey, *Complexity and Creativity in Organisations*, 65; Marion, *The Edge of Organization: Chaos and Complexity Theories of Formal Social Systems*, 41.
30 McGlade and Garnsey, "The Nature of Complexity", 5.
31 See, for example: Edward N. Lorenz, "Deterministic Nonperiodic Flow", *Journal of the Atmospheric Sciences* 20, no. 2 (1963); Edward N. Lorenz, "Predictability: Does the Flap of a Butterfly's Wings in Brazil Set Off a Tornado in Texas?", in *American Association for the Advancement of Science, 139th Meeting* (Sheraton Park Hotel, 1972).
32 Rihani, *Complex Systems Theory and Development Practice*, 8.
33 Glenda H. Eoyang, "The Practitioner's Landscape", *Emergence: Complexity & Organization* 6, no. 1–2 (2004): 58.
34 A 'Periodic Attractor' is where a system moves through its phase space repeatedly and periodically (e.g. un-dampened pendulum), whilst a 'fixed point attractor' is a system phase space where the system behaviour tends towards a single centre of gravity (e.g. dampened pendulum).
35 The 'edge of chaos' is a systemic state that occurs between two extreme states where a system's equilibrium is never fixed, nor disintegrated entirely – also referred to as the 'Chaotic', 'Butterfly' or 'Lorenz' attractor.
36 Coveney and Highfield, *Frontiers of Complexity: The Search for Order in a Chaotic World*, 232.
37 Kevin Dooley, "A Nominal Definition of Complex Adaptive Systems", *The Chaos Network* 8, no. 1 (1996).
38 Mitleton-Kelly, "Ten Principles of Complexity and Enabling Infrastructures", 1, 7.
39 Heylighen, *The Science of Self-Organization and Adaptivity*, 4–5.
40 Frans M. van Eijnatten, "Chaordic Systems Thinking: Some Suggestions for a Complexity Framework to Inform a Learning Organization", *The Learning Organization* 11, no. 6 (2004).
41 E. Garnsey and J. McGlade, eds., *Complexity and Co-Evolution: Continuity and Change in Socio-Economic Systems* (Cheltenham, UK: Edward Elgar, 2006), 3–4.

42 Mitleton-Kelly, "Ten Principles of Complexity and Enabling Infrastructures", 26.
43 Glenda H. Eoyang, "Human Systems Dynamics: Complexity-Based Approach to a Complex Evaluation", in *Systems Concepts in Evaluation – an Expert Anthology*, eds. Bob Williams and Iraj Imam (Point Reyes, CA: EdgePress/American Evaluation Association, 2006), 125.
44 Mitchell, *Complexity: A Guided Tour*, 13.
45 See: Byrne, *Complexity Theory and the Social Sciences: An Introduction*.
46 For example, realism and liberalism, that have implicitly grown out of linear paradigms borrowed from Newtonian science although it has been argued that the linear paradigm emerged from ideas of Hobbes, Descartes and Locke – see: Rihani, *Complex Systems Theory and Development Practice*, 3. When the study of complexity is applied to human systems, it is often assumed to imply constructivist perspectives. This confusion is easy to understand because both complexity and constructivism share some basic principles, including emergence, high levels of interdependence in a system, unreliable causality and continuing transformation over time. Indeed, these common principles result in overlapping practices between the two perspectives. G. Eoyang and T. H. Berkas, *Evaluating Performance in a Complex Adaptive System* (Chaos Limited/Search Institute, 1998), 2–3.
47 See, for example: Jervis, *System Effects: Complexity in Political and Social Science*; N. E. Harrison, ed. *Complexity in World Politics, Concepts and Methods of a New Paradigm* (Albany: State University of New York, 2006); Emilian Kavalski, "The Fifth Debate and the Emergence of Complex International Relations Theory: Notes on the Application of Complexity Theory to the Study of International Life", *Cambridge Review of International Affairs* 20, no. 3 (2007); Antoine Bousquet and Simon Curtis, "Beyond Models and Metaphors: Complexity Theory, Systems Thinking and International Relations", *Cambridge Review of International Affairs* 24, no. 1 (2011); Robert Geyer and Steve Pickering, "Applying the Tools of Complexity to the International Realm: From Fitness Landscapes to Complexity Cascades", *Cambridge Review of International Affairs* 24, no. 1 (2011); J. Urry, *Global Complexity* (Cambridge: Polity Press, 2003).
48 See, for example: Rihani, *Complex Systems Theory and Development Practice*; Ben Ramalingam, *Aid on the Edge of Chaos: Rethinking International Cooperation in a Complex World* (New York: Oxford University Press, 2013); Robert Chambers, *Whose Reality Counts? Putting the First Last* (s.l.: Stylus Publishers Llc, 1997); Alan Fowler, "Complexity Thinking and Social Development, Connecting the Dots", *The Broker*, no. 7 (2008); Mark Cabaj, *Understanding Poverty as a Complex Issue and Why That Matters* (Ottawa, Ontario: Caledon Institute for Social Policy, 2009).
49 See, for example: Lawrence E. Blume and Steven N. Durlauf, eds., *The Economy as an Evolving Complex System, III: Current Perspectives and Future Directions*, Santa Fe Institute Studies on the Sciences of Complexity (Oxford: Oxford University Press, 2005); R. H. Day, *Complex Economic Dynamics: An Introduction to Dynamical Systems and Market Mechanisms* (Cambridge, MA: MIT Press, 1994); W. B. Arthur, "Complexity and the Economy", *Science* 284 (1999); P. Krugman, "What Economists Can Learn from Evolutionary Theorists", in *European Association for Evolutionary Political Economy* (1996); P. Ormerod, *Butterfly Economics: A New General Theory of Social and Economic Behaviour* (London: Faber and Faber, 1998); Erik Beinhocker, *The Origin of Wealth: Evolution, Complexity and the Radical Remaking of Economics* (Harvard Business School Press, 2007).
50 See, for example: Peter Senge, Charlotte Roberts, and Bryan J. Smith, *The Fifth Discipline: The Art and Practice of the Learning Organization* (Bantam Dell, 1990); Eve Mitleton-Kelly, ed. *Complex Systems and Evolutionary Perspectives on*

Organisations: The Application of Complexity Theory to Organisations (Oxford: Elsevier, 2003); R. D. Stacey, *Strategic Management and Organisational Dynamics: The Challenge of Complexity to Ways of Thinking About Organisations* (New York: Prentice Hall, 2007).

51 Sylvia Walby, "Complexity Theory, Systems Theory and Multiple Intersecting Social Inequalities", *Philosophy of the Social Sciences* 37, no. 4 (2007); R. Mayntz, "Chaos in Society: Reflections on the Impact of Chaos Theory on Sociology", in *The Impact of Chaos on Science and Society*, eds. Celso Grebogi and James Yorke (Tokyo: United Nations University Press, 1997).

52 John A. Smith and Chris Jenks, *Qualitative Complexity: Ecology, Cognitive Processes and the Re-Emergence of Structures in Post-Humanist Social Theory* (New York: Routledge, 2006).

53 R. Axelrod, *The Evolution of Cooperation* (New York: Basic Books, 1984); Niklas Luhmann, *Social Systems* (Stanford: Stanford University Press, 1995).

54 Hendrick, "Complexity Theory and Conflict Transformation: An Exploration of Potential and Implications", 17–21.

55 Hendrick, "Complexity Theory and Conflict Transformation: An Exploration of Potential and Implications", 20. However, Mitleton-Kelly states that we mustn't be afraid to move beyond metaphor in applying Complexity to the social world as human communities are complex evolving systems in their own right. See: Mitleton-Kelly, "Ten Principles of Complexity and Enabling Infrastructures", 4.

56 Ben Ramalingam, "Aid on the Edge of Chaos: Exploring Complexity Sciences in International Development and Humanitarian Work" (paper presented at the LSE Complexity Research Programme, Events 2010, London, 22 April 2010).

57 O. Sorenson, "'Book Review' of Eve, R., Horsfall, S. And Lee, M. 'Emergence'", *Chaos, Complexity and Sociology* 1, no. 149–51 (1999); Ramalingam, "Exploring the Science of Complexity Ideas and Implications for Development and Humanitarian Efforts", 7; J. Paley, "Complex Adaptive Systems and Nursing", *Nursing Inquiry* 14, no. 3 (2007): 234.

58 Ben Ramalingam, "Evaluation and the Science of Complexity", in *International Conference on Evaluating the Complex* (Oslo, Norway: Norwegian Agency for Development Cooperation [NORAD], 2008), 78.

59 See EN 34 above. Ramalingam, "Evaluation and the Science of Complexity", 78.

60 Notable exceptions all emanating in the last decade, include: Walter C. Clemens Jr., "Complexity Theory as a Tool for Understanding and Coping with Ethnic Conflict and Development Issues in Post-Soviet Eurasia". *International Journal of Peace Studies* 6, no. 2 (2011); D. Körppen, N. Ropers, and Hans J. Gießmann, eds., *The Non-Linearity of Peace Processes: Theory and Practice of Systemic Conflict Transformation* (Opladen/Farmington Hills: Barbara Budrich Verlag, 2011); Wendell. Jones, "Complexity, Conflict Resolution, and How the Mind Works", *Conflict Resolution Quarterly* 20, no. 4 (2003); Peter T. Coleman, "Conflict, Complexity, and Change: A Meta-Framework for Addressing Protracted, Intractable Conflict – III", *Journal of Peace Psychology* 12, no. 4 (2006); Peter Coleman, "Protracted Conflicts as Dynamical Systems: Guidelines and Methods for Intervention", in *The Negotiator's Fieldbook*, eds. Andrea Schneider and Christopher Honeyman (Chicago: American Bar Association, 2006); G. Eoyang and Lois Yellowthunder, "Complexity Models and Conflict: A Case Study from Kosovo", in *Conference on Conflict and Complexity* (University of Kent, Canterbury: Conflict Research Society and Conflict Analysis Research Centre, 2008); Hendrick, "Complexity Theory and Conflict Transformation: An Exploration of Potential and Implications".

61 For recent examples that touch on this, see: S. P. Campbell, "(Dis)Integration, Incoherence and Complexity in UN Post-Conflict Interventions", *International Peacekeeping* 15, no. 4 (2008); de Coning, "Planning for Success"; Clement and Smith, "Managing Complexity: Political and Managerial Challenges in United Nations Peace Operations".
62 By 'peace operations environment', I mean systemic context within which peace operations exist and function.
63 Ramalingam, "Exploring the Science of Complexity Ideas and Implications for Development and Humanitarian Efforts", 12.
64 Cedric de Coning, "Coherence and Coordination in United Nations Peacebuilding and Integrated Missions: A Norwegian Perspective", (Oslo: Norwegian Institute of International Affairs, 2007), 14; Chiyuki Aoi, Cedric de Coning, and Ramesh Thakur, "Unintended Consequences, Complex Peace Operations and Peacebuilding Systems", in *Unintended Consequences of Peacekeeping Operations*, eds. Chiyuki Aoi, Cedric de Coning, and Ramesh Thakur (Tokyo: United Nations University Press, 2007) 5; de Coning, "Planning for Success", 26–7.
65 Mitleton-Kelly, "Ten Principles of Complexity and Enabling Infrastructures", 16.
66 C. Hunt, "Public Information as a Mission Critical Component of West African Peace Operations", in *KAIPTC Monograph No. 5* (Accra, Ghana/New York: Kofi Annan International Peacekeeping Training Centre/United Nations Peacekeeping Best Practices Section, 2006).
67 Others have labelled this uncertainty in terms of 'peacekeeping ambiguity'. See, for example: Michael Lipson, "Performance under Ambiguity: International Organization Performance in UN Peacekeeping". *The Review of International Organizations* 5, no. 3 (2010).
68 Marion, *The Edge of Organization: Chaos and Complexity Theories of Formal Social Systems*, 29–32.
69 See, for example: Kathleen Jennings and Anja Kaspersen, "Introduction: Integration Revisited". *International Peacekeeping* 15, no. 4 (2008).
70 Campbell, "(Dis)Integration, Incoherence and Complexity in UN Post-Conflict Interventions".
71 Hendrick, "Complexity Theory and Conflict Transformation: An Exploration of Potential and Implications", 55.
72 See, for example: Oliver Wils *et al.*, *The Systemic Approach to Conflict Transformation Concept and Fields of Application* (Berghof Foundation for Peace Support, 2006), 35–6; Coleman *et al.*, "Intractable Conflict as an Attractor: Presenting a Dynamical Model of Conflict, Escalation, and Intractability", 341–3; Hendrick, "Complexity Theory and Conflict Transformation: An Exploration of Potential and Implications", 24–31.
73 See for example: Clement and Smith, "Managing Complexity: Political and Managerial Challenges in United Nations Peace Operations".; de Coning, "Planning for Success", 24; see also Cedric thesis.
74 This reality has become more pertinent as these operations have increasingly engaged in early peacebuilding efforts, regularly getting involved in institutional change in support of social transformation. See: Menkhaus, "State Fragility as a Wicked Problem", 85–98.
75 See for example: Paul Diehl and Daniel Druckman, *Evaluating Peace Operations* (Boulder; Lynne Rienner, 2010).
76 Interview: Office of Operations Official, UN DPKO – New York, February 2009.
77 "Exit Strategies and Peace Consolidation in State-Building Operations", In *Report on Wilton Park Conference 965* (CIS; University of Oxford, 2009), 4.

78 Longstaff, "Security, Resilience, and Communication in Unpredictable Environments Such as Terrorism, Natural Disasters and Complex Technology", 88.
79 Commonly cited examples are: incentivising and/or contributing to corruption and organised criminality such as trafficking in people, arms and drugs; producing distortions of the host country economy and labour markets; and, peacekeepers have at times perpetrated sexual gender-based violence as well as contributed to the transmission of HIV/Aids. See: Aoi, de Coning, and Thakur, "Unintended Consequences, Complex Peace Operations and Peacebuilding Systems".
80 The likely existence of exogenous factors and the impact of unintended consequences further violate the principle of *ceteris paribus*.
81 Eoyang, "Human Systems Dynamics: Complexity-Based Approach to a Complex Evaluation", 124.
82 Hendrick, "Complexity Theory and Conflict Transformation: An Exploration of Potential and Implications", 14.
83 See section on 'Context-(In)Sensitivity' below.
84 Schumacher, "What to Measure in Peace Operations", *The Pearson Papers* 10, no. 1 (2007), 45; Downs and Stedman, "Evaluation Issues in Peace Implementation", In *Ending Civil Wars: The Implementation of Peace Agreements*, eds. John Stedman, Donald Rothchild, & Elizabeth Cousens (Boulder; Lynne Rienner, 2002), 43.
85 See, for example: Michael Barnett, "Illiberal Peacebuilding and Liberal States", in *Roundtable on Humanitarian Action* (Social Science Research Council, 2005).
86 Jervis, *System Effects: Complexity in Political and Social Science*, 35.
87 William J. Durch and Madeline L. England, "The Purposes of Peace Operations", in *Annual Review of Global Peace Operations 2009* (New York: Centre on International Cooperation, 2009).
88 See, for example: Roland Paris, "Peacekeeping and the Constraints of Global Culture", *European Journal of International Relations* 9, no. 3 (2003); Séverine Autesserre, *The Trouble with the Congo: Local Violence and the Failure of International Peacebuilding*, Cambridge Studies in International Relations (Cambridge: Cambridge University Press, 2010).
89 James McGlade, "Ecohistorical Regimes and La Longue Duree: An Approach to Mapping Long-Term Societal Change", In *Complexity and Co-Evolution: Continuity and Change in Socio Economic Systems*, eds. Elizabeth Garnsey & James McGlade (Cheltenham, UK; Edward Elgar, 2006), 82–3.
90 Ramalingam, "Exploring the Science of Complexity Ideas and Implications for Development and Humanitarian Efforts", 44.
91 That is, tightly coupled or intimately interacting.
92 That is, human agents sense and react to their environment in different ways; process information; make decisions; take actions; have diverse goals; react and adapt to the system; self-organise with each other. Adaptive agents bring perception, reflection and conscious action into the complexity science lens.
93 Marion, *The Edge of Organization: Chaos and Complexity Theories of Formal Social Systems*, 173–6.
94 Eoyang, "Human Systems Dynamics: Complexity-Based Approach to a Complex Evaluation", 138.
95 See, for example: Bob Williams and Iraj Imam, eds., *Systems Concepts in Evaluation – an Expert Anthology*, Aea Monograph (Point Reyes, CA: EdgePress/American Evaluation Association, 2006); Robert Schwartz, Kim Forss, and Mita Marra, eds., *Evaluating the Complex* (New Brunswick, USA: Transaction

134 *Theory and framework building*

Publishers, 2011); Marian Barnes, Elizabeth Matka, and Helen Sullivan, "Evidence, Understanding and Complexity", *Evaluation* 9, no. 3 (2003); Eoyang and Berkas, *Evaluating Performance in a Complex Adaptive System.*

96 See, for example: Michael Quinn Patton, *Developmental Evaluation: Applying Complexity Concepts to Enhance Innovation and Use* (Guilford Press, 2010); Eoyang, "Human Systems Dynamics: Complexity-Based Approach to a Complex Evaluation". See also: real-time evaluation; emergent evaluation; action evaluation; and, adaptive evaluation in Michael Quinn Patton, "Evaluating the Complex: Getting to Maybe", in *International Conference on Evaluating the Complex* (Oslo, Norway: Norwegian Agency for Development Cooperation [NORAD], 2008), 102.

97 Eoyang and Berkas, *Evaluating Performance in a Complex Adaptive System*, 2. See also: Patricia Rogers, "Implications of Complicated and Complex Characteristics for Key Tasks in Evaluation", in *Evaluating the Complex*, eds. Robert Schwartz, Kim Forss, and Mita Marra, (New Brunswick, USA: Transaction Publishers, 2011); Irene Guijt, *Seeking Surprise. Rethinking Monitoring for Collective Learning in Rural Resource Management* (Wageningen, The Netherlands: Wageningen University Press, 2008); Gerald Midgley, "Systems Thinking for Evaluation", in *Systems Concepts in Evaluation – an Expert Anthology*, eds. Bob Williams and Iraj Imam (Point Reyes, CA: EdgePress/American Evaluation Association, 2006); Jonathan. A. Morell, *Evaluation in the Face of Uncertainty: Anticipating Surprise and Responding to the Inevitable* (New York: Guilford Press, 2010); Bob Williams and Richard Hummelbrunner, *Systems Concepts in Action: A Practitioners Toolkit* (Stanford, CA: Stanford University Press, 2011).

98 Eoyang and Berkas, *Evaluating Performance in a Complex Adaptive System*, 9.

99 Otto Hospes, "Evaluation Evolution?", *The Broker*, no. 8 (2008): 24.

100 Ray Pawson, "Nothing as Practical as a Good Theory", *Evaluation* 9, no. 4 (2003): 472.

101 Rogers, "Implications of Complicated and Complex Characteristics for Key Tasks in Evaluation".

102 List from: Eoyang, "Human Systems Dynamics: Complexity-Based Approach to a Complex Evaluation", 126.

103 Patton, "Evaluating the Complex: Getting to Maybe"; Westley, Zimmerman, and Patton, *Getting to Maybe: How the World Is Changed?*

104 Rogers, "Implications of Complicated and Complex Characteristics for Key Tasks in Evaluation"; Rogers, "Matching Impact Evaluation Design to the Nature of the Intervention and the Purpose of the Evaluation".

105 Albeit with some motivation to render 'best practices' for the subsequent application across temporal and spatial difference.

106 Peter Woodrow and Diana Chigas, "Connecting the Dots: Evaluating Whether and How Programmes Address Conflict Systems", in *The Non-Linearity of Peace Processes: Theory and Practice of Systemic Conflict Transformation*, eds. Daniela Korppen, Norbert Ropers, and Hans J. Giebmann (Opladen/Farmington Hills: Barbara Budrich Verlag, 2011), 210–11; Midgley, "Systems Thinking for Evaluation", 18–19.

107 Patton, "Evaluating the Complex: Getting to Maybe", 71; Fowler, "Complexity Thinking and Social Development, Connecting the Dots", 12; PANOS, "How Can Complexity Theory Contribute to More Effective Development and Aid Evaluation?" (London; PANOS, 2009), 4.

108 Patton, "Evaluating the Complex: Getting to Maybe", 113.

109 Eoyang, "Human Systems Dynamics: Complexity-Based Approach to a Complex Evaluation", 127–8.

110 Paul Cilliers, "Complexity, Deconstruction and Relativism", *Theory, Culture & Society* 22, no. 5 (2005): 257.

111 Patton, *Developmental Evaluation: Applying Complexity Concepts to Enhance Innovation and Use*, 151.
112 Eoyang, "Human Systems Dynamics: Complexity-Based Approach to a Complex Evaluation", 126; Patton, *Developmental Evaluation: Applying Complexity Concepts to Enhance Innovation and Use*, 126–31, 50.
113 Jonathan A. Morell, *Evaluation in the Face of Uncertainty: Anticipating Surprise and Responding to the Inevitable* (New York: Guilford Press, 2010); Guijt, *Seeking Surprise. Rethinking Monitoring for Collective Learning in Rural Resource Management*.
114 Woodrow and Chigas, "Connecting the Dots: Evaluating Whether and How Programmes Address Conflict Systems", 226.
115 Eoyang and Berkas, *Evaluating Performance in a Complex Adaptive System*, 3; Gürkaynak, Dayton, and Paffenholz, "Evaluation in Conflict Resolution and Peacebuilding", 290–3.
116 Patton, *Developmental Evaluation: Applying Complexity Concepts to Enhance Innovation and Use*, 132, 150–1.
117 Eoyang and Berkas, *Evaluating Performance in a Complex Adaptive System*, 1.
118 Patton, *Developmental Evaluation: Applying Complexity Concepts to Enhance Innovation and Use*, 131–3.
119 Ramalingam, "Evaluation and the Science of Complexity", 67–8.
120 Iraj Imam, Amy LaGoy, and Bob Williams, "Now What? How to Promote Systems Concepts in Evaluation", in *Systems Concepts in Evaluation – an Expert Anthology*, eds. Bob Williams and Iraj Imam (Point Reyes, CA: EdgePress/American Evaluation Association, 2006), 212.
121 Woodrow and Chigas, "Connecting the Dots: Evaluating Whether and How Programmes Address Conflict Systems", 226.
122 Hendrick, "Complexity Theory and Conflict Transformation: An Exploration of Potential and Implications", 72.
123 Boyd *et al.*, "Systemic Evaluation: A Participative, Multi-Method Approach", 1306.
124 Treat 'fixing a mess' by identifying/isolating a 'problem' then attempting to solve it as if it were a 'puzzle' – i.e. as reasonably predictable activity that responds to universally applicable 'laws'. See: Ackoff, *Redesigning the Future: A Systems Approach to Societal Problems*; Ramalingam, "Exploring the Science of Complexity Ideas and Implications for Development and Humanitarian Efforts", 11.
125 de Coning, "Planning for Success", 25.
126 Virginia Lacayo, "What Complexity Science Teaches Us About Social Change", in *MAZI Articles* (South Orange, NJ: Communication For Social Change Consortium, 2007).
127 Clement and Smith, "Managing Complexity: Political and Managerial Challenges in United Nations Peace Operations", 2.

4 A framework for monitoring and evaluating the impact of UNPOL

Introduction

The previous chapter explored the potential value-add of complexity theory to understanding change and impact in peace operations. The purpose of this chapter is to outline a framework for doing M&E that is informed by complexity theory in order to overcome the challenges facing UNPOL and the M&E thereof identified in Chapters 1 and 2. The framework is not meant to be an exhaustive methodology for conducting M&E per se. Instead, it draws together the central tenets of what I propose to be an improvement in extant thinking and praxis into a framework for context-specific application. The framework is underpinned by ideas and concepts synonymous with complexity theory in two key ways. First, complexity concepts inform the circular and systemic design of the overarching framework such that it is iterative, context-sensitive and incorporates feedback processes. These qualities render the approach more responsive to the emergent nature of change and more capable of facilitating both first-level and second-level organisational learning. Second, the field-level M&E process embedded within the framework is grounded in complexity principles that pertain to issues of causality and attribution in dynamic and unpredictable circumstances. It therefore details three key areas. First, it specifies demands for foregrounding assessments to ensure context-awareness. Second, it introduces important criteria for the selection of data sources and methods to ensure the approach is outcome/impact-focused, has the capacity for flexibility, and privileges participation – advocating a methodologically ecumenical approach that utilises a combination of methods as appropriate. Third, it lays out the imperatives for careful interpretation and response to findings. Overall, the framework presents an approach to M&E that not only provides an innovative way of tracking the impact of UNPOL activities in the field but is also tailored to contribute to and enable organisational learning objectives.

The chapter proceeds in three main parts. The first section introduces the overarching framework, presenting its architecture, the rationale for its design and its key features. The second section explicates the internal field-level 3-step M&E process, describing each step in turn and suggesting the possible tools and methods for its execution as well as relating each step to the others. The third section articulates how the framework facilitates learning processes, including how this is designed to feed back into and inform mission planning. The chapter concludes by summarising the main elements of the framework and its potential benefits as a foundation for the primary field research in subsequent chapters.

A framework for M&E of UNPOL in peace operations

The overarching M&E framework constitutes an organisational learning cycle. That is, it is an architecture that delineates the relationships between: information gathering and interpretation as the mission proceeds; first-level organisational learning in the field and second-level organisational learning at headquarters; as well as the way in which this learning feeds back to inform planning for ongoing as well as new missions. It contains a sub-process relating specifically to the field-level preparation, data collection and information handling, including the methodological choices and challenges associated. The following diagram illustrates the overarching framework.

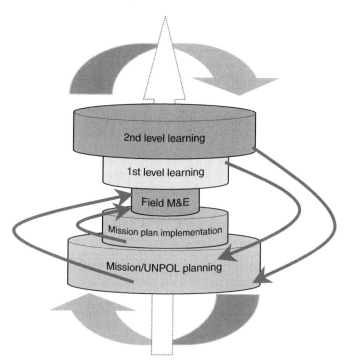

Figure 4.1 Diagram of overall M&E framework.

Complexity theory informs the design of the framework as a whole. It is pervaded by two key features that derive from this thinking. First, the whole process laid out by this framework is intended to be 'circular'. To do so, the framework is typified by perpetual M&E *practice* that is *iterative* and *reflexive*. This fundamental design feature is intended to overcome the current orthodoxy generally comprising a series of inchoate, truncated and discrete events or static after-action-reviews.[1]

The framework's *iterative* nature is achieved by focusing on short and recurring cycles with high contextual specificity rather than longitudinal assessments that are more general in scope and relevance. M&E practice is *reflexive* in that it guarantees ongoing deliberation on what is working and what is not, rather than one-off assessments of the status quo at a singular point in space and time. That is, in addition to producing accounts of progress over time it can also better question the assumptions of the underlying logic of UNPOL operations. For example, whilst in a managerial sense M&E can help to enhance police reform by tracking activity and efficient implementation, it can also enable a critical awareness of the effectiveness of particular police reform modes and methods. This involves asking more about whether UNPOL are 'doing the right things' rather than if they are 'doing things right'. Ultimately, this reflexive process is promoted primarily as a means of enhancing the efficacy of operations rather than a tool for critiquing performance and directing punitive action.[2] This is what was referred to in the previous chapter as moving M&E away from a 'fear of failure' towards a 'hunger for learning'.

By embedding these *iterative* and *reflexive* qualities the framework is circular over time. This more recursive M&E practice adheres to complexity-oriented-M&E principles that emphasise the importance of including regular feedback loops. Consequently, by creating the space for revision and adaptation, it promises to better serve the objectives of organisational learning, both in real-time for course correction in the field as well as in slower time for developing and managing knowledge at headquarters.

The second key feature of the framework is that it is 'systemic'. The benefits of tailoring M&E to the idiosyncrasies of UNPOL in conflict-affected environments are clear and evidenced in Chapter 2. However, it was also highlighted that extant orthodoxy is either too broad such that it lacks specificity for UNPOL or, more commonly, that it is overly siloed such that M&E loses sight of the larger system of which UNPOL objectives are a part. UNPOL activities involve and implicate the agendas of numerous stakeholders. Systematising M&E for UNPOL is therefore motivated by the need to imbue the framework with an awareness of the complex system(s) that UNPOL inhabits. Consequently, the framework is designed to synergise with existing UN frameworks, mechanisms and tools. For example, the process is tailored to be compatible with the *Integrated Missions Planning Process* (IMPP) which has its own reporting requirements[3] and does not duplicate but rather harnesses efforts such as the nascent *Rule of Law Indicators Project* (ROLIP).[4] Similarly, UN entities beyond the purview of the mission – for example the DPET Evaluation Unit or the Office of Internal Oversight Services (OIOS) – will usefully continue to play their unique role in the architectural M&E. Furthermore, in activities such as combating transnational crime or police reform, UNPOL efforts will be in partnership with host governments, regional arrangements and other bilateral partners. Country-wide transitional policy frameworks such as the UN's Development Assistance Frameworks (UNDAF), national poverty reduction strategies or broad efforts to attain the Millennium Development Goals also include their own large-scale M&E components. Therefore the M&E regimen for UNPOL is designed to 'speak to' their respective performance management and accountability frameworks.[5]

Explicitly situating UNPOL within its systemic context is an essential element of complexity-oriented-M&E for understanding its place, interrelationships and contribution to goals in a complex system. It therefore creates the opportunity for assessments of UNPOL to be contextualised as part of the system they inhabit as well as ensure it has the capacity to co-operate with the broader M&E architecture invariably in place.[6] Such cross-fertilisation and efficiency (i.e. avoiding duplication) promises a more harmonised and coherent M&E architecture that can better reflect the impact of collective (often integrated) endeavours. Despite these critical design features, the utility of the overall framework is dependent on the type, quality and timeliness of data gathering and interpretation that takes place in the field. The following section explicates the framework's embedded process for conducting these assessments.

Field-level M&E process

The process is comprised of three steps that relate to: foregrounding assessments; design and implementation; and, interpretation of and response to the findings. For ease of presentation the steps are introduced sequentially. However, it is important to emphasise in advance that the ideas and content from each step is intended to feed back into the others iteratively and not necessarily according the sequence below. The diagram below illustrates the process.

Step 1: Foregrounding

The first step and the fundamental point of departure for field-level M&E involves foregrounding. That is, furnishing M&E with an awareness of the contextual conditions and exigencies that underpin and interact with the mission as well as how they should inform assessment.[7] The step serves two purposes. Firstly, given the ambiguous nature of mission mandates and paucity of guidance and doctrine for many UNPOL tasks, it is vital that

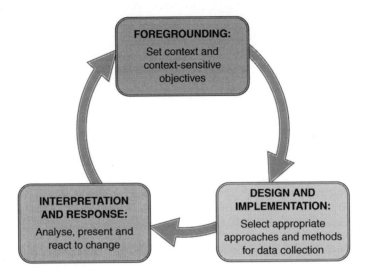

Figure 4.2 Field-level M&E process.

M&E begins by clarifying mission objectives based on activities being conducted and realistic expectations of what can be achieved. Secondly, if the situation at the beginning of an M&E cycle (i.e. pre-deployment or preceding a particular phase of a mission) is not analysed and documented, it will be difficult to ascertain the extent to which there have been positive or negative changes in the areas UNPOL is working on.[8] This step is therefore also concerned with producing baseline assessments to establish a platform from which to build arguments of change.[9] Therefore, the dual purpose of this step is to construct a clear picture of what a mission is required to do as well as the circumstances into which it is deploying. In line with insights on sensitive dependence from complexity theory, the step is underpinned by the idea that if M&E is to reflect the realities on the ground, it should be cognisant of and sensitive to the specific context in which it is applied.

Mission objectives and realistic expectations

The mission type assessment is concerned with ascertaining a detailed picture of the mission's mandate, scope and the level of resources at its disposal. This should include understanding the tasks and objectives mandated to UNPOL, as well as locating the UNPOL component in relation to interdependent programming taking place under the auspices of an integrated Rule of Law strategy.

To date, there has been a tendency for M&E to measure against unrealistic objectives that can have the effect of setting up missions to fail.[10] The dominant vision of change will invariably emerge from consensus sought in the Security Council with the host state's consent. The views of the UN as a major stakeholder (and financier), are legitimate and will necessarily inform a major portion of a peace operation's strategic 'thinking'. However, UN peace operations and the police components therein are rarely provided with a detailed vision of what success looks like. Peace operations are politically sensitive undertakings and consequently mandates promulgated by the Security Council are notoriously – sometimes intentionally – vague and have tended to focus on grand objectives such as the restoration of peace and security. Whilst mandates have become more detailed, with extensive operative paragraphs on thematic issues and sectoral priorities,[11] in many ways, they remain uninstructive and goals are rarely articulated in operational terms conducive to their transposition into criteria and indicators for M&E.[12] The upshot is that these strategic documents fail to identify particular changes the mission is required to achieve.[13] It is therefore important to understand the tasks being commonly implemented under these mandates so as to establish key objectives and realistic expectations for M&E to measure against.

As examined in Chapter 1, there is a disparate range of operational tasks that may be required of UNPOL in different operational settings.[14] Nevertheless, UNPOL missions are invariably tasked with combinations of objectives relating to 'operational support' and 'policebuilding' with additional 'supplementary activities'. The table below (Table 4.1) captures the primary activities that have recurred in UNPOL missions and can reasonably be expected to occur in future ones.[15]

These three 'tasks' categories constitute the elements that the rest of the framework is designed to address. Prior determinations relating to mission type serve to narrow and focus the scope of assessments. It is important to recognise that these tasks have variable scope. That is to say, some constitute discrete activities or slightly longer projects (e.g. operational support activities), whereas others (e.g. police reform) constitute programmes with multiple elements and components. This has ramifications for how they should be assessed.[16]

Identifying UNPOL tasks is a necessary but insufficient precursor to M&E assessments. M&E must also include a process for identifying mission goals that are pragmatic and feasible in the given context. Whilst clear leadership and good management can help to clarify mission goals and objectives, drawing upon consensus-derived visions of change is likely to be integral to establishing realistic objectives. Given the array of stakeholders with disparate and often competing agendas, it is important to explicitly target the different conceptions of success for the mission to help facilitate answers to the questions such as what is success and according to whom? Satisficing and notions of 'good enough' outcomes are important in arriving at realistic objectives and supporting feasible M&E.[17] This requires a process that reaches consensus on the main problems

Table 4.1 UNPOL tasks

UNPOL TASKS (*individual officers and FPUs*)			
Operational support	*Policebuilding*		*Supplementary activities*
Executive law enforcement (e.g. protection of property and lives)	Reform (e.g. community-based policing, public relations, gender mainstreaming)		Supervision of ceasefire
Public disorder response and management (e.g. riot/crowd control, area security)	Restructuring (e.g. vetting, selection and recruitment, civilian oversight/investigation of misconduct)		DDR (e.g. securing law and order in demobilisation and cantonment zones, ensuring basic rights of ex-combatants when reintegrating, integration into police, developing firearms legislation)
Joint patrols	(Re)building and capacity-building (e.g. emergency/armed response units, provision of resources and building core infrastructure [e.g. training facilities, police stations, communications equipment, vehicles and uniforms]; HR development, establish administration and financial management arrangements, planning)		Electoral assistance (e.g. pre-election [i.e. security for voter registration, campaigning, etc], election day [i.e. security for candidates, voters at ballot boxes, integrity of polling booths], post-election [i.e. secure transportation of ballot boxes, public order during installation/transition of government, general security in fragile aftermath])
Operational supervision	Technical assistance/advisory support (e.g. review and renew technical guidance – SOPs, etc.)		Facilitate safe returnees
Investigation of crimes and criminality	Training and mentoring (see Stimson Report, p. 91 for full list)		Combat organised crime
Maritime/border control	Logistical support		Protection of civilians
			Protecting UN personnel and facilities (mostly FPUs but sometimes UNPOL)

through asking what stakeholders' goals are, why and suggested pathways to achieve them – including the obstacles to it.[18] Regardless of where these visions of change emanate from or what the underpinning theory of change might be; in this framework M&E is about assessing progress against realistic expectations of what UNPOL can achieve, qualified by its interdependencies with the rest of the mission and other stakeholders in accomplishing these goals.

Mission context

The mission context assessment includes two facets. The first dimension concerns the political, economic and social circumstances in the host country. In the context of UNPOL, such assessments should focus on the rule of law sector, including the historic legacy and current manifestation of the criminal justice institutions and their governance. This includes asking questions relating to the role of the police in the conflict and the levels of politicisation/ethnicisation of the security sector, provisions for external oversight of security actors, as well as prevailing levels of organised criminality (particularly where this is deemed to have linkages to or complicity within the state). Assessments should also include the country's form of governance (e.g. democratic, autocratic, transitional, hybrid, etc.) as well as its capacity and perceived legitimacy and the socio-economic conditions of the population, including the ways in which predicaments vary along demographic lines. Such analyses of local context are crucial in order to remain cognisant of the broader systemic environment.

Assessments should also include general accounts of the conflict dynamics and degree of stability. For example, is the mission in a crisis phase with a mandate to enforce law and order, or relatively stable and focusing on police reform? This is an important determinant as the permissibility and utility of approaches and methods discussed below will be contingent on the prevailing security conditions. Whilst the security situation is liable to fluctuate, the so-called 'phase' of the mission will likely be the main factor in determining which approaches can be employed and when.[19] Determinations regarding what phase a mission is currently in and, as it progresses, when it is deemed to have transitioned into a new phase space, are an important prerequisite for ensuring context/conflict-sensitive assessments. These 'initial conditions' in terms of host country and mission phase are integral starting points for attempts to assess change in a way that is suitably grounded in the specific context.

The second dimension of mission context assessments concerns identifying and understanding the various actors or stakeholders relevant to UNPOL activities.[20] In line with complexity-oriented-M&E, change is seen as a product of the intricate interactions of system elements and therefore attempts to gauge system change must seek to understand the nature of these key actors and their interrelationships. This involves asking two fundamental questions: who are the stakeholders? And, what are the relationships between them? Regardless of their constituency (i.e. who stakeholders are and who they represent), there will be varying power relationships between different stakeholders and these relationships are likely to change over time.[21] Therefore, once identified, it is important to understand how stakeholders are networked and the consequences regarding two key analytical points: first, what is their importance to the UNPOL mission?; and second, what is their capacity to influence outcomes that relate to UNPOL objectives?[22] This will necessarily require an assessment of the traditional state-based security actors such as national police, but also demands an identification of alternative provision of policing and rule of law services by non-state providers. As described in Chapter 1, many of the countries in which peace operations have occurred have weak central state institutions and display culturally specific normative and/or legal pluralism. Thus, this assessment also lays the foundations for a culturally sensitive approach, such that holistic changes in the local 'experiences' of safety and security can be educed and the effect of competing normative frameworks on outcomes in the mission can be captured.[23]

It is evident that accurate baselines are difficult to obtain in peace operations environments.[24] However, there will inevitably be some information sources that can be drawn upon to make these foregrounding assessments. Their importance to M&E dictates that where information is scarce or common sites of data do not exist, using innovative approaches and diversifying information sources to create baselines will be better than nothing. However, in keeping with complexity-inspired approaches, this also requires deeper assessments that engage a broader cross-section of stakeholders and employ methods that elicit different perspectives.[25]

Step 1: Summary

This initial step is concerned with producing a comprehensive assessment of the mission environment and type to contextualise UNPOL activities for M&E.[26] Given the diversity in mission objectives and settings, it is important that M&E targeting the impact of UNPOL is founded on clear, unambiguous notions of these areas. This step is, therefore, about ensuring a *context-sensitive* process. Detailed foregrounding assessments present a number of benefits for the rest of the design and implementation of the M&E process. First, they have the potential to depict a more accurate picture of the conditions and challenges faced by UNPOL in implementing their mandate. By including a broad array of stakeholders in both the substance and production of foregrounding assessments, these analyses provide a way of setting, substantiating and encouraging more realistic expectations regarding what success looks like for different stakeholders – i.e. what can be achieved and in what timeframe. Second, these realities can form baselines to inform subsequent progress and impact assessment.

Therefore, collecting and interpreting baseline data and the analysis conducted during this foregrounding exercise constitutes the bedrock upon which the rest of the M&E process can be built.[27]

It is important to highlight that these conditions are likely to be dynamic. Hence, to retain currency, assessments need to be regularly updated.[28] Irrespective of whether they are conducted before a peace operation deploys or at any point in its life cycle, it is important that the foregrounding assessments/baseline data collected relates to the changes under analysis and is relevant to the focus of subsequent impact assessments. It is therefore vital that subsequent steps of the framework feed back into this foregrounding step to direct and guide what types of information should be sought. This is an exemplar of how this process – like the framework as a whole – is purposefully iterative, such that the information gleaned in each step of its implementation feeds back into and informs other elements of the system. These foregrounding analyses only realise their potential if they are used as the basis for the subsequent design step.

Step 2: Design and implementation

The second step relates to formulating an appropriate approach to assessing the impact of UNPOL within the parameters delineated in the foregrounding step. The purpose of this step is to guide answers to two key questions: first, what and whose knowledge is important to evidencing what progress is being made against objectives? (i.e. sources of monitoring data); and second, how can this information be solicited and captured? (i.e. methods for accessing it). Building on insights from complexity theory relating to nonlinearity and emergence, this section describes the *criteria* proposed for guiding the approach as well as potential *data sources* and *methods* required to execute this and other steps.

Criteria

OUTCOME/IMPACT-FOCUSED

M&E in this framework is about gauging progress towards mission objectives and therefore its design should be unambiguous regarding the distinctions between 'results levels' and guided by a focus of analyses on *outcomes* and *impacts*. That is to say, the approach facilitates a move beyond reporting what police in peace operations 'do' – i.e. their *output* – towards asking about what they 'achieve' and the quality and effect of their actions – i.e. their *impact*, such as improved public safety. Whilst this is more difficult to achieve, it is at this level that the critical issues can be addressed. This requires that the 'M' and the 'E' are blended and more akin to 'impact-oriented monitoring'[29] than separated and distinct activities as in the conventional dichotomy.

146 *Theory and framework building*

Notwithstanding the privileging of outcomes/impact, results at the output level may occasionally need to suffice as a measure of progress. The stage of the mission may dictate that outputs are the best – or indeed the only – indication of progress in a particular programme with a protracted implementation and achievement horizon.[30] For example, attempts to gauge progress in the early stages of police restructuring might rely on results at the output level as an indicator of activity before any associated impact can be determined. This is why the framework advocates for using mixed methods such that each of these different results levels can be targeted as necessary.[31] Nevertheless, generally speaking output measures remain, at best, a partial indicator of short-term progress in mandate implementation as it is difficult to fashion output indicators that capture local perceptions and are indicative of socio-cultural transformation synonymous with UNPOL objectives such as police reform.[32] Even where outputs are temporarily relied upon, assessments should be focused on the way in which these outputs may or may not have contributed to broader change. Furthermore, it should be clear that the focus will move to outcomes/impacts as soon as is practicable. Whilst this is a straightforward statement of the priority level of analysis of M&E, this has important ramifications for the means by which progress is tracked and the way in which the issue of attribution is handled.

Another key element in that sense relates to external influences and unintended consequences of action. Given the contingent nature of outcomes/impacts in UNPOL endeavours, a variety of factors beyond the control of UNPOL and the mission in general affect outcomes and impacts in the mission area. This relates to the emergent quality discussed in the previous chapter insofar as outcomes/impacts are phenomena that are irreducible to their constituent inputs and as a result are difficult to predict accurately. Incorporating exogenous factors and potential externalities is vital to understanding change as well as being able to identify, isolate and qualify problems and challenges.[33] It is at the outcome and impact levels that the combination of real-world forces manifests, including positive or negative unintended consequences.[34] Therefore, this criterion embeds an approach that emphasises the centrality of seeking out the unexpected and identifying and contextualising both exogenous factors and externalities as they relate to UNPOL.

FLEXIBILITY

Nonlinearity and unpredictability of outcomes dictate that the M&E approach must be amenable to capturing a moving picture rather than a snapshot. In this sense it needs to be flexible and tailored to not only recognise but also harness and optimise the information that emerges from UNPOL-specific tasks, experiences, reporting methods and their associated timelines. Therefore, it is important that the approach employed is conducive to an iterative implementation process so that change can be continuously contextualised with clear and frequent reference to regularly updated baselines. This is to ensure that M&E is not set to improbable timeframes due to political agendas, arbitrary institutional reporting requirements and budget cycles. As identified in Chapter 2, this is vital given that these schedules are rarely suitable for the dynamics of change associated with the types of activities UNPOL engage in.[35] Whilst UNPOL are under pressure to deliver (and be seen to deliver) results quickly following deployment, it is important that the M&E process acknowledges that objectives of many UNPOL tasks targeting sustainable change will take time.[36] Gauging the impact of these efforts therefore requires clear reference back to the phase of the mission to situate objectives and furnish assessments with temporal caveats commensurate with context-sensitive understandings of progress in this setting.

Furthermore, as operational environments are liable to change dramatically and quickly,[37] it is important that attempts to document change are not trapped in mechanistic structures that fail to adapt to differing contexts and inevitable changes – or lose their relevance when they do.[38] For instance, in more volatile crisis environments, M&E needs to be responsive to erratic circumstances in which timeframes, benchmarks and planning assumptions may change frequently and unpredictably. Similarly, as missions move through different phases of their lifetime, adjustments to strategy and/or tactics are inevitable. Consequently, M&E needs to allow managers to make decisions on when to adhere to the original design and when it should be adjusted in line with an evolving situation.[39] *Flexible* M&E privileges and caters for an approach that is agile and adaptive in the face of changing conditions and objectives but retains its relevance and utility for assessing change despite interim alterations to intended outcomes.[40] An important caveat, however, is that this flexible design must safeguard against becoming opportunistic. That is to say, flexibility is vital for accurate reflections of reality, not to facilitate a diversion towards easy wins or neglect where realities are difficult to grapple with. It is therefore about a shift away from the perversity of 'what cannot be measured easily will not get done' and/or 'what goes well gets measured' towards a more insightful 'what is happening and why'.

PARTICIPATION AND COOPERATION

The third criterion underpinning the M&E approach relates to participation and issues of ownership. Whilst revealing the myriad of relevant actors in the system is a crucial first step, an approach that facilitates their involvement in the process is fundamental to overcoming exclusive and narrow participation in conventional M&E processes – often to the omission of disadvantaged segments of society.[41] The concepts in complexity-oriented-M&E that call for perspectives from a cross-section of actors dictate that methods used should be governed by a participatory imperative. In other words, it is vital that M&E secures buy-in from and participation by a broader group of stakeholders. This is important for two main reasons. Firstly, to increase access to information and various perspectives – importantly including those that are well placed to observe and/or experience change.[42] Secondly, an inclusive approach renders local stakeholders as participants in, rather than objects of, the M&E process. This has the potential to build credibility, legitimacy and support – or at a bare minimum, the acquiescence – of key stakeholders.[43] Furthermore, deeper participation and cooperation increase reach and engagement and mean that local people are more aware that efforts are being made in line with local expectations and what stage these efforts are at. This may lead to the identification of simple indicators of impact that would not be apparent to other stakeholders but participatory approaches importantly have the potential to deepen buy-in and enhance local ownership of M&E.[44]

Therefore, the M&E approach should engender a sense of ownership in the relevant constituencies. However, the most relevant constituency will differ throughout the life cycle of a peace operation.[45] In the early phases it is highly likely that by default the mission will 'own' the M&E. The majority of UNPOL activities immediately following deployment demand that UNPOL are in the M&E 'driving seat'. Similarly, elements of UNPOL work towards reforming police organisations will unavoidably and necessarily challenge the interests of some of the major stakeholders, making initiatives to enhance local ownership such as collaborative goal-setting a difficult endeavour.[46] As intervening actors, UNPOL are the ones implementing the initial programmes and therefore need to have responsibility for, and ownership over, gauging their impact and responding to it. However, in the medium term all parties (and the M&E itself) will benefit if the process is "joint-owned" by the peace operation and broader group of stakeholders.[47] This means involving actors from beyond the employ of the mission in mechanisms for managing, reviewing and overseeing the M&E. In the case of UNPOL, this demands that a broad cross-section of rule of law stakeholders are engaged as early as possible. In particular, the participation of non-state providers of policing type services is vital in this regard.[48] Ultimately, by embedding what is relevant, important and well-understood locally, the process incrementally entrenches and facilitates local awareness and understanding of the M&E and with it the potential for genuine sense of accountability. And this is also more likely to lead to M&E findings being acted upon collaboratively.[49]

From the beginning, M&E designed in this way can constitute a collaborative tool for peacebuilding, rather than a compulsion to adopt a particular style of management or set of measures handed down by outsiders. Indeed, if and when this is the case, the process itself can be understood as capacity-building for the host country and its security sector stakeholders.[50] This transfer or development of specific M&E 'knowledge' has important ramifications for the sustainability of the process as a peace operation draws down and transitions out. Therefore, the M&E approach should entrench participation and an inclusive approach from the outset. Adhering to complexity-oriented-M&E principles which jettison any attempt to depict M&E as impartial or objective, assessments should involve the full gamut of actors that matter most to the decisions that matter most.[51]

These three criteria provide the guiding principles necessary to overcome the major design flaws in M&E of current convention. That is, by prioritising *outcome/impact-focused* design furnished with an awareness of the effects of exogenous factors and externalities it navigates the major conceptual challenges; and, by embedding ideas of *flexibility* and *inclusivity* it ensures that the design is not only influenced by these important notions, but intrinsically engineered to repeatedly reflect on the issues that are too often overlooked or buried in the modalities conventionally employed. The aim is to avoid the scenario whereby M&E becomes driven by a particular instrument or tool – with corollary prescriptive risks – rather than an M&E process and its questions. These criteria are intended to govern the collection of suitable information. Therefore, the subsequent elements of this step concerns the identification and selection of data sources and methods for accessing them.

Data sources

As has been mentioned, the environments into which peace operations deploy are not typically data rich and existing information is often not readily accessible. Conventional sources of information are often scarce and unreliable, logistical challenges are many and security concerns prevail. For UNPOL, this can be exacerbated by the cultures of secrecy synonymous with security institutions.[52] The current reliance on these conventional and predominantly quantitative sources risks presenting a partial or even flawed account.[53] When available, these conventional sources of information will continue to be vital fodder for the process. However, given the informational realities it is necessary to look beyond these common data and seek out alternative sites of knowledge to access similar information. In keeping with the criteria for complexity-oriented-M&E compliance, remedying this requires the identification of what Harry Jones describes as "an eclectic mix of knowledge sources at different levels and times",[54] and involves leveraging existing reservoirs of knowledge as well as exploring potential alternatives.

Alternative sites of knowledge include a range of qualitative sources.[55] For example, NGOs can also provide a rich source of data in information-poor environments. Whilst police may not have the competencies to disaggregate crime statistics by ethnicity, local human rights NGOs may record incidences of crime against particular vulnerable minorities. Beyond these formal avenues, community-based organisations and informal networks constitute an important fount of knowledge that is rarely used in extant M&E. Existing networks and information gathering entities amongst recipient communities are a prime source of information that can feed into M&E. These alternative sites will necessarily vary with context, but what is common about them is that they are likely to be available and practical in the circumstances. Incorporating alternative sources has the added benefit of mitigating the risk of letting the commonly available data dictate the substance of the M&E (i.e. 'what can be measured (easily), will be measured'). It also has the potential to reveal vital local dimensions, dynamics and perspectives in the environment, too often overlooked at the mission level.[56] Furthermore, this is another way of ensuring that certain types and categories of information (e.g. western/outsider) are not privileged to the detriment of a representative picture of what is happening and why.[57]

It is by diversifying and expanding the pool of knowledge that this framework promises to add better depth and breadth to analyses. The important thing is for M&E to recognise the value and validity of information that is circulating in alternative fora and informal meetings. In order to avoid inefficient data collection that serves little purpose, the fundamental principle guiding the choice of data sources is whether or not it is 'good enough' given the operational environment and informational realities.[58] Such judgments should be based on what they can and cannot be relied upon to evidence, based on their relevance to the subject in question, their perceived legitimacy amongst stakeholders, the availability of potential alternatives, and the fidelity of data collection methods.[59] Therefore, the selection of methods for gathering information and acquiring knowledge are also vital.

Methods

Data collection processes for the express purposes of assessing the impact of UNPOL efforts are in their infancy, and consequently, underdeveloped. The ways in which the aforementioned types of knowledge can be mined are many and it is impractical to attempt to cover them all here. Indeed, in keeping with the flexible and adaptive character of the framework, the most appropriate modes of data collection may have been infeasible or unsuitable elsewhere and should be expected to emerge in a particular context. Nevertheless, in order to demonstrate the types of methods that satisfy the criteria laid out and are necessary to complement/augment conventional methods, the following section points to a collection of methods that are deemed appropriate.

Quantitative methods are useful for representing large numbers of people and are often sufficient for output measures.[60] However, these approaches are not without their limitations and their shortcomings mean that they are best used in combination with other methods.[61] Whilst qualitative methods are less amenable to generalisation of trends and themes, they provide for a more nuanced understanding of complex issues.[62] Where UNPOL tasks target organisational and behavioural change ends – by whatever means – methods used to target data must be more attuned to eliciting intangibles such as the perceptions, attitudes, beliefs and knowledge of change in relation to desired outcomes and impacts. Capturing changes in public opinion has a huge significance in these settings due to their focus on outcomes/impacts. For example, these methods can be particularly useful for ascertaining perceptions of changing public security dynamics and determining public preferences between statutory and non-state providers.

In this regard, qualitative methods that revolve around narrative accounts are particularly salient.[63] These are methodological techniques that map and trace contribution through the construction of 'performance narratives'.[64] Such methods involve M&E practitioners as facilitators rather than expert assessors and constitute a collaborative process of data collection and analysis. They employ focus group discussions and individual or group interviews with a wide range of stakeholders to develop narratives of change and generate indicators of achieving objectives, as well as realistic timelines for their attainment.[65] Narratives are an effective way to elicit and help to understand context, culture and participants' experiences in relation to mission activities and outcomes. Contribution stories also provide a good source of information about relationships between participants and entities and have the benefit of creating the space to identify additional relevant data sites/indicators to use for gauging the impact of activities, progress towards intended goals and perceptions of the extent to which such programming has met expectations.

Importantly, contribution narratives are an effective way of explicating the hypothetical programme logic or theory. That is, this method allows for the exploration of cause-and-effect relationships as perceived by those in the field and recipients of UNPOL efforts.[66] In this way they can be used to focus on ascertaining how UNPOL *activities* and their corresponding *outputs* contribute to certain trends at this macro level.[67] For example, can an increase in public confidence in police in a certain area be linked, at least in part, to a training programme to enhance police responsiveness? Though causation cannot be quarantined at this level because of the many other factors likely to be affecting an outcome,[68] the narrative approach constitutes a way of accumulating multiple perspectives articulating how *activities, outputs* and the related *outcomes* may have impacted and affected these shifts in social conditions. Furthermore, contribution narratives provide a means of identifying the presence and consequences of pertinent exogenous factors and potential unintended consequences.[69] That is, they are suitable for seeking out and capturing the unexpected, non-linear and surprising. For example, they provide a way of eliciting how changes in the policing domain have affected, and may have been affected by, other elements of mission and other stakeholders. Ultimately, narrative-based approaches that build contribution stories provide an account of both why causality cannot be claimed as well as proffering alternative opinions towards demonstration of contribution. Furthermore, it does not assume that incremental progress is inevitable, but rather enables a design that can account for regression and articulate the potential contribution of UNPOL to such outcomes.

Another major benefit of these methods is that they lend themselves to an iterative process. This is true both in terms of continual and ever-increasing data gathering and collation, as well as repetitive reflection and updating and strengthening of the contribution narrative; along with incremental validation or revision of undergirding assumptions and theories of change, and areas of priority. In general, these constitute methods that prioritise context-sensitivity, the construction of narratives around contribution to target impacts and offer an effective means of creating short and cost-effective feedback loops that can enable rapid and timely assessments to influence learning and the decision-making based upon it in an iterative manner. Moreover, these methods meet the participatory imperative and point to the inclusion of perspectives from a variety of disparate constituencies in the information gathering exercise.

Methods that set about constructing narratives around change offer ways of accessing large quantities and a rich diversity of information and constitute an approach that satisfies many of the criteria for complexity-oriented-M&E laid out above.[70] However, no single tool constitutes the panacea in all cases – any particular method is only useful for addressing specific types of questions.[71] Given the range of questions emerging from the design above, numerous options applied in a careful and context-sensitive manner are necessary to provide sufficient methodological leverage.[72] To reflect this, the framework is methodologically ecumenical. That is to say it promotes a multi-method approach that, whilst coherent, allows for choice in selecting the most suitable methods for accessing, managing, analysing and presenting information about change. As one related account suggests, "there is no need to reinvent the wheel, but it may need off-road tyres to work in more difficult environments."[73] In short, when M&E is implemented in the context of scarce budgetary, temporal and informational resources and importantly under political constraints, the selection of methods needs to be governed by feasibility and relevancy but it also needs to maximise participation and the value of data that does exist and harness rapid data collection methods.[74] However, it is important to acknowledge that the choice of these methods is also values-laden. Every method brings with it trade-offs due to, for example, timelines and costliness, and these choices can be understood to establish path dependencies. It is therefore important to be transparent about the methods being used, the assumptions that underpin them and their consequent limitations.

Step 2: Summary

In sum, step 2 provides the 'blueprint' for the selection of information sources and data collection methods that ensures an outcome/impact-focused; flexible and participatory approach. This enables information to be solicited from a wide range of actors and data sources in a way that targets collective understandings of UNPOL contributions to desired outcomes/impacts. The selection and gathering of information/knowledge as evidence of impact needs to strike a careful balance between accuracy, utility, feasibility and ethics.[75] Therefore, this step advocates for an approach whereby the appropriate tools are matched to the question or task under analysis. It is tailored to the full gamut of UNPOL tasks and should ensure that there is a deep reservoir of data to supply the interpretation and response needs of the process captured by the following step.

Step 3: Interpretation and response

The third step concerns the utilisation of data and knowledge emanating from the previous steps and its purpose is twofold. First, to interpret the findings from the multiplicity of data and perspectives collated in the previous steps in a way that makes sense of uncertain causal relationships and diverse opinion relating to progress and change. Second, to ensure that these findings reach the necessary constituencies for subsequent stakeholder responses that feed into future iterations of the M&E process. In this sense, the step is underpinned by insights from complexity theory that suggest emergent outcomes will not be self-evident and that feedback and continuous practice is crucial to understanding dynamical change.

Interpretation

Interpretation relates to answering the question of what can reasonably be concluded from the information ascertained and how can we interpret it in a way that reliably says something useful about the impact of UNPOL endeavours? It encompasses issues of validation, disaggregation and reflection.

The framework's privileging of multiple perspectives and data sources presents perennial questions about the *validity* (i.e. strengths and weaknesses) of particular pieces of the data. This is particularly true where subjective perceptions and attitudes are under assessment as they are particularly difficult to interpret.[76] Whilst the informational landscape and the derivative assessments will be imperfect, acknowledging this reality need not de-legitimate them. Rather, it must underpin the need for validation in interpretation of the findings.[77] As a result, there is an enduring need to reflect on the fidelity of the information gleaned from these multi-stakeholder processes. Validation is achieved through the triangulation of sources. Like all good intelligence assessments, one piece of information

154 *Theory and framework building*

or one perspective is never enough. Therefore, it is by using the confluence of inter-subjectivities (e.g. subjective perspectives of multiple stakeholders) to inform 'cause-and-effect'/contribution narratives (introduced in the previous step) that the reality of what UNPOL are doing in the field can be most usefully mapped. In this sense, the framework advocates for interpretation based on abductive reasoning whereby a representative explanation is derived from contribution analyses which include a systematic search for evidence that corroborates or indeed disconfirms emerging themes.[78] Furthermore, this cross-referencing approach can be used to control, to as great an extent as is possible, for unreliable or incomplete information and bias or points of divergence from the mean such that data is 'good enough' for learning purposes. The circular manner of the process further promises to corroborate or contradict earlier findings in subsequent iterations.

Regarding the need for *disaggregation* of findings, even if success is conceptualised similarly across different constituencies, the impact of missions is unlikely to be felt the same way by everybody, everywhere, all of the time. Horizontal inequalities dictate that the experiences of vulnerable or marginalised groupings such as women, children, ethnic or religious minorities will differ from those in the traditionally privileged demographics such as the political elite, men, etc. Similarly, the reality for people in urban locales with large UN presence will likely compare favourably to others stricken by destabilising factors such as presence of militia or resource extraction possibilities. Therefore, to avoid misleading generalisations and aggregations (particularly when these divisions are potential drivers of instability), assessments need to – wherever possible – code and disaggregate findings along geographic and other demographic dimensions (e.g. sex, ethnicity, religion, income level, level of education) to render a nuanced reflection of reality. Similarly, UNPOL activities can have an intended impact at differing levels of analysis. For example, some missions are only ever intended to operate in a particular region of a country such as UNAMID in the Darfur region of Sudan. Conversely, others straddle two territories such as the MINURCAT mission working in both Chad and the Central African Republic. It is vital, therefore, that interpretation of findings do not elide 'results' and 'environment' levels of aggregation by, for example, assuming that impacts always manifest at the national level. Interpretation of M&E data must look for impacts at differing geographic levels.

Dedicated *reflection* in interpretation is primarily to identify any challenges to effective implementation. Once a contribution story has been constructed through participatory techniques it can then be critically examined and the robustness of the narrative can be interrogated.[79] In this stage, patterns are detected and the strengths and weaknesses of the contribution story are highlighted. The central element of this reflective assessment is highlighting which, if any, exogenous factors are having significant effects on progress and what unintended consequences of action have transpired. The former can include, for example, UNPOL activities and their impact vis-à-vis political commitment of host governments – i.e. are transitional/newly elected governments committed to police reform or placating international will and acquiescing? How is this changing over time? The latter should include assessments of any negative unintended consequences of policing actions, for example, is UNPOL doing inadvertent harm by reinforcing problematic power relations or horizontal inequalities? The reflective process constitutes a way of identifying how UNPOL is affecting as well as being affected by the conflict dynamics and consequently what UNPOL should and should not be held responsible for. Furthermore, it allows for the disaggregation of specific *activities* from the whole of mission perspective whilst at the same time depicting the system-level net effects in a way that can account for UNPOL contribution.[80] In addition to identifying what has worked, this reflective assessment seeks to understand what did not work and why it did not.

In sum, the information emanating from earlier steps of the process is only as good as its interpretation. No indicator of impact will be universally self-evident, and therefore careful and context-sensitive interpretation of the data is crucial to the ultimate utility of assessments.[81] M&E in these settings requires the employment of experience and political analysis, as well as common sense in deciphering and drawing conclusions about the information emanating from the M&E process.[82] Where possible, this should include the explicit recognition of the weaknesses of particular sources and how this has been navigated to avoid over-stating the findings. These interpretation provisions can be undertaken in similar ways to earlier participatory methods – gaining a wide range of perspectives.

Response

Consolidated M&E findings need to be shared widely to multiply and diversify the recipients of information relating to progress. This offers the chance to elicit responses as feedback to ongoing M&E, adding further richness to the analyses and the effectiveness of future iterations of the process. Therefore, it is essential that the findings are rapidly disseminated and accessible to potential end-users – both physically and intellectually. As Menkaus has suggested, the aim should be to infuse findings with a greater appreciation of complexity "without making our analyses indigestible for policymaking processes and programming."[83] Lessons identified or recommendations must therefore be purveyed in an actionable format. However, this desire for useability must be balanced against the tendency to over-simplify findings which can obscure nuances and risk leading to corollary distortions in policy-making.[84] In order to reach all intended audiences, it will be important to tap into and harness dominant modes of information-sharing in society. Harnessing a wide range of media including mission radio stations, myriad information sources, and tapping into informal networks through community outreach – e.g. use of musicians, theatre troupes and comedians – constitutes a valuable enabler for the consistent distribution of information about the mission and its progress.[85] The important thing is that the process is capable of informing the reporting, avoiding the scenario where the reporting format and demands end up dictating the process and information sought.

Once the findings have been articulated and distributed, an important element of this step relates to how recipients react to change or lack thereof implied by the findings. Embedding a way of capturing responses pertains to feedback from the broader group of actors about perceived accomplishments, problems, patterns and trends. In current practice, this is often where linkages break down and the findings have little effect on continuing M&E implementation. Such feedback is vital in this framework for refinements to impact assessments and subsequent cycles of the M&E process. In short, this design feature is intended to avoid the unsatisfactory scenario whereby reports and findings are 'filed and forgotten' – a situation that runs the risk of important feedback loops being broken and subsequent action being ill-informed.

Step 3: Summary

This final step in the process is concerned with interpreting the data emanating from the previous steps, presenting and distributing the consolidated accounts of what is happening to the myriad stakeholders as well as embedding the feedback mechanisms for reactions to their content. This presents the opportunity to further reflect on what is working, to what extent, for whom, in what conditions and why. Consequently, it promises to entrench the participatory imperative and reflexive character of the M&E process in ways that benefit the iterative and incremental adaptation qualities of this process.

Field-level M&E process summary

This internal M&E process mainstreams an awareness of the complexity involved in UNPOL operations in key ways. First, it is tailored to facilitate an understanding of the systemic nature of the problems being addressed and how these problems evolve over time, bringing an emergent perspective to understanding outcomes and attribution. Complexity theory permeates the process, recognising that the desired effects of many UNPOL programmes and activities are difficult to attribute to the mission per se. Consequently, rather than a design that looks to 'shoe-horn' data into attribution-focused assessments, this internal M&E process privileges a nuanced understanding of contribution to outcomes/impacts. Doing so embeds the capacity to demonstrate that UNPOL might be doing all they can to contribute to a certain desired outcomes/impacts whilst providing substantiating evidence of other disabling factors standing in the way. That is, focusing on contribution also restricts to more realistic change what UNPOL are held accountable for. This is not only useful in justifying performance management assessments, but it is crucial for informing the adaptation of future strategies based on more modest accounts of what has been achieved. Furthermore, it implants feedback processes to enable the continuous updating of baselines, objectives and relevant data sources.

Second, it is customised to include the participation of stakeholders beyond the mission. The framework is not intended as a 'one-size-fits-all' approach – on the contrary, it does not stipulate the indicators to produce M&E results. UNPOL missions and their locations are too diverse for standardised indicators. Appositely, the process promotes an approach which is to be populated with appropriate content by those most important to the process at the relevant time. It is therefore a process whereby the right people (i.e. stakeholders broadly defined) can be asked – and themselves ask – the right questions which will, in turn, generate the most relevant data and assessments of progress and change. Consequently, a core quality of this framework is that it mitigates the all-too-common occurrence where the selection of a particular approach henceforth dictates the information seeking and analysis and becomes a prescriptive instrument.

It is important to reiterate that the three steps of this internal process are not discrete finite events or fixed in sequence. Each step is envisaged as a continuous process and as the content of each stage is consistently updated, it in turn feeds into and affects the other steps.[86] Ultimately, the findings of this internal process are intended as a means to learning ends. For these to be realised, the pathways and processes for enabling real-time learning in field operations and feeding into a repository of organisational knowledge should be explicitly tied to the findings of M&E. The following section highlights the nature of the linkages between the internal M&E process explicated above and organisational learning.

Relationship between M&E and organisational learning

If peace operations are to achieve learning objectives and draw optimal benefit from M&E in this regard, it is vital that the insights garnered and lessons identified in the field-level information gathering and analysis process above are captured in the corporate memory of the peace operations apparatus.[87] However, there is currently a lack of institutional mechanisms for translating M&E results into organisational learning.[88] This framework is capable of facilitating learning in three key ways.

First, the real-time and continuous nature of M&E herein means that learning can occur for adjustments at the field level.[89] The observations and findings emanating from the M&E approach laid out above are a prerequisite for what has been referred to as 'first-level organisational learning'. That is, the ability of missions to actively learn from their environment and experiences – 'learning while doing'. The focus on learning as the mission proceeds supports this type of learning irrespective of whether a mission is deemed to be an overall success or a failure after the fact. It is in the use of these insights for adaptation and improvement in responses that learning can be said to have occurred.[90] For example, through improved problem diagnosis and understanding, possible solutions missions can craft more effective programming to address them. Given that outcomes/impacts are perceived to have no unique causal pathway, neither can they be believed to have a single 'silver bullet' solution. Therefore, the substance of the learning made possible by this M&E is firstly the identification of multi-causal relationships and secondly to identify the combinations of activities that might contribute to tangible improvements. Consequently, the field-level M&E can inform the management of missions by feeding valuable information into ongoing planning processes that in turn can inform refinements in practice.

Second, knowledge accumulated through first-level learning in the field is the prerequisite ingredient for 'second-level organisational learning'. The reflexive qualities of the M&E framework – asking questions such as, is this approach suitable for the context? Are there alternative approaches that could meet the same objectives in a more efficient or effective manner? – mean that reflections on the overall strategies and operational concepts employed can feed into headquarters learning. Given that the assumptions underpinning UNPOL activities are largely unproven and certainly under-tested, interrogating the implicit change theories underpinning much of what UNPOL do can lead to developments in how mandates are implemented. Therefore, M&E findings provide the ammunition for testing the credibility of the modes and methods employed, or even the rationale of the entire endeavour, and learning from the insights gleaned.[91] To re-apply the surgery analogy used above,[92] this promises to avoid the situation where 'the operation was a success but the patient died' – in other words, UNPOL implements all of its activities effectively, but the overall endeavour continues to be based on a faulty premise. Where lessons arise about what works and what doesn't across the gamut of UNPOL tasks, such generalisable insights can be captured and shared. For the good and bad experiences gleaned in M&E to become lessons learned requires clear and robust mechanisms to ensure that these practices are captured in the UN's institutional memory. When this knowledge permeates thinking at the strategic level and becomes codified in organisational policies and doctrine, it can be said to have informed 'second-level organisational learning'. This M&E-driven learning is then able to feed into mission design and mandate implementation planning. In this way, the flow of knowledge loops back, feeds into and can have an effect on how existing missions are updated and adapted and how generalities gleaned from the UN's past and present portfolio of missions can support mission design and subsequent implementation planning for new missions.

Finally, the iterative character of the process means that observations can and should lead to learning that informs the adaptation of M&E itself. The findings of M&E and the associated gaps and shortcomings constitute the fuel for learning to aid reflection on and improvement/recalibration of the M&E framework for subsequent cycles. For example, insights emerging from complete cycles of the M&E process can feed into the next iteration, at which point decisions can be made to realign the approach such that it is better matched to the scenario. Furthermore, it presents the opportunity to reflect on each step to adjust and improve the process. For example, how has the context changed? Are there new data opportunities or conversely redundant information sources? Are new data collection methods permissible or more appropriate? Has the political landscape changed to the extent that interpretation needs to adjust accordingly?

In sum, the learning orientation of the framework pertains to organisational learning for adaptation of policies and practices (i.e. first- and second-level learning) as well as adjustments to the M&E process itself. That is, the design is tailored so that field-level impact assessments facilitate multi-level organisational learning – heeding widespread calls for more cross-fertilisation of impact assessment and organisational learning.[93]

Conclusion

In this chapter I have developed a framework for holistic M&E of UNPOL in peace operations. The fundamental argument here is that attempting to enhance M&E in these settings requires the development of M&E *practice* rather than the design of a discrete M&E *methodology* or indicator set. Based on these insights and the deductions from the previous chapters, a framework has been developed to guide this practice in a way that aims to surmount the challenges identified in Chapters 1 and 2. It is based on the argument that improvements in this area can be made by drawing on the insights of complexity theory which underpins the framework in a number of key ways.

Complexity theory informs the overall design of a circular and systemic M&E framework. Consequently, the framework is inherently process-oriented, privileging a recursive/iterative, reflexive practice with multiple critical operational feedback processes to mitigate circuit-breakers and enhance knowledge transition. That is, it is as much about how it is executed as it is about what is done. The chapter presented a field-level M&E process that articulates the important facets of *foregrounding, design and implementation* and the imperatives for *interpreting* and *responding* to findings. Complexity concepts ensure that the approach is tailored to suit the distinguishing conditions unique to – or exacerbated in – conflict-affected environments and the idiosyncrasies of UNPOL endeavours.

Furthermore, it is primarily concerned with robust demonstration of how UNPOL contribute to emergent outcomes/impacts, including when and why they cannot and should not be attributed to their efforts, per se. It is less about asking did 'A cause B', more about asking 'what happened?' and 'why?' As a result, it presents a more systematic modality for tracking and assessing the impact of UNPOL. That is, the framework promises to provide a timelier and much richer reflection of the impact of UNPOL than extant approaches, whilst heeding calls for greater modesty in what these assessments can claim to prove. This necessitates a re-orientation towards legitimising alternative data sources and methods, as well as interpretative lenses that draw on complexity theory.

Current M&E orthodoxy assumes UNPOL missions to be a fixed programme with a clearly delineated time frame where the purpose of M&E is to evidence the achievement of discrete goals for accountability. On the contrary, this framework privileges a scenario where goals are emergent and changeable according to timelines that are undefined and where the overriding purpose of M&E is to facilitate organisational learning as a means to more effective peace operations. The unique insights emanating from field-level M&E conducted in this way can be systematically utilised in real-time to inform adaptation in the field, feed into institutional learning systems at the headquarters level, as well as constitute the evidence for adjusting and refining the M&E process itself. In these ways, the framework promises to invigorate and strengthen the linkages between impact assessment and organisational learning.

Personnel in peace operations and the broader set of stakeholders in the mission environment undergo a continuous and daily process of learning lessons. They experience firsthand what change looks like, as well as the best indicators of it. This framework is a way of eliciting and capturing that experience and understanding in a more flexible way such that it does not depart the mission with rotating contingents or continue to be excluded from what constitutes legitimate knowledge for the M&E process. The next part of this book, comprising three chapters, proceeds to 'test' this framework in the case of the United Nations Mission in Liberia (UNMIL) with the aim of revealing where and how this approach can improve upon current convention, as well as identifying any stumbling blocks and outstanding challenges to its effective implementation. In light of this framework's commitment to extensive foregrounding and a context-sensitive approach, the following chapter addresses the need to provide a detailed background to the conflict and the UNPOL mission in Liberia.

Notes

1 Christian van Stolk, Tom Ling, Anais Reding, and Matt Bassford, *Monitoring and Evaluation in Stabilisation Interventions: Reviewing the State of the Art and Suggesting Ways Forward.* (Santa Monica, CA: RAND Corporation, 2011), 4.

2 Sarah Dalrymple, "Survey of the United Nations Organisation's Arrangements for Monitoring and Evaluating Support to Security Sector Reform", In *Research Report* (London: SAFERWORLD, 2009), 32; Sarah Jane Meharg, "Practitioner Perspectives and Policy Options", In *Measuring What Matters in Peace Operations and Crisis Management*, ed. Sarah Jane Meharg. (Montreal: McGill-Queen's University Press, 2009), 226; Craig Cohen, "Measuring Progress in Stabilization and Reconstruction", In *Stabilization and Reconstruction Series*, ed. USIP (2006), 11.
3 "United Nations Integrated Missions Planning Process (Impp) Guidelines Endorsed by the Secretary-General on 13 June 2006" *International Peacekeeping* 15, no. 4 (2008), 588–607.
4 See: "The United Nations Rule of Law Indicators: Implementation Guide and Project Tools". (New York: United Nations Department of Peacekeeping Operations/Office of the High Commissioner for Human Rights, 2011).
5 This coherence is attained by establishing a reasonably common lexicon and compatible reporting formats, whilst acknowledging that these complementary frameworks will vary in their amenability to the demands of M&E in conflict-affected societies. See: USAID, "Monitoring and Evaluation in Postconflict Settings", (Washington DC: USAID, 2006), 6.
6 Cedric de Coning and Paul Romita, "Monitoring and Evaluation of Peace Operations", (New York/Oslo: International Peace Institute & Norwegian Institute of International Affairs, 2009), 7–8.
7 Cheyanne Church and Julie Shouldice, "The Evaluation of Conflict Resolution Interventions: Framing the State of Play", (Letterkenny: INCORE, 2002), 5.
8 David C. Becker and Robert Grossman-Vermaas, "Metrics for the Haiti Stabilization Initiative", *Prism* 2, no. 2 (2011), 151.
9 Michael Dziedzic, Barbara Sotirin, and John Agoglia, "Metrics Framework for Assessing Conflict Transformation and Stabilization", in *Measuring Progress in Conflict Environments (MPICE)* (New York: United States Institute for Peace, 2008), 5.
10 Jake Sherman, "Measures of Effectiveness in Peacebuilding and State-Building", in *Measuring What Matters in Peace Operations and Crisis Management*, ed. Sarah Jane Meharg (McGill – Queens University Press, 2009), 211.
11 Ellie B. Hearne, "From New York to the Field: A Dialogue on UN Peace Operations", (New York: International Peace Institute, 2010), 6.
12 Dalrymple, "Survey of the United Nations Organisation's Arrangements for Monitoring and Evaluating Support to Security Sector Reform", 31.
13 de Coning and Romita, "Monitoring and Evaluation of Peace Operations", 4–7.
14 The mission typology used to describe UNPOL missions in Chapter 1 is useful to illustrate the chronological progression, but it is important to unpack those tasks that fall under the multidimensional policing type for the express purposes of M&E.
15 The content is primarily drawn from an exhaustive analysis of 'task frequency' in UNPOL mission mandates from 1999 to 2010 conducted by the Stimson Center (See: Table A1.2: 'Prioritizing UNPOL Tasks and Skill Sets Based on Task Frequency in Mission Mandates from 1999 to 2010' in Durch and England, eds., *Enhancing United Nations Capacity to Support Post-Conflict Policing and Rule of Law*, 89–91.). However, additional facets such as tackling organised crime or the protection of civilians do not appear as headline objectives for UNPOL in analyses of the mandate language for previous missions. These thematic involvements have become increasingly implicit in UNPOL concepts of operations and are at the heart of visions articulated for the future of UNPOL in peace operations (See: "Core Business of UN Police and Its Key Partners", in *UN Peacekeeping PDT Standards, Specialized Training Material for Police – 1st Edition* (New York: United Nations, 2009), 7–10. See also: UN,

"United Nations Police", in *Report of the Secretary-General* (New York: United Nations, 2011), 2–6.). It is therefore important that these understated and emerging practices are also revealed and incorporated into the foregrounding of M&E if a representative impact of UNPOL is to be ascertained.
16 See Design and Implementation step below.
17 Otwin Marenin, "Understanding Mission Environments: Local Contexts and the Legitimation of Reforms", in *Making Sense of Peace and Capacity-Building Operations: Rethinking Policing and Beyond*, eds. Bryn W. Hughes, Charles T. Hunt, and Boris Kondoch (Leiden: Martinus Nijhoff, 2010), 21–5.
18 Jay Rothman, "Action Evaluation", in *Beyond Intractibility*, eds. Guy Burgess and Heidi Burgess (Boulder: Conflict Research Consortium, University of Colorado, 2003). Methods for eliciting these perspectives are addressed in subsequent sections below.
19 UN peace operations generally move through phases of: 'Start-up'; 'Stabilisation'; 'Peace Consolidation'; 'Drawdown'; and, 'Withdrawal'. The hypothetical transition through the phases lead to presumed improvements in stability and access and in turn to changing circumstances for M&E.
20 Actors/Stakeholders should be understood as "individuals, groups, and organisations who have an interest (stake) and the potential to influence the actions and aims of an organisation, project, or policy direction" Brugha and Varvasovszky (2000: 239) cited in Mehrizi M., F. Ghasemzadeh, and J. Molas-Gallart, "Stakeholder Mapping as an Assessment Framework for Policy Implementation", *Evaluation* 15, no. 4 (2009).
21 Wibke Hansen, Tobias Gienanth, and Roderick Parkes, "International and Local Policing in Peace Operations: Lessons Learned and the Way Forward to Integrated Approaches", In *International Berlin Workshop Report* (Berlin: ZIF, 2007), 18.
22 See: UNDP, "Handbook on Planning, Monitoring and Evaluating for Development Results", (UNDP, 2009), 25–9.
23 S. Rynn and D. Hiscock, "Evaluating for Security and Justice: Challenges and Opportunities for Improved Monitoring and Evaluation of Security System Reform Programmes", (Saferworld, 2009), 19.
24 Stolk *et al.*, *Monitoring and Evaluation in Stabilisation Interventions: Reviewing the State of the Art and Suggesting Ways Forward*, 9; USAID, "Monitoring and Evaluation in Postconflict Settings", 3–4.
25 For more discussion of expanding data sites and seeking out alternative information sources, see subsequent step.
26 This is not commonplace in the initial stages of M&E; however, in many ways it is similar to recent developments in conflict assessment/analysis. See, for example: USAID, "Conducting a Conflict Assessment: A Framework for Strategy and Program Development", (Washington, DC: U.S. Agency for International Development, 2005).
27 BCPR, "Guidelines for Planning, Monitoring and Evaluation in Conflict Prevention and Recovery Settings", (Bureau Conflict Prevention and Recovery, UNDP), 4.
28 M. H. Ross, "'Good Enough' Isn't So Bad: Thinking About Success and Failure in Ethnic Conflict Management", *Peace and Conflict: Journal of Peace Psychology* 6, no. 1 (2000): 6.
29 Irene Guijt *et al.*, "Evaluation Revisited: Improving the Quality of Evaluative Practice by Embracing Complexity", in *Conference Report* (Wageningen/Randwijk/Utrecht: Centre for Development Innovation, Wageningen University and Research Centre/Context, International Cooperation/Learning by Design, 2011), 20.
30 USAID, "Monitoring and Evaluation in Postconflict Settings", 4.

31 For more detail on suitable methods, particularly those methods capable of achieving impact-oriented assessments, see subsequent step.
32 Sarah Jane Meharg, "Measuring the Effectiveness of Reconstruction and Stabilization Activites", *The Pearson Papers* 10, no. 1 (2007), 42.
33 J. A. Morell, *Evaluation in the Face of Uncertainty: Anticipating Surprise and Responding to the Inevitable* (New York: Guilford Press, 2010), 211–14.
34 Charles Hunt and Bryn Hughes, "Assessing Police Peacekeeping: Systemisation Not Serendipity", *Journal of International Peacekeeping* 14, no. 3–4 (2010): 422–3.
35 Meharg, "Measuring the Effectiveness of Reconstruction and Stabilization Activites", 32.
36 Stolk *et al.*, *Monitoring and Evaluation in Stabilisation Interventions: Reviewing the State of the Art and Suggesting Ways Forward*, 7–8; USAID, "Monitoring and Evaluation in Postconflict Settings", 3.
37 Paul F. Diehl and Daniel Druckman, "Dimensions of the Conflict Environment: Implications for Peace Operation Success", *Journal of International Peacekeeping* 13, no. 1–2 (2009).
38 Caty Clement and Adam C. Smith, "Managing Complexity: Political and Managerial Challenges in United Nations Peace Operations", (New York: International Peace Institute, 2009), 26.
39 Parsons *et al.*, "Developing Indicators to Measure the Rule of Law: A Global Approach" In *VERA International Indicators Group.* (Vera Institute of Justice, 2008), 23; USAID, "Monitoring and Evaluation in Postconflict Settings", 3.
40 'Flexibility' is achieved as a result of the design elements related to data source choices and agile and ecumenical methods – see below.
41 Dalrymple, "Survey of the United Nations Organisation's Arrangements for Monitoring and Evaluating Support to Security Sector Reform", 32; UNDP, "Handbook on Planning, Monitoring and Evaluating for Development Results", 25; Rynn and Hiscock, "Evaluating for Security and Justice: Challenges and Opportunities for Improved Monitoring and Evaluation of Security System Reform Programmes", 18.
42 Stolk *et al.*, *Monitoring and Evaluation in Stabilisation Interventions: Reviewing the State of the Art and Suggesting Ways Forward*, 14.
43 L. Nathan, *No Ownership, No Commitment: A Guide to Local Ownership in Security Sector Reform*, (UK Government: Global Conflict Prevention Pool, University of Birmingham, 2007), 51–2.
44 Ebo Adedeji, "Local Ownership and Emerging Trends in SSR: A Case Study of Outsourcing in Liberia", in *Local Ownership and Security Sector Reform*, ed. Timothy Donais (Geneva/Vienna: DCAF/LIT Verlag, 2008), 154.
45 Annika S. Hansen, "Local Ownership in Peace Operations". In *Local Ownership and Security Sector Reform*, ed. Timothy Donais. (Geneva/Vienna: DCAF/LIT, 2008), 39–58.
46 Sherman, "Measures of Effectiveness in Peacebuilding and State-Building", 211; Robert Egnell and Peter Haldén, "Laudable, Ahistorical and Overambitious: Security Sector Reform Meets State Formation Theory", *Conflict, Security and Development* 9, no. 1 (2009), 32.
47 Harry Jones, "Taking Responsibility for Complexity", in *Briefing Paper 68* (London: Overseas Development Institute [ODI], 2011), 3.
48 Rynn and Hiscock, "Evaluating for Security and Justice: Challenges and Opportunities for Improved Monitoring and Evaluation of Security System Reform Programmes", 19; Bruce Baker, "Grasping the Nettle of Non-State Policing", *Journal of International Peacekeeping* 14, no. 3–4 (2010).
49 Michael Quinn Patton, *Developmental Evaluation: Applying Complexity Concepts to Enhance Innovation and Use*, (New York: Guilford Press, 2010), 14.
50 Jodie Curth and Sarah Evans, "Monitoring and Evaluation in Police Capacity

Building Operations: 'Women as Uniform?'", *Police Practice and Research* 12, no. 6 (2011), 492–505.
51 William Frej and Ben Ramalingam, "Foreign Policy and Complex Adaptive Systems: Exploring New Paradigms for Analysis and Action", in *SFI Working Paper*, Santa Fe Institute (SFI) (2011), 6.
52 Rynn and Hiscock, "Evaluating for Security and Justice: Challenges and Opportunities for Improved Monitoring and Evaluation of Security System Reform Programmes", 11–12.
53 For example, a range of official/formal quantitative sources such as government statistics (e.g. national census records and crime rates and trends); police administrative data (e.g. police deployment records, police logistics units tracking equipment such as vehicles, radios, weapons, office equipment, etc, budgets, training records); the existence and content of legislative documents (e.g. oversight arrangements for police [internal and external], constitutional division of responsibilities between security agencies, etc); policies and procedures (e.g. police SOPs, strategic plans, organisational charts, and domestic performance management frameworks). Whilst qualitative sources are fewer, ad hoc surveys, expert opinion (e.g. UNPOL senior management and advisers) and anecdotal evidence (e.g. insights emanating from exchange of views captured in minutes of formal meetings) capture much of what is frequently utilised in M&E.
54 Jones, "Taking Responsibility for Complexity", 4.
55 For example, other similar evaluations (e.g. other UNPOL missions) and existing research including relevant case studies and independent studies conducted by academic and research institutions. In addition, third-party narrative reports such as those produced by foreign embassies, government agencies, local and international NGOs/civil society groups and the media (e.g. newspaper reports of people killed as result of police action) can shed light on social phenomena of interest. Other sites include branching out to the private sector/business community and even the military.
56 See, for example: Severine Autesserre, *The Trouble with the Congo: Local Violence and the Failure of International Peacebuilding*, Cambridge Studies in International Relations (Cambridge: Cambridge University Press, 2010).
57 Michael Barnett, "Illiberal Peacebuilding and Liberal States", in *Roundtable on Humanitarian Action* (Social Science Research Coucil, 2005), 5.
58 DfID, "Monitoring and Evaluation", in *Stabilisation Issues Note* (London: Stabilisation Unit, UK Government, 2010), 1.
59 Stolk *et al.*, *Monitoring and Evaluation in Stabilisation Interventions: Reviewing the State of the Art and Suggesting Ways Forward*, 9, 20.
60 For example, victimization surveys that ask respondents about their experience of crime as well as their fear of crime and their confidence in police and rule of law sector are salient to the challenge of M&E in UNPOL. See, for example: Robert C. Davis, *The Use of Citizen Surveys as a Tool for Police Reform* (New York: Vera Institute of Justice, 2000); David H. Bayley and Clifford D. Shearing, "The Future of Policing", in *Policing: Key Readings*, ed. Tim Newburn (Portland, OR: Willan, 2005), 720.
61 For example, high quality surveys are notoriously difficult to execute. Large household surveys are both labour- and time-intensive and expensive; need to be conducted with care (conflict-sensitivity); are beset with cultural/linguistic problems; and, can be susceptible to dramatic swings in response. See: DfID, "Measuring and Managing for Results in Fragile and Conflict-Affected States and Situations", 30.
62 Sabine Garbarino and Jeremy Holland, "Quantitative and Qualitative Methods in Impact Evaluation and Measuring Results", in *Issues Paper* (London: Governance and Social Development Resource Centre (GSDRC), 2009), 11–17.

63 Meharg, "Measuring the Effectiveness of Reconstruction and Stabilization Activites", 41–3.
64 John Mayne, "Addressing Cause and Effect in Simple and Complex Settings through Contribution Analysis", in *Evaluating the Complex*, eds. R. Schwartz, K. Forss, and M. Marra (New Brunswick, USA: Transaction Publishers, 2011).
65 Annabelle Nelson, *Storytelling for Prevention* (Evergreen, CO: The WHEEL Council, 1998); Jess Dart, "Report on Outcomes and Get Everyone Involved: The Participatory Performance Story Reporting Technique", in *2008 Australasian Evaluation Society conference* (Perth, 2008); Tineke Abma, "Learning by Telling: Storytelling Workshops as an Organizational Learning Intervention", *Management Learning* 34, no. 2 (2003).
66 Charles McClintock, "Using Narrative Methods to Link Program Evaluation and Organization Development", *The Evaluation Exchange* IX, no. 4 (2004); J. Mayne, "Addressing Attribution through Contribution Analysis: Using Performance Measures Sensibly", *The Canadian Journal of Program Evaluation* 16, no. 1 (2001).
67 Mark Friedman, *Trying Hard Is Not Good Enough: How to Produce Measureable Improvements for Customers and Communities* (Victoria: British Colombia: Trafford Publishing, 2005), 2.
68 Howard White, *A Drop in the Ocean? The International Development Targets as a Basis for Performance Measurement* (Institute of Development Studies, 2002), 7–9.
69 Mayne, "Addressing Cause and Effect in Simple and Complex Settings through Contribution Analysis".
70 Methodologies that employ similar techniques include: 'Outcome mapping' (See: Sarah Earl, Fred Carden, and Terry Smutylo, *Outcome Mapping: Building Learning and Reflection into Development Programs* (Ottawa: International Development Research Centre (IDRC), 2001); 'Contribution analysis' (See: Fiona Kotvojs and Bradley Shrimpton, "Contribution Analysis – a New Approach to Evaluation in International Development", *Evaluation Journal of Australasia* 7, no. 1 (2007).); 'Most Significant Change' (See: Jess Dart and Rick Davies, "A Dialogical, Story-Based Evaluation Tool: The Most Significant Change Technique", *American Journal of Evaluation* 24, no. 2 (2003)); 'Success case method' (See: Robert O. Brinkerhoff, *The Success Case Method: Find out Quickly What's Working and What's Not* (San Francisco: Berrett-Koehler Publishers, 2003).); 'Qualitative case studies' (See: Jennifer Costantino and Tracie Greene, "Reflections on the Use of Narrative in Evaluation", *American Journal of Evaluation* 24, no. 1 (2003)); 'Appreciative Inquiry' (See: Frank Barrett and Ronald Fry, "Appreciative Inquiry in Action: The Unfolding of a Provocative Invitation", in *Appreciative Inquiry and Organizational Transformation: Reports from the Field*, eds. Ronald Fry and Frank Barrett (Westport, CT: Quorum Books, 2002)). See also: 'Multiple Levels and Lines of Evidence' (MLLE); 'List of Possible Causes' (LOPC); and, 'General Elimination Methodology' (GEM).
71 WKKF, "Designing Initiative Evaluation: A Systems-Oriented Framework for Evaluating Social Change Efforts", (W.K. Kellogg Foundation [WKKF], 2007), 28–9.
72 Guijt *et al.*, "Evaluation Revisited: Improving the Quality of Evaluative Practice by Embracing Complexity", 6.
73 INCAF, "Draft Justice and Security Monitoring and Evaluation Toolkit – Version 2", OECD International Network on Conflict and Fragility – Task Team on Peacebuilding, Statebuilding & Security (2010), 5.
74 Michael Bamberger, Jim Rugh, and Linda Mabry, *Realworld Evaluation: Working under Budget, Time, Data, and Political Constraints* (SAGE Publications, Inc, 2011).
75 Patricia Rogers, "Four Key Tasks in Impact Assessment of Complex Interventions", in *Rethinking Impact: Understanding the Complexity of Poverty and Change* (Cali, Colombia, 2008).

76 Stolk *et al.*, *Monitoring and Evaluation in Stabilisation Interventions: Reviewing the State of the Art and Suggesting Ways Forward*, 22.
77 Todd Foglesong and Vera Institute of Justice, "Measuring Progress toward Safety and Justice: A Global Guide to the Design of Performance Indicators across the Justice Sector", (New York: Vera Institute of Justice, 2003), 6.
78 Patton, *Developmental Evaluation: Applying Complexity Concepts to Enhance Innovation and Use*, 284–7.
79 John Mayne, "Contribution Analysis: An Approach to Exploring Cause and Effect", in *ILAC Brief 16* (Rome, Italy: Institutional Learning and Change [ILAC] Initiative, 2008), 3.
80 That is, this approach allows one to identify, for example, that UNPOL *activity* x achieved positive *output* y even though the overall *outcome* z did not show a positive movement, owing to problems in other parts of the mission or environmental factors. As such, it seeks to handle the analogy offered by Smith that, "Even if the surgery (i.e. *activity*) is a success (*output*), the patient may still die (*outcome*)". See: Dennis Smith, "Managing Civpol: The Potential Performance Management in International Public Services", in *Rethinking International Organizations: Pathology and Promise*, eds. Dennis Dijkzeul and Yves Beigbeder (New York: Berghahn, 2003) 275.
81 Ken Menkhaus, "Measuring Impact: Issues and Dilemmas", in *Occasional Paper Series* (Geneva: InterPeace, 2003), 12.
82 Sarah Jane Meharg, "Emerging Trends in a Common Tradespace", in *Measuring What Matters in Peace Operations and Crisis Management*, ed. Sarah Meharg. (Montreal: McGill – Queen's University Press, 2009), 249.
83 Menkhaus, "State Fragility as a Wicked Problem". *Prism* 1, no. 2 (2010): 85–100.
84 Meharg, "Emerging Trends in a Common Tradespace", 249.
85 Charles T. Hunt, "Public Information as a Mission Critical Component of West African Peace Operations", *KAIPTC Monograph No. 5* (New York: United Nations Peacekeeping Best Practices Section, 2006).
86 For example, changes in the security conditions and the phase of the mission surfaced in the foregrounding step will necessarily feed into and influence the implementation and utilisation steps, as well as the design step that follows it in the process sequence.
87 Susanna Campbell, "When Process Matters: The Potential Implications of Organisational Learning for Peacebuilding Success", *Journal of International Peacebuilding and Development* 4, no. 2 (2008).
88 Clement and Smith, "Managing Complexity: Political and Managerial Challenges in United Nations Peace Operations", 5; Thorston Benner, Stephan Mergenthaler, and Philipp Rotmann, *The New World of UN Peace Operations: Learning to Build Peace?* (Oxford: Oxford University Press, 2011), 211–14.
89 Stolk *et al.*, *Monitoring and Evaluation in Stabilisation Interventions: Reviewing the State of the Art and Suggesting Ways Forward*, 4.
90 Lise Morjé Howard, *UN Peacekeeping in Civil Wars* (Cambridge: Cambridge University Press, 2008), 16.
91 Menkhaus, "Measuring Impact: Issues and Dilemmas", 4.
92 See note 80 above.
93 Guijt *et al.*, "Evaluation Revisited: Improving the Quality of Evaluative Practice by Embracing Complexity", 20; Campbell, "When Process Matters: The Potential Implications of Organisational Learning for Peacebuilding Success".

Part III
Empirical case study and implications

5 Conflict and consequence in Liberia

Introduction

The previous chapter outlined a framework for doing M&E that is informed by complexity theory in order to overcome the challenges facing UNPOL and the M&E thereof. This included a dedicated stage in order to ensure subsequent impact assessments and organisational learning processes are context-sensitive. The purpose of this chapter is to provide a background to the events, causes and consequences of the protracted conflict in Liberia and the UNPOL mission deployed by the UN in response. In keeping with the tenets and principles of the framework introduced previously, this includes a nuanced conflict analysis and identifies a range of influential stakeholders and variables relating to public safety in post-conflict Liberia.

The chapter has two main parts. The first presents a brief background to Liberia's genesis including the political, economic and social development that occurred between formation and the outbreak of civil war. It proceeds to chronicle the two phases of violent conflict in Liberia stretching from 1989 to 2003, addresses the competing narratives regarding the root causes of the conflict and documents the major consequences of protracted insecurity. The second part introduces the UN peace operation in Liberia, first detailing its mandate then analysing the mission's milestone achievements and examining the UNPOL experience to date. This includes a description of the UNPOL component from inception through to contemporary operational circumstances, including significant changes during the mission lifetime and its primary activities. The final section charts the drawdown of the mission to date and its relevance to UNPOL objectives.

A short history of Liberia: 'the love of liberty brought us here'

On the stretch of coast between modern day Sierra Leone and Côte d'Ivoire, known by European traders and slavers as the 'Pepper Coast' after the ubiquitous Malagueta pepper,[1] Liberia was established in 1822. A project of the American Colonization Society (ACS), it was conceived of as a sanctuary for 'free people of colour' – who Moran describes as "descendents of Africans who by luck, birth, or their own efforts, were no longer legally enslaved".[2] A combination of manumitted slaves from America, the Caribbean and other 'recaptives' from across Africa taken from impounded slave ships, this settler group assumed the mantle as the national elite and became known as the 'Americo-Liberians' or 'Congoes'.[3]

This invasion brought dominant systems of war, trade and government as well as a mission to proselytise and civilise the 'natives'[4] in what effectively subjugated Liberian indigenes to an era of indirect rule that has been labelled as 'Black Colonialism'.[5] The indigenous population, between 2 and 3 million, draw their identities from one or more of over sixteen ethno-linguistic groupings, commonly referred to by Liberians as 'tribes'.[6] Liberia, located in the Mano River basin, declared independence in 1847, making it Africa's oldest republic.

What followed, basically uninterrupted until 1980, has been described as a "political autocracy and economic anomie".[7] This was overseen and perpetuated by the Americo-Liberian oligarchy manifest in the one-party rule of the True Whig Party,[8] the machinery of the Church and the Masonic Order, whereby a mere 5 per cent of Liberia's population oppressed the majority indigenous population through political exclusion and socio-economic subordination.[9] In the 'hinterland', this indigenous population were refused the privileges of settler Liberians and subjugated by the often barbaric Liberian Frontier Force. Consequently, social order in the arcadian areas consisted of myriad localised 'stateless communities',[10] governed by a range of alternative sources of political legitimacy, including the influential 'secret societies' such as the Poro authority.[11]

Despite reforms by the post-World War II administrations of Presidents Tubman and Tolbert aimed at incorporating the 'natives',[12] these achieved little beyond creating patrimonial rule and clientism.[13] This reality was further entrenched through the self-serving control, selection and removal of customary Chiefs by the autocratic Presidency.[14] In the context of a clamour for independence in the sub-region and Africa more broadly, disgruntled elements of society organised resistance movements which came to a head in the infamous 'rice riots' of 1979, during which a number of protestors were shot dead in the streets of Monrovia.[15] These events instigated a steep descent into crisis.

As Adedeji has described, "the Liberian social contract had been breached by a self-serving elite which misgoverned the people to the point of rebellion and anarchy."[16] In 1980 a group of low-ranking soldiers launched a bloody coup d'état. Led by Master-Sergeant Samuel K. Doe, the uprising overthrew Tolbert and the long-reigning True Whig Party. Portrayed as an indigenous revolution, it removed the Americo-Liberian elite from power for the first time in the country's history.[17] Tolbert and 13 senior officials were assassinated on a central Monrovia beach following show trials.[18]

With promises of return to civilian control, constitutional reform and inclusive democratic elections within five years, the People's Redemption Council (PRC) with Doe increasingly at the helm initially drew the support of intellectuals and other elements of society agitating for political transformation.[19] However, Doe's decade-long reign proved to be a brutal one, including political assassinations and the decimation of civil society, precipitating a 'brain drain' of the educated class into exile.[20] His regime went about consolidating its power, inserting members of his own Krahn ethnic group – themselves only 5 per cent of the population – in high-ranking positions in parliament and other institutions of state.[21] A major component of this strategy occurred through his ethnic reconstitution of the security apparatus, purging the Armed Forces of Liberia (AFL) of ethnic Gios and Manos, replacing them with Krahn brethren – traditionally marginalised in the Non-Commissioned Officer ranks – in senior positions.[22] The ethnicized security forces morphed into an 'instrument of oppression' for Doe and his base.[23]

Doe's "clumsy theft"[24] of rigged but US-endorsed elections in 1985 consolidated his tightening grip on executive authority.[25] This was closely followed by a failed coup attempt led by General Thomas Quiwonkpa – a key player in the 1980 coup and original member of the PRC before fleeing. Quiwonkpa and his fellow putschists were executed and, in retaliation, the AFL was sent to 'pacify' his homeland of Nimba County where they rampaged, looted and burned villages, raping and killing thousands of ethnic Gios and Manos in the process.[26] Adebajo has claimed that, "this single episode, more than any other, set the stage for the exploitation of ethnic rivalries that would eventually culminate in Liberia's civil war."[27]

14 years of civil war

> The Liberian conflict topped and surpassed all other wars in form and character, in intensity, in depravity, in savagery, in barbarism and in horror.[28]

Liberia was in a state of civil war, punctuated by temporary lulls, for approximately 14 years. This era of disarray and violence is often depicted as two discrete wars: the first from 1989 until the election of Charles Taylor in 1997; and the second, beginning around 2001 until a peace agreement in 2003. It is, however, somewhat misleading to categorise these as two separate wars. In reality, fighting ended shortly before and resumed soon after the 1997 elections, rendering almost a decade and a half of violent conflagrations and a plethora of broken peace agreements involving around ten rebel factions that destabilised the broader Mano River basin.

The first phase began when Charles Taylor, a former official in Doe's government,[29] led his *National Patriotic Front of Liberia* (NPFL) across the Ivorian border into Nimba County on Christmas Eve, 1989. Little more than 100 fighters armed by and trained in Libya at Col. Qaddafi's notorious Benghazi camp for African Revolutionaries[30] but with the express aim – communicated primarily through histrionic interviews with the BBC World Service – of removing Doe and his regime. Residents of Nimba – predominantly Gio and Mano peoples, targeted so brutally by the AFL pogroms – responded to Taylor's anti-Doe message and rushed to join the NPFL. Primarily Gio former soldiers, farmers and mercenaries recruited from neighbouring countries, their ranks swelled to as much as 20,000 in just a few months.[31]

The first year of the war is estimated to have internally displaced 700,000, with tens of thousands more seeking refuge in Ghana and Nigeria.[32] Despite predictable outsider assessments characterising it a product of 'ancient tribal hatreds'[33] – more nuanced analyses summarised the conflict as one that defied easy characterisation as, "[i]t lacked an ideological motivation or direction, and was characterised by sordid opportunism".[34] Celebrated academic and former interim Liberian President, Amos Sawyer, captured this nefarious marauding in the following:

> Whatever discipline and revolutionary principles instilled by [their] training seemed to have been undermined by the NPFL leadership's exhortation to 'capture what you can' and 'keep what you capture'. Thus, banditry was the ideology of the NPFL right from the start ... In the absence of political ideology, terror, use of drugs and opportunity for booty served to drive the group and underpin personal loyalty to its leader ... Far from seeking to establish a social order, educate or indoctrinate villagers and thereby win their support – behaviour typical of the guerrilla movements of the 1970s – the NPFL and its cohorts in plunder so terrorised local populations that they fled.[35]

By 1990, Doe's dictatorship teetered on the precipice of collapse. After a decade of mismanagement, his administration was riddled with corruption and the economy was in dire straits – a result of declining revenues from resource exports and the significant termination of US economic assistance. Meanwhile, despite gaining territory, by July 1990 the NPFL began to fragment and disintegrated into two, spawning the Independent NPFL (INPFL) led by Prince Johnson.[36]

None of the factions were able to gain the upper hand and the Economic Community of West African States' (ECOWAS) Mediation Committee talks in Banjul, Gambia, in August led to the creation of the ECOWAS Cease-Fire Monitoring Group (ECOMOG) comprised initially of 3,000 troops from five West African countries.[37] It was mandated to supervise a ceasefire, establish an interim government and organise elections within a year.³⁸ Whilst its deployment was credited with halting the NPFL's assault on Monrovia, its overall effectiveness was contested due to perceived lack of legitimacy amongst key stakeholders as well as its own malfeasance. The Nigerian-led mission was politically controversial for the international community, lacked support from key Francophone ECOWAS member states³⁹ and was outright opposed by Taylor's NPFL.⁴⁰ Regarding its conduct, ECOMOG was implicated as a partial player and at times an exploitative one,⁴¹ engaging in its own share of abusive behaviour and pillage.⁴²

On 9 September 1990, under the less than watchful eye of ECOMOG, President Doe was captured by INPFL forces at the Freeport of Monrovia. He was taken to their nearby base, where Johnson presided over his protracted torture and eventual murder.⁴³ Following Doe's demise, the hapless AFL scattered to Sierra Leone and ECOMOG secured Monrovia to allow for the installation of an 'Interim Government of National Unity' (IGNU). As it transpired, the IGNU was severely limited due to Taylor's rejection of its authority and its complete reliance on ECOMOG for its survival.⁴⁴ Meanwhile, Taylor had erected parallel government structures in Gbarnga, Bong County, which enabled him to exploit the vast natural resources of the hinterland.

The following seven years would be characterised by over a dozen abrogated and failed peace agreements. From 1990–3 the NPFL mounted numerous unsuccessful attempts to take Monrovia by force.⁴⁵ Taylor's cross-border meddling in Sierra Leone and Guinea, plus spillover issues in Côte d'Ivoire, led to destabilisation of the Mano River basin. It also saw the emergence of the United Liberation Movement for Democracy in Liberia (ULIMO) – primarily remnants of Doe's disintegrated army – who joined the conflict attacking the NPFL from Sierra Leone.⁴⁶

The Cotonou Peace Accord of July 1993 called for the replacement of the IGNU with a Liberian National Transitional Government (LNTG), the expansion of ECOMOG to include more Francophone troops, the scheduling of elections in which all faction leaders could stand, and the creation of the United Nations Observer Mission in Liberia (UNOMIL) – comprising 368 military observers, mandated to assist ECOMOG in implementing the accord.⁴⁷ This failed to stick and in late 1994, ECOWAS-driven mediation efforts changed tack, moving away from enforced peace in Liberia towards the inclusion of rebel leaders in transitional arrangements. The Akosombo Agreements led to a ceasefire and the creation of a Council of State to reflect a balance of main factions. However, this too faltered and fighting resumed. Subsequent shifts in the balance of military power led to peace talks in Abuja, Nigeria.⁴⁸ Peace talks culminated in the 'Abuja II' peace agreement which stipulated a reconstitution of the Council of State, headed by Ruth Perry,⁴⁹ rescheduled elections and included the provision for disarmament of rebel fighters.⁵⁰

Presidential elections went ahead in July 1997. Through unparalleled capacity for patronage, bullying and the popular fear of renewed conflict

– an atmosphere of resignation epitomised by an oft-cited rally song "You killed my Ma, you killed my Pa; I'll still vote for you" – Charles Taylor swept to a landslide victory with over 75 per cent of the vote declared 'free and fair' by the UN and ECOWAS and finally assumed *de jure* executive power, bringing to an end the first phase of the conflict.[51] Taylor's election as Liberia's twenty-second President precipitated a withdrawal of the international community's security presence and diminished support to a government deemed untrustworthy and abusive. It signalled the end of UNOMIL, as the Secretary-General reluctantly created the UN's first peacebuilding support office, UN Office in Liberia (UNOL), in its stead. This office was poorly resourced and had a weak mandate – in no small part due to Taylor's contestations – yet was chastised for being an apologist for him.[52] Taylor came under increasing criticism for his support to the Revolutionary United Front (RUF) in Sierra Leone as they battled with ECOMOG – further exacerbated by his refusal to cooperate with ECOMOG in its efforts to reinstate Tejen Kabbah's legitimately elected government in early 1998. Taylor also refused to allow ECOMOG to fulfil its role under the Abuja agreement in disarming Liberia's combatants.[53] Never on good terms with ECOMOG, these events accelerated the departure of the remaining ECOMOG troops from Monrovia by the end of 1998.

Despite apparently conciliatory attempts to include his enemies in government, Taylor quickly became tyrannical and cracked down on his political opponents.[54] Almost six years of Taylor in the Executive Mansion led to little more than continued exploitation of the state and its wealth and further degradation of its infrastructure and institutions. He formalised his brand of warlordism in the Presidency and used it as a launching pad for continued adventurism in the sub-region.[55] Despite handsome gains from the privatisation of mineral resources in the interior, there was little investment in improving the lot of ordinary Liberians.[56] No genuine attempt was made to heal the wounds of war or to build the state into anything beyond a replica of the shadow state – engineered for regime security and wealth accumulation – that Doe's administration left behind.[57]

Following suit with his predecessors, Taylor reconfigured the security apparatus into one which would be committed to his survival in executive power.[58] This involved reconstituting the AFL, replacing many Krahn soldiers with thousands of his erstwhile NPFL troops.[59] However, this trend went wider and deeper than inserting faithful fighters into the army. The practice of including long-time comrades – many of whom had fought with him as child soldiers – was pervasive throughout the security sector. Taylor's son, 'Chucky', was placed at the helm of the conspicuous Anti-Terrorism Unit (ATU), whilst his cousin, Joe Tate, was made Chief of the Liberian National Police (LNP). His reputation for having commanded political death squads throughout the conflict was only reinforced by the conduct of the LNP under his leadership, staffed with many former fighters who wielded considerable power and acted with impunity.[60] The Special Operations Division (SOD) – parochially known as "Sons of the Devil" – was another notorious and terrifying component of this deviant network of security agencies and militia. As Adedeji has described, "Taylor used the armed and security forces to suppress and oppress Liberians to levels hitherto unknown."[61]

The country relapsed into violence shortly after Taylor's election as insurgency intensified in mid-1999 with the emergence of the Liberians United for Reconciliation and Democracy (LURD). Formed from the remnants of the ULIMO factions and other anti-Taylor elements, the LURD was allegedly supported by Guinea – the base from which they attacked into Liberia's north-western Lofa County.[62] Subsequently, in response to the outbreak of insurrectionary violence in neighbouring Côte d'Ivoire believed to involve former RUF/Liberian fighters as soldiers of fortune, the Ivorian government supported a breakaway faction of LURD called the Movement for Democracy in Liberia (MODEL).[63]

These groups advanced on Monrovia from the northwest and southeast, respectively. Fighting inflicted a huge toll on civilian populations as massacres were committed by rebels and government forces alike against defenceless civilians.[64] Furthermore, the LURD's indiscriminate shelling of Monrovia left civilians trapped and scared.[65] By the middle of 2003, LURD and MODEL forces controlled most of Liberia's interior and encircled Monrovia.[66] This predicament and mounting international pressure compelled Taylor's beleaguered government to participate in peace talks with rebels, opposition political parties and civil society. During negotiations, the Special Court for Sierra Leone (SCSL) indicted Charles Taylor for atrocities committed in the conflict there and issued a warrant for his arrest. Soon thereafter, Taylor relinquished power in Liberia and went into exile in Nigeria on 11 August 2003. On 18 August 2003, the Comprehensive Peace Agreement (CPA) was signed in Accra, Ghana.[67]

Bringing to an end this second phase of fratricidal conflict, amongst its provisions, the CPA stipulated two major pillars for implementing the peace agreement. First, it called for the creation of an interim coalition government comprised of LURD, MODEL, residual Taylor government elements and civil society. The National Transitional Government of Liberia (NTGL) formed in October 2003, under the Presidency of Liberian businessman, Gyude Bryant. Second, it requested the deployment of a UN stabilisation force to help restore peace and stability and assist the transitional government in preparing to conduct national elections in October 2005. As the UN force was generated, the ECOWAS Mission in Liberia (ECOMIL) with approximately 3,500 troops deployed shortly after signatory.

Root causes and drivers of protracted conflict

The proximate causes of the protracted civil war were many and complex.[68] Indeed, explanations for recurrence of civil war following Charles Taylor's election are also contested.[69] No single variable can explain the causes of war. However, there is consensus that the drivers of the first phase featured in the reversion to the second phase.[70] These are commonly split between issues to do with the policies of exclusion and reasons of political economy; however, the failure of the security sector to afford basic protections to Liberians is also a significant factor. This section briefly addresses each of these causes/drivers.

First, some have claimed that Liberia's recurrent conflict was the product of exclusionary socio-economic and political policies.[71] Many others go further to suggest that Liberia's creation and discriminatory constitution laid the foundations for what followed.[72] They point to the exclusionary governance of successive administrations, including economic and political marginalisation, that has entrenched enmities between indigenous and 'settler' groups and the corollary land disputes and inequitable distribution of benefits from natural resource extraction and trade. Ellis has posited that "Americo-Liberians, in fact, were as much a social and political class, a type of aristocracy, as they were a true ethnic group."[73] These social strata were transformed into significant political cleavages in quick order when the conflict began in 1989.

Others highlight the importance of parochial identities (e.g. (sub-) ethnic, religious, regional) as well as alliance and allegiances between different ethnic groups and the Liberian state in perpetuating cycles of inter- and intra-ethnic violence.[74] This is particularly salient in relation to the demonisation of the Mandingos, often described as 'strangers' or non-Liberians; and the targeting of the Gio and Mano tribes during Doe's purges of Nimba County and subsequent retaliatory attacks against the Krahn. Some have specifically identified the religious and spiritual dimensions of Liberian social order – particularly in the countryside – as a contributing factor to the trajectory of the conflict.[75] In basic terms, issues of identity-based alienation, exclusion and inequity have been identified as a key factor in the ease with which ethnicity could be exploited and mobilised during the conflict.

The second commonly forwarded explanation relates to the political economy of war. In the context of economic collapse – a result of falling export commodity but rising oil and food prices – the plunder and illicit trade in Liberia's natural resources became an increasingly attractive proposition and a war economy emerged out of the ruins of the formal economy.[76] Rebel factions occupied resource-rich locations or transit hubs and economic benefits reaped from the control of territory subsequently produced a potent incentive to perpetuate the war.[77] For example, in 1995 alone, diamonds and gold amounting to somewhere between US$300 million and US$500 million, US$27 million worth of rubber and timber worth US$53 million were exported to markets in Europe and Southeast Asia by Liberia's warlords.[78] Whilst these two narratives are important elements of repeated relapse into conflict, another lesser cited reason for the intensity, longevity and recurrent nature of conflict in Liberia relates to the politicization and degradation of the security sector.

Since its creation as a republic, Liberia's security institutions have been politicised to some extent and have never been a protector of the people, but rather abusive instruments of regime-security and perpetuation of political power.[79] As described above, the powerful office of the President has repeatedly personalised and invariably militarised the security sector from their genesis as the 'home guards' through the Liberian Frontier Force (LFF) to the AFL, the Liberian National Police (LNP) and other specialist security agencies such as the Special Security Services (SSS) and the notorious Anti-terrorist Unit (ATU).[80] It is argued that these conditions not only failed to prevent but may have contributed to the descent into civil conflict.[81]

During the war years, the security sector was synonymous with violent practices, corruption and abuse of power. It became highly factionalised and agencies were tightly controlled by the Presidency or had close connections with particular rebel groups, who respectively brandished considerable clout over their actions.[82] Liberia's security institutions were a constant threat to the civilian population throughout the many years of war.[83] A key feature of the security sector was its abuse of official authority for private gain as well as its proclivity for human rights abuses, including arbitrary detention, torture and extrajudicial killings, often with impunity.[84] In effect, the Liberian security sector underwrote what had become a praetorian society. This lack of internal public security also allowed for and was perpetuated by a pervasive presence of organised crime (with transnational characteristics) – ranging from the illicit trade in natural resources such as timber and diamonds to the trafficking in arms, drugs and people.[85] Whilst there is little data available to validate anecdotal accounts common in reports of the Panel of Experts and reports by organisations such as Global Witness, official Liberian government peacebuilding strategy documentation states that, "[t]he breakdown of law and order and the over centralization of rule of law institutions have been identified as having been central root causes of Liberia's conflict."[86]

The consequences of protracted civil war

Fourteen years of almost continuous civil conflict exacted a tremendous toll on Liberia politically, economically and socially, leaving Liberia in "a state of decrepitude".[87] The war witnessed widespread human rights abuses and atrocities by all parties. It is estimated that as many as 270,000 people died – amounting to around 10 per cent of the pre-war population[88] – and over half of these were thought to be non-combatants. A devastating hallmark of the Liberian civil war was the extremely high rates of sexual and gender-based violence that accompanied it. According to a co-convened World Health Organisation-Government of Liberia study in 2005, 91.7 per cent of women and girls interviewed had been subjected to multiple violent acts during Liberia's conflict when rape was a frequently employed weapon of war.[89]

Cumulatively, around 1.8 million Liberians were displaced, most internally but at least 700,000 sought refuge in neighbouring countries. This voluminous displacement, severe dislocation and the associated fracture of family units led to a breakdown of communities and the degeneration of social fabric.[90] Civil society emerged severely disempowered with deleterious consequences for social cohesion – particularly in rural areas.[91] Consequently, post-war Liberia is replete with social cleavages – some simply revealed, but others deepened or created during the fighting. For example, the issue of ethnic and communal disputes over land and resources were exacerbated by the war and continue to pose serious threats to the long-term stability of Liberia.[92]

Regarding infrastructure, it is estimated that 80 per cent of dwellings were damaged or destroyed during the fighting.[93] The country's roads are generally in a poor state and largely unpassable during the lengthy wet season, leaving rural populations and other urban centres disconnected from the capital and each other with negative consequences for economic activity as well as security agency coverage. Basic utilities were not functioning throughout the conflict and – despite some progress since 2007 – electricity, access to drinking water and sanitation are still not to be expected beyond metro-Monrovia. Similarly, public health services are basically unavailable or at least inaccessible to the majority of Liberians.[94] In addition to the exodus of skilled people during the war years, the education system ground to a halt such that the UN has suggested that Liberia might be the only country in the world where the younger generation is less educated/literate than their parents.[95]

Governance and institutional degradation

In terms of governance, by the end of Taylor's rule, the Liberian state was akin to a criminal enterprise.[96] Arms dealers, diamond merchants, timber loggers and traffickers of drugs and people had free run and often protection of the Liberian state.[97] The personal control over and corruption of the apparatus of the state, linkages to criminal and terrorist organisations as well as the regional and international facilitation and distribution networks had transformed the Liberian Presidency into the *capo di tutti capi* of a vast criminal empire where high-level political office became a means of self-enrichment with impunity and the licit and illicit were oftentimes indistinguishable.[98]

As the architects of the conflict sought lucre through plunder, the national economy was in free fall. Traditional measures such as GDP per capita plummeted from $1,269 in 1980 to $280 in 2003 – which goes down as one of the largest reversals ever recorded[99] – leaving national government with paltry budgets. This has been a major contributing factor to the lack of opportunities for job creation and in part explains the enduring unemployment rates estimated to be as high as 85 per cent – at least in the formal sphere.[100] Widespread income disparities have also contributed to rendering crippling poverty where as many as 64 per cent of the population live on less than US$1 a day.[101] Eight years after the end of the war, Liberia was 182nd out of 187 countries ranked in the UNDP's Human Development Index for 2011, making it one of the world's poorest countries.[102]

A decade and a half of manipulating the machinery of government and neglect of public service provision led to the severe degradation of government institutions. The prolonged insecurity precipitated or facilitated the collapse of fundamental institutions of governance.[103] Nowhere is this shortfall more conspicuous than in relation to the security sector.[104] This includes the various Ministries of Defence, Justice and National Security, but was particularly true in the case of the criminal justice system as the judiciary, corrections and policing institutions essentially warped and fell into a state of disrepair.[105] The conflict eroded the capacities of the armed forces, the police and the plethora of additional security sector agencies.[106] This left the police and other internal security agencies dysfunctional,[107] incompetent and beset by lack of professionalism.[108] Police were largely unpaid and encouraged to extort bribes from civilians so as to 'pay yourself' – a modality akin to that of the old LFF.[109] As described above, the LNP – as with the security sector more broadly – was personalised, politicised and militarised. When all was said and done, the LNP and the rest of the security agencies performing policing roles were able to operate with impunity.[110]

This has left a legacy of a besmirched reputation for Liberia's security institutions and led to a heavy stigma that has proven hard to shake.[111] This, in turn, has contributed to a deep-seated lack of confidence amongst Liberians in relation to the security sector,[112] nowhere stronger than the distrust and contempt directed towards the Liberian National Police – the front line of the formal security sector and interface between the state and the public.[113] As Malan has noted, "not surprisingly, by the time of the August 2003 Comprehensive Peace Agreement 10 (CPA), [p]olice and military officers were not regarded as a source of protection, but rather as powers to be feared."[114] A further consequence of the lack of state protection was the emanation of non-state alternatives.

180 *Empirical case study and implications*

Role of non-state providers of security and justice

As a result of this individual and community vulnerability and the dysfunction or absence of the formal trappings of the state, particularly outside of urban centres, traditional systems and alternative sources of governance were important to new social and political orders emerging as a result of these shocks to the system. Over the course of protracted insecurity, informal social institutions were a vital source of conflict resolution within and between ethnic communities as well as integral players in the provision of basic public goods and management of local level development and even crucial infrastructure projects.[115] Most pertinent to this inquiry, such actors were particularly salient in the areas of public safety and justice.[116]

Liberia has a long history of legal dualism and non-state security and justice systems have long since existed, particularly in areas neglected or beyond the reach of the state.[117] Indeed, in terms of underwriting public safety, since its creation the Liberian state and its national security agencies have been unable to establish or maintain a monopoly on the use of force throughout Liberia's territory.[118] Given the nature of the conflict in Liberia, at all stages since 1989, the government security apparatus had very little authority in large tracts of the territory. In the absence of state-based protection amidst chronic insecurity, alternative security arrangements often filled the vacuum. For example, during the conflict, communities initiated a range of ad hoc arrangements as self-protection strategies. Whilst spontaneous, these often utilised or were borne out of long-standing social institutions or drew on customary pan-ethnic organisations for implementation. Sawyer presents two major examples, in terms of physical security, concerning the Poro authority[119] in the northwest and formation of community-anchored auxiliary forces in the southeast.[120]

It is important to note that many of these non-state providers also suffered during the conflict. Like formal state institutions, traditional systems were corrupted, degraded and at times denigrated and discredited. As the war destroyed social capital, traditional governance systems were eroded, in part or in whole, including corruption and or infiltration of traditional societies like the Poro.[121] A major factor in this was the rise of youth to positions of authority and power in rebel groups which often led to them to challenge and demean the traditional authority of elders, including the chieftaincies.[122] Nevertheless, some non-state mechanisms and arrangements endured and even thrived throughout conflict – indeed the concept and local legitimacy of non-state security and justice provision itself is an important consequence. As a result, they have played an important role in the rural security sector and now constitute important elements of the security environment.[123]

It is such that in post-conflict Liberia, most people are faced with a dual system when it comes to security and justice where many turn to the non-state realm to meet their basic needs. As Kantor and Persson have explained, "on a day to day basis most Liberians find themselves navigating a continuum of choices for both their security and justice."[124] As described in Chapter 1, these sources of non-state policing capture how citizens turn to various security actors depending on their specific security needs[125] and can be commercial or community-based and informal in nature.[126] Whilst the private security companies present in post-conflict Liberia are significant in both number and function,[127] it is the community-based mechanisms such as the civil defence forces, known as Community Watch Teams or Groups, which have been most influential in the Liberian setting and present more of a challenge to post-conflict policing endeavours. Such groups – sometimes operating under the auspices of traditional chiefs or local 'big men';[128] sometimes retaining pre-existing (para-) military structures and chains of command from the war[129] – have persisted and even proliferated in the aftermath of the conflict as UNMIL and the nascent LNP have struggled to prevent crime and public disorder.

There are competing ideas about the utility of these watch groups. On the one hand, there are perceived benefits given that they can plug a public security gap, often with high levels of local legitimacy and furthermore they occupy young potentially unemployed often marginalised (men) ex-combatants. On the other hand, concerns remain over the lack of oversight and code of conduct as well as the latent risks of escalating violence and potential for re-mobilisation.[130] Notwithstanding these unresolved issues, as Kantor and Persson state, "vigilantes, like other forms of informal security provider networks, are an important part of the Liberian security context."[131]

Studies in 2007 and 2010 showed that Liberians generally point to UNMIL as their main guarantor of security. However, the capacities and perceptions of sources of protection thereafter are less clear.[132] Similar research conducted in 2009 suggested that the preference of most Liberians would remain with informal sources – focusing alternatively on restorative justice and social reconciliation – even if the formal criminal justice system was able to provide timely, affordable and impartial results.[133] These suggestions are buttressed by 2011 population-based survey research on security and dispute resolution.[134]

Security (and justice) services in Liberia have always been – and continue to be – provided by a myriad of state and non-state actors. Whilst Liberia's protracted civil war has had an effect on the functioning and public perceptions of all of these providers, the enduring existence and local legitimacy of informal providers means that they have important implications for the post-conflict security sector and in the formations of public perceptions of the formal state apparatus.[135] Non-statutory sources of security are a preeminent factor in post-conflict Liberia and many argue that they need to be part of the equation in addressing the provision of public safety going forward.[136] Regardless, it is apparent that non-state providers of policing services need to be acknowledged and their influence understood in any effort to gauge the progress of human-centred security sector reform.

182 *Empirical case study and implications*

In sum, the social, economic and political consequences of the war have significant ramifications for the ways in which peace in Liberia is consolidated and built from the ruins of war. They are vital starting points in the challenge of addressing post-conflict public security and the rule of law. In particular, given the state-complicity in human rights abuses of the very people it has the primary responsibility to protect and the legacy of predatory security agencies acting with impunity, one of the major challenges facing post-conflict Liberia is building a capacity to provide for public safety capable of earning the trust and respect of ordinary Liberians. Indeed, some have gone as far as to say that the success and sustainability of Liberia's war-to-peace transition is largely dependent upon this.[137]

Support and assistance to the security and rule of law architecture is deemed to be essential for the consolidation of peace in Liberia and the wider sub-region. These realisations led to strong calls for holistic Security Sector Reform in post-War Liberia. Importantly, and in keeping with the section discussing the importance of informal providers above, Aboagye and Rupiya contend that, "the reform of the security sector should be informed by the dynamics of Liberia's politico-military history, which have dealt a deadly blow to the monopoly of the state over the use of coercive violence, and should involve the broad spectrum of state and non-state actors."[138] The post-conflict challenge for Liberia might not just be about restoring state structures, but rather reinventing a state system for public safety. In order for Liberia to move towards just, equitable and sustainable peace and prosperity, it cannot reproduce the security structures of the past. The perceived centrality of addressing the abusive legacy of Liberian security agencies saw UNPOL and Security Sector Reform (SSR) objectives placed at the heart of UN efforts to support fledgling post-conflict governments to build a new peace in Liberia. The following section details the mandate of the UN Mission in Liberia (UNMIL) and analyses the milestone achievements and UNPOL experience to date.

The United Nations mission in Liberia

In September 2003, determining that the situation in Liberia constituted a threat to international peace and security, and in accordance with the CPA, the UN SC passed resolution 1509, creating the United Nations Mission in Liberia (UNMIL). Initially authorised with 15,000 military personnel and 1,115 UNPOL (including FPUs), UNMIL was the largest such peace operation ever established. It assumed control of the mission on 1 October 2003 as around 3,500 ECOMIL troops were 're-hatted' as UN peacekeepers. UNMIL was authorised under Chapter VII of the Charter to use 'all necessary means' to implement four key elements:[139]

1 Support the Transitional government implement the Ceasefire Agreement (including DDRR) and the CPA.

2   Protection of UN Staff, Facilities and Civilians (under imminent threat of physical violence, within its capabilities).
3   Support for Humanitarian and Human Rights Assistance.
4   Support for Security Reform.

The police component of the mission has been a critical part of UNMIL since the start. UNPOL was charged with temporarily substituting for, and longer-term resuscitation of, Liberian policing agencies. It was therefore tasked with the twin imperatives of restoring law and order whilst also assisting the transitional government in transforming Liberia's public security apparatus from militant misrule to one that would abide by – and ultimately become the guardian of – the rule of law. The international community's SSR mandate derives from 'Part Four' (articles VII and VIII) of the CPA which included the provisions for wide-ranging SSR.[140] As per these articles, responsibilities for SSR were shared between: the United States government – tasked with the re-creation of the AFL; the government of Liberia – responsible for addressing the governance mechanisms in Ministries of Defense and Justice; and, UNMIL – assuming the role of overseeing police reform.[141]

UNMIL's police reform mandate is enshrined in Article VIII of the CPA and SC Resolution 1509. The former refers to restructuring and where necessary disarming the LNP and other statutory security entities including the Immigration Force, Special Security Service (SSS), customs security guards, Anti-Terrorist Unit, SOD and paramilitary groups that operate within the National Ports Authority (NPA), Liberian Telecommunications Corporation (NTC), Liberian Refining Corporation (LPRC) and the airports. Restructuring was aimed at a "professional orientation that emphasizes democratic values and respect for human rights, a non-partisan approach to duty and the avoidance of corrupt practices." It further stipulated the responsibilities of an interim police force for law and order until the deployment of newly trained national police and the corollary expectations on UNPOL to monitor the activities of the interim police force and assist in the maintenance of law and order throughout Liberia. Finally, it lays out the call on UNPOL to assist in the provision of training programmes for the LNP.[142]

The latter stipulated that UNMIL shall:

> …assist the transitional government of Liberia in monitoring and restructuring the police force of Liberia, consistent with democratic policing, to develop a civilian police training programme, and to otherwise assist in the training of civilian police, in cooperation with ECOWAS, international organizations, and interested States.[143]

These responsibilities were written into the Secretary-General's Mission Plan which emphasised "restructuring and reorganizing the Liberian

National Police",[144] as well as the Concept of Operations which also specified a "long-term [focus] on the redrafting and development of police legislation, policies, and guidelines which will create the foundation for an accountable and responsive police institution answerable to the law of the country."[145]

UNMIL mandate implementation and performance

The deployment of UNMIL helped to restore relative calm to the country. Following the basic stabilisation of the situation, one of the initial programmes undertaken was the Disarmament, Demobilisation, Rehabilitation and Reintegration (DDRR) of the armed groups. Despite initial faltering and gross underestimations of the numbers involved,[146] UNMIL eventually oversaw the disarmament of over 103,000 combatants and the disbanding of the former armed factions as the 'DD' components were declared complete by November 2004.[147] Whilst the intention was to lead into specific skill training and community-based reintegration, these 'RR' elements of the process were much less successful and led to what Paes referred to as a "dangerous mismatch between the DD and RR phases".[148]

Gyude Bryant's NTGL – a mixture of aspirational politicians and erstwhile warlords – oversaw what has been described as a 'grand theft' of national treasure in two short years, including granting of long-term leases on raw material mining dispensations with exorbitant kick-backs.[149] This seamless continuation of politics-as-plunder – facetiously referred to by some Liberians as "business more than usual"[150] – occurred despite the international community's attempts to regulate the management of natural resources. Subsequent attempts to address this larceny led the international community to create the Governance and Economic Management Assistance Program (GEMAP) in 2005 that, *inter alia*, included intrusive measures to oversee economic functions of the state – most notably revenue collection.[151] This was symptomatic of attempts to rectify the kleptocracy that had plagued Liberia in recent history.

A significant milestone for UNMIL was the successful conduct of relatively peaceful, internationally accredited, multi-party elections in October/November 2005. Ellen Sirleaf-Johnson emerged victorious following a run-off, assuming office in January 2006 as the first African female elected Head of State.[152] These elections were heralded as an indication of emerging democratic order in Liberia.

One of UNMIL's priority and enduring objectives relates to the maintenance of law and order and police reform. In addition to the military contingent, UNPOL have been an important stabilising presence. In pursuit of its law enforcement mandate, UNPOL created an Operations Section, tasked with supporting the LNP to tackle crime. To do so, various configurations of UNPOL officers and formed units performed joint patrols to address issues of public disorder and criminality. Furthermore,

UNPOL units were co-located with advisors in urban and rural sectors and assisted in crime analysis.

In keeping with previous endeavours in Bosnia and Sierra Leone, the UN became a chief architect amongst the international partners in designing a SSR approach for post-War Liberia.[153] This was premised on two central tenets of SSR: (1) establish efficient, effective, equitable and accountable security agencies; (2) establish effective civilian oversight of the security sector.[154] However, the CPA explicitly apportioned responsibility for military restructuring to the US government who outsourced the recruitment, training and reconfiguration of the AFL to US-owned private contractors DynCorp and Pacific Architects and Engineers Inc. This was much to the chagrin of many Liberians and other commentators due to the perceived democratic transparency and accountability deficits associated with private security industries – particularly given bitter regional experiences with private military companies in recent history.[155] Nevertheless, this led to the creation of a relatively small force, approximately 2,000-strong, and primarily responsible for protecting the territorial integrity of Liberia. As of 1 January 2010, the AFL assumed control of its own training provision, the US army has been providing mentoring whilst UNMIL have begun ongoing training and joint operations with the AFL as they move towards full operational capability.[156]

UNPOL's police reform efforts reflected the overarching SSR goals. In the early life of the mission, UNPOL were partnering with a few hundred officers quickly selected from the remnants of the LNP as an interim police force to maintain law and order. However, from the start, UNPOL were simultaneously required to restructure, retrain and equip a reformed LNP. Following initial demobilisation efforts, this basically required building the LNP from 'scratch'. Despite the magnitude of the task, as the mission deployed there was no dedicated assessed funding for reconstituting the LNP. As Malan recounts,

> From their personal allowances, UNPOL officers bought black T-shirts with "POLICE" printed in white bold lettering as a makeshift uniform for this small cadre of officers. They also purchased stationery and basic office supplies for the new LNP officers; there was simply no budget line or funding within UNMIL for creating and operationalizing the LNP.[157]

Shortfalls and a piecemeal approach in donor funding has hampered police reform efforts from the start and continues to be a significant constraint. Furthermore, despite the clear prioritisation of police reform in the mandate, UNMIL lacked any clear guidance or doctrine from headquarters for realising this objective.[158]

A target to vet, recruit and train 3,500 LNP officers was set by UNMIL and the NTGL (to be reached by 2006). It is hard to say how that figure was arrived at,¹⁵⁹ but it was deemed to be "adequate and in line with available resources".¹⁶⁰ In conjunction with the NTGL, UNPOL developed a vetting, selection and training programme.¹⁶¹ Over 2,000 former LNP officers who registered failed to meet the criteria for retraining but efforts to demobilise these individuals were hampered by insufficient funds to pay the severance packages. This was eventually covered by the UK government and, with the help of further sporadic donor contributions, by August 2007, 3,522 officers had graduated from the National Police Academy.

Despite meeting the benchmark for trained LNP officers, assessments of the police reform process remained unfavourable. As of 2008, Malan summarised that "…the LNP remains ineffective, largely because of critical shortages of essential police equipment … addressing urgent leadership and management challenges will improve the present low morale and poor discipline of the LNP."¹⁶² However, challenges also remained regarding the lack of an overarching national security strategy, delays in passage of the 'National Security Reform and Intelligence Act', as well as the meagre extension of authority and service provision throughout the territory.¹⁶³

A UN Technical Assessment Mission (TAM) conducted in April/May 2009, contained a section dedicated to the progress of police reform.¹⁶⁴ It noted that stakeholders regarded the LNP as "ineffectual" and highlighted that a combination of poor service conditions, ineffective management and inadequate resources and logistics were perpetual problems. It further emphasised that "police relations with the communities they serve remain poor" and that Liberians still feared the LNP.¹⁶⁵ The report indicated that the reform of the public security apparatus had retarded and was in need of a new injection of energy and resources.¹⁶⁶ Despite the focus of the mandate on holistic reform of the LNP, in reality UNPOL's work had mainly consisted of vetting and training the new recruits.¹⁶⁷

UNSC resolution 1836 (2008), endorsed the Secretary-General's recommendation to increase the number of personnel deployed as part of UNMIL's police component to provide strategic advice and expertise in specialised fields, provide operational support to regular policing activities and react to urgent security situations.¹⁶⁸ In terms of frontline policing, as the LNP stood up in increasing numbers, UNPOL officers have become less involved in operational support functions. However, UNPOL have continued to provide assistance when needed, primarily from FPUs, such as joint patrolling at night. Furthermore, UNPOL continued to provide operational supervision to the LNP, particularly in relation to crime investigations.

Regarding police reform, UNPOL became increasingly involved in assisting the LNP in areas deemed vital to the reform and restructuring process – assisting in the implementation of programmes and initiatives, as well as monitoring and facilitating the deployment of LNP units to the counties.¹⁶⁹ In the context of a more clearly articulated national security architecture,¹⁷⁰ UNPOL RRR efforts moved towards building specialist capabilities. Having established the core complement of LNP officers and seeing the ranks swell to around 4,000,¹⁷¹ focus shifted to building a 500-strong Emergency Response Unit (ERU). The ERU is designed as an armed capacity mandated with the lethal use of force, to deal with insurgent threats to security from within the national borders including arrest of armed criminals, hostage situations, violent crimes in progress and armed terrorist activities.¹⁷² It is also intended to patrol in high crime areas and provide assistance in major disaster situations. These efforts produced a contingent of around 330, at which point priority shifted towards creating complementary 'Police Support Units' (PSU).¹⁷³

The PSUs are envisaged to provide basic armed support to patrolling officers or to respond to incidents of public disorder, short of the lethal use of force, more for crowd control and corporeal threats against civilians – tasks akin to those conducted by UNPOL FPUs.¹⁷⁴ Furthermore, PSUs were designed to improve self-sustaining capacity of the LNP by plugging the logistical and maintenance support gaps that UNMIL has hitherto been covering.¹⁷⁵ Such a unit was deemed to be critical in preparing to police the 2011 elections.

UNPOL have continued to address infrastructure shortfalls through the renovation of LNP HQ and regional HQ, as well as the rehabilitation or construction of LNP facilities. These efforts have been particularly focused on the counties – where oftentimes they have never had police stationed before. These reflect continued 'Quick Impact Project' efforts to equip LNP police stations and barracks, both old and new, to provide the amenities for a sustained presence.

Since 2009, UNPOL have been focused on strategic advisory support such as the development of the LNP Strategic Plan 2009–2013. This has been complemented by concerted efforts – with varying degrees of success – to develop organisational policies and procedures such as an oversight system and investigation of police misconduct.¹⁷⁶ Another core area for UNPOL has been providing advanced and specialist training. For example, there has also been a focus on capacity development at the executive level through the Senior Advisory Programme and in support functions such as administration and planning, public relations, payroll and logistics, as well as ongoing leadership training and human resource development.

Other thematic capacity-building with the LNP has focused on a number of key areas. Firstly, efforts have been made to enhance 'Community-Oriented Policing' aimed at breaking down the barriers of apathy and mistrust and improving relations between civilians and security institutions through community policing forums (CPF).¹⁷⁷ Secondly, gender mainstreaming in accordance with SC Resolution 1325 has been a major pillar of UNPOL work, including continued efforts to hit the 20 per cent target for female members of LNP. Furthermore, gender training throughout Liberian security institutions and the creation of 52 LNP Women & Child Protection Sections as a means for addressing enduring SGBV are all part of that drive.[178] Thirdly, UNPOL have also been heavily involved in efforts to tackle organised crime including drugs, arms and people trafficking through the West African Coast Initiative (WACI). This included the creation of a Transnational Crime Unit (TCU) within the LNP.[179]

Towards a more holistic rule of law approach

As of late 2005, there was little concentration on reform and capacity-building in the judiciary and correctional services.[180] Furthermore, there was little attention to other critical components of the security sector such as immigration, intelligence, special forces, customs and corrections.[181] This is an important omission given the Liberian security sector was saturated with agencies, often with overlapping responsibilities.[182] Reports of corruption amongst agencies such as immigration and customs have had deleterious consequences on pubic impressions of the LNP as more often than not, civilians do not draw distinctions between police officers and other uniformed personnel.[183] Similarly, when those detained by the LNP are released back into the community without charge, failures of the judiciary to prosecute within the 48 hours stipulated by Liberian law or simply institutional opacity and corruption are oftentimes not differentiated from the performance of the LNP which is presumed to be corrupt. Following consultations for national security strategy formulation, the need for corresponding activities to assist and build the capacity of the judicial system and belatedly the Bureau of Corrections and Rehabilitation (BCR) was eventually recognised. Thereafter, the need to pay attention to the National Bureau of Investigation (NBI), Drug Enforcement Agency (DEA), Bureau of Immigration and Naturalisation (BIN) and the National Fire Service were also increasingly recognised as important to holistic rule of law and security sector reform. However, these efforts have remained chronically under-resourced and have not kept pace with even modest improvements in the police.[184]

UNMIL's police component has in some ways been a crucible for the increasing utilisation of police in peace operations. Whilst UNPOL were required to perform both operational duties and RRR activities, in reality, their de facto programming responsibility became more wide-ranging. Due to the lack of provision and resourcing for efforts to reform the criminal justice system, in effect UNPOL responsibilities extended to include corrections, customs and immigration, as well as legal/judicial.[185] While the primary focus remained on the development of the LNP, UNPOL provided a small compliment of advisors to the BIN and increasingly corrections experts. In this sense, UNPOL became increasingly engaged in a more holistic security sector reform project.

Although gradually recognised in the progress reports of the Secretary-General, it was a report of the OIOS that emphasised the need for greater integration of UNMIL's security sector reform endeavours.[186] This shift was reflected by the structuring of the mission to include a Deputy-Special-Representative of the Secretary-General for Rule of Law and the creation of the SSR Advisor position. The need for a systemic approach was further acknowledged in the 22nd progress report of the Secretary-General, which stated that:

> There is growing recognition that rule-of-law issues, especially an efficient criminal justice system, need to be addressed comprehensively, including in the context of security sector reform. The Government of Liberia and the United Nations are developing a joint justice and security programme that will partly address this challenge, as will the Peacebuilding Commission's focus on decentralized security and justice service delivery.[187]

Despite the increasing recognition and measures taken to employ a systemic approach to rule of law and security sector reform, efforts have faltered.[188] To be sure, they have been hampered by a lack of funding, but also by a persistence with a planning and mandate implementation approach that separates 'security' and 'rule of law' concerns in strategic thinking and subsequent operational planning. Such an approach continues to 'silo' these thematic areas in different pillars at the expense of an interdependent and holistic vision.

Non-state actors in the rule of law domain

UNMIL efforts to assist in building sustainable rule of law have focused almost exclusively on the machinery of the state, in particular reconstituting the LNP.[189] Despite the multi-layered security and justice environment, UNMIL efforts have been predominantly state-centric. That is to say, UNMIL has been reluctant to address the phenomenon of non-state security and justice providers. This has significant ramifications given the big problems facing the LNP in covering the territory.

As Stephen Ellis has noted, "Liberia, more by accident than design, has become a laboratory, a place where the interaction between the citizens of a failed state and international policy-makers may be observed and experimented with."[190] In this vein, UNMIL had significant latitude to push the envelope and enhance the way peace operations conceive of and attempt to enhance local ownership when it comes to post-conflict security sector reform. However for the UN, developing an approach for engaging with and harnessing the utility of non-state policing mechanisms in immediate post-conflict security sector reform remains controversial and fraught with challenges. For example, in reference to the extreme 'trial by ordeal' procedures,[191] one senior mission official explained, "We cannot help but undermine some of those age-old practices because we know that, apart from being a gross abuse of the rights of the victims ... they only appear to solve problems because the people don't survive."[192] However, even these more extreme practices retain high levels of popular support.[193]

Nevertheless, there has been an attempt by UNMIL and the wider UN presence to engage and even partner with some non-statutory actors. For example, the Community Policing Forum arrangements were set up as a way of bringing together a wide cross-section of stakeholders – from traditional chiefs to representatives of civil society, women's groups and vigilante groups – to discuss and address issues of public safety. Moreover, the President was behind a policy of creating vigilante groups to 'police' suburbs of Monrovia against high rates of armed robbery. However, a number of challenges associated with these arrangements arose. In particular, the tendencies for some of these community-based arrangements to see themselves as a parallel entity as opposed to one designed to partner and assist the state to support the main policing function.

There was a process based on nationwide consultations attempting to reconcile the state and non-state provision of law and justice services.[194] The aim was to harness the existing strengths of the customary mechanisms and harmonise with the statutory criminal justice system in order to increase access to justice for ordinary Liberians.[195] In other words, this is an attempt to 'formalise the informal'. The findings of a national conference were scheduled to go through another round of regional consultations; however, at the time of writing the process had reached an impasse. The UN, through UNMIL and increasingly the Peacebuilding Fund, supported the government in this process – a commitment that demonstrates willingness on behalf of the UN to acknowledge and work with informal providers of security and justice.

Despite these developments, the incorporation of non-state providers into reform programming has been minimal. This neglects emerging consensus that these actors are important to sustainability in Liberia post-UNMIL.[196] Moreover, Sawyer has cautioned that any efforts that fail to reflect the desires and capabilities of local communities, but instead stifle or override them, could represent little more than an attempt to reconstitute the over-centralised state that was arguably one of the root causes of the decade and a half of violence and predation.[197]

Aside from the potential incompatibility with human rights standards, there is a risk of reproducing or at least further entrenching a multi-tiered system whereby there is one system for the urban-wealthy elite and another for the rural-poor majority. In the extreme, this dualism has the potential to polarize society, foster discord and even lead to further unrest and violent conflict.[198] The enduring challenge in this regard is tied up with balancing the recognition of utility of non-state sources with the need for those very systems to also transform from any inequitable and discriminatory practices into a system that is fair and just and will ensure protection and justice for all Liberians – not just a few.

Current progress and priorities: an interim assessment of UNPOL in UNMIL

Whilst some argue that the reform of the LNP has been relatively successful,[199] others point to remaining challenges as evidence of the distance left to travel before national authorities can effectively assume control of policing duties.[200] For example, Gberie points out that, "the UN has now been in Liberia for seven years ... but still most of the important policing functions in the country are provided by the UN."[201] Similarly, in relation to the situation beyond urban locales, Kantor and Persson note that, "UNMIL troops and the armed UN Formed Police Units are still the primary actors safeguarding rural areas when conflicts break out."[202]

As with many UN peace operations, the UNPOL component in UNMIL has suffered from a lack of suitable human resources and has often been left with little option but to deploy wrongly-skilled officers in unfamiliar roles. Recent developments have seen some movement in the SC and within DPKO regarding the process for recruiting specialised capabilities such as forensics, pathologists as well as other civilian expertise such as information management and communications, HR and institutional planning to complement police-specific skill sets. However, structural and operational challenges endure. As Malan has noted, "[w]here United Nations (UN) peacekeeping missions are deployed, SSR continues to slip into a systemic funding vacuum, with the Security Council mandating missions to conduct SSR and hoping that a 'lead nation' will step forward."[203] Whilst the US has increasingly led the way, the financial assistance for police and broader SSR in Liberia has been unreliable to the point of stagnation.

Consequently, the LNP suffers from serious shortage of equipment and logistics necessary to facilitate and sustain its presence.[204] It has been said that this is particularly conspicuous in terms of the lack of armed emergency response capacity;[205] however this is arguably true across the range of LNP functions. The inadequate capability to effectively address issues such as rape, domestic violence and petty theft ensure that 'everyday policing' remains the biggest deficit. The procurement of basic equipment for the LNP continues to lag behind training, leaving officers with limited resources to perform their duties.[206] Capacity shortfalls persist in the critical areas of administration, logistics, finance and community relations.[207] For example, vehicle scarcity means that LNP officers are almost entirely dependent upon UNPOL for their mobility. This was demonstrated during the 2011 post-election crisis in neighbouring Côte d'Ivoire whereby the LNP demonstrated increased capacity to mount complex operations but were beset by worrisome shortfalls in logistics. This remains a significant factor as the LNP shapes up to be the primary provider of internal security.

Moreover, the LNP is still largely absent in leeward areas of the country and consequently the extension of state authority and protection is severely limited.[208] Public frustrations regarding the lack of police responsiveness frequently manifest in extra-judicial measures being taken which can escalate into mob violence.[209] Furthermore, accusations of human rights abuses and endemic corruption persist and are often linked to ineffectual vetting of some senior LNP members.[210] The result is that confidence in the LNP and prevalence of formal rule of law is low. In a 2011 population survey, only one third of respondents identified the police as a source of protection – many adding that they were required to pay for services rendered.[211] Despite what has been heralded as a "new paradigm of civil society involvement and engagement in influencing and shaping the processes and ends of peace-building, including ... security reforms",[212] there has been slow progress in relation to shifting public perceptions of the reformed security and justice agencies. This has been identified repeatedly in both internal reporting and external evaluations as a major reason for shortcomings in UNMIL's effectiveness and ongoing fragility in Liberia.[213] For example, one Secretary-General report stated that, "low public confidence in the State's capacity to deliver justice frequently leads to rapid flare-ups, threatening overall law and order."[214] It also noted that, "[i]t is crucial that the development of the security sector becomes a main priority for the Government and the international community so that those institutions become independently operational, and are sufficiently resourced."[215] As a senior UNMIL official stated, "Things are now relatively stable on the surface, however, people don't feel safe ... there is a mindset of insecurity ... despite a strong quest for peace here in Liberia."[216]

Consolidation, drawdown and withdrawal

The perennial desire of UN member states and major contributors to UN peace operations to scale back these expensive endeavours, and the pressure on DPKO to demonstrate an ability to manage transition and work towards a clearly defined exit strategy, means that UNMIL is currently undergoing what has been labelled a 'Consolidation, Drawdown and Withdrawal' plan (CDW).[217] The CDW was approved in August 2007 under Security Council resolution 1777 and constitutes a phased approach to gradually reducing the military strength of the mission and downsizing/reconfiguring the police component, whilst adjusting the civilian elements in line with evolving priorities as the mission moves towards its eventual withdrawal and handover to successor arrangements.

In 2007, a report of the Secretary-General laid out a three-phased drawdown of military personnel, reducing troop levels significantly by December 2010.[218] An important caveat was included, stating that the drawdown would remain contingent on meeting a decisive benchmark to stand up the ERU by July 2009.[219] This is an example of the way in which policing concerns have become integral in the design and management of the CDW. The 'Consolidation' phase of the UNMIL CDW plan formally ended on 31 December 2007[220] and the military gradually reduced its troop strength in line with these plans from 15,250 to the authorised strength of 7,952 troops scheduled to be maintained until after the 2011 elections.[221] However, as the military strength gradually reduced, the UNPOL presence actually increased.

The need for early planning of drawdown and withdrawal strategies has led to a concerted focus on building security sectors capable of sustaining peace and laying the foundations for the eventual exit of peace operations.[222] In the case of UNMIL, this is particularly true in relation to efforts to reconstitute the public security agencies. In 2007, the CDW planned for "gradual reduction of 498 police advisers in seven stages between April 2008 and December 2010."[223] However, this was later adjusted, in light of continued challenges faced by the LNP, with the Secretary-General recommending to, "freeze the drawdown of the police advisory component and deploy two additional formed police units."[224]

UNMIL remains one of the UN's largest multidimensional peace operations although it is now well into its phased drawdown to eventual withdrawal. In late 2013, it was comprised of 7,343 total uniformed personnel including 5,760 troops and 127 military observers and was complemented by 415 international civilian personnel, 916 local staff and 205 UN volunteers.[225] UNMIL's police component had 1,474 personnel deployed of an authorised 1,795. The authorised UNPOL ceiling included 468 police advisers, 983 officers comprising eight formed police units, 23 immigration advisers, and 32 uniformed corrections personnel. There were 181 women in the police component.[226]

There has been some concern amongst Liberians and external commentators alike regarding the readiness of the Liberian security sector for maintaining peace amidst the spectre of a retreating UNMIL. This has led to careful discussion and a change in rhetoric away from talk of 'withdrawal' towards less dramatic language of 'transition'. Nevertheless, the CDW is in train and the success in police reform is amongst the most integral elements of UNMIL's exit strategy.[227] It is therefore vital that UNMIL to have a firm handle on the effects they are having and the impact it is realising amongst the LNP and the wider population.

Conclusion

After a long history of inequitable governance and a decade and a half of devastating internecine conflict, Liberian society has been undergoing a process of profound change. UNMIL has been credited with partially restoring state authority throughout Liberia's 15 counties. However, building sustainable peace remains a daunting challenge and the government of Liberia faces significant challenges in providing basic services beyond Monrovia where the dividends of peace have not been experienced evenly. Many ongoing challenges ranging from widespread poverty and high unemployment to a frail economy render the peace process in Liberia precarious.[228] Nevertheless, since the signing of the CPA and the arrival of UNMIL, attempts have been made to reform, and in certain ways transform, the system of governance to overcome and leave behind the maladies of the past.

Amongst the many causal factors, which contributed to the descent into fratricidal conflict in Liberia, the long history of co-option, politicisation and the eventual collapse of the security sector is a lesser cited, but significant factor. Therefore, the reconstitution of the security sector into one which relinquishes its history of predation and embraces a responsive, service and civilian-protection orientation has been deemed a critical prerequisite for overcoming the imbroglio and building sustainable peace in Liberia. UNMIL has been a major player in the design and implementation of such efforts, particularly given its responsibilities for police reform, and has invested much – both in material and reputational terms. However, despite its clear mandate and concerted efforts, progress in improving public safety and changing perceptions about the statutory security agencies, primarily through the reform and capacity-development of the LNP, have been underwhelming. Questions remain about the effectiveness of country-wide policing capabilities, as well as their sustainability in light of withdrawing international support. Whilst this is often attributed to resource shortfalls, in this chapter I have identified two major issues that are contributing factors to the impact of UNMIL in this regard.

First, the recognition of the importance of a systemic approach to reforming the security, law and justice sector was belated. This has led to uneven development of the criminal justice institutions with knock-on effects for effectiveness and public perceptions. This has ramifications for how and why police reform efforts lead to overall mission objectives. Second, a primarily technocratic and state-centric approach has resulted in the neglect and/or underplaying of the existence and importance of a multitude of non-state providers of security and justice that pre-dated, but in some cases also grew stronger, during the war. Whilst this is entirely consistent with UN practice to date, it is increasingly clear that it is inconsistent with the realities of security and justice provision in Liberia. This has not adequately addressed questions surrounding the politics, legitimacy and prevalence of alternative non-state providers, as well as their relationship with the state. In turn, this has contributed to a blinkered vision of the complex system that constitutes Liberia's security environment. Such awareness is even more important given that as UNMIL withdraws, the likelihood is that these informal networks and actors will take on greater importance in filling the security vacuum left in its wake. Whilst the longer-term questions of statebuilding and how the security sector should look in Liberia might challenge this idea, in the short-term – i.e. the timeframe that UN peace operations are a major factor in SSR – revealing existing strengths and legitimate sources of authority is important to understanding the impact of efforts in this domain.[229]

Despite a decade of stabilisation and peacebuilding efforts, Liberia is often described as stable but fragile.[230] Gberie paints a slightly more alarming picture claiming that, "Liberia remains a highly volatile, and deeply divided, nation."[231] Whilst the 2011 elections were heralded as a demonstration of how far Liberia has come in its post-war transformation towards democratic order, other integral elements of democratic statehood and fulfilling the government's side of the social contract are yet to materialise sufficiently. This should not be surprising. As McGoven has posited "Liberia took decades to decay and will take decades to restore sustainable security, political and economic structures."[232] Ultimately, much remains to be done to realise effective, sustainable peacebuilding in Liberia and holistic security sector reform is indisputably a central component of it. Whilst in more recent times individual donors (particularly the USA) have stepped up to the mark in providing more reliable material assistance to holistic security system reform, some still go as far as to suggest that lack of progress in rebuilding the security sector holds the "potential of undermining all the gains made so far."[233]

In this context, UNMIL, like other missions before it, is under concerted pressure to demonstrate progress towards an exit strategy. The historical account of Liberia's bastardised security sector, UNPOL activities and the major challenges faced presented in this chapter are important contextualising factors for any assessment of UNMIL's progress and impact in this area. The ways in which existing approaches attempt to do this and how this might be enhanced with the application of the framework developed in the previous chapter are the subject of the following chapters.

Notes

1 Also referred to as the 'Grain Coast'.
2 Mary H. Moran, *Liberia: The Violence of Democracy* (Philadelphia: University of Pennsylvania, 2006), 2.
3 J. G. Liebenow, *Liberia: The Evolution of Privilege* (Ithaca, New York: Cornell University Press, 1969), 1–8.
4 Stephen Ellis, *The Mask of Anarchy: The Destruction of Liberia and the Religious Dimension of an African Civil War*, 2nd edition (London: Hurst, 2007), 41.
5 Yekutiel Gershoni, *Black Colonialism: Liberian Struggle for the Hinterland* (Boulder and London: Westview Press, 1985).
6 These 'tribes' are rough units of analysis and to some extent artificial constructs invalid until quite recently. However, they are the political and administrative groupings commonly used by central government in Liberia. For a more nuanced rendering of ethnic identities in Liberia, see: Liebenow,

196 *Empirical case study and implications*

     Liberia: The Evolution of Privilege, 30–8; Ellis, *The Mask of Anarchy: The Destruction of Liberia and the Religious Dimension of an African Civil War*, 31–3.
7 Adekeye Adebajo, *Building Peace in West Africa: Liberia, Sierra Leone and Guinea Bissau* (Boulder: Lynne Rienner Publishers, 2002), 43.
8 The True Whig Party ruled Liberia for all but 6 years between 1877 and 1980. See: Funmi Olonisakin, "Liberia", in *Dealing with Conflict in Africa: The United Nations and Regional Organizations*, ed. Jane Boulden (New York: Palgrave Macmillan, 2003), 112–14.
9 Adebajo, *Building Peace in West Africa: Liberia, Sierra Leone and Guinea Bissau*, 45.
10 Ellis, *The Mask of Anarchy: The Destruction of Liberia and the Religious Dimension of an African Civil War*, 32.
11 For detailed explanation of the Poro and other secret societies, see note 119.
12 Festus B. Aboagye and Martin R. Rupiya, "Enhancing Post-Conflict Democratic Governance through Effective Security Sector Reform in Liberia", in *A Torturous Road to Peace: The Dynamics of Regional, UN and International Humanitarian Interventions in Liberia*, eds. Festus Aboagye and Alhaji M. S. Bah (Pretoria: Institute for Security Studies, 2005), 250.
13 Paul Richards, Steven Archibald, Beverlee Bruce, Watta Modad, Edward Mulbah, Tornorlah Varpilah, and James Vincent, *Community Cohesion in Liberia: A Post-Conflict Rapid Social Assessment*, vol. No. 21, Social Development Papers: Conflict Prevention & Reconstruction (Washington DC: The World Bank, 2005), 40.
14 Amos Sawyer, *Beyond Plunder: Toward Democratic Governance in Liberia* (London: Reinner Publishers, 2005), 163.
15 Robert M. Press, "Candles in the Wind: Resisting Repression in Liberia (1979–2003)", *Africa Today* 55, no. 3 (2009): 7; Dunn and Tarr, *Liberia: A National Polity in Transition*, 90–2.
16 Adedeji, "The Challenges and Opportunities of Security Sector Reform in Post-Conflict Liberia", 15.
17 Adekeye Adebajo, "Liberia: A Warlord's Peace", in *Ending Civil Wars: The Implementation of Peace Agreements*, eds. Stephen John Stedman, Donald Rothchild, and Elizabeth M. Cousens (Boulder, CO: Lynne Reinner, 2002), 601.
18 Christopher Clapham, "Liberia", in *Contemporary West African States*, eds. Donal Cruie O'Brien, John Dunn, and Richard Rathbone (Cambridge: Cambridge University Press, 1989), 102.
19 Dunn and Tarr, *Liberia: A National Polity in Transition*.
20 Mike McGovern, "Liberia: The Risks of Rebuilding a Shadow State", in *Building States to Build Peace*, eds. Charles T. Call and Vanessa Wyeth (Boulder, CO: Lynne Rienner, 2008), 335.
21 As mentioned, 'Krahn' as a tribal grouping is a blunt descriptor as in reality such groupings comprise complex sub-divisions, often with distinctive cultural differences such as language. In reality, Doe privileged only particular sub-divisions of those commonly referred to as Krahn. See: Ellis, *The Mask of Anarchy: The Destruction of Liberia and the Religious Dimension of an African Civil War*, 35.
22 Clapham, "Liberia", 103.
23 Comfort Ero and Jonathan Temin, "Sources of Conflict in West Africa", in *Exploiting Sub-Regional Conflict for Prevention*, eds. Chanfra Sriram and Zoe Nielsen (Boulder and London: Lynne Rienner, 2004), 105.
24 ICG, "Liberia: Uneven Progress in Security Sector Reform", in *Africa Report No. 148* (International Crisis Group, 2009), 3.
25 Doe's Liberia was supported by the USA's Cold War strategy in Africa, an outspoken critic of the Arab world and a recipient of military training and assistance from Israel. For an excellent account of the fraudulent 1985 presidential

elections and its international legitimation, see: Patrick L. N. Seyon, "The Results of the 1985 Elections in Liberia", *Liberian Studies Journal* 13, no. 2 (1988).
26 HRW, "Liberia: Flight from Terror. Testimony of Abuses in Nimba County", in *Africa Watch Report* (New York: Human Rights Watch, 1990); Adebajo, "Liberia: A Warlord's Peace", 601.
27 Adebajo, *Building Peace in West Africa: Liberia, Sierra Leone and Guinea Bissau*, 46.
28 Liberian resident cited in Stephen Ellis, "Liberia 1989–1994: A Study of Ethnic and Spiritual Violence", *African Affairs* 94, no. 375 (1995): 165.
29 Taylor had only a few years earlier suspiciously 'escaped' from a Massachusetts prison where he was being held, facing extradition to Liberia, on embezzlement charges alleged to have occurred during his tenure as Doe's Chief of the General Services Agency. For further details, see: Mark Huband, *The Liberian Civil War* (London: Frank Cass, 1998), 45–7.
30 Known as 'al-Mathabh al-Thauriya al Alamiya' roughly translating as 'World Revolutionary Headquarters'. NPFL fighters were also trained in guerrilla warfare techniques with the support of Blaise Compaore in Burkina Faso and further support from Côte d'Ivoire. Arms were provided to Taylor's NPFL from both Tripoli and Ouagadougou throughout the civil war. See: Ellis, *The Mask of Anarchy: The Destruction of Liberia and the Religious Dimension of an African Civil War*, 69–70.
31 Kwesi Aning, "Managing Regional Security in West Africa: ECOWAS, ECOMOG, and Liberia", in *Working Paper No. 94.2* (Copenhagen: Centre for Development Research, 1994), 12.
32 David Wippman, "Enforcing the Peace: ECOWAS and the Liberian Civil War", in *Enforcing Restraint: Collective Intervention in Internal Conflicts* ed. Lori Damrosch (New York: Council on Foreign Relations Press, 1993), 179.
33 Oversimplifying the predominantly Krahn Government forces facing off against a primarily Gio and Mano NPFL. See: Moran, *Liberia: The Violence of Democracy*, 16.
34 Lansana Gberie, "Liberia's War and Peace Process: A Historical Overview", in *A Torturous Road to Peace: The Dynamics of Regional, UN and International Humanitarian Interventions in Liberia*, eds. Festus Aboagye and Alhaji M. S. Bah (Pretoria: Institute for Security Studies, 2005), 54.
35 Amos Sawyer, "Violent Conflicts and Governance Challenges in West Africa: The Case of the Mano River Basin Area", in *Political Theory and Policy Analysis* (Indiana University, 2003), 16.
36 A further splinter group, the Central Revolutionary Council (CRC) led by erstwhile senior NPFL figures, emerged subsequently. See: Adebajo, "Liberia: A Warlord's Peace", 601.
37 These were Nigeria, Ghana, Sierra Leone, the Gambia and Guinea (Conakry) – the only Francophone contributor.
38 Adebajo, *Building Peace in West Africa: Liberia, Sierra Leone and Guinea Bissau*, 52.
39 Particularly Burkina Faso and Côte d'Ivoire.
40 Adebajo, *Building Peace in West Africa: Liberia, Sierra Leone and Guinea Bissau*, 52.
41 Herbert Howe, "Lessons from Liberia: ECOMOG and Regional Peacekeeping", *International Security* 21, no. 3 (1997); Klaas Van Walraven, *The Pretence of Peace-Keeping: ECOMOG, West Africa, and Liberia* (The Hague: Netherlands Institute of International Relations, 1999); Karl Magyar and Earl Conteh-Morgan, eds., *Peacekeeping in Africa: ECOMOG in Liberia* (Hampshire, London: Macmillan, 1998).

42 As Gberie has stated, "Looting was so common among the [ECOMOG] troops – with stolen cars and household furniture and other goods being routinely shipped to Nigeria and elsewhere – that Liberians corrupted the acronym ECOMOG to stand for 'Every Car Or Moving Object Gone'". Gberie, "Liberia's War and Peace Process: A Historical Overview", 57. See also: Christopher Tuck, "'Every Car or Moving Object Gone': The ECOMOG Intervention in Liberia", *African Studies Quarterly* 4, no. 1 (2000).
43 An event sadistically captured on videotape by a correspondent of a Middle Eastern news agency willing to capture and disseminate the graphic detail of the humiliation and downfall of an outspoken supporter of Israel against the Arab world. See: Huband, *The Liberian Civil War*, 193.
44 Cynical Monrovians later referred to the IGNU as the 'Imported Government of No Use'. Ellis, *The Mask of Anarchy: The Destruction of Liberia and the Religious Dimension of an African Civil War*, 14.
45 Abiodun Alao, John Mackinlay, and Funmi Olonisakin, *Peacekeepers, Politicians, and Warlords: The Liberian Peace Process* (New York: United Nations University Press, 1999), 35.
46 ULIMO eventually splintered into Krahn and Mandingo factions, i.e. ULIMO-J (around 4,000 strong, headed by Roosevelt Johnson) and ULIMO-K (around 7,000 strong, led by Alhaji Kromah), respectively. See: Adebajo, "Liberia: A Warlord's Peace", 602.
47 See: Wentworth Ofuatey-Kodjoe, "Regional Organizations and the Resolution of Internal Conflict: The ECOWAS Intervention in Liberia", *International Peacekeeping* 1, no. 3 (1994).
48 Adebajo also highlights the important timing and consequences of the military coup/regime change in Nigeria in November 1993. Adebajo, "Liberia: A Warlord's Peace", 622.
49 First female head of state in Africa, albeit unelected.
50 Adebajo, "Liberia: A Warlord's Peace", 614–16.
51 Ibid., 599, 618–20; Terrence Lyons, *Voting for Peace: Post Conflict Elections in Liberia* (Washington, DC: Brookings Institution, 1998).
52 Adebajo, *Building Peace in West Africa: Liberia, Sierra Leone and Guinea Bissau*, 67.
53 "Truth and Reconciliation Commission: Consolidated Final Report", 167.
54 Adedeji, "The Challenges and Opportunities of Security Sector Reform in Post-Conflict Liberia", 5.
55 L. Wantchekon, "The Paradox of 'Warlord' Democracy: A Theoretical Investigation", *American Political Science Review* 98, no. 1 (2004): 27.
56 George Klay Kieh Jr, "The Roots of the Second Liberian Civil War", *International Journal on World Peace* 26, no. 1 (2009): 17–20.
57 Gberie, "Liberia's War and Peace Process: A Historical Overview", 62.
58 Ero and Temin, "Sources of Conflict in West Africa", 105.
59 "Taylorland under Siege", *Africa Confidential* 40, no. 4 (1999): 7.
60 Mark Malan, "Security Sector Reform in Liberia: Mixed Results from Humble Beginnings", (Strategic Studies Institute, 2008), 9.
61 Adedeji, "The Challenges and Opportunities of Security Sector Reform in Post-Conflict Liberia", 15.
62 Adebajo, *Building Peace in West Africa: Liberia, Sierra Leone and Guinea Bissau*, 67.
63 ICG, "Liberia: Security Challenges", in *Africa Report N°71* (Freetown/Brussels: International Crisis Group, 2003), 9–12.
64 "Truth and Reconciliation Commission: Consolidated Final Report", 167–8.
65 For detailed account of the formation, support and escapades of the LURD, see: James Brabazon, *My Friend the Mercenary* (Edinburgh: Canongate Books, 2010).

66 Pham, *Liberia: A Portrait of a Failed State*, 180–90.
67 Comprehensive Peace Agreement Between the Government of Liberia and the Liberians United for Reconciliation and Democracy (LURD) and the Movement for Democracy in Liberia (MODEL) and Political Parties, Accra, August 18, 2003.
68 Martin Lowenkopf, "Liberia: Putting the State Back Together", in *Collapsed States: The Disintegration and Restoration of Legitimate Authority*, ed. I. William Zartman (Boulder and London: Lynne Rienner, 1995), 99–101; Ero and Temin, "Sources of Conflict in West Africa", 95–105.
69 For discussion of these factors, see: Charles T. Call, "Liberia's War Recurrence: Grievance over Greed", *Civil Wars* 12, no. 4 (2010); Kieh Jr, "The Roots of the Second Liberian Civil War".
70 Kieh Jr, "The Roots of the Second Liberian Civil War", 9.
71 See, for example: Adedeji, "The Challenges and Opportunities of Security Sector Reform in Post-Conflict Liberia", 5; Adebajo, "Liberia: A Warlord's Peace", 601.
72 Gershoni, *Black Colonialism: Liberian Struggle for the Hinterland*; Clapham, "Liberia".; G. K. Kieh, "The Crisis of Democracy in Liberia", *Liberian Studies Journal* 22, no. 1 (1997); Liebenow, *Liberia: The Quest for Democracy*; Moran, *Liberia: The Violence of Democracy*.
73 Ellis, *The Mask of Anarchy: The Destruction of Liberia and the Religious Dimension of an African Civil War*, 43.
74 "Report on Peace Committees", (Monrovia: UNMIL Civil Affairs, 2009), 8.
75 See, for example: Ellis, *The Mask of Anarchy: The Destruction of Liberia and the Religious Dimension of an African Civil War*; Ellis, "Liberia 1989–1994: A Study of Ethnic and Spiritual Violence".
76 See: William Reno, "The Business of War in Liberia", *Current History* 95, no. 601 (1996).
77 Adebajo, "Liberia: A Warlord's Peace", 620.
78 Philippa Atkinson, *The War Economy in Liberia: A Political Analysis* (London: Overseas Development Institute, 1997), 9.
79 Luseni Sayon Bangalie Kromah, "The Study of the Behavior of the Liberian Police Force During the Americo-Liberian Administration, First Republic and up to the Administration of the Second Republic" (Tennessee State University, 2007); Aboagye and Rupiya, "Enhancing Post-Conflict Democratic Governance through Effective Security Sector Reform in Liberia", 258–60.
80 Adebajo, *Building Peace in West Africa: Liberia, Sierra Leone and Guinea Bissau*, 70; Gompert *et al.*, "Making Liberia Safe: Transformation of the National Security Sector", 1; Adedeji, "The Challenges and Opportunities of Security Sector Reform in Post-Conflict Liberia", 4; ICG, "Rebuilding Liberia: Prospects and Perils", in *ICG Report No. 75* (Freetown/Brussels: International Crisis Group, 2004), 19.
81 Adebajo, *UN Peacekeeping in Africa: From the Suez Crisis to the Sudan Conflicts*, (Boulder, CO: Lynne Reinner, 2011), 146; Cecil Griffiths, "Promoting Human Rights Professionalism in the Liberian Police Force", in *Tactical Notebook – New Tactics Project*, ed. Liam Mahony (Minneapolis, MN: The Center for Victims of Torture, 2004), 6–7.
82 Thomas Jaye, "Liberia: Setting Priorities for Post-Conflict Reconstruction", *Journal of Security Sector Management* 1, no. 3 (2003): 5; David C. Gompert, Robert C. Davis, and Brooke Stearns Lawson, "Oversight of the Liberian National Police", in *Report prepared for the Office of the U.S. Secretary of Defense* (RAND Corporation, 2009), 2.
83 Adedeji, "The Challenges and Opportunities of Security Sector Reform in Post-Conflict Liberia", 17; Janine Rauch and Elrena van der Spuy, "Recent

Experiments in Police Reform in Post-Conflict Africa: A Review", (Institute for Democracy in South Africa, 2006), 144.
84 David Zounmenou, "Managing Post-War Liberia: An Update", in *Situation Report* (Institute for Security Studies, 2008), 6.
85 Nika Stražišar Teran, "Peacebuilding and Organised Crime: The Cases of Kosovo and Liberia", in *Working Paper 1/2007* (Bern: Swisspeace, 2007), 28.
86 "Justice and Security in Liberia", (Monrovia: Ministry of Justice, Republic of Liberia, 2009).
87 Gberie, "Liberia's War and Peace Process: A Historical Overview", 67.
88 Different sources cite that number dead totalled 200,000 by 1997 (See: Final Report of Secretary-General on UNOMIL, S/1997/712, 12 September 1997, p. 5) and at least 250,000 by 2003 (See: CIA World Factbook. Available at www.cia.gov/cia/publications/factbook/geos/li/html). For detail on final figure, see: "Liberia Poverty Reduction Strategy", (Monrovia: Republic of Liberia, 2008), 14. Liberia's pre-war population was approximately 2.6 million inhabitants (See: Ellis, *The Mask of Anarchy: The Destruction of Liberia and the Religious Dimension of an African Civil War*, 37.)
89 See: "Ninth Progress Report of the Secretary-General on the United Nations Mission in Liberia", (New York: United Nations, 2005), 9.
90 Zounmenou, "Managing Post-War Liberia: An Update", 3.
91 Richards *et al.*, *Community Cohesion in Liberia: A Post-Conflict Rapid Social Assessment*.
92 Morten Boas, "Beyond Plunder: Toward Democratic Governance in Liberia, by Amos Sawyer", *African Affairs* 108, no. 431 (2009). In addition, in 2008 land conflict was identified by the Governance Commission as the most important consequence of the war and security issue facing post-war Liberia.
93 Richards *et al.*, *Community Cohesion in Liberia: A Post-Conflict Rapid Social Assessment*.
94 ICG, "Liberia: How Sustainable Is the Recovery?", in *Crisis Group Africa Report, N°177* (Dakar/Brussels: Internaitonal Crisis Group, 2011), 16.
95 UNMIL, "Building Liberia's Capacity", *UN Focus* 7, no. 1 (2010): 26.
96 McGovern, "Liberia: The Risks of Rebuilding a Shadow State", 335.
97 Teran, "Peacebuilding and Organised Crime: The Cases of Kosovo and Liberia", 31–3.
98 William Reno, *Warlord Politics and African States* (Boulder, CO: Lynne Reinner, 1998), 81, 94–9.
99 "Liberia Poverty Reduction Strategy", 16.
100 Andreas Mehler and Judy Smith-Höhn, "Security Actors in Liberia and Sierra Leone – Roles, Interactions and Perceptions", in *State failure revisited II: actors of violence and alternative forms of governance – INEF Report 89*, eds. Tobias Debiel and Daniel Lambach (Duisburg: INEF 2007), 55.
101 CWIQ Survey, 2007 cited in "Liberia Poverty Reduction Strategy", 16.
102 "Human Development Report 2011 – Sustainability and Equity: A Better Future for All", in *Summary* (New York: United Nations Development Programme (UNDP), 2011), 19.
103 Sawyer, *Beyond Plunder: Toward Democratic Governance in Liberia*, 1.
104 "Security Sector Reform in Liberia: A Case of the Liberian National Police and Its Capacity to Respond to Internal Threat in the Wake of UNMIL Drawdown in 2012", (Monrovia: Search for Common Ground/SIPRI, 2011), 12.
105 Mehler and Smith-Höhn, "Security Actors in Liberia and Sierra Leone – Roles, Interactions and Perceptions", 54.
106 Adedeji, "The Challenges and Opportunities of Security Sector Reform in Post-Conflict Liberia", 16.
107 J. Shola Omotola, "Beyond Transition: Challenges of Security Sector Reform

and Reconstruction in Liberia", *Journal of Security Sector Management* 4, no. 4 (2006): 5.
108 Adedeji, "The Challenges and Opportunities of Security Sector Reform in Post-Conflict Liberia", 61.
109 ICG, "Liberia: Uneven Progress in Security Sector Reform", 4.
110 Griffiths, "Promoting Human Rights Professionalism in the Liberian Police Force", 6–7.
111 Omotola, "Beyond Transition: Challenges of Security Sector Reform and Reconstruction in Liberia", 3.
112 Jaye, "Liberia: Setting Priorities for Post-Conflict Reconstruction", 5.
113 "Security Sector Reform in Liberia: A Case of the Liberian National Police and Its Capacity to Respond to Internal Threat in the Wake of UNMIL Drawdown in 2012", 12.
114 Malan, "Security Sector Reform in Liberia: Mixed Results from Humble Beginnings", 9.
115 Amos Sawyer, "Social Capital, Survival Strategies, and Their Potential for Post-Conflict Governance in Liberia", in *WIDER Research Paper No. 2005/15* (Helsinki: World Institute for Development Economics Research, 2005).
116 Jörgel, "The Mano River Basin Area – Formal and Informal Security Providers in Liberia, Guinea and Sierra Leone".
117 Ezekiel Pajibo, "Traditional Justice Mechanisms: The Liberian Case", in *Traditional Justice and Reconciliation after Violent Conflict: Learning from African Experiences* (Stockholm: International IDEA, 2008), 16; Stephen C. Lubkemann, Deborah H. Isser, and Philip A. Z. Banks III, "Unintended Consequences: Constraint of Customary Justice in Post-Conflict Liberia", in *Customary Justice and the Rule of Law in War-Torn Societies*, ed. Deborah H. Isser (Washington DC: United States Institute of Peace, 2010), 193–214.
118 Mehler and Smith-Höhn, "Security Actors in Liberia and Sierra Leone – Roles, Interactions and Perceptions", 53. The 'Hinterland' had been administered under a system of indirect control up until 1963, when the 'hinterland' designation was scrapped and replaced by four administrative counties. This represented the first time in Liberian Republic's history that it had an administrative arrangement that extended central governance over the entirety of its territory. However, in actuality, central government authority and provision of public safety through the national police failed to stretch into the countryside.
119 The Poro authority is a "pan-ethnic social institution embracing the collective social and historical experiences of most Mel and Mande-speaking groups in Liberia, Sierra Leone and Guinea. It is considered to be of a deeper order of legitimacy than any group of secular rulers and commands a wider pool of resources than those available to any single ethnic community. With deep roots in vast sections of the rainforest, Poro institutions have been embedded in social organization from the level of the village to higher levels of authority". (Sawyer, "Social Capital, Survival Strategies, and Their Potential for Post-Conflict Governance in Liberia", 4–5). The Poro and equivalents are often referred to as a 'secret society' with elaborate initiation rituals and clandestine nature. However, their importance does not lie in their secrecy, but rather in the social order they are constitutive of. They are inherently networked such that disparate elements of society from Paramount Chiefs to police officers are likely to be members. These bonds transcend national borders, leading to strong connections between peoples throughout the Manu River basin. The Poro is not present everywhere but equivalent pan-ethnic social institutions do exist across much of Liberia. For further detail, see: Beryl Bellman, *The Language of Secrecy: Symbols & Metaphors in Poro Ritual* (New Brunswick, NJ:

Rutgers University Press, 1984); James L. Gibbs, "Poro Values and Courtroom Procedures in a Kpelle Chiefdom", *Southwest Journal of Anthropology* 18(1962): 341, 49–50; Christian Kordt Højbjerg, "Masked Violence: Ritual Action and the Perception of Violence in an Upper Guinea Ethnic Conflict", in *Religion and African Civil Wars*, ed. Niels Kastfelt (London: Palgrave Macmillan, 2005); Ellis, *The Mask of Anarchy: The Destruction of Liberia and the Religious Dimension of an African Civil War*, 220–80; Jörgel, "The Mano River Basin Area – Formal and Informal Security Providers in Liberia, Guinea and Sierra Leone", 58–62; Deborah Isser, Stephen Lubkemann, and Saah N'Tow, *Looking for Justice: Liberian Experiences with and Perceptions of Local Justice Options*, (Washington DC: The United States Institute of Peace, 2009), 23–4.
120 Sawyer, "Social Capital, Survival Strategies, and Their Potential for Post-Conflict Governance in Liberia", 4–6.
121 "Liberia Poverty Reduction Strategy", 15; ICG, "Rebuilding Liberia: Prospects and Perils", 21.
122 Anna Kantor and Mariam Persson, "Understanding Vigilantism: Informal Security Providers and Security Sector Reform in Liberia", (Folke Bernadotte Academy, 2010), 25.
123 Isser, Lubkemann, and N'Tow, *Looking for Justice: Liberian Experiences with and Perceptions of Local Justice Options*, 4, 23–4.
124 Kantor and Persson, "Understanding Vigilantism: Informal Security Providers and Security Sector Reform in Liberia", 33.
125 Bruce Baker, *Security in Post-Conflict Africa: The Role of Nonstate Policing*, Advances in Police Theory and Practice (Boca Raton, FL: CRS Press, 2009), 27–45.
126 Some accounts identify sources as disparate as: voluntary vigilante groups; customary chiefs; work-based associations; market vendors' committees, taxi/mini-bus drivers' associations; local NGOs. For more examples, see: Bruce Baker, "Law Enforcement Capacity-Building in African Postconflict Communities", *Prism* 2, no. 3 (2011): 55.
127 Particularly in relation to the protection of property and natural resource sites. See, for example: Mehler and Smith-Höhn, "Security Actors in Liberia and Sierra Leone – Roles, Interactions and Perceptions", 56.
128 For more detail on the patron-client relations and networks of 'big men', see: Jörgel, "The Mano River Basin Area – Formal and Informal Security Providers in Liberia, Guinea and Sierra Leone", 13.
129 Kantor and Persson, "Understanding Vigilantism: Informal Security Providers and Security Sector Reform in Liberia", 24–7.
130 David H. Bayley, "The Morphing of Peacekeeping: Competing Approaches to Public Safety", *International Peacekeeping* 18, no. 1 (2011), 55–9.
131 Kantor and Persson, "Understanding Vigilantism: Informal Security Providers and Security Sector Reform in Liberia", 30; Deborah H. Isser, "Introduction: Shifting Assumptions from Abstract Ideals to Messy Realities", in *Customary Justice and the Rule of Law in War-Torn Societies*, ed. Deborah H. Isser (Washington DC: United States Institute of Peace, 2010), 1–10.
132 Kantor and Persson, "Understanding Vigilantism: Informal Security Providers and Security Sector Reform in Liberia"; Mehler and Smith-Höhn, "Security Actors in Liberia and Sierra Leone – Roles, Interactions and Perceptions", 56; Jörgel, "The Mano River Basin Area – Formal and Informal Security Providers in Liberia, Guinea and Sierra Leone", 40–4.
133 Isser, Lubkemann, and N'Tow, *Looking for Justice: Liberian Experiences with and Perceptions of Local Justice Options*, 3.
134 Vinck, Pham, and Kreutzer, "Talking Peace: A Population-Based Survey on Attitudes About Security, Dispute Resolution, and Post-Conflict Reconstruction in Liberia", 59.

135 Sarah Meharg and Aleisha Arnusch, "Liberia: Nonstate Security Actors", in *Security Sector Reform: A Case Study Approach to Transition and Capacity Building*, eds. Sarah Meharg, Aleisha Arnusch, and Susan Merrill (Carlisle, PA: Strategic Studies Institute, 2010), 56.
136 Richard Hill, Jonathan Temin, and Lisa Pacholek, "Building Security Where There Is No Security", *Journal of Peacebuilding & Development* 3, no. 2 (2007): 47–8; Jimmy Carter, "Reconstructing the Rule of Law: Post-Conflict Liberia", *Harvard International Review* Fall (2008); Sawyer, "Social Capital, Survival Strategies, and Their Potential for Post-Conflict Governance in Liberia"; Bruce Baker, "Resource Constraint and Policy in Liberia's Post-Conflict Policing", *Police Practice and Research: An International Journal* 11, no. 3 (2010).
137 Malan, "Security Sector Reform in Liberia: Mixed Results from Humble Beginnings", 20; Aboagye and Rupiya, "Enhancing Post-Conflict Democratic Governance through Effective Security Sector Reform in Liberia", 275.
138 Aboagye and Rupiya, "Enhancing Post-Conflict Democratic Governance through Effective Security Sector Reform in Liberia", 275.
139 United Nations Mission in Liberia Homepage, 'Mandate', http://unmil.org/1content.asp?ccat=mandate&zdoc=1.
140 Jaye, "Liberia: Setting Priorities for Post-Conflict Reconstruction", 4.
141 "Comprehensive Peace Agreement between the Government of Liberia and the Liberians United for Reconciliation and Democracy (LURD) and the Movement for Democracy in Liberia (Model) and Political Parties", (Accra: Ghana, 18th August 2003), 11–12.
142 Ibid.
143 United Nations Security Council, Resolution 1509 (2003), S/RES/1509 (2003), September 19, 2003, p. 4.
144 "Report of the Secretary-General to the Security Council on Liberia", (New York: United Nations, 2003), para 66.
145 UN DPKO, "Guidelines for Formed Police Unit in United Nations Mission in Liberia (UNMIL)", (New York: Civilian Police Department, DPKO, United Nations, 2004), 18.
146 UNMIL originally estimated that approximately 38,000 ex-combatants would register for demobilisation benefits. See: Wolf-Christian Paes, "The Challenges of Disarmament, Demobilisation and Reintegration in Liberia", *International Peacekeeping* 12, no. 2 (2005): 254.
147 DDRR Consolidated Report Phase (Status of Disarmament and Demobilisation Activities as at 1/16/2005). 1, 2 and 3. Available at: http://humanitarian-info.org/liberia/coordination/sectoral/DDR/index.asp.
148 Some accounts suggest as many as 82,000 demobilised ex-combatants were unaccounted for in the 'RR' phase. This has, in part, been attributed to the fact that UNMIL were only responsible for the DD components, the RR being handled by the UNDP through a separate Trust Fund. See: Paes, "The Challenges of Disarmament, Demobilisation and Reintegration in Liberia", 258–60.
149 McGovern, "Liberia: The Risks of Rebuilding a Shadow State", 335, 39.
150 Stephen Ellis, "How to Rebuild Africa", *Foreign Affairs* 84, no. 5 (2005): 1.
151 This was followed by the creation of the Governance Reform Commission (GRC).
152 See: Ellen Johnson-Sirleaf, *This Child Will Be Great: Memoir of a Remarkable Life by Africa's First Woman President* (New York: Harper, 2009).
153 These partners included ECOWAS, the US and other pivotal states. See: Thomas Jaye, "An Assessment Report on Security Sector Reform in Liberia", (Monrovia: Governance Reform Commission of Liberia, 2006).

154 Omotola, "Beyond Transition: Challenges of Security Sector Reform and Reconstruction in Liberia", 5; Adedeji, "The Challenges and Opportunities of Security Sector Reform in Post-Conflict Liberia", 2–3.
155 Aboagye and Rupiya, "Enhancing Post-Conflict Democratic Governance through Effective Security Sector Reform in Liberia", 267.
156 "Republic of Liberia Poverty Reduction Strategy: Second Annual Progress Report", (Monrovia: IMF, 2011), 19; "Twenty-Second Progress Report of the Secretary-General on the United Nations Mission in Liberia", 5–6; "Twenty-Third Progress Report of the Secretary-General on the United Nations Mission in Liberia", (New York: United Nations, 2011), 7. Whilst originally intended to be fully operational by 2012, hold-ups with security sector legislation as well as procurement of equipment, look set to delay the AFL reaching full operational functionality until 2014.
157 Malan, "Security Sector Reform in Liberia: Mixed Results from Humble Beginnings", 49.
158 Thorsten Benner, Stephen Mergenthaler, and Philipp Rotmann, *The New World of UN Peace Operations: Learning to Build Peace?* (Oxford: Oxford University Press, 2011), 104.
159 For example, despite differences in the size of national territory, comparative numbers in neighbouring Sierra Leone (which has approximately 12,500 police) equate to roughly double the number of police per capita. This mismatch was said to be even more salient given that the SSR concept in Liberia has the AFL postured to deter external military incursion and therefore is not configured nor does it have the capacity to provide for internal stability.
160 Aboagye and Rupiya, "Enhancing Post-Conflict Democratic Governance through Effective Security Sector Reform in Liberia", 263.
161 For full account of the process, see: Malan, "Security Sector Reform in Liberia: Mixed Results from Humble Beginnings", 50.
162 Malan, "Security Sector Reform in Liberia: Mixed Results from Humble Beginnings", ix.
163 "Special Report of the Secretary-General on the United Nations Mission in Liberia", (New York: United Nations, 2009), 7–10.
164 Ibid., 7–9.
165 Ibid., 7.
166 Ibid., 8.
167 Benner, Mergenthaler, and Rotmann, *The New World of UN Peace Operations: Learning to Build Peace?*, 103.
168 "Security Council Resolution 1836", (New York: United Nations 2008).
169 "Special Report of the Secretary-General on the United Nations Mission in Liberia", 7.
170 This vision was largely provided for between the National Security Strategy (January 2008) and the national Poverty Reduction Strategy, which employed consultative approaches to building on the goals laid out in the CPA and UNSC 1509.
171 PRS, "Fact Sheet: Progress in the Peace & Security Pillar", (Monrovia, Liberia: Liberia Reconstruction and Development Committee, 2010), 2.
172 The main intention for this was to limit the need for the AFL being required to respond to matters of internal security. See: Gompert *et al.*, "Making Liberia Safe: Transformation of the National Security Sector".
173 "Republic of Liberia Poverty Reduction Strategy: Second Annual Progress Report", 20; "Security Sector Reform in Liberia: A Case of the Liberian National Police and Its Capacity to Respond to Internal Threat in the Wake of UNMIL Drawdown in 2012", 14.
174 "Security Sector Reform in Liberia: A Case of the Liberian National Police

and Its Capacity to Respond to Internal Threat in the Wake of UNMIL Drawdown in 2012", 6.
175 Ibid., 14.
176 Gompert, Davis, and Lawson, "Oversight of the Liberian National Police".
177 UNMIL, "Winning Hearts through Community Policing", *UN Focus* 7, no. 3 (2011): 18–19.
178 UNMIL, "WACPS Makes Strides in Combatting SGBV", *UN Focus* 7, no. 3 (2011).
179 "Twenty-Third Progress Report of the Secretary-General on the United Nations Mission in Liberia", 5.
180 ICG, "Liberia: Resurrecting the Justice System", in *Africa Report no. 107* (Dakar/Brussels: International Crisis Group, 2006).
181 Aboagye and Rupiya, "Enhancing Post-Conflict Democratic Governance through Effective Security Sector Reform in Liberia", 262.
182 One account describes fifteen different agencies. See: Gompert *et al.*, "Making Liberia Safe: Transformation of the National Security Sector", 42.
183 "Security Sector Reform in Liberia: A Case of the Liberian National Police and Its Capacity to Respond to Internal Threat in the Wake of UNMIL Drawdown in 2012", 17.
184 "Security Sector Reform in Liberia: A Case of the Liberian National Police and Its Capacity to Respond to Internal Threat in the Wake of UNMIL Drawdown in 2012", 17.
185 The judicial system in Liberia was particularly degraded and stigmatised by the end of the conflict and, like the police, has struggled to lose its reputation as elitist, inaccessible and inequitable as well as a culturally alien institution. This has been exacerbated by an inability to overcome extremely high rates of pre-trial detention (81 per cent of prison population according to the "Twenty-Second Progress Report of the Secretary-General on the United Nations Mission in Liberia", 7.) See: Isser, Lubkemann, and N'Tow, *Looking for Justice: Liberian Experiences with and Perceptions of Local Justice Options*, 39–46.
186 OIOS, "Programme Evaluation of the Performance and the Achievement of Results by the United Nations Mission in Liberia", in *Report of the Office of Internal Oversight Services* (New York: United Nations, 2010), 12–13.
187 "Twenty-Second Progress Report of the Secretary-General on the United Nations Mission in Liberia", 5.
188 Blume, "Implementing the Rule of Law in Integrated Missions: Security and Justice in the UN Mission in Liberia", 12.
189 Baker, "Resource Constraint and Policy in Liberia's Post-Conflict Policing", 191.
190 Ellis, *The Mask of Anarchy: The Destruction of Liberia and the Religious Dimension of an African Civil War*, xxvii.
191 The most controversial of these in Liberia is called 'sassywood', actually a range of customary practices that, *inter alia*, involves administering a poisonous brew made from indigenous plants which when imbibed is believed to lead to guilt being determined by instantaneous death; survival bringing a verdict of being innocent. Other elements include the application of a hot machete to the skin (usually the feet) whereby a burn or retraction indicates guilt. For more detail, see: Pajibo, "Traditional Justice Mechanisms: The Liberian Case". The Liberian Supreme Court officially outlawed the use of 'sassywood' as unconstitutional in 2008 but the practice remains widespread and retains popular support and legitimacy. For more detail, see: Amanda C. Rawls, "Policy Proposals for Justice Reform in Liberia: Opportunities under the Current Legal Framework to Expand Access to Justice", in *Traditional Justice: Practitioners' Perspectives, Working Paper Series, No. 2* (Viale Vaticano: International Development Law Organization [IDLO], 2011).

206 *Empirical case study and implications*

192 Author interview: senior UNMIL official – Monrovia, Liberia, September 2010.
193 ICG, "Liberia: How Sustainable Is the Recovery?", 14.
194 'National Conference on Access to Justice' (Government of Liberia, 2010).
195 Rawls, "Policy Proposals for Justice Reform in Liberia: Opportunities under the Current Legal Framework to Expand Access to Justice", 2–3.
196 Mehler and Smith-Höhn, "Security Actors in Liberia and Sierra Leone – Roles, Interactions and Perceptions", 64.
197 Sawyer, "Social Capital, Survival Strategies, and Their Potential for Post-Conflict Governance in Liberia", 11.
198 Pajibo, "Traditional Justice Mechanisms: The Liberian Case", 24.
199 See, for example: ICG, "Liberia: How Sustainable Is the Recovery?", 11–14, 26.
200 "Security Sector Reform in Liberia: A Case of the Liberian National Police and Its Capacity to Respond to Internal Threat in the Wake of UNMIL Drawdown in 2012", 12–15.
201 Gberie, "Liberia: The 2011 Elections and Building Peace in the Fragile State", 5.
202 Kantor and Persson, "Understanding Vigilantism: Informal Security Providers and Security Sector Reform in Liberia", 16. See also: ICG, "Liberia: How Sustainable Is the Recovery?", 26.
203 Malan, "Security Sector Reform in Liberia: Mixed Results from Humble Beginnings", ix.
204 Baker, "Resource Constraint and Policy in Liberia's Post-Conflict Policing", 4.
205 "Security Sector Reform in Liberia: A Case of the Liberian National Police and Its Capacity to Respond to Internal Threat in the Wake of UNMIL Drawdown in 2012", 15.
206 ICG, "Liberia: How Sustainable Is the Recovery?", 12.
207 "Security Sector Reform in Liberia: A Case of the Liberian National Police and Its Capacity to Respond to Internal Threat in the Wake of UNMIL Drawdown in 2012", 13–15.
208 Meharg and Arnusch, "Liberia: Nonstate Security Actors", 63.
209 "Security Sector Reform in Liberia: A Case of the Liberian National Police and Its Capacity to Respond to Internal Threat in the Wake of UNMIL Drawdown in 2012", 15, 36; ICG, "Liberia: Resurrecting the Justice System", 2.
210 A survey question asking how often police ask for a bribe returned 47 per cent of people with the answer 'every interaction'. See: "Security Sector Reform in Liberia: A Case of the Liberian National Police and Its Capacity to Respond to Internal Threat in the Wake of UNMIL Drawdown in 2012", 13–14, 25; Meharg and Arnusch, "Liberia: Nonstate Security Actors", 64.
211 Vinck, Pham, and Kreutzer, "Talking Peace: A Population-Based Survey on Attitudes About Security, Dispute Resolution, and Post-Conflict Reconstruction in Liberia", 55–7.
212 Aboagye and Rupiya, "Enhancing Post-Conflict Democratic Governance through Effective Security Sector Reform in Liberia", 266.
213 See, for example: OIOS, "Programme Evaluation of the Performance and the Achievement of Results by the United Nations Mission in Liberia", 1, 10–13.
214 "Twenty-First Progress Report of the Secretary-General on the United Nations Mission in Liberia", 16.
215 Ibid., 16.
216 Author interview: UNMIL Senior Management – Monrovia, Liberia, September 2010.
217 See: "Special Report of the Secretary-General on the United Nations Mission in Liberia".
218 "Fifteenth Progress Report of the Secretary-General on the United Nations Mission in Liberia", (New York: United Nations, 2007).

219 Ibid., 15.
220 "Sixteenth Progress Report of the Secretary-General on the United Nations Mission in Liberia", (New York: United Nations, 2008), 14.
221 "Twenty-First Progress Report of the Secretary-General on the United Nations Mission in Liberia", 14.
222 Mehler and Smith-Höhn, "Security Actors in Liberia and Sierra Leone – Roles, Interactions and Perceptions", 54.
223 "Fifteenth Progress Report of the Secretary-General on the United Nations Mission in Liberia", 15.
224 "Seventeenth Progress Report of the Secretary-General on the United Nations Mission in Liberia", (New York: United Nations, 2008).
225 'UNMIL Facts and Figures', www.un.org/en/peacekeeping/missions/unmil/facts.shtml.
226 "Twenty-Sixth Progress Report of the Secretary-General on the United Nations Mission in Liberia", 15.
227 These claims are evidenced in UNMIL's benchmarking approach to the CDW. This will be addressed in detail in the following chapter.
228 Mehler and Smith-Höhn, "Security Actors in Liberia and Sierra Leone – Roles, Interactions and Perceptions", 57.
229 Carter, "Reconstructing the Rule of Law: Post-Conflict Liberia", 17.
230 See, for example: Adebajo, *UN Peacekeeping in Africa: From the Suez Crisis to the Sudan Conflicts*, 147.
231 Gberie, "Liberia: The 2011 Elections and Building Peace in the Fragile State", 7.
232 McGovern, "Liberia: The Risks of Rebuilding a Shadow State", 341.
233 Gberie, "Liberia: The 2011 Elections and Building Peace in the Fragile State", 5.

6 M&E in practice

Strengths, comparative advantages and potentialities

Introduction

The previous chapter chronicled the major developments in Liberia's protracted civil conflict and the UN peace operation deployed there. In particular, it identified the importance of the decaying security sector as both a cause and consequence of the conflagrations and the centrality of UNPOL efforts to visions of sustainable peace in Liberia. Building on this analysis, the purpose of this chapter is to examine the extent to which the framework developed in chapter 4 helps to overcome practical challenges in the field. The case of UNMIL in Liberia demonstrates many of the issues germane to the challenge of M&E in peace operations deployed to conflict-affected settings. That is to say, the environment and mission type display many of the characteristics that make M&E in peace operations uniquely difficult. Furthermore, the UNPOL mandate is broadly reflective of police peacekeeping in most contemporary UN missions.

Based on field research in the case of UNMIL in Liberia, the argument developed throughout is that the framework for M&E of UNPOL proposed herein can be seen to offer a number of advantages when compared to existing practice.[1] The empirical insights from the field support the hypothesis that principles and methodological advancements proposed in this study can lead to enhancements in the way M&E is designed and implemented, and with it bring the potential for improvements in the practice of peace operations. In particular, the chapter argues that the framework in this book strengthens M&E by better reflecting the complexity of the situation under analysis. In the first instance, the overall design – embedding M&E in a framework that privileges a recursive and systemic modality – promises to be more responsive to the dynamics and uncertainties at play. In addition, the internal field-level M&E process has the potential to enhance M&E through its context-sensitive, impact-focused, flexible and participatory design, as well as dedicated attention to interpretation of multiple perspectives and creating the space for critical and reflective feedback and responses. Finally, by developing linkages between field-level impact assessments and institutional learning, the framework presents comparative advantages for facilitating a learning focus through an embedded organisational learning cycle. In doing so, the chapter demonstrates the framework's value-add regarding a number of issues that have heretofore constituted significant stumbling blocks or been simply omitted/sidelined in approaches of current convention. These have implications for the way in which UN peace operations, and specifically UNPOL efforts, should be conceived of, designed, assessed and ultimately managed.

The chapter proceeds in two parts. The first briefly accounts for the M&E frameworks and approaches currently employed in UNMIL, including strategic frameworks as well as operational/tactical level tools. The second identifies the comparative advantages of this framework vis-à-vis current orthodoxy. It brings empirical insights and examples to bear on the purported strengths of the framework and emphasises a number of ways in which it has the potential to improve on current practice.

Extant M&E architecture for UN presence in Liberia

In order to assess the comparative advantages of the proposed framework, it is first necessary to identify the M&E tools that are currently employed in UNMIL. This section therefore introduces the main M&E instruments that will be compared and contrasted in subsequent sections. It is not intended to be an exhaustive review, but rather a primer to foreground what follows. Based on a review of publicly available reporting, documents provided by mission officials and responses of interviewees in the field, there are a range of provisions and requirements that govern M&E in UNMIL. These can be categorised as either *strategic frameworks* or *operational/tactical tools*.

A number of tools employed by the UN and the government of Liberia to monitor and evaluate its progress towards post-conflict recovery are *strategic-level frameworks* located at the nation/mission-wide level. The first, produced in February 2004 by the NTGL, along with the UN and the World Bank, was the 'Results-Focused Transitional Framework' (RFTF).[2] The RFTF was the core framework guiding the implementation of the CPA until it was replaced by the 'interim Poverty Reduction Strategy' (iPRS) in late 2006, later to be replaced by its sequel the 'Poverty Reduction Strategy' (PRS), developed under Ellen Johnson-Sirleaf's elected government, released in April 2008. In its own words, the PRS "articulates the Government's overall vision and major strategies for moving toward rapid, inclusive and sustainable growth and development during the period 2008–2011."[3] The final strategic framework of note is the 'United Nations Development Assistance Framework' (UNDAF), originally launched in 2003 and updated in 2007 for the period 2008–12. This constitutes the UN system's joined-up response to the Liberian government's goals as laid out in the PRS.[4] These strategic frameworks are holistic in nature insofar as they are comprised of all the pillars deemed central to an effective war-to-peace transition and from internationally underwritten security to Liberian owned and self-sustaining peace and poverty reduction. Each contains a focus on the objectives of UNPOL and broader security sector reform, falling under pillars relating to 'security' or 'governance and the rule of law'.

Significantly, each contains its own M&E provisions largely predicated on broad targets such as the Millennium Development Goals (MDGs) or those that form the basis of the UN's benchmarking approach.[5] Notwithstanding this attention, these M&E arrangements have not been effective at capturing progress towards outcomes and impacts associated with the various pillars. As the mid-term review – relevant to both the PRS and the UNDAF – noted, "one of the major challenges for the UN system has been the absence of a fit-for-purpose M&E framework including baselines and indicators."[6]

Whilst these strategic frameworks include a focus on areas that UNPOL contribute to – i.e. consolidation of peace and security and strengthening rule of law – and the UN is heavily involved in their conception and implementation, they are neither policy frameworks nor M&E tools for UNMIL and the UNPOL component itself. That is, they target overarching national goals and are intended to coordinate the efforts of the international community but do not necessarily capture the specific expectations of UNMIL and particularly UNPOL's contribution to these. Rather, they exist as overarching elements of the M&E architecture in the mission area.

There are also a number of M&E tools focused on assessments at the *operational/tactical levels*. Most M&E mechanisms employed by UNMIL in this locus are fragmented and different components of the mission invariably have their own reporting, monitoring and self-evaluation approaches.[7] Whilst a number of these ad hoc approaches have offered some flexibility and context-specific development, their lack of formalisation or systemisation has limited learning beyond the individual managers and their units.[8] Other M&E tools are intended to be cross-cutting and mission-wide. As described in Chapter 2, the two approaches pervasive in all UN missions, and entrenched in UNMIL, are RBB and Benchmarking. The most task-oriented tactical level micro-management tool used to track progress in-mission is without doubt RBB which has been present in UNMIL since its inception. The primary objectives of RBB are twofold: first, to provide demonstrable accounting for activity and the use of resources in the preceding financial period; and second, to propose and defend sustained or increased budgetary needs for the subsequent financial period. One official heavily involved in the process described RBB as "a management tool, focused on tactical level activities conducted on a daily basis – e.g. meetings held, nature of joint-programming with government".[9] At the beginning of each financial year, mission managers are required to disaggregate their particular mandated objectives into actionable programmes, set associated targets and then report back against these at the end of the reporting period. The process sometimes involves auditors from HQ who come to check back against RBB submissions.[10]

Benchmarking – a technocratic means of monitoring mandate implementation and gauging progress towards peace consolidation and eventual withdrawal of the mission – has existed in UNMIL since 2006.[11] An offshoot of the overarching benchmarking approach is the Integrated Mission Priorities and Implementation Plan (IMPIP) and associated Mandate Implementation Plan (MIP). These were established in late 2006, including benchmarks for all parts of an integrated UN endeavour, purported to be a tool for joint programming and monitoring the efforts of UN integrated missions.[12] All three manifestations use benchmarks for regular comparison between planned and actual achievements to track progress. Whilst these are seen as an "essential management tool" that can "enable monitoring of the progress in achieving the mission's mandate", in relation to UNPOL, the lack of clarity regarding the format and procedures for following MIPs had undermined their utility for M&E purposes. This finding was supported by an OIOS report assessing the management of UNPOL operations.[13]

Other noteworthy elements of the UNMIL M&E architecture are those associated with Knowledge Management implemented incrementally since 2006.[14] This includes the 'Knowledge Management Toolkit' comprising four tools for capturing experiences[15] and a Best Practices Officer.[16] In addition, the complementary but inconsistent OIOS Evaluations (up to four per year) have been a fixture of UNMIL's evaluation culture.[17] The M&E tools and instruments specific to the police component are few and far between, but since UNMIL initially deployed performance appraisals of UNPOL personnel, they have become obligatory.

This collection of tools and processes constitutes the M&E architecture that overlays and occupies those in UNPOL when it comes to assessing progress and determining the impact of mission activities. The remainder of this chapter draws on insights garnered in extensive field research to draw comparisons between these approaches and the one developed in this book to identify the benefits of the framework proposed herein.

Strengths, comparative advantages and potentialities

The field research highlighted a range of strengths, comparative advantages and potentialities relating to the framework's overall design, field-level M&E process and its focus on facilitating organisational learning. This section presents the findings in each of these areas in turn.

Overarching design

Circularity

The frustration with extant M&E most consistently flagged by mission officials was the issue of inappropriate implementation timeframes. For example, a number of peacekeepers experienced in RBB stated that the annual time horizons associated with RBB were too elongated to offer much real-time value to decision-makers on a day-to-day basis.[18] Moreover, some contended that the corollary demands for precise forecasting of programme objectives and likely indicators of their attainment ahead of time (i.e. one full year) were inappropriate for and ill-suited to objectives where outcomes are inherently unpredictable.[19] In the opinion of many respondents, this further reduced the utility of RBB for accurate real-time assessments and these timeframes became stringent pre-commitments to report against.

Similarly, many of those interviewed highlighted the lag associated with infrequent evaluations conducted by a visiting team from the OIOS or DPKO's DPET Evaluation Unit. For example, a 2010 OIOS evaluation on 'UNMIL mandate implementation effectiveness' identified a lack of focus on reform of the rule of law elements as a system.[20] However, according to respondents this finding only really served to formalise what had been recognised within the mission years earlier (i.e. a need for a more integrated or comprehensive approach to SSR[21]) and to legitimate steps already undertaken to address this problem (e.g. adjusted structure of mission, creating a DSRSG pillar to reflect the centrality of holistic Rule of Law approach as well as the creation of the position of 'SSR Advisor to the SRSG').[22] In this case, the OIOS evaluation was not deemed to be timely enough for its results to feed back to the mission to inform adjustments – albeit this can be understood as making a contribution to second-level learning.[23] This view was reinforced by others referring to the questionable wisdom of the timing of current M&E undertakings. For example, one respondent explained that the "urgency of arbitrary timelines for progress reporting incentivizes people to massage the data even more" to meet objectives and that this was an additional concern.[24] This led to discussions about a perceived lack of effective linkages between M&E findings and their application.[25]

The circular – i.e. iterative and reflexive – character of the framework proposed was deemed to hold great potential to mitigate the problems and risks associated with ad hoc and inconsistent timeframes synonymous with extant orthodoxy. Respondents highlighted the benefits of the framework for moving beyond intermittent assessments to meet periodic reporting, towards dedicated and wider analysis that could provide more useful information for adjustments to tactics and programming in real time. Furthermore, it was suggested that these qualities could help overcome some of the resistance to M&E associated with unexpected/impromptu evaluations. For example, one interviewee said, "if operatives know that M&E is taking place as a continuous process then they will be better able to reconcile the perceived threat it poses and potentially even go on to embrace it as a supportive management tool".[26]

Systemic approach

It became clear during field research that, despite there being numerous M&E mechanisms in and around UNMIL which address the security situation and progress in relation to the security sector and rule of law reform,[27] these frameworks and reporting procedures did not cohere well, nor were there clearly identified channels for feeding back into ongoing planning or strategic decision-making. As one respondent insisted, "they are of an ad hoc nature with little or no systemization".[28] Another pointed out that multiple reporting chains from the local/sub-national level tended to overwhelm the capacity of any centralised mechanism to analyse and synthesise this real-time information flow.[29]

Whilst some interviewees claimed that strategic planning has reached a level of coherence, they were also at pains to highlight that this planning coherence did not translate into implementation coherence which was deemed to be much harder.[30] In other words, whilst overarching post-conflict recovery frameworks are designed to complement each other and avoid duplication of efforts, there remains a degree of dissonance in their implementation, beset by unclear sequencing and lopsided focus. A number of interviewees felt that the lack of cross-cutting or at least complementary M&E was a decisive factor in this. For example, the SSR advisor emphasised the importance of M&E in reconciling this disconnect, explaining how:

> One of the problems with M&E is it always comes across as an afterthought. If you ever read a book it's always in an Annex, or "Chapter 10, the M&E chapter!" So, the only way we're going to resolve the coherence deficit in implementation, is by having stronger monitoring and evaluation from the outset so that we ensure we're coherent. It means that..., in terms of the programme cycle, [M&E] must *be* the programme cycle.[31]

He and others believed, therefore, that the framework's focus on ensuring systemic awareness of and coherence with the rest of the M&E architecture was not only important for more effective impact assessments, but moreover, could have positive knock-on effects for better implementation coordination and policy harmonisation.

In the same vein, one official claimed that the lack of feedback from existing approaches into ongoing planning processes were in part due to

214 *Empirical case study and implications*

the fact that M&E is not entrenched in the day-to-day practice of peace operations.[32] Another respondent captured the organisational challenge underlying this, saying that "[existing] M&E elements are not continuous ... they are more like a snapshot assessment of a particular issue area based on urgent need. The immediate needs supersede the holistic and systematic – people are constantly putting out fires."[33] This reactive posture and lack of attention to process and continuity in M&E was repeatedly identified as a major cause of dysfunctional feedback between M&E and mission planning and consequently a contributing factor to variance witnessed in meeting mission objectives. For instance, numerous interviewees pointed to uneven progress in the reform of the various criminal justice institutions as a prime example of this.[34]

These insights echo the findings of others that UNMIL demonstrates the need to link planning processes to qualitative assessments of progress on the ground.[35] Therefore, a more holistically conceived framework that embeds M&E in overall mission management, avoiding the 'afterthought-ism' typical of extant approaches, would be better placed to support enhanced congruency in planning and implementation. Participants generally believed that the framework's design with cognisance of the complex systemic environment, explicit linkages between field M&E and multi-tiered organisational learning as well as entrenched feedback loops to planning and implementation hold considerable promise for addressing these systemic issues. Overcoming the inconsistent and unsystemic nature of current orthodoxy represents genuine, if simple, value add in this domain.

Field-level M&E process

This section addresses the areas of importance arising in the fieldwork relating to the field-level M&E process. It explains strengths and comparative advantages of the framework in relation to: context-sensitive foregrounding and baselines; the impact/outcome focus, addressing issues of exogenous factors and unintended consequences, questions of attribution and multiple data sources; flexibility; inclusive/participatory approach; and interpretation and response elements.

Context-sensitive foregrounding/baselines

A recurrent criticism of M&E in UNMIL concerned the extent to which analyses were situated in the specific operating context. Many interviewed pointed to insufficient attention to the specific and historically contingent conditions that constituted UNMIL's operating environment. Regarding UNPOL, a senior leader in UNPOL emphasised the "[h]uge importance of contextual considerations" and was adamant that M&E "[s]hould not and cannot generalise!"[36] This notion was supported by another senior UNPOL official who explained that "...we have to understand the cultural factors and the working environment which impact on your ability to achieve change."[37] A major associated issue highlighted concerned the resources available to not only implement police reform programmes but also to sustain the new entities thereafter. As one respondent noted, "We can't do these assessments without also looking at the state of the economy they have to operate in – and every post-conflict economy is weak. So, that is a chicken and egg problem."[38]

It was highlighted that the contextual assessments proposed in the framework would go a long way towards improving this predicament. Furthermore, it was noted that dedicated foregrounding would importantly allow for an accounting of important facets of the mission environment commonly omitted/sidelined in current M&E orthodoxy. One frequently cited example was the prevalence of non-state providers of policing type services.[39] Whilst incorporating an awareness of these stakeholders will provide a clearer and fuller picture of the providers of public safety, it was also believed to be a precursor to determining preferences amongst the population for their use and a vital element of understanding the extent to which the state police are (or are not) the first port of call for matters of protection and criminal justice. It was believed that this, in turn, could be used to provide insight into changing perceptions of the LNP.

A corollary shortcoming identified repeatedly concerned baseline assessments. When asked about the existence and reliability of baselines for tracking change and gauging impact in M&E, the most common response was that there was little or no accurate and useful baseline data collected or assessments made.[40] This, many concluded, left assessments lacking a 'how things were' measurement against which relative improvements could be gauged.[41] Indeed, in relation to UNPOL undertakings, one official went as far as to say that for "[m]ost of these things we're doing, there has never been a baseline taken."[42]

One possibility for plugging the baseline gap identified by a number of interviewees across the rule of law components was the fledgling ROLIP.[43] Many believed this was a positive development given its focus on producing an appraisal of current capacities across the rule of law institutions. However, there remained some doubts about the suitability of the indicators proposed for the ROLIP. One official pointed to a lack of cultural/context sensitivity in the selection of some indicators included in final drafts for ROLIP, giving the example of standards for daily costs per prisoner to assess whether or not corrections institutions were functioning effectively and satisfactorily. In this official's opinion, these standards were alien to the realities of Liberia in terms of welfare available to any citizen, let alone those who had committed serious crime. The related concern was that these indicators may hold UNPOL efforts to standards that are simply not realistic or sustainable in the context of post-conflict environments such as Liberia.[44] Perhaps worse, one official explained how these targets can serve to dictate reform efforts and in doing so produce perverse consequences such as, "making going to prison attractive to people who would otherwise try and stay out of it."[45] Ultimately, some in the police component claimed that even if it could ascertain accurate baseline studies and subsequent snapshot analyses, ROLIP's shortcoming in this regard emphasised the need for context-sensitive design and implementation of all M&E elements. The framework's development of indicators of change through participatory approaches was believed to hold promise in mitigating the risk of inappropriate measures.[46]

Notwithstanding these challenges, a large proportion of those interviewed argued that it was important to have baseline data to work against. Furthermore, given the state of incapacity of the LNP at the inception of the UNMIL reform programme, it was stressed that baselines must accurately reflect such realities to be useful.[47] In addition, it was regularly cited that as the process unfolded, it was especially important that baselines are updated in an iterative way, but that this was rarely the case with existing instruments.[48] These qualities are at the core of the framework offered in this book with its purposeful context sensitivity and the foregrounding step for constructing relevant baselines, as well as its circular iterative and updating modality. In these ways, many respondents believed that the framework has the potential to overcome a fundamental problem identified with existing approaches and build the foundations for more precise and reliable findings. Another potential value-add of targeting baselines and enhanced context awareness identified relates to the framework's focus on assessing impact.

Impact/outcome focus

Some senior mission staff interviewed argued that gauging the impact of UNMIL activities was the focus of ad hoc evaluations commissioned by HQ or the UNMIL Senior Mission Leadership Group (SMLG).[49] However, most respondents agreed that the absence of an impact-focus in ongoing M&E within the mission was conspicuous. Regarding focus, many of those interviewed – irrespective of their place in the operation's hierarchy – lamented the fact that the majority of current practice was preoccupied with demonstrating accountability rather than ascertaining the impact of action. A senior official summarised the current state of play in this regard, explaining that:

> I think there are two issues at stake: The first is that program officers on the ground have to be accountable for the money they spend – so there's an accountability issue. The other issue of course relates to impact – whether what we're doing is actually making a difference. And I think impact and accountability are actually two completely different things and we somehow have conflated both into one with this M&E stuff – to be accountable to our financiers and show that the

money has been spent but at the same time to show that there is value in spending that money.[50]

As a result of accountability eliding impact motivations, extant approaches were not highly thought of as a modality for reporting on the actual impact of actions or enabling learning from findings. Many respondents highlighted that the techniques employed in benchmarking and RBB struggled to get at the issue of impact due to their overdependence on output level and quantitative measures synonymous with accountability audits.[51] The perspective of one civil society organisation typified these sentiments, noting that, "the UN may focus on the numbers, but in doing so the actual challenges on the ground are not captured."[52] As one senior staff officer said, "RBB is very good at counting things, but not so good at getting at the associated impacts of the activities we do."[53] Another official concurred, describing current orthodoxy as "limited" because it is "using predominantly quantitative indicators to demonstrate productivity without much attention paid to the effect or impact of those activities."[54] According to mission officials, benchmarking and derivative IMPIP/MIP are beset by similar problems, given that they generally employ the same predominantly quantitative metrics found in the other instruments to assess progress on mandate implementation.[55] Some claimed that conventional approaches were particularly inappropriate for demonstrating impact in some instances. For example, measuring success of the Political, Policy and Planning Section towards elections involved counting the number of meetings held with political parties. The official referred to the metrics employed as "absolute nonsense", adding that "it is not the number, but the substance of those meetings that matters."[56] He continued that these measures "might make some sense to those demanding [them], but not to people on the ground", further adding that "...in the political realm these approaches are not only insufficient, but also risk distorting the work of our departments to meet these targets".[57]

Senior members of UNPOL dismissed the output orientation of current M&E approaches, or what one called "wooden numbers",[58] asserting in relation to police reform,

> we may have ten nice new police stations but whether anybody bothers to go and make a report is a separate question altogether and if they don't bother to make a report, then you want to know why ... It's easy to count how many buildings you have put up; but not so easy to assess the impact [of doing so].[59]

An example of inappropriate measures given numerous times was the UNPOL Quick Impact Projects (QIPs) to construct Women and Children Protection Centres (WCPCs) as part of LNP infrastructure where the indicator of success was simply the number of centres built. The isolated output focus missed the reality that, despite having a new building, staff had too few vehicles to transfer perpetrators and victims of sexual violence separately and no money to buy food for the women and children once at the centre.[60] That is, the existence of the building alone was not enough to facilitate better services to women/child victims of crime – a nuance absent in the measure used.[61] This example is indicative of the wider challenges with output metrics employed under current M&E orthodoxy.

One senior mission leader asserted that, contrary to current approaches, it was important for M&E to tease out the 'quality' of police performance.[62] This is a view firmly supported by the GRC that has repeatedly emphasised the need to measure police performance rather than training output.[63] Others in the UNPOL establishment agreed that there was a need to gain better clarity on what is being measured, why and what it can tell us, stressing that, "we need to be clear about the differences between inputs, outputs, outcomes and impacts."[64] In relation to police reform objectives in particular, one senior mission leader agreed that going deeper and broader when attempting to assess impact was critical, stating that "M&E is crucial to the issue of sustainability. Getting at 'impact' is the only way to get an idea of how sustainable productivity has been."[65]

When asked to explain why current practice failed to address impact, many replied that it was too difficult to produce meaningful impact assessments with the existing tools at their disposal. For example, one official stated that, "Contextual accounts or 'thick descriptions' are hard to construct and harder to justify and substantiate to 'bosses' than simple metrics. In this way, non-quantifiable attributes are left unattended to – the focus is elsewhere."[66] Furthermore, respondents gave examples where even qualitative benchmarks were tracked and measured using quantitative metrics. For instance, the overriding benchmark for the reform of the LNP uses the term 'operational' to be indicative of successful attainment of standing up the new LNP. However, as a senior UNPOL leader stated, "Practices and procedures are what makes [the LNP] operational, not numbers ... Concepts like 'operational' are qualitative, subjective and intangible and cannot be quantified and measured in the ways we are required to under these systems."[67] Despite this recognition, one criticism that figured prominently was the lack of tools available for doing so.[68] One official was forthright in proclaiming that UNMIL is beset by a "complete lack of sophisticated methodologies for measuring impact"[69] and stated that in reality UNMIL personnel had to use their individual acumen to draw on templates developed in other UN peace operations, not to mention different contexts, due to a lack of in-mission options.[70] A senior UNPOL leader similarly lamented the paucity of suitable models, stating that, "I don't think there are currently any ready-made mechanisms or tools that can measure the things UNPOL would like to measure – that being the impact of UNPOL activities."[71]

This is not to suggest that these dominant practices were dismissed as useless. On the contrary, mission personnel were at pains to highlight when primarily quantitative output measures could be useful. Almost without fail, interviewees stated that any M&E architecture needed a modality for tracking implementation of project outputs, if only as a basic management tool.[72] Nevertheless, the majority of those questioned believed that this was a necessary, but not sufficient, element of M&E. Consequently, despite the difficulties identified in terms of conducting and 'selling' impact-focused M&E there was a widespread acceptance that the impact of activities needed to be the focus of M&E to make it more effective. One respondent epitomized this, noting, "There is clearly a need to move beyond reporting outputs and target the outcomes and impact associated with those outputs."[73] Summarising the challenge, one official noted, "As a mission, we need to be sure that, beyond the numbers and the buildings, the impact is being understood and reacted upon."[74]

When asked about the most pertinent means of understanding UNPOL impact, many were of the opinion that, given the stage of the mission, it was necessary to focus on the extent to which the LNP and other law enforcement agencies had improved. In addition to looking at the quality and quantity of human resources in the LNP, there was a general belief that the best way of determining improvements in the LNP was by ascertaining how Liberians' experiences of the police were changing.[75] For example, a senior UNPOL manager noted, "Given that UNMIL are now primarily here to develop the LNP, it is important that public perceptions of how the LNP is improving are used as the indicator of 'success'."[76] As many emphasised, this sits in stark contrast to current convention which lacks focus on eliciting public perceptions but remains heavily output-centric – both in terms of the 'expected accomplishments' identified and the indicators used to demonstrate this. Whilst these are often employed as proxies for improved perceptions, as one official asserted, "Public confidence is not built by doing one act, or doing one act well; but a series of activities done well over time."[77]

For these reasons, and as others have shown, UNMIL demonstrates the need to "think beyond short-term goals and quantitative indicators for benchmark evaluations".[78] This is increasingly recognised in rhetorical statements and internal audit reports,[79] but the evidence from the field is that practice lags behind significantly. The framework proposed here was therefore seen to be advantageous in its focus on outcomes/impacts whilst simultaneously contextualising outputs when necessary. Furthermore, the range of methods proposed in the framework for doing so, particularly the participatory ones, were deemed better suited to ascertaining a valuable picture of progress and impact by eliciting public perceptions. The focus on impact triggered discussions about the effect of external influences and seeking out the unexpected or unintended consequences.

EXOGENOUS FACTORS AND UNINTENDED CONSEQUENCES

Interviews frequently revealed that current M&E is not good at revealing and incorporating the presence and effect of exogenous factors and unintended consequences. In relation to external influences, respondents highlighted two major considerations. First, there was a widespread agreement that UNMIL was just one actor amongst many that contribute towards change in Liberia and that this should be better reflected in M&E. As one senior official admitted, "Ultimately, we – the mission – are not in control of all the factors."[80] In particular, the centrality of the Liberian government as a partner in post-conflict reconstruction was singled out as an important variable insufficiently captured in existing practice.[81] For instance, one respondent noted that "at this stage of the mission, partnership with the government is crucial. After all, UNMIL's mission is to support and assist the government. M&E needs to get at that."[82] This is an equally salient concern for UNPOL, particularly when engaging in a political process like law enforcement reform. In the same vein, UNPOL is just one of many influencing agents in producing change in the Liberian criminal justice architecture given the involvement of bilateral donor governments and private companies in SSR.

Second, in line with emerging consensus, mission personnel pointed to the importance of understanding police effectiveness in the context of an interdependent rule of law system. For example, one official explained that, "There is a sense in which the reputation of the police is really in the hands of the courts."[83] She further asserted that, "If the courts are not functioning then what confidence do people have that people they report won't come back and threaten them, if they go in and come back right out again and come and beat them on the head for having made the report to begin with."[84] In this sense, interviewees argued that the dysfunction of other parts of the criminal justice system should be conceptualised as negative exogenous factors in the outcomes of police reform. However, it was commonly remarked that the recognition of multiple external influences was not sufficiently reflected in the design and findings of current M&E. Despite rhetorical commitments and organisational arrangements to integrate thematic rule of law efforts, interviewees stated that UNPOL M&E remained siloed and isolated from UNMIL assistance to the broader criminal justice system, not to mention a deeper-seated security and justice landscape.[85] For example, some argued that understanding non-state actors as exogenous actors with significant influence was vital to overall impact assessments.[86]

One official emphasised that examples such as these reflect the lack of appreciation of the systemic nature of change in this domain more generally.[87] Many described how the M&E tools at their disposal were unable to include variables beyond the strict remit of their programme – as one interviewee lamented, "We are trapped in a bureaucratic straitjacket."[88] In this regard, a number of interviewees also questioned the indicators employed under extant M&E regimes. For example, a mission expert explained how indicators such as 'number of arrests' can become "a faulty measurement of how we are doing".[89] In reference to the lack of a systemic focus in extant M&E, one interviewee declared that, "Any attempt to assess the performance of the police alone – that fails to see how things trickle further down the line – are less valuable. Without all of those things working, the police will never inspire confidence."[90]

When asked about unintended consequences, common responses coalesced around the belief that extant M&E only reports what it is looking for and generally fails to include an account of the externalities associated with UNMIL implementation – be they positive or negative.[91] The example given above of WCPCs provides further insight into the limitations of current M&E in this regard. The simple metric utilised to count the number of WCPCs built neglects the unintended consequences of producing new buildings, whereby in one case, the WCPC was commandeered by the LNP as it was a much better facility than the local LNP station.[92] This perverse effect is missing from the account which assumes creating WCPCs will have an automatic and exclusively positive intended effect. In regard to follow-up M&E of these QIPs that might pick up these contextual factors and externalities, an UNMIL official admitted that, "this is just not happening".[93] This exemplifies how M&E that reveals negative consequences associated with UNPOL activities is scarce.

In trying to gain a clearer picture of what change is (not) taking place and why, one official noted, "We must be able to recognize the existence of external influences on outcomes. It is vital that we acknowledge the context within which these developments are taking place."[94] Another senior staffer was clear about this matter, noting that, "The existence of exogenous factors and unintended consequences means it is vital that UN peacekeeping develops a way of incorporating these phenomena into its M&E approach."[95] This was indicative of widespread agreement amongst interviewees that for M&E to be more useful for all stakeholders, it must be able to present a more systemic picture of what is happening and why.[96] The framework's systemic focus and the methods proposed to seek out the unexpected was said by many to offer great advantage in ways that can overcome the shortcoming of existing approaches regarding external forces and unintended consequences. Furthermore, these examples add further weight to the argument for the iterative assessments of impact embedded in the framework. Issues of impact, external influences and externalities were further believed to have important ramifications for the challenge of attribution.

ATTRIBUTION: CAUSALITY VS. CONTRIBUTION

When asked about the question of attribution – i.e. what achievements can be attributed to the work of UNPOL and to what extent? – many stated that the way M&E is currently designed means that it lacks humility when claiming causality for certain outcomes and prevailing conditions. Numerous respondents stated that they believed extant M&E over claims what UNMIL components have achieved collectively/individually, without acknowledging the influence of other actors and factors.[97] Many identified the aforementioned overlooking of exogenous factors and unintended consequences – as a major reason for the lack of convincing attribution of accomplishments, particularly those at the most macro level. Furthermore, it was often said that ambiguous understandings of cause-and-effect curtailed M&E's utility for learning.[98]

One long-serving official pointed to, "methodological inelegance regarding the attribution question".[99] UNPOL officers concurred, describing how extant approaches lack the methodological leverage to construct a compelling case for cause-and-effect between UNPOL programming and observable outcomes, rendering such claims as largely inferential and contingent on assumptions in the theories of change underpinning assessments.[100] For example, referring to the reality that outcomes are the product of multiple influences, a mission official in the political affairs section said that, "...we are part of a multi-actor implementing team ... in these circumstances there can be no single causal agent and M&E should not be trying to assert otherwise."[101]

Consequently, most respondents advocated for M&E that produced more humble findings, focusing on explaining potential influence on strategic goals, as opposed to attempting to demonstrate a direct cause-and-effect relationship between the actions of UNPOL and changes in the security sector. In this regard, one official simply implored that any approach used "needs to be underpinned by a sense of realism".[102] Another respondent emphasised the importance of getting at how things had changed – i.e. what has the peace operation actually done to influence outcomes and impacts – rather than rudimentary indications that something had indeed happened.[103] These findings suggest that the framework's alternative approaches to measuring the impact of mission activities focused on emergent outcomes as well as greater humility in what can be attributed to UNPOL offer potential advantages over current orthodoxy. The framework's focus on contribution analysis techniques in league with other methods capable of constructing narratives about change reflects this consensus and it was strongly believed that such an approach could add genuine value in this regard. The framework's multi-method character appears to better reflect the changing needs on the ground whilst remaining appropriate, such that the approach is uncomplicated and practical yet careful and insightful. Many experts interviewed believed that such an approach held promise for providing the necessary focus on the realities of change on the ground as well as the avoidance of distorting practice or pandering to political masters unnecessarily.[104] A large part of these methods pertains to broadening the scope of what constitutes 'good enough' data.

MULTIPLE DATA SOURCES

In this regard, the majority of those interviewed identified the framework's focus on multiplying and diversifying the sites and sources of data for M&E as a key strength. Many attested that government statistics are not readily available or particularly trustworthy in Liberia.[105] The government has focused on building the capacity of formal information gathering and analysing entities.[106] However, when asked whether this had garnered positive improvements in the type and quality of information available for assessment of UNPOL and the LNP, most suggested that it had not.[107] For instance, it was remarked that there are few sources of authoritative statistics to measure rates or trends in crime.[108] Ultimately, according to the majority of respondents, the lack of conventional data should not detract from the important realisation that statistics – however trustworthy – are not the panacea to M&E in these settings.

Furthermore, it was frequently said that attempts to substitute this type of information had proven to be inadequate. For example, one previous employee of the monitoring unit of the Legal/Judicial Unit explained how, despite having dedicated monitors in all areas of the field, the low quality of reporting left analysts at headquarters with primarily anecdotal evidence and little reliable information to work with in producing their own assessments. The lack of a systematic approach to credible data collection and analysis was perceived as a "serious circuit-breaker in planning, monitoring and evaluation",[109] and a major stumbling block to effective interpretation and utilisation of field-level experiences.

These findings suggest that due to a dearth of adequate conventional data sources, a peace operation may need to look elsewhere, and be innovative in doing so, in order to construct a nuanced but reliable picture of what is happening. The framework's focus on utilising alternative data sources was highlighted as a major strength in this regard. For instance, one interviewee claimed that, "there is a need to seek out and cultivate sites of information and networks through which data can be harvested".[110] As mentioned, many interviewees highlighted the fact that this needs to include a range of both quantitative and qualitative sources.[111] The framework's call for being more creative when deciding what constitutes 'good enough' data was also emphasised as a positive development. For example, a senior government official stated that things like the ability of money-changers to operate on the streets, the attendance of children in schools, and even the presence of foreign researchers like myself, could be understood as indicative of progress in re-establishing the rule of law.[112] Another official highlighted that UNPOL and LNP officers themselves were a rich source of information and feedback for M&E – particularly given their vantage point to observe and experience changes in organisational behaviour.[113]

In addition, a number of interviewees identified a myriad of community-based actors and networks as a rich source of information about local perceptions of the public security system as well as a means of tracking change over time.[114] For example, one interviewee spoke about the role of hybrid arrangements such as the Community Policing Forums.[115] Similarly, another official pointed to the fledgling County Security Mechanisms as a potential site of valuable input given their local level location and composition that includes stakeholders from both formal (e.g. head of the LNP, the local district attorney, prosecutor) and informal (e.g. the Paramount, local, clan chiefs, religious leaders and respected and influential CSOs) spheres.[116] Another representative of civil society spoke about the latent value of other community-based forums such as the County Peace Councils and Country Development Committees as rich sources of information.[117] It is, however, important to note that the same interviewee highlighted that despite the burgeoning of committees and mechanisms, those serving on them were often fewer, insofar as the same individual often represented a particular community on many of these.[118] Others pointed to the role of the media, in particular the example of a daily 'Crimewatch' programme on local radio from 2–4am where the general public can call in to report crime, directly linked to the LNP, but also creating a forum for sharing perceptions of the LNP.[119]

However, it is clear from the field research that these sites and sources of information are not systemically utilised in extant M&E. For example, the measures synonymous with RBB/benchmarking do not tap into informal data sources. Similarly, qualitative evaluations undertaken rarely interview or survey host populations to ascertain their perceptions about impact and change.[120] Ultimately, however trustworthy and abundant conventional sources, insights from the field research emphasised that the peace operations environment dictates that alternative sources of data are both available and vital in producing a textured picture of what is happening. As one interviewee asserted, "It makes sense – in addition to the traditional form of information gathering – to use this alternative approach of working with local organisations, community groups, chiefs, etc., to get information."[121] There was agreement that M&E needs to be more malleable in terms of what constitute 'good enough' data sources and types. These empirical findings emphasise how the framework therefore promises to add value by broadening the criteria for what constitutes good enough data to inform M&E.

Flexibility

Issues of flexibility were addressed above in relation to the overarching design of the framework.[122] Whilst there are some similarities between the terminology and the issues covered in those findings and the analysis that follows, this section is specifically focused on the benefits and advantages derived from inbuilt flexibility in the field-level M&E process and warrants a dedicated discussion.

A key issue described by many respondents concerned the rigidity of UNMIL's current M&E approaches. It was often stated that mission phases are important and – as one official put it – "there is a need for different types of M&E for different stages of a mission".[123] However, the general consensus was that current orthodoxy was inflexible such that it was lethargic and rendered incapable of responding effectively to inevitable changes to mission circumstances and objectives.

This was deemed to be the case at both the macro and micro level. For instance, whilst initially in partnership with the transitional government, police reform programmes were significantly rejigged following the election of President Johnson-Sirleaf.[124] UNPOL officials regularly noted that the inability of extant M&E to adjust to changing objectives led to disconnect between expected accomplishments and the focus of altered programming. At the operational level, UNPOL officials intimated that targets embedded in extant M&E are problematic when there is a strict definition attached to a benchmark but it is misguided. One senior UNPOL official gave the example of the ERU creation, whereby a benchmark of '500 members trained' was "set in stone", explaining that it was only when his office insisted that it was an operational imperative to shift focus towards up-skilling the PSU that a reduction of the ERU target/benchmark to its current strength was accepted.[125] As it was described, this required an adamant stance by senior UNPOL figures to "break the sanctity of the benchmark".[126] In addition to losing relevance to changing objectives, numerous interviewees warned that the inflexibility of implementation tracking mechanisms also risked distorting the action of peacekeepers in line with prescriptive instruments.[127] For example, some described how resources were increasingly earmarked to meet particular targets rather than to fund holistic programming. One official explained how in this case, the demand to report on particular targets can, at times, alter the original intent of the reporting process, adding that, "The framework [for M&E] has essentially become a series of numbers that dictates what is collected in the field", in effect flip-siding the M&E process such that "the data comes last!"[128]

Similarly, it was lamented that – rare as it might be – good data from the ground cannot influence benchmarks or prevent the perverse diversion of work towards attaining them.[129] This dysfunction in the transmission of meaningful information from and back into the M&E process was identified as a major breakdown in feedback loops that could enable learning.[130] This perception was corroborated by another official who said, "It is important in the peace operations setting that M&E has the built-in flexibility to adapt to changing objectives over time."[131] Furthermore, there was a general belief that changes in missions and their operating environment are not necessarily discrete or self-evident, and therefore M&E would be most useful if it was designed to allow for recursive adaptation to unpredictable circumstances.[132] As a senior manager in UNPOL asserted, "There is a need for greater flexibility and adaptability to be built in to [M&E] so that it can be calibrated along the way as the mission progresses."[133]

It was emphasised that the proposed framework was potentially more capable of dealing with this dynamical change. The insights in this domain therefore suggest that the framework's design to be adaptive to the realities of post-conflict environments and UNPOL idiosyncrasies is not only desirable, but also achievable. Built-in flexibility promises a more responsive approach, allowing for those with awareness of the situation to select the most appropriate methods to match the circumstances at any given time. This is further buttressed by the embedded reflexivity which also presents an opportunity to continuously revisit elements of the M&E process to ensure its currency.[134] A number of respondents also pointed to these advantages as a way of mitigating pressure from above to fit a corporate accountability model and the prescriptive and distortive tendencies of existing approaches that are governed more by political objectives than operational realities.

Inclusive/participatory approach

As already touched upon, insights from UNMIL point to advantages of the framework in relation to its inclusive nature, the participatory approaches embedded in it and the spin-off benefits for ownership. This was deemed to be the case regarding setting objectives, carrying out the process for measuring against them and inculcating a sense of ownership and cooperation in the implementation of M&E. Regarding objective setting, when asked about the value of the benchmarks/targets used in current approaches, respondents regularly disputed the wisdom of the selection of these milestone targets. For example, many questioned what criteria were considered in setting the targets in the first place.[135] Similarly, a number of officials in UNPOL highlighted issues relating to the 'framing' of the benchmarks and queried whether or not the prescribed target/benchmark for number of LNP personnel was sufficient to meet the real needs of public security throughout Liberia – before any questions about its sustainability in the longer term.[136] One official stated that this was indicative of the reality that, "there exists a huge gap between the 'imposed benchmarks' set elsewhere and the emergent challenges and associated targets which arise from on-the-ground knowledge and experience".[137] It was said that the framework's enhanced participation would constitute valuable feedback opportunities to inform the generation of locally grounded and realistic objectives and a "collaborative way of driving the process forward".[138]

In addition, many identified the narrow participation in extant approaches as an inhibiting factor that had ramifications for the utility and even the credibility of findings.[139] Members of government interviewed stated their displeasure with M&E that was overly mission-centric, failed to adequately incorporate national and local perspectives and led to unilateral decision-making. For instance, a former LNP Deputy Inspector-General pointed to the initial vetting of former LNP officers as a prime example of a "non-consultative and non-participatory approach that was ill-conceived and failed to appreciate local concerns".[140] She went on to explain that she firmly believed that this deficit was a major factor in the significant problems encountered in early LNP reform efforts. One example given was the reluctance of people in the leeward counties to testify against the wartime activities of candidates for the new LNP for fear of retribution. This, she said, severely limited the effectiveness of that component of the vetting procedure.[141] Furthermore, she and others added that when subsequent improvements occurred, they were largely due to enhanced collaboration between the UN, the LNP and local communities in the implementation and tracking of reform activities.[142]

Regarding execution of M&E, it was commonly stated that existing M&E instruments lack any significant participation in information gathering and analysis beyond a small number of mission personnel. Even then, the involvement and input of mission personnel is filtered through the stringent orthodoxy. For example, many respondents claimed that they saw first-hand when progress, or indeed regression, occurred but felt that the mission did not have appropriate tools to capture this. One official echoed this conviction in saying that, "The challenge is formalizing what is usually individual intuition and sensitivity based on contextual knowledge: 'we know it when we see it!'"[143]

This lack of participation in M&E was further emphasised as an issue at the sub-national level where partnership with government heralded at the national level was not reflected at the local level.[144] Many of those interviewed felt strongly about the potential value add of the framework for expanding this pool of participants. In addition to their value as data sites, many respondents believed non-governmental and community-based actors had much value to add as potential contributors and collaborators in conducting M&E. For example, one NGO official noted, "Community-based networks for feeding into M&E and disseminating M&E findings do exist and have the potential to broaden the perspective."[145] However, challenges remain in regard to sustainable funding for their continued work in the long haul.[146] CSOs and local community members also stated that they have a lot to offer to M&E processes, due to their 'on-the-ground' knowledge and intuitive sense of progress, as well as experience of the unintended consequences of action and the exogenous factors inhibiting progress.[147] These opinions were repeated by others; for example, the Minister for Justice implored that the valuable contributions of ordinary Liberians "...should be harnessed by the UN and others in their assessments of impact".[148]

In addition, many emphasised that the conspicuous absence of non-state actors in conceptualising and implementing SSR and its M&E belies the importance of informal provision of public safety and justice to large populations in Liberia.[149] How an appreciation of this reality feeds into M&E is largely without precedent in the peace operations setting and interviews revealed strongly held views on how the issue of non-state providers should be addressed and/or incorporated. Nevertheless, respondents were broadly agreed that M&E tools available to them are generally blinkered to the existence and effect of non-statutory policing actors in relation to the impact of UNPOL activities.[150] Notwithstanding disparate perspectives on their rightful role, as important stakeholders in SSR, it was widely agreed that non-state providers are well-placed and have both capacity and knowledge to provide unique information and feedback into the M&E process. A senior UNPOL manager explained that, "In Liberia, there is no precedent for the state – specifically the police – as conceived by UNMIL."[151] Consequently, what cannot be ignored is that public perceptions of the LNP are not only on a relative scale including their own historical legacy, but on a comparative scale vis-à-vis alternative sources of protection and security. As another senior official explained,

> [Liberians] have been used to looking elsewhere. Getting them to look at the state is, in itself, an exercise in reorientation, so they had better get something concrete from it, or they aren't ever going to have confidence in it.[152]

These findings suggest that M&E has a lot of distance to travel if it is to incorporate the importance of the pluralistic nature of security and justice provision in the Liberian context. Nevertheless, it was remarked that the inclusivity and systemic awareness built in to this framework presented the opportunity to bring important contributions to the process, as well as much-needed balance to the state-centrism of extant approaches.

Importantly, many respondents pointed out that the framework's participatory approach to M&E would not be a radical proposition as Liberia has been a crucible for innovative approaches to consultative and participatory reform, in particular through initiatives of the GRC, as well as nationwide consultations on developing a national security strategy and the PRS.[153] It was regularly noted that a major perceived benefit of this participatory modality was enhanced local ownership of the processes underway. Insights from the field supported the argument that this framework's focus on shared, 'transitional' and local ownership has the potential to facilitate these aims. For instance, a senior UNPOL official claimed that the example of the performance management system developed to track the implementation of the LNP Strategic Plan demonstrated the advantages of formalising transitional ownership of M&E as police reform priorities are increasingly deemed to be the responsibility of the host government.[154]

It was suggested that an enhanced sense of ownership amongst relevant stakeholders promises to facilitate better relations between communities and security actors (international and/or domestic) through improved interaction, cooperation and building of mutual trust and confidence between police and those they serve. This potentially has corollary added value of facilitating successful community policing initiatives. Many interviewees emphasised that at the local level, where much of UNPOL programming was targeted, relationships with community-based stakeholders and CSOs such as the Rotary Club, religious institutions and familial/informal networks were vital to eliciting information for M&E.[155] The framework's ability to (semi-)formalise these relationships and take them out of the remit of individuals was universally deemed to be a comparative advantage of the framework.[156] Ultimately, the case of UNMIL points to the value in embedding shared ownership of M&E and with it the broad-based participation and cooperation of a wide range of stakeholders in a process that will eventually become their responsibility.

This framework's focus – where practicable – on broad-based stakeholder participation in the design, implementation and utilisation of M&E was believed to constitute an effective antidote to the inhibitive exclusivity and associated tunnel vision of extant M&E in UNMIL. Furthermore, the privileging of consensus-derived notions of success and the most appropriate means of assessing progress towards them, offers an alternative way of increasing relevance that is intrinsically more grounded in local perspectives and understanding of the challenges and opportunities at play. The framework provides the means of entrenching these governance and monitoring mechanisms and promoting shared ownership to ensure that they do not erode and fall away but instead become an integral part of sustainable and ongoing reform.[157] Consequently, many pointed to the foreseeable utility for many different stakeholders at all levels of operation and hierarchy as one of the major benefits of the proposed framework.

Interpretation and response

Whilst implicit in some of the previous discussion, it is important to note that findings from the field research reinforce the framework's dedicated focus on interpretation and acting on findings as critical to the relevance and value of M&E. Drawing meaning from information collated was said to be particularly important in the peace operations setting due to the causal ambiguity at play. The specifics of making sense of data was said to be the even more important in the realm of policing and public safety, particularly where public perceptions were involved.[158] Emphasising this challenge, a senior mission manager underscored that, "First of all, we have to admit that in no country in the world are the citizens entirely happy with the police."[159]

Consequently, some interviewees applauded the design of the framework for its use of multiple perspectives to validate insights in the interpretation of information. That is, increasing the data pool and diversifying participation allows for triangulation to verify and/or repudiate particular perspectives. Given the paucity of reliable traditional sources of data discussed above, a number of those interviewed highlighted the shortage of cross-referencing of indicators and lack of verification and/or triangulating data sources as adding to the problems with current M&E such as the RBB and benchmarking.[160] As one respondent asserted, "You can collect [information] from within, but you always need something like a check – an alternative source."[161] Most of those interviewed extolled the importance of having multiple, and even competing, perspectives to form a textured picture of what is happening and why that might be the case.[162] The framework's focus on developing narratives about change based on broad stakeholder participation was generally deemed to be an important facilitator of this. Contribution stories that are the synthesis of multiple perspectives and portray a textured account of what is happening, as well as the possible reasons why, were universally deemed to be a useful way of augmenting current modes of M&E.

Many respondents lamented what they perceived to be a lack of reflection in any of the current M&E approaches used in the mission. It was emphasised that this shortage of critical introspection related to the strategic approach taken, as well as the derivative operational concepts and tactical level activities conducted in pursuit of this. Many believed that in effect, current M&E was preoccupied with validating prescriptive intervention logic rather than reflecting upon and interrogating the strength of assumptions undergirding the day-to-day activities of the mission/UNPOL.[163] In other words, a number of respondents identified that extant M&E is concerned with demonstrating and reporting on 'planned' change at the expense of emergent and unforeseen change.[164]

Numerous participants therefore welcomed the idea of a more reflexive process inherent in this framework. A number of section heads and senior managers pointed out that it was particularly advantageous to have this reflexivity built in to the system, given the limited time and freedom afforded to them to reflect on these 'bigger questions' when preoccupied with pressing day-to-day tasks and problem-solving.[165] Others concurred, highlighting that it was precisely these reflective insights they felt were missing in much of the extant practice.[166] Similarly, at the operational level, many remarked that even simple reflections would help identify areas of issue, counter-intuitive developments or reasons for unpredicted lack of progress in key areas. For instance, one official described an example where entrenched cultural perceptions of the police cut against the grain of what the UNPOL efforts were hoping to produce in terms of behavioural change. She described how:

> The average Liberian behaves in the manner of someone who has been subjected to years of abuse. They have been used to being hammered on the head by heavily armed police who shoot if provoked. Now we are forcing them to get used to the notion that a police officer need not be armed to do police duties. We have a crisis of confidence founded on this disconnect, between what they consider to be an effective police officer – one who is heavily armed and who 'brokes' no nonsense and who will break a head or two,... [and] the officer imbued with human rights principles who is not necessarily armed. But you can tell by the way that they hail the [militarised police] that it has nothing to do with the fact that they are more effective on the job than other police, but they just look more impressive and more like the American-type, macho, heavily armed, police officer on the street who swaggers and puts fear into everybody.[167]

In this case, a number of UNPOL officials said that the ability to identify this phenomenon and feed realisations such as these into planning might have facilitated more suitable restructuring and ongoing capacity development of the LNP and its specialised agencies.[168] Examples such as these demonstrate that a more reflexive modality would constitute a significant breakthrough compared to existing practice. The framework's focus on continual reflection and using information analysis and interpretation to seek out the unexpected as a way of informing adaptation of operational concepts and tactical activities appears to constitute a positive development in that direction.

The framework's focus on *response* and in particular the dissemination of M&E findings further reflects the belief of many in the field that results need to be widely shared in suitable forms for learning to occur. UNPOL interviewees emphasised that this was particularly important with regard to police reform due to the dependency on improving public perceptions and both meeting and managing expectations about change in this domain. It was remarked that the format commonly used was a major issue in communicating what was happening, many pointing to the simplified 'traffic lights' system as a problematic approach due to its bluntness,[169] and a senior UNPOL leader stating that, "there is a preoccupation with painting pictures – the UN is very good at it – but they don't tell us much."[170] These findings reflect the recommendations for more targeted dissemination in recent UN self-evaluation, such as an OIOS report which stated

232 *Empirical case study and implications*

that the "compilation and dissemination of lessons learned through chief of staff bulletins, magazines and flyers, UNMIL broadcasts and the intranet"[171] was an area that warranted attention.

Ensuring that M&E findings elicit a suitable response is another advantage of the framework evidenced by insights from the field. Many respondents gave examples of how existing approaches tend to induce reactions when it comes to controversial issues but less so in regard to the seemingly mundane. For instance, one official spoke of how monitoring of issues such as corruption and human rights abuses by the LNP and accusations of sexual abuse by peacekeepers tended to preoccupy the reactions of section heads.[172] Whilst these are obviously important to the mission's image and that of reforming security apparatus, it was suggested that this focus was to the detriment of other issues that were not making headlines. Furthermore, some emphasised how this tendency contributed to the distortion of M&E towards searching out evidence of criminal activity at the expense of other useful information.[173] It was noted that the framework's provisions for broadening the scope for response to M&E findings promised to facilitate larger quantities and better quality of feedback to inform future cycles of the M&E process.

Learning focus

The final major area of comparative advantage of the framework identified during the field research relates to its focus on and facilitation of organisational learning. Whilst a recent internal assessment of UNPOL in UNMIL pointed to effective reporting structures between UNPOL and senior mission management, as well as between the mission and headquarters level,[174] many of those interviewed for this research identified a number of fragilities and blockages in information exchange when it comes to the transition of information leading to institutional learning within the mission as well as at HQ. Indeed, when asked about the relationship between impact assessment and organisational learning, most agreed that learning, both within the mission (i.e. first-level learning) and for the peace operations apparatus more generally (i.e. second-level learning), was the primary unoptimised benefit of field-level M&E.[175]

Respondents described how they perceived extant mission M&E to be ineffective learning tools. As one official stressed, "good auditing does not always enable the most innovative and effective response because sometimes effective auditing will end up curtailing an innovative risky approach that may yield more dividends."[176] Many highlighted the potential for M&E to play an integral role in learning, but were also quick to emphasise how current M&E did not and that on the contrary it had the tendency to "cement bad plans" and risked institutionalising misguided programming due to its veneration in a benchmark or indicator. One official captured these frustrations, summarising that, "Sometimes the M&E tools employed are largely self-serving, predominantly attend to bureaucratic needs and do little to further the strategic goals of the organization or mission beyond sustaining the funding to perpetuate its existence."[177] Many believed that the linkages between M&E and the learning infrastructure within the mission as well as at HQ were inadequate and consequently the learning cycle invariably breaks down. For example, some pointed to enduring cultural rigidities within the military vis-à-vis the police and uniformed vis-à-vis civilian sections as resisting cross-mission learning through existing M&E mechanisms.[178] Furthermore, an evaluation of the strategic frameworks introduced above suggested that whilst decision-makers knew of their existence they do not appear to use the M&E findings emanating from them to inform their own engagement.[179] For instance, even the M&E provisions in Strategic Frameworks (e.g. PRS and UNDAF) were perceived to offer little by way of reflection on the validity of overall political strategies, despite the pre-planned written in (bi-)annual evaluations. Therefore, these tools and frameworks and the reporting upon them do not appear to be guiding strategic policy-making as intended.

Notwithstanding the inefficiencies of extant practice, most agreed that the potential benefits of doing so implored a shift towards a learning focus. For example, regarding first-level learning, referring to the UNPOL objectives, respondents emphasised the central importance of learning on the go due to the 'newness' of this work to these particular people, in this peculiar context. One official noted, "This is organisational learning both for UNPOL – don't forget there are 39 different police cultures in the mission – and also the LNP."[180] Interviewees across the mission stressed that, for UN peace operations in general, the wholesale reform of security sectors from scratch is also a nascent practice and constitutes "not just a cultural shift, it's a paradigm shift."[181] Summing up the potential value add of M&E in identifying and capturing good practices in this regard, a senior UNPOL policy advisor described how the whole endeavour should be understood as the "business of learning", adding that a learning focus for field-level M&E was vital, "because you're never 'there' – you recognise that you've got to continually improve this process, pick at it and say: how can we improve it and what are the weak spots?"[182] This need was deemed to be accentuated in light of the short rotations synonymous with UNPOL personnel and the need to furnish arriving personnel with the learning of their predecessors. In general, it was emphasised that credible and reliable information informing real-time learning would be a huge 'force multiplier' to the existing arrangements for capturing 'best practices' at the field level.

Regarding second-level learning, the extent to which extant M&E tools are feeding into institutional knowledge is unclear. Although some respondents remarked upon recent innovations such as the increasing use of Knowledge Management tools, including online CoPs and regular sharing of experiences between missions,[183] there remained a general sense of dissatisfaction with the way UNPOL experiences in the field had fed back into organisational knowledge management processes at headquarters level.[184] Interviewees across the mission highlighted the framework's focus on learning as a positive development in this regard. For instance, numerous interviewees emphasised UNMIL's pioneering experience, including the deployment of all-female FPUs and breakthroughs on police-military division of labour and interoperability as important opportunities for organisational learning that were being missed. Another example of the value of learning related to the early identification of any mismatch between the activities undertaken and the human resources at the mission's disposal, particularly regarding reform and capacity-building activities. For example, a member of the senior leadership team emphasised that reflective M&E might have brought to their attention earlier that, "what UNPOL needs are not police on the beat, but rather civilian specialists on management, forensics, pathology and suchlike".[185] As one senior mission manager noted, "If we have the ability to measure impact and identify gaps, maybe we can use this information to address through advocacy to member states/GA about the need for different capacities within missions – particularly in the area of UNPOL."[186]

One of the most commonly cited benefits of the learning orientation of the framework related to the issue of non-state policing entities. In addition to challenges of a technical nature (e.g. resources, recruiting, training and retaining UNPOL), learning more about how to address and deal with non-state actors – what works and what doesn't – was deemed to be one of the most pressing challenges for UNPOL today both within ongoing missions and as an organisation. As a senior UNPOL leader said,

> Although the plans are ad hoc and characterised by impromptu decision-making, the reality is that UNMIL and UNPOL in particular are about creating new systems and social orders. They are extremely state-centric at that, so we need to keep asking ourselves whether our approach is the right one or not.[187]

UNMIL demonstrates that a major part of M&E utility is capturing how the shoots of engagement with non-state actors in law and justice domain – rare in UN peace ops – play out and what this means for future strategy and operational concepts. In addition, and more generally, some respondents suggested that insightful assessments from the ground would be better placed to populate periodic reporting to the Security Council such that, in keeping with recommendations of the Brahimi Report, the peace operations apparatus stresses to the Council "what it needs to know and not what it wants to hear".[188] As one senior mission leader explained, "If we can find a way to assess the effect of our actions so we can take corrective measures, perhaps it also gives the latitude for future missions to learn from the experience of other missions."[189]

The framework's focus on clarifying and developing the linkages between the field and HQ such that pragmatic and innovative solutions in the field can feed up into the organisational learning infrastructure of the peace operations bureaucracy was said to constitute real value add to the overall endeavour of M&E. Furthermore, some respondents believed the framework approach could shift the incentive structure by providing the impetus for dampening the perception that rewards flow from a meeting of fixed goals and benchmarks. It was therefore deemed to present an opportunity to include learning objectives as well as performance and productivity goals, such that there is a promotion of 'M&E for improving' rather than 'evaluation for proving' – making clear that career opportunities will be advanced by embracing learning culture and contributing to collective memory.[190] These reflections from the field lend significant support and advocacy for the framework's proposed shift from 'fear of failure' to 'hunger for learning'.

Conclusion

Despite a bewildering array of M&E frameworks, tools and demands at multiple levels aimed at disparate audiences, the impact of UNPOL in UNMIL thus far has primarily been measured by indications of productivity such as the number of patrolling hours clocked up, quantity of material resources deployed, and in particular by the number of graduates from the police training academy who have become LNP officers and members of the various specialised units and agencies. This latter focus on training output as the barometer of police reform has neglected to address the issue of performance, whether through the appraisal of LNP conduct or through measurement of changes in public perceptions of their service. Furthermore, this approach offers little insight into the impact of UNPOL in providing assistance in the restructuring and capacity-building of Liberian law enforcement entities – let alone uncovering the effect of exogenous factors on the process or the unintended consequences of these intrusive interventions. Moreover, it is has done little to assess the extent to which the reformed LNP have contributed to positive change in wider rule of law experiences and broader issues of peace and security in Liberia. Finally, these approaches have offered little in terms of learning for UNMIL as it has progressed or to the peace operations apparatus as a whole. In short, UNPOL in UNMIL has lacked an effective means of monitoring and evaluating the impact of its work or contributing to institutional learning from these efforts since it deployed.

This is not to underestimate the challenge. It is extremely difficult to monitor and evaluate change in policing services where there was no police service to speak of as recently as 2003; where the process of recruitment, training and equipping the new corps is ongoing; where there is a paucity of trustworthy data from which to analyse crime and victimization patterns; and where until recently there has been no clearly articulated national security strategy nor national visions and polices for crime prevention.[191] Furthermore, enduring ambiguity around where the responsibilities of UNMIL end and where those of the government of Liberia begin regarding the resurrection of the rule of law dictate that measuring progress against the objectives of UNPOL endeavours will remain an imperfect and difficult task. The realistic expectations for what UNPOL can achieve and expect to attribute to themselves need to be placed in the context of the lengthy time horizon for behavioural and organisational change implicit in SSR processes. However, this has left mission managers and political decision-makers with little evidence to go on when trying to be responsive, adjust their practices on the ground and calibrate the CDW and move towards UNMIL transitioning out of Liberia.

The primary research findings presented in this chapter make evident a number of ways in which the framework proposed in this book offers strengths, advantages and potentialities when compared with the M&E approaches currently in use in UNMIL. In particular, it highlighted numerous advantages to augmenting existing approaches with new thinking proposed in this framework. The framework's ongoing and systematic process was believed to better reflect the dynamical change typical of peace operations environments. It was further seen to alleviate the distortive risks associated with inappropriate timeframes. The focus on impact and an explicit treatment of the issue of causality were deemed to promise more realistic and humble assessments. The framework's flexibility was understood to lead to increased relevance in the way M&E could track change as well as contribute to it. Its inclusive and participatory imperative was said to offer multiple benefits including incentivising buy-in and facilitating critical local relevance and ownership. The reflexive nature of the approach was deemed to be crucial for enabling the improvement in the modalities and methods of early peacebuilding, particularly given the relative 'newness' of efforts to reconstitute police services to the UN's peacebuilding project. The findings also supported the argument that the non-state realm is significant to everyday experiences of public safety and consequently incorporating the influence of non-state actors was seen as a key strength of the framework. Finally, insights from the field suggested that the framework would be well-placed to contribute to organisational learning for real-time decision-making in the field as well as knowledge management at HQ level.

In sum, the empirical insights from the field offer much support to the overarching framework, the design and content of each of the steps in the field-level M&E process, as well as their inclusion in a holistic framework to guide and facilitate multi-level organisational learning. Whilst the case of UNMIL demonstrates a range of strengths, comparative advantages and potentialities of the framework proposed in this book, the empirical case study research also serves to bring into focus a number of experiences that could challenge the suitability and practicalities of some of the principles and elements of the framework. The following chapter highlights and addresses these potential weaknesses, latent problems and naïveté within the framework.

Notes

1 All interviews cited below were conducted by the author during extensive fieldwork in late 2010. Interview references have been deliberately depersonalised to adhere to ethical considerations that authorised the author to gather and utilise this information.
2 "Results Focused Transitional Framework (RFTF)". (Monrovia: National Transitional Government of Liberia/United Nations/World Bank, 2005).
3 "Liberia Poverty Reduction Strategy", (Monrovia: Republic of Liberia, 2008), 13. This version was perceived to be 'home-grown' and more locally owned than its predecessors in that, whilst it was still developed collaboratively by the government of Liberia, the UN and international partners/donors, it was based on an extensive participatory and broad-based consultative approach. Ibid., 45–7.
4 "United Nations Development Assistance Framework Liberia 2008–2012: Consolidating Peace and National Recovery for Sustainable Development", (Monrovia: Government of Liberia & United Nations 2007).
5 For further discussion, see below.
6 Michael Dalton, "Mid-Term Review of the United Nations Development Assistance Framework 2008–2012", (Monrovia: United Nations, 2010), 42–4.
7 Interview: UNMIL Senior Official, Legal and Judicial Unit – Monrovia, Liberia.
8 Interview: UNMIL Senior Management, Political, Policy and Planning Section – Monrovia, Liberia.
9 Interview: UNMIL Senior Management – Monrovia, Liberia.
10 Interview: UNMIL Senior Management, Political, Policy and Planning Section – Monrovia, Liberia.
11 See: "Sixteenth Progress Report of the Secretary-General on the United Nations Mission in Liberia", (New York: United Nations, 2008) 14–20.
12 Till Blume, "Implementing the Rule of Law in Integrated Missions: Security and Justice in the UN Mission in Liberia", *Journal of Security Sector Management* 6, no. 3 (2008), 6.
13 OIOS, "Management of UN Police Operations", in, *Audit Report*. (New York: UN Office of Internal Oversight Services, 2008), 4–5.
14 Interview: UNMIL Senior Official, Office of the Special Representative of the Secretary General – Monrovia, Liberia.
15 These four mechanisms are the after action review; survey of practice; end of assignment report; and handover note.
16 In UNMIL, up until the time of the field research, this has not been a dedicated position, but additional responsibility for an existing staff member.
17 Interview: UNMIL Senior Management, Political, Policy and Planning Section – Monrovia, Liberia.
18 Interviews: UNMIL Officials – Monrovia, Liberia.
19 Ibid.
20 OIOS, "Programme Evaluation of the Performance and the Achievement of Results by the United Nations Mission in Liberia", In *Report of the Office of Internal Oversight Services* (New York: United Nations, 2010), 12–13.

238 *Empirical case study and implications*

21 Despite UNMIL's SSR mandate being initially disaggregated between US government, UN and Liberian government responsibilities. Nevertheless, there was little mention of judicial and legal reform in the CPA.
22 Interview: UNMIL Senior Management – Monrovia, Liberia.
23 Albeit some respondents suggested that the process may have encouraged the pre-emptive moves.
24 Interview: UNMIL Senior Official, Legal and Judicial Unit – Monrovia, Liberia.
25 For further discussion, see section below on 'Learning Focus'.
26 Interview: UNMIL Official – Monrovia, Liberia.
27 e.g. PRS, UNDAF, benchmarking, RBB, etc.
28 Interview: UNMIL Senior Management – Monrovia, Liberia.
29 Interview: UNMIL Senior Official, Field Office – Montserrado County, Liberia.
30 Interview: UNMIL Senior Official, Security Sector Reform – Monrovia, Liberia.
31 Ibid.
32 Interview: UNMIL Senior Management – Monrovia, Liberia.
33 Ibid.
34 Interview: UNMIL Senior Official, Security Sector Reform – Monrovia, Liberia.
35 See, for example: Blume, "Implementing the Rule of Law in Integrated Missions: Security and Justice in the UN Mission in Liberia", 12.
36 Interview: UNMIL Senior Management, UNPOL – Monrovia, Liberia.
37 Interview: UNMIL Senior Official, UNPOL – Monrovia, Liberia.
38 Interview: UNMIL Senior Mission Leadership – Monrovia, Liberia.
39 Interviews: UNMIL Officials – Monrovia, Liberia.
40 Ibid.
41 Ibid.
42 Interview: UNMIL Senior Official, UNPOL – Monrovia, Liberia.
43 The ROLIP was being piloted in UNMIL at the time of the field research; the project has since been completed. See: "The United Nations Rule of Law Indicators: Implementation Guide and Project Tools". (New York: United Nations Department of Peacekeeping Operations/Office of the High Comissioner for Human Rights, 2011).
44 Interview: UNMIL Senior Mission Leadership – Monrovia, Liberia.
45 Ibid.
46 See section below on 'Inclusive/Participatory Approach'.
47 Interview: Liberian Government Minister – Monrovia, Liberia.
48 Interview: UNMIL Senior Management, UNPOL – Monrovia, Liberia.
49 Interview: UNMIL Senior Management – Monrovia, Liberia.
50 Interview: UNMIL Senior Official, Security Sector Reform – Monrovia, Liberia.
51 Interview: UNMIL Senior Management, Political, Policy and Planning Section – Monrovia, Liberia.
52 Interview: Official, West African Network for Peacebuilding (WANEP) – Liberia Chapter – Monrovia, Liberia.
53 Interview: UNMIL Senior Management – Monrovia, Liberia.
54 Interview: UNMIL Senior Management, Training – Monrovia, Liberia.
55 Interview: UNMIL Senior Official, UNPOL – Monrovia, Liberia.
56 Interview: UNMIL Senior Management, Political, Policy and Planning Section – Monrovia, Liberia.
57 Ibid.
58 Interview: UNMIL Senior Mission Leadership – Monrovia, Liberia.

59 Ibid.
60 Interview: Liberian Government Assistant Minister – Monrovia, Liberia.
61 Interview: Official, West African Network for Peacebuilding (WANEP) – Liberia Chapter – Monrovia, Liberia; Interview: UNMIL Senior Management – Monrovia, Liberia.
62 Interview: UNMIL Senior Mission Leadership – Monrovia, Liberia.
63 Interview: GRC Official – Monrovia, Liberia; Amos Sawyer cited in Mark Malan, "Security Sector Reform in Liberia: Mixed Results from Humble Beginnings", (Strategic Studies Institute, 2008), 52.
64 Interview: UNMIL Senior Official, UNPOL – Monrovia, Liberia.
65 Interview: UNMIL Senior Official, UNPOL – Monrovia, Liberia.
66 Interview: UNMIL Senior Management, Political, Policy and Planning Section – Monrovia, Liberia.
67 Interview: UNMIL Senior Management, UNPOL – Monrovia, Liberia.
68 Interviews: UNMIL Staff – Monrovia, Liberia.
69 Interview: UNMIL Official – Monrovia, Liberia.
70 Ibid.
71 Interview: UNMIL Senior Management, UNPOL – Monrovia, Liberia.
72 For example, one senior mission manager said that in relation to disarmament, counting the number of AK-47s collected makes perfect sense as an empirical measure of successful disarmament.
73 Interview: UNMIL Senior Management, Training – Monrovia, Liberia.
74 Interview: UNMIL Senior Management – Monrovia, Liberia.
75 Interview: UNMIL Senior Mission Leadership – Monrovia, Liberia.
76 Interview: UNMIL Senior Management, UNPOL – Monrovia, Liberia.
77 Interview: UNMIL Senior Mission Leadership – Monrovia, Liberia.
78 Blume, "Implementing the Rule of Law in Integrated Missions: Security and Justice in the UN Mission in Liberia", 12.
79 See, for example: OIOS, "Audit of United Nations Police in UNMIL", ed. Internal Audit Division (New York: United Nations Office of Internal Oversight Services, 2009), 3; OIOS, "Management of UN Police Operations".
80 Interview: UNMIL Senior Management – Monrovia, Liberia.
81 Interview: UNMIL Senior Management, Political, Policy and Planning Section – Monrovia, Liberia.
82 Interview: UNMIL Senior Management – Monrovia, Liberia.
83 Interview: UNMIL Senior Mission Leadership – Monrovia, Liberia.
84 Ibid.
85 Interviews: UNMIL Officials – Monrovia, Liberia.
86 Interview: UNMIL Senior Official, Security Sector Reform – Monrovia, Liberia.
87 Interview: UNMIL Senior Mission Leadership – Monrovia, Liberia.
88 Interview: UNMIL Senior Management, Political, Policy and Planning Section – Monrovia, Liberia.
89 Interview: UNMIL Senior Mission Leadership – Monrovia, Liberia.
90 Interview: UNMIL Senior Mission Leadership – Monrovia, Liberia.
91 Interviews: UNMIL Officials – Monrovia, Liberia.
92 Interview: UNMIL Senior Management – Monrovia, Liberia; Interview: Official, West African Network for Peacebuilding (WANEP) – Liberia Chapter – Monrovia, Liberia.
93 Interview: UNMIL Senior Management – Monrovia, Liberia.
94 Interview: UNMIL Senior Management, Political, Policy and Planning Section – Monrovia, Liberia.
95 Interview: UNMIL Senior Management, Training – Monrovia, Liberia.
96 Ibid.

240 *Empirical case study and implications*

97 Interviews: UNMIL Staff – Monrovia, Liberia.
98 See section below – 'Learning focus' – for further discussion.
99 Interview: UNMIL Senior Official, Legal and Judicial Unit – Monrovia, Liberia.
100 Interviews: UNMIL Senior Officials, UNPOL; UNMIL Senior Management, UNPOL – Monrovia, Liberia.
101 Interview: UNMIL Senior Management, Political, Policy and Planning Section – Monrovia, Liberia.
102 Interview: UNMIL Senior Mission Leadership – Monrovia, Liberia.
103 Interview: UNMIL Senior Management, Political, Policy and Planning Section – Monrovia, Liberia.
104 Interview: UNMIL Senior Official, UNPOL – Monrovia, Liberia.
105 For instance, whilst the first National Population & Housing census since 1984 was conducted in 2008, a number of those interviewed during this field research explained how the fidelity of its outcomes was debated in some quarters. Interview: UNMIL Senior Official, UNPOL – Monrovia, Liberia; Interview: Official, West African Network for Peacebuilding (WANEP) – Liberia Chapter – Monrovia, Liberia.
106 For example, the Liberia Institute for Statistics and Geo-Information Services (LISGIS) has been an explicit part of the PRS and the National Strategy for the Development of Statistics (NSDS) [The NSDS is the government strategy aimed at creating a coordinated and efficient statistical system for Liberia by 2012]. Interview: UNMIL Senior Management, UNPOL – Monrovia, Liberia.
107 At the time of this research the general perception was that there had been little notable progress with government statistics emanating from this and other complementary institutions. Interviews: UNMIL Senior Official, UNPOL; UNMIL Police Commissioner; UNMIL Senior Management, UNPOL – Monrovia, Liberia.
108 Interviews: UNMIL Senior Official, UNPOL; UNMIL Senior Management, UNPOL – Monrovia, Liberia.
109 Interview: UNMIL Senior Official, Legal and Judicial Unit – Monrovia, Liberia.
110 Interview: UNMIL Senior Official, Security Sector Reform – Monrovia, Liberia.
111 Interview: UNMIL Senior Official, UNPOL – Monrovia, Liberia.
112 Interview: Liberian Government Minister – Monrovia, Liberia.
113 Interview: UNMIL Senior Official, UNPOL – Monrovia, Liberia.
114 Interview: Senior Official, Truth and Reconciliation Commission, Republic of Liberia – Monrovia, Liberia.
115 Interview: Liberian Government Assistant Minister – Monrovia, Liberia.
116 Interview: UNMIL Senior Official, Security Sector Reform – Monrovia, Liberia.
117 Interview: Official, West African Network for Peacebuilding (WANEP) – Liberia Chapter – Monrovia, Liberia.
118 Ibid.
119 Interviews: UNMIL Senior Official, Field Office, Montserrado County – Monrovia, Liberia; Senior Official, Public Information – Monrovia, Liberia; Liberian Government Assistant Minister – Monrovia, Liberia. See also: "UN Development Assistance Framework 2008–2012: Joint Annual Review Report 2008", (Monrovia: United Nations Liberia, 2008), 17.
120 For further discussion on the relevance and value of survey-based techniques see Chapter 7, pp. 249–250.
121 Interview: UNMIL Senior Official, Security Sector Reform – Monrovia, Liberia.

M&E in practice 241

122 See section above on 'Overarching Design'.
123 Interview: UNMIL Senior Management, UNPOL – Monrovia, Liberia.
124 Interview: UNMIL Senior Management – Monrovia, Liberia.
125 Interview: UNMIL Senior Management, UNPOL – Monrovia, Liberia.
126 Interview: UNMIL Senior Management, UNPOL – Monrovia, Liberia.
127 Interviews: UNMIL Senior Official, UNPOL; UNMIL Senior Management, UNPOL – Monrovia, Liberia.
128 Interview: UNMIL Senior Official, Legal and Judicial Unit – Monrovia, Liberia.
129 Ibid.
130 Interviews: UNMIL Staff – Monrovia, Liberia.
131 Interview: UNMIL Senior Management, Training – Monrovia, Liberia.
132 Interviews: UNMIL Staff – Monrovia, Liberia.
133 Interview: UNMIL Senior Management, UNPOL – Monrovia, Liberia.
134 See section below on 'Interpretation and Response'.
135 Interview: UNMIL Senior Management – Monrovia, Liberia.
136 C.f. Chapter 5.
137 Interview: UNMIL Senior Management, UNPOL – Monrovia, Liberia.
138 Interview: UNMIL Senior Official, UNPOL – Monrovia, Liberia.
139 Interview: UNMIL Senior Official, Field Office, Montserrado County – Monrovia, Liberia.
140 Interview: Liberian Government Assistant Minister – Monrovia, Liberia.
141 Ibid.
142 Ibid.
143 Interview: UNMIL Senior Management, Political, Policy and Planning Section – Monrovia, Liberia.
144 Interview: UNMIL Senior Official, Field Office, Montserrado County – Monrovia, Liberia.
145 Interview: Official, West African Network for Peacebuilding (WANEP) – Liberia Chapter – Monrovia, Liberia.
146 Ibid.
147 Ibid.
148 Interview: Liberian Government Minister – Monrovia, Liberia.
149 The challenge of understanding the relevance of informal provision of security and justice services to post-conflict SSR has been identified in previous chapters as important both in general and in the particular context of Liberia. Non-state provision is a characteristic of most peace operations environments. Indeed, large portions of the Liberian population have never really experienced the presence of the formal state in providing for their day-to-day personal safety.
150 Interviews: UNMIL Senior Official, UNPOL; UNMIL Senior Management, UNPOL – Monrovia, Liberia.
151 Interview: UNMIL Senior Management, UNPOL – Monrovia, Liberia.
152 Interview: UNMIL Senior Mission Leadership – Monrovia, Liberia.
153 Interview: Director, ICTJ Liberia – Monrovia, Liberia; Interview: Senior Official, Truth and Reconciliation Commission, Republic of Liberia – Monrovia, Liberia.
154 Interview: UNMIL Senior Official, UNPOL – Monrovia, Liberia.
155 Interview: UNMIL Senior Official, Field Office, Montserrado County – Monrovia, Liberia.
156 Ibid.
157 Interview: UNMIL Senior Official, UNPOL – Monrovia, Liberia.
158 Interviews: UNMIL Senior Official, UNPOL; UNMIL Police Commissioner; UNMIL Senior Management, UNPOL – Monrovia, Liberia.

159 Interview: UNMIL Senior Mission Leadership – Monrovia, Liberia.
160 Interview: UNMIL Senior Official, UNPOL – Monrovia, Liberia.
161 Interview: UNMIL Senior Mission Leadership – Monrovia, Liberia.
162 Ibid.
163 Interviews: UNMIL Officials – Monrovia, Liberia.
164 Ibid.
165 Interviews: UNMIL Senior Management, UNPOL – Monrovia, Liberia; UNMIL Senior Management, Political, Policy and Planning Section – Monrovia, Liberia.
166 Interview: UNMIL Senior Mission Leadership Team – Monrovia, Liberia.
167 Interview: UNMIL Senior Mission Leadership – Monrovia, Liberia.
168 Respondents were also at pains to point out that the level of US influence over SSR in Liberia also factored into the penchant for armed policing units.
169 Interview: UNMIL Senior Official, Office of the Special Representative of the Secretary General – Monrovia, Liberia.
170 Interview: UNMIL Senior Management, UNPOL – Monrovia, Liberia.
171 OIOS, "Audit of United Nations Police in UNMIL", 4.
172 Interview: UNMIL Senior Official, Legal and Judicial Unit – Monrovia, Liberia.
173 Ibid.
174 OIOS, "Audit of United Nations Police in UNMIL", ed. Internal Audit Division. (New York: United Nations Office of Internal Oversight Services, 2009), 3.
175 Interview: UNMIL Senior Mission Leadership Team – Monrovia, Liberia.
176 Interview: UNMIL Senior Official, Security Sector Reform – Monrovia, Liberia.
177 Interview: UNMIL Senior Management, Political, Policy and Planning Section – Monrovia, Liberia.
178 Interview: UNMIL Senior Official, Field Office – Montserrado County, Liberia.
179 Dalton, "Mid-Term Review of the United Nations Development Assistance Framework 2008–2012".
180 Interview: UNMIL Senior Official, UNPOL – Monrovia, Liberia.
181 Ibid.
182 Ibid.
183 Interview: UNMIL Senior Management, Political, Policy and Planning Section – Monrovia, Liberia.
184 Interviews: UNMIL Senior Officials, UNPOL – Monrovia, Liberia.
185 Interview: UNMIL Senior Management – Monrovia, Liberia.
186 Ibid. See also paragraph above in 'Reflexivity' section: "what UNPOL needs are not police on the beat, but rather civilian specialists on management, forensics, pathology, and suchlike".
187 Interview: UNMIL Senior Management, UNPOL – Monrovia, Liberia.
188 Interview: UNMIL Senior Management – Monrovia, Liberia.
189 Ibid.
190 Interview: UNMIL Senior Official, Security Sector Reform – Monrovia, Liberia.
191 Malan, "Security Sector Reform in Liberia: Mixed Results from Humble Beginnings", 52. Interview: Assistant Liberian Government Minister – Monrovia, Liberia.

7 M&E in practice II
Weaknesses, latent problems and naïveté

Introduction

The previous chapter identified the many ways in which the framework developed in this book presents comparative advantages over the approaches of current convention that pervade practice and therefore demonstrated how it promises to strengthen M&E. The purpose of this chapter is to highlight a number of potential weaknesses with the framework in relation to what the case of Liberia reveals, but also what its particular operating environment, mission phase at the time of the field research, and specific mandate may conceal vis-à-vis the settings and possible mandates of UNPOL in other UN peace operations.

Identifying weaknesses and/or enduring challenges to effective implementation of the framework are an important endeavour for a number of reasons. Firstly, in order to credibly test the framework it is vital to balance the evidenced strengths with the perceived problems and fragilities. To do so reflects the absence of consensus and enduring difference in opinion on how to do M&E in these settings. Importantly, testing the framework in this way enables the identification of possible refinements and revisions. Doing so also helps to avoid falling into the trap of other frameworks that presume a 'good fit' but are subsequently inflexible to adaptation. This is also in keeping with iterative and learning-oriented philosophy of the approach undergirded by the retroductive research design of this study.

This chapter therefore addresses critiques arising during the field research concerning the focus, approach/methods and practicalities of the framework.[1] I argue that, whilst these criticisms are valid, many can be assuaged with further refinement and clarification of the framework. Moreover, I posit that others are more indicative of the fundamental challenges facing M&E in peace operations and therefore should be understood as limitations on rather than weaknesses with the framework. Notwithstanding these caveats, I demonstrate that: (1) opinion may remain divided over the utility of the framework due to the expectations such an approach places on missions but that it constitutes a necessary shift in the right direction; (2) M&E of this type will not satisfy everybody's preconceptions of what it should do and how, but will be a valuable addendum to extant efforts; and, (3) practical constraints appear daunting/insurmountable in the foreseeable future and the arrival of this framework will not bring change without corollary garnering of political will and structural adjustment to facilitate the approach, but that the framework nevertheless creates the space for doing so.

Weaknesses, latent problems and naïveté

The potential stumbling blocks for the framework made evident in the case of UNMIL can be categorised as relating to three broad areas: focus; approach/methods; and, practicalities.

Focus

The first set of criticisms relates to the focus of the framework. They question the wisdom of its impact-orientation and the validity of its organisational learning credentials.

Overly impact-oriented?

Despite the benefits of an impact-focused framework substantiated here, some respondents warned of the potential dangers of such an approach in the specific context of UNPOL in peace operations. Given the lengthy timelines associated with effective SSR, some argued that peace operations and UNPOL are only in the business of laying the foundations for sustainable reform (i.e. early peacebuilding, at most).[2] This modality means that UNPOL necessarily operate under a 'first things first' imperative where missions cannot be expected to achieve sustainable ROL capacity without first creating the enabling environment, including (infra)structures, materials and resources. For example, according to one official, whatever their competency at the time of the 2005 national elections, the LNP would not have been able to achieve much with their fleet of three vehicles for the whole service.[3] This led to the suggestion that UNPOL should only be held accountable for putting such preconditions in place and planting the seeds of reform for follow-on arrangements such as the UNCT and bilateral donors to cultivate and for them to be held responsible, in partnership with host governments, for achieving longer-term sustainable outcomes and overall impact.[4] The risk, they believed, was that grand goals of achieving sustainable reform and institutional transformation in the lifetime of a peace operation was setting a mission up for failure. As one senior official explained:

> UNMIL [is] trying to build police stations in many areas – clearly they've never had police there. So, if they've never had police there in

the 163 years the country has been independent that in itself tells a story. You're not going to "undo" those habits in the 7 years that UNMIL has been here. So, we also have to be realistic in how we measure some of those things, or else we will beat ourselves on the head for nothing. You cannot undo 160 years by 7. Nor can you even undo the harm that 14 years of a lack of options by way of state protection [has produced].[5]

In this vein, the lack of realism associated with objectives and claims was regularly brought up as an issue for current M&E practice. For instance, a senior mission leader stated that M&E for the mission must acknowledge and capture the mismatch between the ambitious expectations held by and placed upon the mission, and, the paltry resources at the mission's disposal to achieve them.[6] The main example given by many was that despite being given the responsibility to reform the LNP, there was no assessed funding dedicated to this task. Flagging the potential dangers of incorporating questions of sustainability into assessments, the official went on to caution against judging UNMIL on programmes that are beyond its explicit remit – i.e. M&E should constitute a means of assessing progress for that which is explicit in the mandate, not that which has since evolved as 'mission-creep'.[7] For these reasons, a number of respondents questioned whether the framework's explicit focus on impact risked perpetuating existing problems with expectations in M&E. By extension, there may be ethical considerations associated with a shift towards impact focus. For instance, what does an impact-orientation mean for the question of how impacts are pursued? Could the demands on achieving impact lead to focus on *ends* by whatever *means* necessary?

Whilst these are salient concerns, and the need to manage expectations about what can realistically be achieved and in what timeframe is critical, the framework's focus on appropriateness and relevance, as well as its consensus-based notions of success, are intended to avoid over-inflated objectives. Moreover, the framework is intended to liberate mission managers to learn as they go, rather than pressurise them to achieve the impossible. It may be the case that clarity over definitions can allay some of these fears. For instance, numerous interviewees emphasised the fact that 'impact' was too often an ambiguous concept in extant M&E. Although some recognised that impacts could manifest at multiple levels of analysis, responses consistently identified that dominant conceptions tended to focus only on the most macro level.[8] Being clear that impact is understood to occur at different levels of magnitude – i.e. they are not only that 'police reform is complete' or that 'peace has been restored throughout the country' – may be sufficient in addressing this concern. However, a re-calibration towards greater focus on the intermediary outcomes more closely associated with UNPOL programming could also emphasise this intent.

246 *Empirical case study and implications*

Notwithstanding such refinements in this area, as a senior mission leader put it,

> The question about assessing the impact of peacekeeping operations goes to the core of what we need to do now. Discussions about drawdown and withdrawal with Liberian partners need to be grounded in meaningful assessments of progress and local capacity.[9]

Therefore, although impact always needs to be understood in context, it is the shift in approach and the methods used that come with an impact-orientation that promises to be of most benefit to M&E of police efforts in peace operations.

Prospects for learning?

In a similar vein, some respondents cautioned against expecting too much by way of organisational learning in the short time frames implied by the iterative cycles of the framework (i.e. first-level learning). For example, one respondent asserted that, "lesson learning for peacekeeping cannot be a daily process. Rather it should be a longitudinal profile of operations over a period between one and five years."[10] Others echoed a familiar warning against expecting too many improvements from the transfer of learning from one site to another (i.e. second-level learning). For instance, a senior official spoke of the limitations involved in importing a number of initiatives implemented in neighbouring missions in Sierra Leone and Côte d'Ivoire to the Liberian setting.[11] Another senior official warned that in the longer-term, the reapplication of lessons learned from past experience will – and more importantly should – only be as useful as the new context allows.[12] That is, the specific circumstances of a situation may dictate that successes elsewhere are not replicable by exactly the same means in the new scenario.[13] A number of respondents referred to the different experiences regarding DDR in Liberia compared to other missions. One example given was in Mozambique where the difference in funding for reintegration component was considerable and had significant ramifications for the effectiveness of that programme.[14]

To be sure, the expectations for learning must be modest. Experiences in the field change quickly and yesterday's panacea can be today's faux pas. Similarly, any second-level learning that becomes codified in the rules and procedures of the organisation must be sufficiently generic and qualified with the caveat that the reapplication of such practices is done in a context-sensitive manner. Therefore, what is most important is that the pathways for feeding field-level experiences into first- and second-level organisational learning are clearly demarcated and developed. This is how the framework allows that when good practices *are* established, these lessons do not depart the mission or the organisation altogether at the completion of individual operatives' service, but instead are captured in collective memory for better praxis in future. As one official put it, "...there's no such thing as the perfect programme, but we can probably learn a little bit from what works and what doesn't".[15] In short, the proposed framework has much to offer to organisational learning processes, but it need not and should not become the pursuit of complete or universally applicable knowledge.[16]

Approach and methods

The second area of criticisms broadly relate to the appropriateness of the approach and methods implied by the framework. They refer to the hurdles to realising a participatory imperative, the fallibility of embedded baselines, challenges of handling multiple data sources, and the claims to methodological rigour.

Barriers and risks to participation

A number of interviewees expressed doubts over whether and how the framework could overcome the inertia symptomatic of current M&E practice. People across all sections of the mission pointed to the enduring lack of buy-in to extant M&E processes from mission personnel. This was described in terms of perceptions that M&E is imposed, inappropriate, irrelevant and/or inconvenient.[17] Furthermore, many described how M&E inspires high levels of suspicion, anxiety and resistance in mission personnel and broader stakeholders who perceive M&E as an existential threat to programming and job security and fear critique accordingly. As one respondent put it, "the way M&E is currently viewed means that it is simply not incentive compatible".[18] Whilst the overarching framework advocates for a shift away from a process perceived as ineffectual and potentially punitive, precipitating a 'hunger for learning' rather than a 'fear of failure', it is fair to say that the framework and methods included are not sufficient to guarantee this. Although many agreed that the framework constitutes a suitable model for harnessing increased buy-in and participation by grounding both conception and design in local exigencies, they further proclaimed that field missions and headquarters bureaucracy will require a cultural shift in the way M&E is understood and utilised if this is to be enabled.[19]

The interviews also revealed a number of doubts about the ability to secure the participation of locals in M&E – in terms of both design and information gathering.[20] First, in their opinion, enduring practical constraints – such as physical access to rural locales – limit the ability to secure broad-based participation advocated for in the framework.[21] Second, local stakeholders may be reticent to participate in the process on various grounds. For example, respondents pointed to power dynamics, including social norms (e.g. customary pressures on women), as reasons why locals may be reluctant to contribute to what is a highly politicised process.[22] Another recurring contention related to the issue of exploiting host populations as a data mine. This unease related to the ethical and security concerns associated with extracting information from local communities, as well as the possibility of implicating them in potentially divisive M&E findings. For example, bringing together different stakeholder groups might jeopardise peoples' safety or lead to recriminations for those involved.[23] Similarly, there are risks when peace operations personnel integrate with local communities for information gathering and learning.[24] Whilst there are stringent rules and regulations governing the conduct and discipline of mission personnel, there have been high-profile allegations of abuse and exploitation by UNMIL peacekeepers that some emphasised must be factored in when advocating for this level of inter-mingling.[25] These risks cast shadows of doubt in the minds of some over the ability of the framework to 'do no harm' and realise its purported 'conflict-sensitive' approach.

Every effort must be made to mitigate the risks associated with tapping varied information sources – particularly where this involves vulnerable individuals/communities. It may be that where these sensitivities are high, more methods that gather information by proxy or through existing informal networks are better suited. Conflict-sensitive M&E is a relatively nascent field and is still embryonic in practice;[26] however, the framework is intentionally – in the foregrounding stage – furnished with the capacity to recognise and mitigate risk to those involved in the process or implicated by its findings and hence better suited to enable conflict-sensitivity.[27]

Whilst it will undoubtedly be difficult to overcome both socio-political and practical barriers to participation in M&E, the desire to make the process as inclusive as is practicable was deemed to be a worthwhile one. Some respondents followed up their contention with suggestions that one solution may involve utilising national staff which often make up a significant proportion of the civilian staff in missions – albeit, there are generally less national staff in UNPOL than some other substantive sections. It was posited that national staff could provide a more culturally acceptable link between the mission and local communities when soliciting their participation/contributions in M&E.

Over-reliance on baselines of limited utility?

It was remarked upon that the framework may risk over-privileging the foregrounding assessments. For example, in relation to policing, a number of interviewees stated that even if accurate baselines could be attained, the utility of such assessments are reduced in the early stages of post-conflict police reform as comparisons to the old discredited or until recently nonexistent police institutions that went before reveal little. One official put it succinctly, saying, "It doesn't help to measure the new police against the old police."[28] Whilst the potential fallibility of baselines is an important point, baseline measurements are only one facet of the foregrounding step. Other components, in particular the context analyses, are intended to ensure that baselines are both produced and used appropriately so as to mitigate counter-productive applications – a quality further buttressed by the flexibility of the framework. These findings serve to emphasise that for baselines to be valuable, they need to be clearly grounded in local exigencies.

Making sense of multiple data sources

Another area of contention related to the framework's increase and diversification of the data sources deemed 'good enough' to inform M&E. Whilst only one of the data sources/methods proposed in the framework, a number of UNPOL officials highlighted the potential risk and challenges of employing survey-based techniques. Victimization surveys were repeatedly suggested as one way to overcome the shortfall in conventional crime trend data and lack of focus on public perceptions. However, other respondents attested to these being conducted infrequently and also tended to be of dubious quality.[29] Moreover, the fidelity of the results of survey-style techniques was brought into question by some UNPOL officials. For instance, one senior official noted that surveys can be misleading and even manipulative if not carefully designed and interpreted, illustrating the "typical and wonderful example relating to domestic abuse – the question asked is: 'have you stopped beating your wife?' Whether they say yes or no, they have made a confession".[30] She went on to highlight the time-dependent nature of these methods, citing that widely reported incidences of police malfeasance could affect peoples' instinctive responses to such questioning, explaining how,

> that kind of survey can be influenced by the timing of one high-profile case ... If there is a big case that is covered by all the newspapers, for example, in the average person's mind they don't see it as one case in which the police did a botch-up job because they've read it 10 times – but it's the same report.[31]

Finally, the way in which these surveys are conducted was also flagged as potentially sullying their results. For example, one interviewee said that, "If people come to you in uniform and want to know what you think of the police, you've got to be foolhardy to tell them the truth!"[32] In sum, it was asserted that there are dangers in trying to measure public perceptions in this way.

Consequently, a number of interviewees feared that the framework's shift towards qualitative methods would render it overly dependent on survey-based techniques and therefore would risk suffering the aforementioned ailments. However, the overarching commitment to a context-/conflict-sensitive approach promises to mitigate some of this risk. Furthermore, the framework advocates that any method should only ever contribute part of the picture, such that survey findings are complemented and triangulated with other sources to validate and make sense of findings.

Regarding the framework's participatory methods, discussions in the field revealed concern amongst some that there was a strong likelihood that irreconcilable/mutually exclusive perspectives would be generated through the inclusive approach to information gathering.[33] The flipside of this equation was also highlighted as a possible problem whereby the semi/un-structured questioning synonymous with participatory methods might not elicit all the most important answers to questions that are important to some stakeholders.[34] First, it is true that contradictory perspectives are likely to arise through the participatory methods advocated in the framework. However, the interpretation process, including provisions for cross-referencing and where necessary weighting these visions and opinions, serve to moderate the level of consensus surrounding particular viewpoints and verify their validity through triangulation. Second, missing information or shortfalls in data is an inevitable consequence of time-constrained and open-ended questioning/focus group discussions synonymous with the methods proposed. However, this is simply remedied given the framework's recursive design. Gaps can be filled and additional information can be solicited in future iterations if deemed to be important. These data validity and coverage realities are crucial to recognise and do present some limitations. However, it can be argued that they do not elide the benefits of locally-driven information gathering, analysis and reflection. These insights reinforce the case for the framework's focus on selecting 'good enough' data based on assessments of their strengths and weaknesses and including explicit qualifications regarding associated limitations.

Not unrelated, numerous interviews pointed to challenges in interpreting information gathered in the framework process. For example, some cautioned against seeing the expansion of data sites and types as the answer to the informational deficit in and of itself. One official conjectured that once information has been gathered from a range of alternative sources "the difficulty then is the skill set required in the mission to do something with that information."[35] He gave an example, explaining,

> If you go to Nimba County and talk to a local chief in Sanniquellie about issues, he will give you very specific information from his mindset about his specific problem and specific bias. Then it's the skill of the UN official to use and understand what that information really means ... so that this type of information can be analysed, deconstructed and a sort of a true narrative put around it.[36]

Many pointed out that UNMIL simply did not have that kind of capacity at present and hence there was a danger this type of information could be wrongly interpreted and become overly influential. This concern led to a number of respondents adding the caveat that any attempt to diversify data sources must guard against the dangers of over-privileging any single perspective – be that the UN or the most grassroots local actor/organisation – i.e. the importance of multiple perspectives.

Undoubtedly, the framework creates a demand for a specific skill set in the personnel involved in managing/conducting M&E.[37] However, as already described, the process and methods employed are purposely designed and selected to identify outlying data points and perspectives that are not corroborated in iterative verification ahead of findings feeding into decision-making and policy shifts. In this way, the burden on mission staff to manage complicated interpretation of data is reduced. Nevertheless, dependency on the competence and integrity of those who are ultimately responsible for compiling/presenting findings was identified as a potential weakness, and an important one at that, of the framework design. Despite appreciating the inclusive nature and shared ownership of the framework's implementation, it became clear in discussions with those in the field that the reliance on key individuals had the potential to undermine the participatory and representative credentials of the framework. This was not deemed to be a problem in general, but some believed that when findings were particularly critical, or when the organisation was faced with controversial failures, the resilience of honest, transparent and inclusive M&E would come under significant pressure.[38]

In short, this is an unavoidable frailty of the framework. Whilst some measures can be put in place as a check and balance on interpretation – particularly regarding conflict sensitivity – there will likely remain a dependence on the fidelity of particular individuals under the mission employ. One point to remember is that all M&E in UNMIL suffers from a similar dependency on the individual. Departing from the current orthodoxy, this framework moves to include enough stakeholders in participatory approaches to interpreting multiple subjectivities to embed a certain level of accountability to local partners as well as to political masters. Furthermore, mission officials with important roles in M&E are entrenched in a continuous process frequently appraised of changing local exigencies, as opposed to current praxis where assessments are both infrequent and oftentimes conducted by external agents as temporary visitors. Nevertheless, this critique points to a significant limitation in the framework that needs to be made explicit and qualified in the framework and its findings.

Sufficiently rigorous model?

The field research also identified a number of concerns that revolved around the framework's level of rigour. There was some trepidation about the scientific credentials of the framework. For example, a number of respondents charged that the proposed approach might be disregarded as it was not a statistical instrument and does not employ so-called scientific methods to 'prove' things.[39] Whilst this is likely due to perennial pressures to demonstrate external legitimacy of evaluations, the potential push-back is grounded in thinking that the framework is an attempt to break free from. The framework is not intended to be a statistical tool; in large part due to the lack of reliable and accessible statistical data in the post-conflict context. Consequently, the framework's design is purposeful to use practical and available information sources that do not jeopardise the safety of participants but need not compromise the rigorous foundations of the findings either.

Similarly, a number of officials pointed out that the methods used in the framework were not impartial and apolitical and do not appear to adhere to universal evaluation standards.[40] The implication was that its findings would be less independent and transparent and suggested that this could delegitimise it as a credible source of assessment in the eyes of some important constituencies for M&E. However, as mentioned, in order to be more responsive to the unique context at play, the framework design is not intended to be uninvolved. OIOS and other DPKO-commissioned external evaluations can and should serve that purpose, complementing this framework. This framework explicitly rescinds any claim to objectivity based on the realisation that M&E can play an important role in achieving sustainable outcomes as well as recording and presenting them. Whilst some respondents spoke about the benefits of 'external' and, as they argued, 'objective' evaluation, all were in agreement that this alone is not sufficient to meet M&E needs or potential. Many added that the major downside to these external 'fly-in-fly-out' assessments was the fact that they lack any iterative process of ongoing monitoring and real-time assessments which in turn inhibited the extent to which M&E could not only track change, but also contribute to it.[41]

In addition to questions around scientific and objective credentials, a recurrent criticism of the methods proposed for information gathering and interpretation related to their susceptibility to human error. These accusations concerned issues of selection, omission and handling bias. Many said such methodological imperfections were likely at every point in a subjective approach as advocated.[42] Another manifestation of bias relates to cultural pluralism. Whilst it was agreed that it was important to recognise competing visions of success, some respondents emphasised that some are likely to be contrary to overall objectives of the UNPOL mission. For instance, respondents pointed to a number of traditional justice practices involving a poisonous concoction known as sassywood were patently incompatible with international human rights obligations.[43] Whilst the potential for these types of bias in contributions is high, the fact that they cannot be eradicated need not be perceived as a problem. As mentioned in relation to data sources above, the iterative and triangulated process of data analysis and interpretation serves to isolate uncorroborated and outlying data points as well as counterintuitive but widely held views. Therefore, the approach in the framework allows for disparate perspectives to be included in findings in a way that informs rather than distorts final results.

In the course of discussions, a number of interviewees also questioned the framework's utility for real-time comparative assessments between multiple missions in different locations. Whilst this is a fair question,[44] it is also true that the framework is not intended for this purpose. That is to say it is not meant to be a way of gauging the progress of UN missions in relation to each other. What the framework does envisage and aim to facilitate is second-level learning (i.e. learning between missions) occurring via complete organisational learning cycles, only after lessons emerging in one locale are mediated through knowledge management systems and institutionalised in policy and doctrine so as to provide guidance and where appropriate permeate practice in other and future missions.[45]

In sum, questions relating to the methodological rigour of the framework are to be expected given the paradigms that dominate current thinking and practice in peace operations and related fields from where many of the interviewees have come. Nevertheless, this framework is purposebuilt to diverge from and ultimately target a shift in the mental models that pervade extant orthodoxy. As a member of the senior management team asserted, "Whilst corporate paradigms increasingly dominate the UN's bureaucracy based on positivist social science thinking ... these might not be the most appropriate tools in this particular setting."[46] This was supported by another senior UNMIL official who suggested that given the unique challenges faced by contemporary peace operations, when it comes to M&E, "modern management techniques such as [RBB/Benchmarking] derived from traditional logical framework philosophies simply do not work well."[47] Therefore, what these insights highlight is that in places and cases where the framework departs from the orthodoxy, the reasons why and benefits of doing so must be clearly articulated. It is also worth reiterating that this framework is ultimately intended to play a specific role as part of the M&E architecture, not be all things to all people.

Practicalities

The final set of criticisms emanating from the field testing relate to practicalities of implementing the framework. These concern issues of whose agenda predominates, resource constraints, potential duplication, applicability across contexts and possible unforeseen consequences of new approaches.

Differentiating hierarchical demands

Whilst many interviewees commended the framework's focus on field-level consensus-based visions of change for setting the objectives against which UNPOL were assessed, many stated that they did not see how the framework had the ability to ensure these objectives superseded external pressures and expectations. For example, referencing a recurrent and problematic "[d]isconnect between strategic visions and the on-the-ground visions",[48] a number of senior mission officials declared that directing their programme of work to meet the expectations of donors/ members states will remain a powerful incentive for mission staff and that the framework's approach would not overcome this per se. Furthermore, some highlighted that these conditions produced a significant disconnect between the theory and practice of M&E in the field. In other words, whatever the shortcomings of the M&E approach employed, the enabling environment for these processes to thrive – be it requisite resources or culture of openness and information sharing – did not exist in UNMIL.[49] In short, the framework creates the space for cultural shift in the way M&E is conceived of and conducted but it will struggle to achieve this shift in the absence of political appetite and will. This salient criticism demands that the potential for the framework alone to achieve these shifts must be qualified as contingent in this sense.

Resource and attention requirements?

One of the most common questions arising in interviews related to the resources required to operationalise and implement an M&E framework such as this. There was a line of argument, usually from those overburdened in the field, that the framework appeared onerous. That is to say they contended that it would require too much capacity and time to grasp the concepts and the multiple methods required to implement it.[50] Many respondents emphasised that current M&E demands already outstripped the capacity of existing personnel and attention/resources at a mission's disposal to implement it.[51] For instance, one interviewee went as far as to say "RBB and benchmarking bog everybody down and ... they are very cumbersome and time-consuming".[52] In addition, the POLCOM declared that there was very limited knowledge and understanding about M&E methods and processes within UNPOL, the integrated rule of law efforts or the mission in general.[53] Indicative of the focus at DPKO on quantity rather than quality of personnel, he stated that, "UNPOL officers deployed to UNMIL lack the expertise to carry out some functions – one of those is certainly M&E."[54] Another explained that, in addition to skill sets, deployment patterns would need to be adjusted for personnel to be effective at activities like M&E as it required "more longevity than the average tour-of-duty allows".[55] As a result of these constraints, UNPOL officials presumed that the proposed framework and approach may require more quantity and quality of human resource than can be reasonably expected at present. For instance, a senior Advisor noted that implementing something like this, "brings its own challenges for an organisation like the UN or a DPKO mission, because do you have the staff that can actually do [it] or that have any experience of that?"[56] One respondent went further to claim that the participatory methods involved, "[w]ould require an overhaul of the personnel".[57]

However, insights from the field also suggest that the human and material resource demands of the framework are less of a concern than perceived by some. For example, one respondent spoke of sufficient quantity of personnel in UNMIL concerned with monitoring but lamented the lack of quality and suitable skill sets.[58] Therefore, answers may lay in clarifying and demanding human resource requirements. Furthermore, existing M&E demands suggested that significant time and resources are already dedicated to this task. For example, one official stated that the mission's in-house training cell had gone to the lengths of devising a curriculum and providing RBB training for UNMIL staff so that they can complete it.[59] These findings suggest M&E in the field is already labour-intensive such that proposals for new approaches need not shy too far away from requests for increased or transferred resources. Furthermore, within the UNPOL structure, the Research and Planning section provides support to the POLCOM in gathering and collating the data used in submission for the dominant M&E products (e.g. RBB and benchmarking).[60] Therefore, ongoing documentation of outputs and managing data is already a requirement of UNPOL components and this framework basically requires more of the same. The participatory nature of the framework dictates that the content of M&E is generated by as many stakeholders as are included. Whilst additional tasks such as facilitating stakeholder involvement as well as managing ongoing risk and conflict-sensitivity assessments constitute an additional burden, the activities necessary to execute the participatory approaches here described are actually similar to the work that police often perform on a daily basis. Although this process may require a more systematic approach to conducting these tasks, investigations, evidence gathering and subsequent verification of sources to construct a feasible and believable narrative are the 'staple' daily duties of police in some parts of the world. It is however important to note that UNPOL as currently contributed by member states and their counterparts in the domestic police in places like Liberia are unlikely to be imbued with these skill sets as a matter of course.[61] This reality adds further weight to arguments advocating a higher standard of training for UNPOL officers, as well as the need to rethink the required competencies of contributing individuals.

Despite more elaborate system and resource demands, the more accurate reflection of reality arrived at through this framework promises a better utilisation of scarce resources in the long run. Furthermore, the process can – and even should – be introduced incrementally without radical departures from the existing or the immediate need to create new and expensive capabilities. To use a well-known idiom, there is no need to throw the baby out with the bathwater![62]

In sum, whilst the framework undoubtedly creates demand for skilled personnel and dedicated attention to M&E, existing competencies and staffing arrangements evidenced in UNMIL suggest the framework's demands are not insurmountable. Nevertheless, these criticisms, including real concerns about diverting existing human resource capacity away from UNPOL activities to M&E tasks potentially undermining the integrity of both, bring into focus important qualifications on the practicalities of the framework – at least in the short-term.

Risk of duplication?

In light of these concerns about resource requirements, interviews highlighted apprehension on the part of some who feared that – as with all new management tools – the framework may lead to inefficient duplications of existing functions.[63] In particular, some questioned whether the orientation of the framework may render it redundant due to the existence of: (1) existing Joint Mission Analysis Cell (JMAC) and Joint Operations Centre (JOC); and, (2) nascent Knowledge Management tools. First, the JMAC/JOC system in UNMIL was identified by some as a centre of gravity for information gathering, analysis and feedback within the mission. However, others believed that whilst there may be a useful role for the JMAC/JOC in M&E, it was not sufficient.[64] The JOC is charged with information gathering, primarily through collation of the weekly SITREPs of each substantive section which it then uses to produce situational awareness assessments. The JMAC is primarily an entity for analysis and assessment, producing an "overarching and multidisciplinary view of what's going on" regarding medium- and long-term security threats to the mission for dissemination as deemed appropriate but predominantly for the consumption of the SRSG.[65] Neither, nor both in tandem, constitute a mission M&E cell for gauging progress in mandate implementation or the impact of particular components of the mission.[66] A number of interviewees explained that the primary flow of information in UNMIL, ultimately mediated through these entities,[67] functions through a very top-down, 'need-to-know' modality.[68] For example, one interviewee said, "Mission structure dictates that information gathering entities don't have sufficient horizontal relationships for sharing information – rather everything is designed to privilege a vertical provision. This inhibits the potential value add of feedback loops."[69] It may be that the JMAC concept could be built upon, to go beyond current political analysis and threat assessment to become a more holistic information gathering and management entity.

However, in its current configuration it is not a suitable substitute for the requirements of M&E.[70]

Secondly, a number of respondents pointed out that the mission had only recently rolled out the nascent Knowledge Management tools, including a range of mechanisms for capturing lessons from the field and envisaged appointment of a dedicated Best Practices Officer to coordinate these efforts. It was emphasised that given the learning orientation of this framework, it appeared to cover similar territory.[71] Some queried whether a competing framework with the same overarching objective was advisable.[72] However, others declared that these initiatives had heretofore struggled to gain traction and consequently were not having their intended impact.[73] Regardless, there was agreement that these needed to be linked into a more systematic process of making sense of field-level experiences if they were to fulfil their potential. The explicit intention to harness and buttress these very tools meant that many deemed the framework to constitute a potential multiplication rather than duplication of their function.

Nevertheless, these concerns demonstrate the clear need to avoid redundancy due to duplication of information gathering, analysis and utilisation efforts. The insights therefore corroborate the need for the framework to cohere with other parts of the M&E architecture, such as the JMAC and existing Knowledge Management tools, if it is to de-conflict with existing mechanisms and ensure efficiency in this regard.

Limits of tailoring to UNMIL-specific context?

A number of respondents suggested that the framework appeared to be weighted towards assessing police reform and transition activities. Whilst most accepted that the full typology of UNPOL missions was tailored for in the foregrounding stage, a few of those engaged nevertheless put it to me that the framework and its methods risked being overly focused on the M&E needs of capacity-building mandates. Their contention was that this might render it less useful for assessing the other regularly mandated tasks of UNPOL, particularly when it comes to the initial stages of a new mission where the stabilisation and restoration of law and order are the priority. Another identified the increasing role of UNPOL (particularly FPUs) in implementing protection of civilians mandates as something that required different approaches and measures of effectiveness.[74] Furthermore, another official challenged that the framework might not be suitable for unforeseen, and potentially unique, future UNPOL mandates or operating environments.[75]

The framework does have a slant towards the methods and approach necessary to assess policebuilding activities. However, this is primarily because it is the complexity of these transformational endeavours that conventional M&E has struggled most to reflect. Furthermore, once a degree of stability has been achieved, effective police reform is invariably the priority for UNPOL. As a senior mission manager explained, at this stage of UNMIL,

> we are here to mentor and train LNP. So, however wonderful our indicators are in-house, they may not translate into anything meaningful if LNP doesn't show signs of having been trained, doesn't show better acumen at doing police duties, doesn't show the managerial control that a police force has, and so on.[76]

Therefore, the framework is primarily designed around existing and priority UNPOL tasks and activities. Moreover, policebuilding in particular is at the heart of modern UNPOL operations and a vital crutch for exit strategies. Nevertheless, the point of contention – i.e. that the circumstances for UNPOL missions differ and future missions may differ dramatically – reiterates the value of the context-sensitive foregrounding intrinsic to the framework. Furthermore, it also adds support to the argument for the framework's in-built flexibility so as to retain its utility for what are accepted, even promoted, to be constantly evolving circumstances. The framework, like the practice of UN policing in peace operations, will inevitably need to evolve in the face of changing demands upon it. These insights serve to reinforce this underlying principle.

Pursuit of complete knowledge through organisational learning?

A fundamental challenge that came up in the field research relates to the normative underpinnings of the framework. That is, a number of respondents asked whether or not the focus on impact assessment as the means to organisational learning (i.e. formalising institutional 'best practices') was premised on the notion that the UN peace operations bureaucracy can eventually learn 'everything there is to learn', at which point peace operations will become ideal? This is an important question given the evolution and rapid expansion of UN peace operations and the experiences of many respondents in witnessing that change. Many who highlighted this issue stated that such an approach was potentially dangerous given the varied record of missions with even quite humble expectations. The framework is predicated on the notion that learning is a never-ending process. However, it is also founded on the assumption that peace operations cannot and should not attempt to do everything. Therefore, contrary to the concerns raised, this framework promises to assist in identifying what cannot (or should not) be part of UNPOL/peace operations based on clearer understandings of the contributions that can be made, as well as revealing the potentially negative consequences of some action. Its reflexive modality is purposefully privileged so as to critically reflect on hitherto ingrained practices, as well as new initiatives and their underlying theories of change to ensure that programming is having its intended impact or else adjusted accordingly with clear pathways for this to inform organisational learning at the headquarters level.

Drilling down into how this learning takes place, participants pointed to the fact that not everything that is done in peace operations is conducive to being enshrined in doctrine and guidance that can be followed in a "paint-by-numbers kind of way", certainly not across different contexts.[77] As Benner et al. argue, "the very cultural and political core of institution-building in a post-war society holds [a high] degree of complexity that defies simple standard operating procedures".[78] Similarly, it was noted that whilst some UNPOL tasks are amenable to standardisation, there are some increasingly central parts of UNPOL mandates that cannot and should not necessarily be generalised for the purpose of developing doctrine and guidance. For example, UNPOL officials highlighted that the technical elements of assistance may be easily reduced to standard operating procedures (SOPs) and the rules of engagement for FPUs are relatively straightforward and reproducible. However, they also emphasised that context-specific elements of building an effective and legitimate police service to work in and with the community based on political decisions are much harder to generalise or formalise.[79] Therefore, some argued that the framework did not seem to have provision for this type of learning. Like the field-level M&E itself, second-level learning infrastructure needs to include innovative ways of capturing and sharing experiences that are not easily formalised in organisational documents like SOPs, doctrine and policy directives. Ultimately, that is the concern of the learning infrastructure rather than the M&E machinery. Nevertheless, these critiques further clarify the need for the framework to enable this type of learning by ensuring that it provides the refined or prepared ingredients for that machinery.

Danger of disempowering already constrained field missions?

Whilst many of the responses were critical of existing approaches for their asymmetry and bias towards the agendas of politico-strategic level stakeholders, a number of interviewees alluded to potentially counterproductive consequences of M&E that produced a more realistic portrayal of effects on the ground. The general tenor of the debate was that, whilst uninstructive and burdensome at times, extant M&E tools can also be convenient for mission managers in the field in their reporting to HQ. One official referred to the CDW/Benchmarking approach as something,

> ..devised to provide the room for creative messaging. It is convenient for the mission to show "fancy" numbers so as to sustain and increase resources forthcoming from member states and donors. After some time, everybody in the system became hooked on it – particularly the

260 *Empirical case study and implications*

Security Council. Ultimately, this is a creative way to sell certain ideas, not necessarily an effective means of furthering strategic goals.[80]

The connotation is that developing more sophisticated approaches for capturing the impact of missions could, in effect, result in disempowering field operatives already constrained in terms of decision-making autonomy and material means for implementing their mandates. In other words, more insightful field-level M&E could be problematic from the perspective of mission leaders attempting to manipulate M&E to convince audiences like the Security Council that, "there has been significant progress but not enough to withdraw."[81] Furthermore, anything that further limits decision-making autonomy for mission managers in the field is likely to inhibit the amount of freedom to realise first-level learning that can be seen to permeate practice. These are important points, not least because such a situation would likely feed into new rationale for resistance to M&E and low buy-in. However, the framework is built upon the idea that political masters will need to recalibrate their expectations of M&E and with it, support change in the relationships between field missions, the peace operations bureaucracy and the decision-making bodies of the UN. Furthermore, in the context of perceptions that political masters in the Security Council are becoming "less impatient and increasingly accepting that it takes time for missions to implement their programmes and for change to occur",[82] the gravitas of depriving mission managers of this Machiavellian avenue is reduced somewhat.

Conclusion

On the basis of the insights gleaned in the field research, a number of experiences in the case of UNMIL, as well as insights about peace operations and UNPOL endeavours in general, challenge the suitability of some of the principles and elements of the framework. This chapter has addressed these alleged weaknesses, problems and naïveté as they relate to the focus, approach/methods and practicalities associated with the implementation of the framework.

The critiques arising from the field research occasionally demonstrated perceived weaknesses and problems with the proposed framework when compared to some existing instruments. However, more commonly, the accusations levelled at the framework were indicative of enduring conceptual, methodological and practical hurdles that epitomise the 'state of the art' when it comes to M&E in peace operations and conflict-affected settings – even in more innovative approaches. It has therefore been argued that some of these critiques point to areas for revision, reinforcement and refinement of the framework. For instance, there is a need to clarify terminology and definitions as well as articulations of the framework's purpose.[83] Also, it is important to highlight where complementary elements of the framework are custom-designed to compensate for fragilities elsewhere. However, it was also argued that other criticisms hold most importance in highlighting limitations of the framework as opposed to problematic weaknesses. Issues relating to focus, methods and practicalities of M&E in the field speak to the need to ensure that whilst efforts are required to push beyond current orthodoxy, any proposals for doing so must be underpinned by pragmatic principles and incorporate checks and balances to ensure they remain appropriate and incentive compatible. Furthermore, there will be an ongoing need to emphasise and evidence the effectiveness of similar approaches in the realm of peace operations and related fields,[84] such that an overall drive towards acceptance of 'complexity-friendly' thinking and methods can begin to infuse institutional culture and structures relating to M&E at the UN. It is clear from the field that this is crucial if new approaches are to gain traction in practice.

Whilst many of those interviewed in this field research identified a slew of significant shortcomings associated with existing approaches to M&E in UNMIL, almost all of them identified M&E as critical to the effective management of peace operations and a potentially powerful tool in contributing to the eventual outcomes and impacts of peace operations.[85] One official captured this by simply stating that "if created today, UNMIL would have ... an M&E unit included".[86] The overall perception of extant M&E at the field-level was summed up well by a senior UNPOL official who said that,

> M&E is integral to the management of UNPOL in peace operations. However, there is a danger that the approach used is not realistic. The mechanisms in place have limitations in the extent to which they can capture the realities on the ground.[87]

However, it was often said by senior mission personnel that alternative tools and techniques are unavailable to them. One official concluded that, "...we simply must develop more realistic mechanisms for monitoring and evaluating these phenomena". Another long-time servant in the mission added that "there is an urgent need for innovation in this area – whilst accepting that we will continually have to live up to expectations."[88] Another summed up the general consensus emerging across all interviews, saying, "You have to make sure, in terms of the measures you put in place, that you 'measure what you value' not 'value what you measure'."[89]

Notwithstanding the need for refinement and recognition of enduring challenges to implementation, the field research presented in these two chapters demonstrates that the framework developed in this study holds a great deal of potential for advancements in the way M&E for UNPOL is conceived of and conducted. Whilst I believe it to be a defensible body of empirical work, the fieldwork from which this and the preceding chapter are derived should be viewed as contingent. That is to say, the information and insights gleaned are a product of a particular space and time in the history of the UN's presence in Liberia.[90] They are also contingent on the responses and insights of the specific sample of participants interviewed – albeit augmented by additional secondary source material and observations from the field. These findings, therefore, validate the preceding framework development to the extent that field research in one case study can be relied upon to do so.

Nevertheless, it is clear from these findings that advancements in the way M&E is conducted hold a great deal of potential for many stakeholders in the business of peace operations, and policing therein, in a context like UNMIL. As a senior mission advisor stated,

> ...the issue of impact assessment is a complex one, but a vital one – i.e. whether the approach was useful in building local ownership and capacity, in building sustainability, in responding to need and all of those issues – and that's a much more subjective issue. Quite clearly we all have much more work to do on that.[91]

Or, as the DSRSG drolly put it,

> I tell you, it is very depressing when you can't see the outcome of a lot of effort that you are putting in.... So, anything that helps operatives and those like us, who have to lead the process, to be able to measure whether we are making any headway at all will certainly be good for morale, if for nothing else![92]

The following and concluding chapter consolidates these findings and provides an overview of the argument developed throughout.

Notes

1 All interviews cited below were conducted by the author during extensive fieldwork in late 2010. Interview references have been deliberately depersonalised to adhere to ethical considerations that authorised the author to gather and utilise this information.
2 Interviews: UNMIL Officials – Monrovia, Liberia.
3 Interview: Liberian Government Assistant Minister – Monrovia, Liberia.
4 Interviews: UNMIL Officials – Monrovia, Liberia.
5 Interview: UNMIL Senior Mission Leadership – Monrovia, Liberia.
6 Interview: UNMIL Senior Management – Monrovia, Liberia.
7 Ibid.
8 Interview: UNMIL Official – Monrovia, Liberia.
9 Interview: UNMIL Senior Management – Monrovia, Liberia.
10 Interview: UNMIL Senior Management, Political, Policy and Planning Section – Monrovia, Liberia.
11 Interview: UNMIL Senior Official, Security Sector Reform – Monrovia, Liberia.
12 Interview: UNMIL Senior Management – Monrovia, Liberia.
13 Interview: UNMIL Senior Official, Security Sector Reform – Monrovia, Liberia; Interview: UNMIL Senior Management – Monrovia, Liberia.

14 Interview: UNMIL Senior Management – Monrovia, Liberia. Similarly, interviewees pointed out that activities and programmes were unlikely to be scalable either, such that effective programmes at a local level may not achieve the same outcomes when scaled up to the national level.
15 Interview: UNMIL Senior Official, Security Sector Reform – Monrovia, Liberia.
16 For further discussion on this point, see section below – 'Pursuit of Complete Knowledge'.
17 Interview: UNMIL Senior Official, Field Office, Montserrado County – Monrovia, Liberia.
18 Ibid.
19 Interviews: UNMIL Officials – Monrovia, Liberia.
20 For further support to these arguments, see: Jodie Curth and Sarah Evans, "Monitoring and Evaluation in Police Capacity Building Operations: 'Women as Uniform?'" *Police Practice and Research* (2011), 11.
21 Interviews: UNMIL Officials – Monrovia, Liberia.
22 Interview: Official, West African Network for Peacebuilding (WANEP) – Liberia Chapter – Monrovia, Liberia; Interview: Director, ICTJ Liberia – Monrovia, Liberia.
23 Interviews: UNMIL Officials – Monrovia, Liberia.
24 L.M. Howard, *UN Peacekeeping in Civil Wars* (Cambridge: Cambridge University Press, 2008), 309.
25 Interviews: UNMIL Officials – Monrovia, Liberia.
26 FEWER, "Conflict-Sensitive Monitoring and Evaluation", in *Conflict sensitive approaches to development, humanitarian assistance, and peace building: tools for peace and conflict assessment* (FEWER, International alert and Saferworld, 2003), 2; Simon Rynn and Duncan Hiscock, "Evaluating for Security and Justice: Challenges and Opportunities for Improved Monitoring and Evaluation of Security System Reform Programmes", (Saferworld, 2009), 14; BCPR, "Guidelines for Planning, Monitoring and Evaluation in Conflict Prevention and Recovery Settings". (Bureau of Conflict Prevention and Recovery, UNDP).
27 OECD-DAC, "Guidance on Evaluating Conflict Prevention and Peacebuilding Activities", in *Working Document for Application Period* (OECD – DAC, 2008), 22; Thomas Winderl and Heather Bryant, "Conflict-Sensitive Monitoring and Evaluation: Monitoring Manual", (Nepal: Monitoring and Evaluation Unit, UNDP, 2006).
28 Interview: UNMIL Senior Management, UNPOL – Monrovia, Liberia.
29 Interview: UNMIL Senior Mission Leadership – Monrovia, Liberia.
30 Ibid.
31 Ibid.
32 Ibid.
33 Interviews: UNMIL Officials – Monrovia, Liberia.
34 Ibid.
35 Interview: UNMIL Senior Official, Security Sector Reform – Monrovia, Liberia.
36 Ibid.
37 In addition to M&E expertise, this was said to include country-specific knowledge/experience and language skills. For more about human resource demands, see section below on 'resource and attention requirements'.
38 Interviews: UNMIL Officials – Monrovia, Liberia.
39 Interview: UNMIL Official – Monrovia, Liberia.
40 Interviews: UNMIL Officials – Monrovia, Liberia.
41 Interview: UNMIL Official – Monrovia, Liberia.
42 Interviews: UNMIL Officials – Monrovia, Liberia.
43 Interviews: UNMIL Senior Mission Leadership – Monrovia, Liberia; Liberian Government Minister – Monrovia, Liberia.

264 *Empirical case study and implications*

44 This subject invariably arose in discussions with those interviewees where this task was part of their job description.
45 CF earlier section in this chapter on 'Prospects for Learning'.
46 Interview: UNMIL Senior Official, Office of the Special Representative of the Secretary General – Monrovia, Liberia.
47 Interview: UNMIL Senior Management – Monrovia, Liberia.
48 Interview: UNMIL Senior Management, UNPOL – Monrovia, Liberia.
49 Interview: UNMIL Senior Official, Legal and Judicial Unit – Monrovia, Liberia.
50 Interviews: UNMIL Officials – Monrovia, Liberia.
51 Interviews: UNMIL Officials – Monrovia, Liberia. See also: Pierre Schori, "Leadership on the Line: Managing Field Complexity", in *Monitoring and Evaluation of Peace Operations*, eds. Cedric de Coning and Paul Romita (New York, Oslo: International Peace Institute & Norwegian Institute of International Affairs, November 2009), 29.
52 Interview: UNMIL Senior Official, Field Office, Montserrado County – Monrovia, Liberia.
53 Interview: UNMIL Senior Management, UNPOL – Monrovia, Liberia.
54 Ibid.
55 Interview: UNMIL Senior Mission Leadership – Monrovia, Liberia.
56 Interview: UNMIL Senior Official, Security Sector Reform – Monrovia, Liberia.
57 Interview: UNMIL Senior Official, Legal and Judicial Unit – Monrovia, Liberia.
58 Ibid.
59 Interview: UNMIL Senior Management, Training – Monrovia, Liberia.
60 Interview: UNMIL Senior Management, UNPOL – Monrovia, Liberia.
61 Ken Menkhaus, "Measuring Impact: Issues and Dilemmas", in *Occasional Paper Series*. (Geneva: InterPeace, 2003), 9.
62 Gerald Midgley, "Systems Thinking for Evaluation", 28–9; Gerald Midgley, *Systemic Intervention: Philosophy, Methodology, and Practice* (New York: Kluwer/Plenum, 2000).
63 Interviews: UNMIL Officials – Monrovia, Liberia.
64 Interview: UNMIL Senior Official, Legal and Judicial Unit – Monrovia, Liberia.
65 Interview: Political Affairs Officer, Joint Mission Analysis Cell (JMAC) – Monrovia, Liberia. See also: Mark Malan, "Intelligence in African Peace Operations: Addressing the Deficit", *KAIPTC Paper* 7(2005): 18–24; Philip Shetler-Jones, "Intelligence in Integrated UN Peacekeeping Missions: The Joint Mission Analysis Centre", *International Peacekeeping* 15, no. 4 (2008); Melanie Ramjoué, "Improving UN Intelligence through Civil–Military Collaboration: Lessons from the Joint Mission Analysis Centres", *International Peacekeeping* 18, no. 4 (2011).
66 Interview: Political Affairs Officer, Joint Mission Analysis Cell (JMAC) – Monrovia, Liberia.
67 Interviews: Political Affairs Officer, Joint Mission Analysis Cell (JMAC) – Monrovia, Liberia; UNMIL Senior Official, Public Information – Monrovia, Liberia.
68 Interview: UNMIL Senior Official, Public Information – Monrovia, Liberia.
69 Interview: UNMIL Senior Official, Legal and Judicial Unit – Monrovia, Liberia.
70 Interview: UNMIL Political Affairs Officer, JMAC – Monrovia, Liberia.
71 Interviews: UNMIL Officials – Monrovia, Liberia.
72 Ibid.
73 Interview: UNMIL Senior Mission Leadership Team – Monrovia, Liberia.
74 Interviews: FPU Commander; UNMIL Police Officials – Monrovia, Liberia.
75 Interviews: UNMIL Senior Official, UNPOL; UNMIL Senior Management, UNPOL; UNMIL Senior Management, UNPOL – Monrovia, Liberia.
76 Interview: UNMIL Senior Mission Leadership – Monrovia, Liberia.
77 Interview: UNMIL Senior Official, Field Office, Montserrado County – Monrovia, Liberia. See also: Thorsten Benner, Stephan Mergenthaler, and Philipp

Rotmann, *The New World of UN Peace Operations: Learning to Build Peace?* (Oxford: Oxford University Press, 2011), 69–70. For similar discussion, see: Michael Barnett and Martha Finnemore, *Rules for the World: International Organizations in Global Politics* (Ithaca: Cornell University Press, 2004).
78 Benner, Mergenthaler, and Rotmann, *The New World of UN Peace Operations: Learning to Build Peace?* 107.
79 Interviews: UNMIL Police Officials – Monrovia, Liberia.
80 Interview: UNMIL Senior Management, Political, Policy and Planning Section – Monrovia, Liberia.
81 Ibid.
82 Ibid.
83 For example, the seemingly esoteric complexity concepts need to be demystified so that they can be understood and worked with (although only really by those with oversight responsibilities). This requires the use of clear and jargon-free language so as to avoid 'drowning' audiences in complexity language.
84 For example, Effects-Based Operations (EBO) in the military domain. For further detail, see: Milan N. Vego, Milan N. "Effects-Based Operations: A Critique". *Joint Force Quarterly* no. 41 (2006): 51–7.
85 Interviews: UNMIL Officials – Monrovia, Liberia.
86 Interview: UNMIL Senior Management – Monrovia, Liberia.
87 Interview: UNMIL Senior Management, UNPOL – Monrovia, Liberia.
88 Interview: UNMIL Senior Management, Political, Policy and Planning Section – Monrovia, Liberia.
89 Interview: UNMIL Senior Official, UNPOL – Monrovia, Liberia.
90 Paul Higate and Marsha Henry, *Insecure Spaces: Peacekeeping, Power and Performance in Haiti, Kosovo and Liberia,* (London: Zed Books, 2009), 6.
91 Interview: UNMIL Senior Official, Security Sector Reform – Monrovia, Liberia.
92 Interview: UNMIL Senior Mission Leadership – Monrovia, Liberia.

Conclusion
Overcoming the convenience of simplicity

> Effective peacekeeping requires flexible structures that can evolve over the different phases of the mission, while consistently providing timely and effective support.[1]

At the outset, this book presented a research puzzle, arguing that despite the increasing centrality of police in contemporary UN peace operations, attempts to understand their effectiveness have evaded dedicated and systematic research in academia and confounded practical steps in the field. The stated objective of this book was therefore to examine how M&E as a means of assessing the impact of mission activity can contribute to making UN peace operations more effective, particularly in the area of UN policing. The primary research question put forward in the introduction was: how should the UN monitor and evaluate the impact of police in its peace operations? The answer put forward here is that in order to enable more efficacious peace operations, the UN should conduct M&E of UNPOL in a way that draws upon and embraces the "spirit of epistemological uncertainty",[2] entrenches flexibility and is embedded in holistic mission management framework that can in turn lead to more effective organisational learning.

This study demonstrated a plethora of shortcomings associated with extant theory and practice of M&E when it comes to reflecting the complex and idiosyncratic characteristics of peace operations and international policing. The research has shown that M&E has myriad potential benefits for multiple constituencies above and beyond its conventional uses and limitations. Moreover, it has been argued that realising these benefits requires that M&E is both re-thought and re-positioned. That is to say: first, it needs to bring new epistemological thinking to bear in the focus and design of an approach and associated selection of methods for its execution; and second, it needs to be embedded in the machinery of peace operations such that it is an intrinsic part of the way peace operations are planned and managed. In conducting such an inquiry I have demonstrated that there is a need for improvements in the way the UN monitors and evaluates the impact of its operations and police components in particular. Furthermore, I have shown that specific developments in the approach to M&E drawing on complexity theory and developing an innovative approach have the potential to contribute to more effective peace operations through organisational learning.

This conclusion reiterates the argument for advancing M&E in this direction. It proceeds to reflect on the book's major contributions, its implications for policy and practice, as well as its limitations, before highlighting potential areas of future research that can enhance the findings herein.

Argument

This study investigated progress and change under the auspices of UN peace operations, how these missions measure themselves and how this process can relate to organisational learning. Peace operations are faced with some of the most daunting challenges at the security-development nexus, restoring stability and spear-heading sustainable development. UNPOL epitomise this location and set of challenges. The book proceeded in three parts. Part I explored how UN policing and M&E are done and identified the problems with current practice, bringing the argument into focus. Part II utilised the value add gained from complexity theory to develop a framework underpinned by the argument. In Part III, the case study research and empirical evidence put forward demonstrated how this argument holds in a real world case – that of Liberia – albeit with the identification of some potential weaknesses that warranted revision and refinement.

In the first part it was shown that the evolution of UNPOL endeavours, particularly towards policebuilding, increasingly target shifts in behaviour and attitudes. It was therefore argued in Chapter 1 that, in addition to the oft-cited technical and logistical challenges, efforts to gauge the impact of UNPOL need to be cognisant of the major political challenges such as the validity of peacebuilding modalities predicated on rule of law change theories, as well as the role of non-state actors in post-conflict public security and justice provision.

Chapter 2 highlighted that recent scholarship has begun to evidence an implicit argument that organisational learning – both within and between missions – is a key factor of effective UN peace operations. Generating and acquiring knowledge and lessons from the field is seen as a prerequisite ingredient for such organisational learning and it was therefore argued that M&E can be understood as a crucial process for doing so. Chapter 2 argued that whilst M&E in these settings is not new, current orthodoxy has proved inadequate for this task. The research demonstrated a variety of shortcomings associated with extant theory and practice of M&E in UN peace operations and argued that it was particularly ill-suited to the unique challenges faced by UNPOL, specifically in assessing their police reform efforts. I further argued that peace operations and UNPOL are a unique case characterised by the dynamic and fluctuating nature of the places in which they operate and fast-changing objectives of the programming they implement, whereby conventional data sources are rare and unreliable and human and material resources for M&E are scarce. Furthermore, contrary to current orthodoxy, the book built the case that the changes sought by UNPOL are the result of intricate interdependencies and hence occur in complex systems. It was consequently argued that impacts/outcomes are the product of multiple and disparate interacting actors with high likelihood of unintended (positive and negative) consequences and therefore cannot be reduced to the actions of single agents, nor predicted with any certainty. I argued that this unique context rendered importing or transposing models and approaches forged in other circumstances an inadequate solution to the problem of impact assessment for UNPOL and therefore, peace operations and UNPOL require a tailored and context-specific framework for monitoring and evaluating their impact.

The second part of the book argued that the insights from complexity theory add significant value to understanding and overcoming these challenges. Chapter 3 demonstrated how complexity theory has important correlations with the characteristics and features of peace operations and their operating environments. In particular, Chapter 3 argued that peace operations environments were characterised by high levels of connectivity, critical feedback processes and emergent outcomes. Furthermore, I argued that complexity concepts and ideas mapped neatly to the challenges facing M&E identified in Chapter 2 and had potential to inform the development of more relevant and appropriate models. Therefore, it was argued that complexity theory adds value by providing an explanatory framework that makes sense of non-linear dynamics and causal ambiguity; prioritises sensitivity to context and initial conditions; privileges a systemic perspective; encourages an inclusive and participatory approach; and constitutes a learning-orientation for 'improving' rather than 'proving'.

In Chapter 4 these theoretical insights and practical applications were used to argue the need to move away from the methodological and philosophical monoculture that predominates and that the design of M&E should therefore be grounded in the same shift in thinking. This argument informed the development of a framework that is both 'circular' – i.e. iterative and reflexive – and 'systemic' – i.e. embedded awareness of interdependence and systemic environment. Within this overarching approach, the argument was made that for M&E of UNPOL to contribute to more effective peace operations, it must be context-sensitive; focused on the impact of mission endeavours; reflective of the emergent nature of change by embedding flexibility/adaptability; reflexive, inclusive and participatory in terms of the data included and methods employed; and oriented towards facilitating organisational learning (both within and between missions) to redress the current imbalance and dominant zeitgeist that entrenches an asymmetric bias towards 'accountability' and audit to enable a shift towards 'learning'.

As it was argued that context-sensitivity and specificity were imperative to accurate analyses using such a framework and methods, testing the utility of the framework required detailed case study research. Hence, in the third part of the book, primary field research in the UN peace operation in Liberia served to test the framework's relevance and comparative advantages over existing approaches. Chapter 5 presented a background to the events of the protracted conflict in Liberia and the UNPOL mission deployed by the UN in response. It argued that the degradation and reconfiguration of a broadly understood security sector – including important non-state elements – was both a cause and consequence of conflict. Moreover, it argued that a detailed rendering of this context was an indispensable precursor to understanding impact and change during UNMIL's presence in Liberia.

The empirical evidence presented in chapter 6 highlighted that M&E is integral to the effective management and implementation of UN peace operations. Moreover, it evidenced that there are numerous advantages to augmenting existing approaches with new thinking and approaches akin to those proposed in this study. It was shown that such adjustments would have significant benefits for the way M&E is conducted and corollary decision-making in the context of UNMIL/Liberia. The ongoing and systematic process entrenched in the framework was believed to better reflect the complex and dynamical change typical of peace operations environments. It was further seen to alleviate the distortive risks associated with inappropriate timeframes. The focus on impact and an explicit treatment of the issue of causality were deemed to constitute important recalibrations, as well as promise more realistic and humble assessments. The framework's flexibility was understood to lead to increased relevance in the way M&E could track change, as well as enhanced utility of the corollary findings for propagating positive change. The inclusive and participatory imperative undergirding the framework was seen to offer multiple benefits including assessments that incentivise buy-in, are more grounded in local exigencies, as well as the potential to facilitate local ownership. The reflexive nature of the approach was deemed to be crucial for enabling the improvement in the modalities and methods of early peacebuilding, particularly given the relative 'newness' of efforts to reconstitute police services to the UN's peacebuilding project. By extension, it was also posited that the logic and theories of change undergirding the UNPOL project can also be interrogated to substantiate or reject normative assumptions about change in these contexts in order to refine the thinking behind ongoing and future missions. The findings also underpinned the argument that when it comes to security and justice provision, the non-state realm is significant to everyday experience of public safety and consequently is part of the calculus of public perceptions of the state security apparatus. It was consequently asserted that a major strength of the framework was incorporating and mainstreaming an awareness of the presence, perspectives and influences of non-state actors. Finally, I made the argument that when done in this way, M&E can contribute to organisational learning. That is, it can improve real-time learning for decision-making in the field as well as knowledge management at headquarters level. It was shown that this can enable improved planning and optimise contributions to desired outcomes/impacts – including mitigating the negative unintended consequences of action – and ultimately lead to more efficacious peace operations.

Despite the many strengths and comparative advantages proffered, the field research also revealed a number of potential weaknesses relating to the focus, approach/methods and practicalities of the framework that were addressed in Chapter 7. It was therefore argued that insights from the field pointed to a number of areas where revision and refinements were necessary to improve upon the framework. Nevertheless, it was also argued that some of the criticisms levelled at the framework were not unique to the proposed framework, but rather indicative of the impediments afflicting M&E in situations where pressure to demonstrate success is high, but predictability of outcomes and impact is low. In these cases, it was argued that critiques should be understood as limitations on the framework as opposed to weak points or problems.

The framework – embracing the "spirit of epistemological uncertainty",[3] entrenching flexibility and embedded in the machinery of holistic mission management – offers a way of facilitating organisational learning processes and providing pathways for overcoming the inertia and rigidity in current approaches and mindsets that ultimately retard and inhibit adaptation. This promises to empower peace operations to be more effective within stringent constraints.

Contributions and implications

The findings of this study have significant implications for research and policy in this field, which has heretofore resided in a narrow sphere. In particular, the book brings M&E in peace operations out of the bureaucratic, technical and external realm into the political, artistic and intrinsic domain.

The findings point to the potential for improvements in the way M&E is both conceptualised and implemented in UNPOL/peace operations. Given that the topic of M&E in peace operations – particularly in relation to international policing – has not been subjected to much detailed study thus far, a major contribution of this book is to conduct the first systematic analysis of M&E for peace operations/UNPOL and to offer a new way of doing it. It uses novel theory and an interdisciplinary approach to generate an innovative critique of current orthodoxy, as well as to build a new framework for M&E that is suitable for use in this setting. In doing so, this study adds much-needed analysis and recommendations to this important area of inquiry.

The interdisciplinary approach, bringing together International Relations[4] with M&E and complexity theory, makes a small but significant contribution to conceptual debates within and across these disciplines. It also presents a modest but unique addition to the repository of research applying complexity theory as a lens for better understanding the system dynamics in the domains of international organisations, peace operations and M&E in conflict-affected environments. This further distinguishes this research from that of others who have addressed similar research questions with different theoretical frameworks.[5] In addition, it provides an alternative perspective to extant studies by providing a more nuanced view of the external and internal factors and conditions that enable or inhibit UNPOL in peace operations to achieve their desired goals and presents a way of opening up the 'black box' and navigating the causal ambiguity inherent in the relationship between peace operations and outcomes of sustainable peace.

The study also contributes to a relatively nascent but growing body of work on the importance, status, evolving objectives, opportunities and challenges associated with the use of civilian police in contemporary peace operations. In doing so, it challenges analysts and implementers to conceptualise how and when non-state actors contribute to and/or are relied upon for progress in peace operations, including how 'progress' is understood and measured. Furthermore, it presents M&E which encourages missions to be reflexive and question the validity of their underlying assumptions – i.e. theories of change largely framed by the liberal peacebuilding paradigm.

M&E that embraces complexity, rather than attempts to simplify and reduce it, presents a potentially useful approach for scholars, analysts and practitioners alike who are attempting to make sense of the 'wicked' problems pervasive in this field. Hence, this research is well-placed to make an innovative, contribution to extant knowledge and thinking about M&E of policing in peace operations, as well as similar challenges in related fields in a number of important ways.

This contribution has a number of potential real-world policy applications. This section reflects on the putative implications and possible applications of the research findings. Regarding this applicability, the research design was purposely tailored to reflect the realities of praxis in the field. In doing so, it is better placed to tackle the enduring disconnects between policy-making and the empiricism/critical literature aimed at improving or developing it.[6] This has enabled the research to address a recurrent criticism in recent research on international policing,[7] and facilitated the generation of more accessible and policy-relevant conclusions and recommendations.

In particular, the book has investigated in depth two key areas of current focus for the UN peace operations bureaucracy – M&E in the field and organisational learning/knowledge management. Regarding the former, recommendations on how M&E in missions can be strengthened to improve impact assessments promises to add more accurate/reflective and defensible information from the field to, *inter alia*, ensure that calls by some member states to "do more with less" do not undermine field imperatives. Regarding the latter, suggestions about how the impact assessments emerging from field-level M&E can be better connected to and feed organisational learning processes and mechanisms for knowledge management at the HQ level promises to enable lessons identified in the field to be more effectively captured in institutional memory and become lessons learned – in turn leading to a more effective peace operations apparatus. These findings present the opportunity for new approaches, as well as the potential to enhance existing and emerging practices in these areas. In doing so, the contribution has potential to facilitate the UN's professionalisation agenda – i.e. the pursuit of more effective individual missions, but also more effective and efficient management of the UN peace operations apparatus.

The findings of this research also have important implications for processes of strategic doctrine development for UNPOL currently underway at HQ. The learning promulgated through this framework could be consolidated in universal guidance and feed into ongoing processes of doctrine development, as well as inform where such attempts to formalise are inappropriate. Given that these doctrinal frameworks are intended for use by all organisations deploying international policing missions, this has further implications for the modalities of the international policing policy community as well.

Another significant implication of these findings relates to ramifications for the planning and management of UNPOL. If the number and type of impacts/outcomes cannot be predicted or measured according to linear thinking, then the UN should consider moving away from a logical framework approach towards one which embraces complexity and empowers M&E to facilitate it. This would require a shift of focus from 'better measuring of results' to 'better managing for results'. The findings of this study therefore have fundamental implications for the way in which UN peace operations, and specifically UNPOL efforts, should be conceived of, designed, assessed and ultimately managed.

Limitations

Having laid out the argument and findings of the study, its major contributions and the most prominent implications, it is worthwhile explaining some limitations associated with the specific research design and process of this study. The first concerns the extent to which one can generalise the findings. Notwithstanding the retroductive research strategy, the insights gleaned from the field research are a product of a particular space and time in the history of one case study – i.e. the UN's presence in Liberia.[8] They are therefore contingent on the observations and responses of the specific sample of participants interviewed – albeit augmented by additional secondary source material and first-hand observations from the field.

Second, the constraints associated with conducting fieldwork in a post-conflict country dictated that access to certain constituencies was difficult to obtain or limited due to restrictions placed upon me. Whilst every effort was made to draw on interviews from a diverse sample, this led to the research findings drawing heavily on interviews with officials from UNMIL. It could therefore be argued that there is a disconnect between on the one hand some of the methods/methodological principles that underpin the proposed framework herein, and on the other hand the method I have employed to test the value of the framework through fieldwork. Whilst this was an unavoidable consequence of these circumstances, this need not discredit the research findings. Rather, it is important that they are placed in the context of this limitation and the need for further research to interrogate the validity of the conclusions drawn herein is clearly articulated. These limitations point to a number of potential avenues for further research.

Further research

As is often the case with time- and space-constrained research, these findings raise as many questions as they answer. Some of these are significant prospects that point to and deserve further consideration and research. In the interests of stimulating scholarly debate and addressing the limitations identified above, it is worth posing some of them here.

First and foremost, this study only constitutes the tip of the iceberg in investigating a crucial area of research and policy-making. Indeed, this research can therefore be understood as an extended introduction for what should be approached as an ongoing retroductive process, whereby theoretical developments continue to be combined with empirical evidence to improve and ensure the currency of M&E in the unique context of peace operations. Therefore, before any supplementary research questions are entertained, there is a need for further attempts to demonstrate empirically the value-add of thinking about M&E in ways proposed herein. Consequently, there is much scope for improvement of the approach proposed in this book with additional in-depth case studies in other UN peace operations to build a robust body of empirical research findings to validate and further refine the emergent conclusions here. As identified, given the inclusive and participatory imperatives in the methodological approach, further research that can expand the breadth and depth of perspectives brought to bear on these developments is also of merit. Furthermore, an additional research dimension would be to apply the thinking here to other organisations deploying police in their peace operations such as the European Union (EU), the African Union (AU), or individual states such as Australia with its IDG.

In addition to further steps to re-test, revise and improve upon the beginnings in this study, this study also opens up a number of promising adjacent research avenues. The findings here suggest the need for research to better understand the entry points for the practical implementation of these ideas – i.e. what are the levers and sites of resistance to applying these ideas in practice? For instance, how, through further empirical research, can these ideas be moved from words to deeds and inform the infrastructure for M&E/learning within DPKO and the Secretariat? One specific dimension that has emerged from this research relates to the need to shift the incentive structure for M&E. That is the need to dampen the perception that rewards flow from meeting of fixed goals and benchmarks and emphasise the inclusion of learning objectives and make clear that career opportunities will be advanced by embracing learning culture and contributing to collective memory.

Another angle would be further research on the relationship between different approaches to knowledge acquisition/information accumulation (i.e. M&E), organisational learning and more effective (UNPOL) peace operations. This could include research questions such as what are the (independent) variables that enable and inhibit this learning cycle to occur and be fruitful? This could be extended to investigate the potential for learning to inform universally applicable doctrine/guidance.

It also opens up the space to conduct studies investigating similar approaches to M&E in related fields. For instance, other components of UN missions, particularly those engaged in early peacebuilding efforts such as rule of law, governance reform and political affairs would be prime candidates; as could other holistic post-conflict agendas managed outside of UN peace operations such as Security System Reform or peacebuilding and development programming more generally.

Two thematic areas highlighted in this book that warrant further research are the validity of normative change theories such as those underpinning the UNPOL project and the role and suitable involvement of non-state providers of security and justice in peace operations recovery plans, as well as incorporating them into assessments of impact. Regarding the former, additional research on the long-term effectiveness of missions with large police components and intrusive mandates will add to the portfolio of these experiences and build a picture of whether or not the dominant modalities and methods of peacebuilding in regard to rule of law are valid or not. Regarding the latter, questions about how UNPOL can and should engage with informal and non-state providers of security and justice at varying points in a mission's life cycle is a critical issue facing the UN's policing missions across the world and warrants further attention.

Finally, but importantly, this project points to the need for further research on conflict-affected contexts and peace operations environments as complex systems. For example, further theoretical explorations to refine and develop the application of complexity theory/concepts to peace operations settings would lend further support to calls for a shift in this direction. For instance, this also points to investigations around the utility of using complexity theory to better understand the nature and value of other management challenges/phenomena in peace operations, such as coordination and integration. Similarly, further interdisciplinary empirical research that aims to test what (additional) methods, tools and instruments are suitable for implementing complexity-oriented M&E would likely contribute new and innovative avenues for practitioners in operationalising M&E in conflict-affected settings. There is a need to build a body of empirical evidence that complexity-oriented-M&E can improve the professionalism, efficiency and effectiveness of peace operations through better agility in the field and improved learning processes at HQ. The more this approach is documented, the more weight it will have to convince the naysayers through descriptions rather than prescriptions.

Research projects such as these have the potential to reinforce and advance the line of reasoning forwarded in this study, as well as add valuable insights in their own right. This list is not exhaustive, but should provide some fodder for making progress in this vital but understudied area.

Overcoming the convenience of simplicity

According to Schumacher, M&E in peace operations "requires a considered mix of audacity and professional realism accounting for the scope of a [peace operation] in its formulation".[9] Despite the plethora of conceptual and practical challenges, trade-offs and compromises this audacity and realism involves, this book constitutes a humble but pragmatic step towards making improvements to M&E in this context.

The jury is still out on how the experiment of attempting to build a liberal peace through UN peace operations will turn out. It may indeed be the case that history will judge this period of grand designs and great expectations as folly or naïveté. On the other hand, time may tell that long-term projects aimed at transforming conflict-affected societies simply require a long time to come to fruition. In this light, improvements and investments in conflict prevention capacities may promise better returns than any cure. Nevertheless, now more than ever before, UN peace operations are heralded as an effective instrument for bringing to an end and preventing the relapse of seemingly intractable conflicts. In real-time the stakes are high as the well-being of millions of people depends on the fragile peace these operations preserve. At the time of writing, missions across the world are being adjusted and adapted to address dynamical and evolving challenges of securing a durable peace. International policing – restoring law and order and building capacities fit for displacing discredited and unresponsive security agencies – is increasingly a centre of gravity in these endeavours. Moreover, this approach does not look likely to wane.[10] The enduring presence of UN policing is matched by the continuous need for adaptation as mandated tasks and priority objectives continue to evolve in areas such as civilian protection and combating organised crime. Despite financial constraints exacerbated by the fiscal austerity amongst primary funders and political sensitivities that frame operations today, the fortitude of consensus around the common objective of stabilising post-conflict countries alone should give the UN and its peace operations architecture the confidence to grasp the nettle of complexity inherent in understanding and assisting societies emerging from conflict.

In Lakhdar Brahimi's personal address to the 2010 General Assembly debate on peacekeeping, reflecting on a decade since the release of the seminal report commonly known eponymously, he recounted recommendations they had made for improving and enhancing the organisation's learning capacity. He asserted that,

> the panel bluntly pointed out that the UN is often taking very serious decisions about how to respond to crises it does not know enough about. We stressed the importance of seriously upgrading the UN's ... general analytical capacities ... The General Assembly did agree to many of the additional staff we suggested, but firmly refused to give the Secretary General the quality analytical capacity he needs.[11]

Over a decade on from the Brahimi Report's calls to professionalise the business of UN peace operations, the need for enhanced M&E as part of a holistic organisational learning infrastructure remains a pressing concern.

To be sure, given the magnitude of the challenges there is a need for humility, modesty and a great deal more self-reflection around claims of what can be achieved through these complex undertakings. However, to equivocate raises the spectre that peace operations – and the police components therein purported to be so important to overall success of a mission – continue to function and be managed in an ad hoc fashion and fail to learn institutionally from their experiences. This would render the peace operations apparatus rudderless and consequently at the mercy of the political games of the Security Council's powerful permanent members – destined to continue 'muddling through'. To do so would be tantamount to adding insult to the injuries of the victims of conflict who have already suffered unspeakably and at the very least deserve a UN that is doing its utmost to learn from its unique experiences. As vastly experienced UN official, Sergio Vieira de Mello, went on record as saying, "history if nothing else has taught us, that what is unlikely usually happens."[12] It is therefore imperative that the UN peace operations apparatus undertakes the necessary retooling for more incisive M&E, fostering of a culture of learning and continuous improvement, and builds a repository of organisational knowledge such that the unfortunate place that requires the UN to deploy a peace operation in future may be the recipient of a mission more capable than those that went before it of assisting resilient people to build a peace they can enjoy.

Notes

1 Then Under-Secretary-General for DPKO Guéhenno's 'Peace Operations 2010' reform agenda, see: "Overview of the Financing of the United Nations Peacekeeping Operations: Budget Performance for the Period from 1 July 2004 to 30 June 2005 and Budget for the Period from 1 July 2006 to 30 June 2007", in *Report of the Secretary General Administrative and budgetary aspects of the financing of the United Nations peacekeeping operations* (New York, United Nations, 2006), 10, para 21.
2 Michael Barnett cited in Thorsten Benner, Stephan Mergenthaler, and Philipp Rotmann, *The New World of UN Peace Operations: Learning to Build Peace?* (Oxford: Oxford University Press, 2011), 225.
3 Michael Barnett cited in ibid., 225.
4 Including Peace and Conflict Studies and Security Studies.
5 See, for example: Ylber Bajraktari, Arthur Boutellis, Fatema Gunja, Daniel Harris, James Kapsis, Eva Kaye, and Jane Rhee, "The Prime System: Measuring the Success of Post-Conflict Police Reform" (Princeton, NJ: Princeton University: Woodrow Wilson School of Public and International Affairs, 2006).
6 IPA, "Counting What Counts: Ten Steps toward Increasing the Relevance of Empirical Research in the UN System", in *Meeting Note* (New York: International Peace Academy, 2006), 1–2.
7 See, for example: Gordon Peake, "Understanding International Police Organisations: What the Researchers Do Not See", in *Making Sense of Peace and Capacity-Building Operations: Rethinking Policing and Beyond*, eds. Bryn W. Hughes, Charles T. Hunt, and Boris Kondoch (Leiden/Boston: Martinus Nijhoff Publishers, 2010); Gordon Peake and Otwin Marenin, "Their Reports Are Not Read and Their Recommendations Are Resisted: The Challenge for the Global Police Policy Community", *Police Practice and Research: An International Journal* 9, no. 1 (2008); Charles T. Hunt and Bryn W. Hughes, "Introduction", in *Making Sense of Peace and Capacity-Building Operations: Rethinking Policing and Beyond*, eds. Bryn W. Hughes, Charles T. Hunt, and Boris Kondoch (Leiden: Martinus Nijhoff, 2010), 5–6.
8 Paul Higate and Marsha Henry, *Insecure Spaces: Peacekeeping, Power and Performance in Haiti, Kosovo and Liberia*, (London: Zed Books, 2009), 6.
9 Joseph Schumacher, "What to Measure in Peace Operations", *The Pearson Papers* 10, no. 1 (2007), 47.
10 William J. Durch and Madeline L. England, eds., *Enhancing United Nations Capacity to Support Post-Conflict Policing and Rule of Law*, Stimson Center Report No. 63, REV 1 ed. Vol. Revised/Updated, Project on Rule of Law in Post-Conflict Settings, Future of Peace Operations Program (Washington DC: The Stimson Center, 2010), 58; Rick Linden, David Last, and Christopher Murphy,

"Obstacles on the Road to Peace and Justice: The Role of Civilian Police in Peacekeeping", in *Crafting Transnational Policing: Police Capacity Building and Global Police Reform,* eds. Andrew Goldsmith and James Sheptycki. (Oxford: Heart Publishing, 2007), 149–76; Annika Hansen, "From Congo to Kosovo: Civilian Police in Peace Operations", *Adelphi Papers* 41, no. 343 (2002), 21.
11 Lakhdar Brahimi, "Contribution to the General Assembly Debate on Peacekeeping", (New York: United Nations, 2010), 4.
12 Sergio Vieira de Mello, "How Not to Run a Country: Lessons for the UN from Kosovo and East Timor", in *Interfet Detainee Management Unit in East Timor,* ed. Michael Kelly. (Chavannes-de-Bogis/Geneve: SLAC, 2000) 7.

Index

African Revolutionaries 172
African Union (AU) 32, 274
African Union-United Nations Hybrid Mission in Darfur (UNAMID) 39–40, 154
An Agenda for Peace (1992) 28, 43
American Colonization Society (ACS) 170
ancient tribal hatreds 172
anti-learning, notion of 120–1
Anti-Terrorism Unit (ATU) 174
Armed Forces of Liberia (AFL) 171
Australian Federal Police's International Deployment Group 32

benchmarking, in peace operations 225, 230; logic for **73,** 78; police reforms and 84; techniques employed in 217
Best Practices Officers (BPO) 66, 211, 257
Black Colonialism 170
Bosnia 29, 34–5, 185
Brahimi, Lakhdar 276
Brahimi Report (2000) 29, 35, 40, 43, 65, 234, 276
brain drain 171
Bryant, Gyude 175, 184
business of learning 233

causality, issue of 269
'cause-and-effect'/contribution narratives 77–8, 80, 111, 151, 154, 222
ceteris paribus 116, 118
child soldiers 174
civil defence forces 181
civil society 111, 114, 171, 175, 178, 190, 192, 217, 224

civilian police, in UN peace operations 32–41; as 'bolt-on' capacity 32; capacity-building and institutional development 34–5; deployment in Congo 33; executive policing 35; in the field and in the office 33; monitoring and advising, role of 33–4; multidimensional and integrated missions 35–41
co-evolution, process of 108; in organisational learning 121
Cold War 1, 6–7, 28, 32–3, 43
Communities of Practice (CoP) 67, 122, 233
community policing forums (CPF) 187, 190, 224
Community Watch Teams 181
community-based networks 227
Community-Oriented Policing 187
Complex Adaptive Systems 107, **108,** 122
Complex Evolving Systems (CES) 107–8, 115
complexity theory, in peace operations 104–11, 138, 156, 159; anti-learning and 120–1; attractors 107; causal ambiguity 116–18; cause-effect relationship 77–8, 80, 111, 119, 151, 154, 222; central tenets of 109–10; context-(in)sensitivity and 118–19; exclusive methods in 120; feedback mechanisms and processes 105–7, 112–13; input-outcome proportionality in 116–17; interactive and interdependent elements of 108; military and non-military components of 114; for overcoming the shortcomings with extant M&E 116–22; peace operations

complexity theory *continued*
  environments and 111–16; properties of 106; punctuated equilibrium 107; ramifications of 122–5; in social sciences 109–11; un-systemic 119–20
COMPSTAT programme 77
conflict management 1, 66
corruption, issue of 232
Cotonou Peace Accord (July 1993) 173
County Security Mechanisms 224
'Crimewatch' programme 224
criminal justice institutions 12, 36, 143, 194, 214
criminal justice system 1, 31, 39, 43, 215; reconstruction of 11
crisis management 36, 88
cybernetics 104

daily costs per prisoner, standards for 215
decision-making 85–6, 152, 213, 227, 234, 251, 260, 269; real-time 236
democratic policing, principles of 38, 42, 44, 183
Department of Peacekeeping Operations (DPKO) 28–9, 32, 35, 47, 65, 76, 111, 274; Integrated Training Service (ITS) 67; Lessons Learned Unit 65–6; Peacekeeping Best Practices Unit 66; Policy and Analysis Unit 66; Policy, Evaluation and Training Division (DPET) 67, 139, 212; RRR policy 38
Disarmament, Demobilisation and Reintegration (DDR) 112–13, 125, 184
division of labour 45; police-military 234
domestic law enforcement services, reforms in 2
DynCorp 185

Economic Community of West African States (ECOWAS) Mediation Committee 172, 174
ECOWAS Cease-Fire Monitoring Group (ECOMOG) 172–4
ECOWAS Mission in Liberia (ECOMIL) 175, 182
Ellis, Stephen 176, 189
emergence, concept of 119
ethnic and communal disputes 178
European Union (EU) 32, 274

financial constraints, for UN peace operations 276
flexibility, issues of 225
'fly-in-fly-out' assessments 252
foregrounding, concept of 139–45; in mission context assessment 143–4; in mission objectives and realistic expectations 140–3
Formed Police Units (FPUs) 42, 47, 234; rules of engagement for 259
framework for M&E 136, 137–9; adaptations of 88; based on abductive reasoning 154; benefits of 211–12, 234; complexity theory *see* complexity theory, in peace operations; development of 14; diagram of **137**; for effective impact assessment 2; evaluation of 233; features of 138; for field-level M&E process 139–57; focus on interpretation and response 229–32; for holistic mission management 2, 14, 48, 126, 214; impact-focused 244; implementation of 243; improvement/recalibration of 159; iterative cycles of 246; for knowledge acquisition 123; learning focus 232–5; level of rigour 251–3; limitations in 251; operational/ tactical tools 209; for organisational learning 8; post-conflict recovery 213; qualities of 158; refinement and clarification of 243; results-based management and 78; Results-Focused Transitional Framework (RFTF) 209; strategic-level 209–10; strengths and comparative advantages of 214; tenets and principles of 169; testing of 243; UN Development Assistance Frameworks (UNDAF) 139, 209; of UNPOL in peace operations 44, 137–9, 208
'free people of colour' 170

global theology 43
good governance 38
Governance and Economic Management Assistance Program (GEMAP), Liberia 184

High-Level Panel on UN Peace Operations 29
Human Development Index 179
human rights abuses 34, 81, 177, 182, 192, 232

Human Security Report Project 7
human social system 126

information-sharing, modes of 155
institutional learning 208
Integrated Mission Priorities and Implementation Plan (IMPIP) 71, 211, 217
Integrated Missions Planning Process (IMPP) 138
Integrated Training Service (ITS) 67
Interim Government of National Unity (IGNU) 173
inter-mission learning 2
internally displaced people 172
international community 1, 29, 120, 173–4, 183–4, 192, 210
international financial institutions 39, 82
International Police Task Force (IPTF) 34
international policing 1, 41; impact of 8; key trends in 9; literature on M&E in 76–8
International Relations (IR) 3, 6, 109–10, 271
interoperability of police-military 234
intra-state conflicts 7, 28–9

job creation, opportunities for 179
job security 247
Johnson-Sirleaf, Ellen 209, 225
Joint Mission Analysis Cell (JMAC) 256–7
Joint Operations Centre (JOC) 256

knowledge management 8, 14, 65–6, 211, 253, 272; organisational 234
Knowledge Management Toolkit 211, 233, 256–7
Kosovo 1, 7, 29, 31, 35, 37, 39, 43

laissez-faire market ideologies 110
learning cycle 66, 137, 209, 233, 253, 274
Le-Roy, Alain 1
level of rigour, of the framework for peace operations 251–3
Liberia: 'Abuja II' peace agreement 173–4; Akosombo Agreements 173; Americo-Liberians 170–1, 176; Anti-Terrorism Unit (ATU) 174, 177; Armed Forces of Liberia (AFL) 171; balance of military power 173; Bureau of Corrections and Rehabilitation (BCR) 188; Bureau of Immigration and Naturalisation (BIN) 188; child soldiers 174; civil war in 171–5; Community Watch Teams 181; Comprehensive Peace Agreement (CPA) 175, 179, 209; consequences of protracted civil war 177–8; Cotonou Peace Accord (July 1993) 173; Drug Enforcement Agency (DEA) 188; ECOWAS Mission in Liberia (ECOMIL) 175; Governance and Economic Management Assistance Program (GEMAP) 184; governance and institutional degradation 178–9; human rights abuses 177; Independent NPFL (INPFL) 172–3; indigenous revolution 170; Liberian Frontier Force (LFF) 170, 177, 179; Liberian National Police (LNP) 37, 174–5, 177, 179, 191–2, 215, 218, 221; Liberian National Transitional Government (LNTG) 173; Liberians United for Reconciliation and Democracy (LURD) 175; mineral resources, privatisation of 174; Movement for Democracy in Liberia (MODEL) 175; National Bureau of Investigation (NBI) 188; National Fire Service 188; National Patriotic Front of Liberia (NPFL) 172–3; National Transitional Government of Liberia (NTGL) 175; non-state providers of security and justice, role of 180–2; parochial identities, importance of 176; People's Redemption Council (PRC) 171; post-conflict public security and the rule of law 182; public security 226; rice riots (1979) 170; root causes and drivers of protracted conflict 176–7; Security Sector Reform 182; short history of 169–71; Special Operations Division (SOD) 175; Special Security Services (SSS) 177; stateless communities 170; Taylor, Charles 171–6, 178; True Whig Party 170; UN Office in Liberia (UNOL) 174; UN stabilisation force, deployment of 175; unemployment rates 179; United Liberation Movement for Democracy in Liberia (ULIMO) 173; United Nations Mission in Liberia (UNMIL) *see* United Nations Mission in Liberia (UNMIL)
Lorenz's 'butterfly effect' 107

282   Index

Mandate Implementation Plan (MIP) 73, 84, 158, 211
Middle East 39; UN peace operations in 27
Millennium Development Goals (MDGs) 139, 210
mission radio stations 156
mission-creep 33, 245
Monitoring and Evaluation (M&E), in peace operations 2–4, 8, 48, 63, 115; accountability demands 85–7; ad hoc evaluations 72; approach and methods for 247–53; approaches in UN field operations 69–76; architecture for UN presence in Liberia 209–11; of barriers and risks to participation 247–8; benchmarking logic **73**; of causality *vs.* contribution 222–3; 'cause-and-effect'/contribution narratives 77–8, 80, 111, 151, 154, 222; circularity of 212–13; classical 'logframe' representation **79**; complexity theory for overcoming the shortcomings with 10, 116–22; in context of post-conflict 'interventions' 64; critiques of dominant approaches in 78–87; danger of disempowering field missions 259–60; data sources for 149–50, 223–4, 249–51; design and implementation of approaches for 145–53; design flaws in 149; diagram of framework for doing **137**; feedback 156; field-level 136, 139–57, 214–32; flexibility, issues of 225; focus on interpretation and response 229–32; foregrounding, concept of 139–45; framework for *see* framework for M&E; further research on 273–5; impact-oriented 145, 219; importance of 6; of inclusive/participatory approach 226–9; infrastructure for 274; interdependent programming 5; interpretation of data 153–5; learning-oriented 121; limits of tailoring to UNMIL-specific context 257–8; literature on 76–8; meaning of 64; of mission objectives and realistic expectations 140–3; Office of Internal Oversight Services (OIOS) 72; at operational/tactical levels 210; overarching design 212–14; over-reliance on baselines of limited utility 248–9; periodic mission reporting 71; practicalities for 253–60; provisions in Strategic Frameworks 233; relation with organisational learning 157–9; of resource and attention requirements 254–6; responses against findings in 155–6; results-based budgeting 69–71; Results-based Management (RBM) 71–2, 78; risk of duplication 256–7; Rule of Law Indicators Project (ROLIP) 75–6; sense of ownership for 148; stakeholders in 143–4, 148; strategic-level frameworks 209–10; strengths, comparative advantages and potentialities of 211–35; systemic approach for 213–14; UN benchmarking for peace consolidation 73–5; in UN peace operations apparatus 65–8

national poverty reduction strategies 139
natural complex systems, characteristics of 126
'New Public Management' (NPM) reform movement 69

Office for Rule of Law and Security Institutions (OROLSI) 40, 68, 75
Office of Internal Oversight Services (OIOS) 72, 139, 189, 211–12, 231, 252
operational support 11, 37, 141, 186
Organisation for Security Cooperation in Europe (OSCE) 32
organisational learning 8, 14, 64, 80, 211, 267, 272; cycles of 253; facilitation of 232; levels of 2, 136–7; objectives of 138; opportunities for 234; of peace operations bureaucracy 235; pursuit of complete knowledge through 258–9; for real-time decision-making 236; relation with Monitoring and Evaluation (M&E) 157–9; role of co-evolution in 121

Pacific Architects and Engineers Inc. 185
Pacific Islands Forum (PIF) 32
'Peace Operations 2010' reform agenda 66, 193
Peace Operations Intranet 67
Peacebuilding Support Office (PBSO) 29, 73, 174

Peacekeeping Best Practices Section (PBPS) 66–7; Communities of Practice (CoP) 67
peacekeeping-peacebuilding nexus 8, 27, 29, 88
Pepper Coast 169
perturbation of the system, notion of 118
police assistance 8
Police Commissioner (POLCOM) 254–5, 261
police peacekeeping 33, 37, 41, 208
police performance, quality of 218
Police Reform Indicators and Measurement Evaluation (PRIME) System 77
police reforms 141; benchmarking of 84; in post-conflict environments 77; wooden numbers 217
policebuilding 37, 39; with additional supplementary activities 141
policing organisations 5; overhaul of 42
post-conflict peace-building, definition of 28
'Principles and Guidelines' document (2008) 30
problem-solving 230
public health services 178
public safety, issues of 190
public sector organisations 69
public security 35–6, 38, 43, 47, 80–2, 117, 151, 177, 181–3, 186, 193, 224, 226, 267

Quick Impact Projects (QIPs), UNPOL 187, 217, 221

reforming, restructuring and rebuilding (RRR) domestic police institutions 34, 38, 42, 76, 188; benchmarking of police reforms 84; budgetary planning and monitoring tool 69; effectiveness of 69; Joint Inspection Unit review of 70; mission planning processes 71; primary objectives of 210; relevance of 69
Regional Assistance Mission to the Solomon Islands (RAMSI) 32
restoration of law and order 1, 4, 11, 80, 257
Results-Based Budgeting (RBB) 69–74, 78–80, 83–5, 87, 210–12, 217, 224, 230, 253–5
Results-based Management (RBM) 69, 71–2, 78

Revolutionary United Front (RUF), Sierra Leone 174
Royal Canadian Mounted Police's International Peace Operations Branch 32
Rule of Law 43, 120, 212; discourse of 31–2, 36; peace operations, concept of 40; and security system 40; theory of change 43–4; triad of 40
Rule of Law Indicators Implementation Guide and Project Tools (2011) 75
Rule of Law Indicators Project (ROLIP) 75–6, 83, 139, 215–16
Rwanda 29, 34, 65

Sawyer, Amos 172, 180, 190
secret societies 170, 201n119
security sector reform (SSR) 6, 11, 15, 30, 40–1, 44, 112, 181–2, 188–9, 195, 210, 212
self-organisation 110, 115, 121; meaning of 107
sexual abuse, by peacekeepers 232
Sierra Leone 7, 29, 112, 169, 173–4, 185, 246; Revolutionary United Front (RUF) 174; Special Court for Sierra Leone (SCSL) 175
small arms and light weapons (SALW) 36, 125
'SMART' policing 34, 38
social capital 180
social science 7, 16, 65, 104–5, 109–10, 125, 253
Somalia 29, 34
"Sons of the Devil" 175
Southwest African Police (SWAPOL) 34
Standard Operating Procedures (SOPs) 4, 113, 259
state security apparatus, public perceptions of 269–70
state-based security 144
statebuilding, notion of 31, 43, 195
sustainable development 267

Taylor, Charles 171–6, 178
Technical Assessment Missions (TAM) 75, 186
Timor-Leste 1, 7, 29, 31, 35, 39, 43, 71
Transnational Crime Unit (TCU) 188

UN Development Assistance Frameworks (UNDAF) 139, 209–10, 233
UN General Assembly 12, 71, 276

284 *Index*

UN Mission in Bosnia and Herzegovina (UNMIBH) 34
UN missions in Rwanda (UNAMIR) 34
UN missions in Somalia (UNOSOM) 34
UN Office in Liberia (UNOL) 174
UN operation in Mozambique (ONUMOZ) 34, 53n59
UN Police (UNPOL) 1–2, 4, 32, 48, 113, 119, 182, 215, 228; capacity-building mandates, implementation of 42–7, 81, 118; criticisms for 79–87; demand for 40; deployment of 11; effectiveness of 6; framework for M&E of 137–9; generating and deploying 41–2; hierarchical demands 254; impact assessment for 268; internal assessment of 232; non-state providers 44–7; objectives of 80, 122, 210; opportunities and challenges for 41–7; performance of 72; planning and management of 272; police reforms 185; policebuilding, politics of 42–4; protection of UN personnel and facilities 39; public perceptions of 85; quantity of 32; Quick Impact Projects (QIPs) 187, 217, 221; role and function of 11, 33; role in institutional civil law enforcement 37; shortage of officers 41; 'SMART' policing 34; strategic advisory support 187; strategic/operational challenges facing 9; success in restoring law and order 84; tasks of *142*; technical capacity-building 38, 42, 118
UN Police Division (UNPD) 41; Governance Indicators 74
UN Security Council 1, 12, 141, 191, 234, 276
UN Technical Assessment Mission (TAM) 75, 186
UN Temporary Executive Authority (UNTEA) 33
UN Transitional Assistance Group in Namibia (UNTAG) 28, 33–4
unemployment rates 179
UNIFEM's Gender and Conflict Indicators 74
United Nations Development Assistance Framework (UNDAF) 139, 209–10, 233
United Nations Mission in Liberia (UNMIL) 10, 13, 17, 160, 173–4, 182–93; causality *vs.* contribution 222–3; Community-Oriented Policing 187; concept of 184; consolidation, drawdown and withdrawal of 192–3; context-sensitive foregrounding/baselines 214–16; current progress and priorities 191–2; deployment of 184; disarmament of armed groups 184; effectiveness of 192; Emergency Response Unit (ERU) 187; exit strategy 193; exogenous factors and unintended consequences 220–1; flexibility, issues of 225; focus of framework for peace operations 244–7; focus on interpretation and response 229–32; Governance and Economic Management Assistance Program (GEMAP) 184; holistic rule of law approach 188–9; impact/outcome focus 216–19; inclusive/participatory approach 226–9; interim assessment of UNPOL in 191–2; interim Poverty Reduction Strategy (iPRS) 209; internal assessment of UNPOL in 232; learning focus 232–5; learning, prospects for 246–7; limitations of 272–3; mandate implementation and performance of 184–91; M&E mechanisms employed by 210; military personnel in 182; non-state actors in the rule of law domain 189–91; objectives of 182–4; overly impact-oriented 244–6; over-reliance on baselines of limited utility 248–9; Peacebuilding Fund 190; police component of 183; police reform mandate 11, 183; Police Support Units (PSU) 187; Poverty Reduction Strategy (PRS) 209; reform programme 216; Results-Focused Transitional Framework (RFTF) 209; security sector reform 188–9; Senior Mission Leadership Group (SMLG) 216; significant milestone for 184; strategic-level frameworks 209–10; Women & Child Protection Sections 188
United Nations (UN) peace operations 1, 7, 218, 266; challenges faced by 267; characteristics of 28; civilian police in *see* civilian police, in UN peace operations; complex aspects of

see complexity theory, in peace operations; convenience of simplicity, overcoming 275–7; core business of multidimensional **30**; criticisms for 79–87; effectiveness of 2; evolution and expansion of 258; failures of 29; financial constraints for 276; framework for 28; High-Level Panel on 29; impacts of 88; in Middle East 27; multiagency character of 114; from peacekeeping to peacebuilding 27–31; Rule of Law Indicators Project 75–6; triple transformation 28

vigilante groups 190

war-to-peace transition 5, 27, 31, 44, 182
West African Coast Initiative (WACI) 188
Women and Children Protection Centres (WCPCs) 217, 221
women/child victims of crime 218
women's groups 190
wooden numbers 217
World Bank 39, 209; Post-Conflict/Governance Indicators 74
World Health Organisation 178

eBooks
from Taylor & Francis
Helping you to choose the right eBooks for your Library

Add to your library's digital collection today with Taylor & Francis eBooks. We have over 45,000 eBooks in the Humanities, Social Sciences, Behavioural Sciences, Built Environment and Law, from leading imprints, including Routledge, Focal Press and Psychology Press.

Choose from a range of subject packages or create your own!

Benefits for you
- Free MARC records
- COUNTER-compliant usage statistics
- Flexible purchase and pricing options
- 70% approx of our eBooks are now DRM-free.

Benefits for your user
- Off-site, anytime access via Athens or referring URL
- Print or copy pages or chapters
- Full content search
- Bookmark, highlight and annotate text
- Access to thousands of pages of quality research at the click of a button.

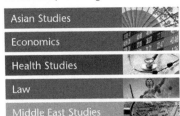

Free Trials Available
We offer free trials to qualifying academic, corporate and government customers.

eCollections
Choose from 20 different subject eCollections, including:

- Asian Studies
- Economics
- Health Studies
- Law
- Middle East Studies

eFocus
We have 16 cutting-edge interdisciplinary collections, including:

- Development Studies
- The Environment
- Islam
- Korea
- Urban Studies

For more information, pricing enquiries or to order a free trial, please contact your local sales team:

UK/Rest of World: **online.sales@tandf.co.uk**
USA/Canada/Latin America: **e-reference@taylorandfrancis.com**
East/Southeast Asia: **martin.jack@tandf.com.sg**
India: **journalsales@tandfindia.com**

www.tandfebooks.com

Printed in Poland
by Amazon Fulfillment
Poland Sp. z o.o., Wrocław